"Andrew Kania's *Philosophy of Western I* dents have been waiting for. Scholarly, l will both enlighten and enthuse anyone w... philosophy of music."

Julian Dodd, University of Manchester

Philosophy of Western Music

This is the first comprehensive book-length introduction to the philosophy of Western music that fully integrates consideration of popular music and hybrid musical forms, especially song. Its author, Andrew Kania, begins by asking whether Bob Dylan should even have been eligible for the Nobel Prize in Literature, given that he is a musician. This motivates a discussion of music as an artistic medium, and what philosophy has to contribute to our thinking about music. Chapters 2–5 investigate the most commonly defended sources of musical value: its emotional power, its form, and specifically musical features (such as pitch, rhythm, and harmony). In Chapters 6–9, Kania explores issues arising from different musical practices, particularly work-performance (with a focus on classical music), improvisation (with a focus on jazz), and recording (with a focus on rock and pop). Chapter 10 examines the intersection of music and morality. The book ends with a consideration of what, ultimately, music is.

Key Features

- Uses popular-song examples throughout, but also discusses a range of musical traditions (notably, rock, pop, classical, and jazz).
- Explains both philosophical and musical terms when they are first introduced.
- Provides publicly accessible Spotify playlists of the musical examples discussed in the book.
- Each chapter begins with an overview and ends with questions for testing comprehension and stimulating further thought, along with suggestions for further reading.

Andrew Kania is Professor of Philosophy at Trinity University in San Antonio; his principal research is in the philosophy of music, film, and literature. He is the editor of *Memento* (in Routledge's series Philosophers on Film, 2009) and co-editor, with Theodore Gracyk, of *The Routledge Companion to Philosophy and Music* (2011).

ROUTLEDGE CONTEMPORARY INTRODUCTIONS TO PHILOSOPHY

Series editor:
Paul K. Moser
Loyola University of Chicago

This innovative, well-structured series is for students who have already done an introductory course in philosophy. Each book introduces a core general subject in contemporary philosophy and offers students an accessible but substantial transition from introductory to higher-level college work in that subject. The series is accessible to non-specialists and each book clearly motivates and expounds the problems and positions introduced. An orientating chapter briefly introduces its topic and reminds readers of any crucial material they need to have retained from a typical introductory course. Considerable attention is given to explaining the central philosophical problems of a subject and the main competing solutions and arguments for those solutions. The primary aim is to educate students in the main problems, positions, and arguments of contemporary philosophy rather than to convince students of a single position.

Recently Published Volumes:

Virtue Ethics
Liezl van Zyl

Philosophy of Language
3rd Edition
William G. Lycan

Philosophy of Mind
4th Edition
John Heil

Philosophy of Science
4th Edition
Alex Rosenberg and Lee McIntyre

Philosophy of Western Music
Andrew Kania

For a full list of published *Routledge Contemporary Introductions to Philosophy*, please visit www.routledge.com/Routledge-Contemporary-Introductions-to-Philosophy/book-series/SE0111

Philosophy of Western Music

A Contemporary Introduction

Andrew Kania

Routledge
Taylor & Francis Group

NEW YORK AND LONDON

First published 2020
by Routledge
52 Vanderbilt Avenue, New York, NY 10017

and by Routledge
2 Park Square, Milton Park, Abingdon, Oxon, OX14 4RN

Routledge is an imprint of the Taylor & Francis Group, an informa business

© 2020 Taylor & Francis

The right of Andrew Kania to be identified as author of this work has been asserted by him in accordance with sections 77 and 78 of the Copyright, Designs and Patents Act 1988.

Library of Congress Cataloging-in-Publication Data
A catalog record for this title has been requested

ISBN: 978-1-138-62872-4 (hbk)
ISBN: 978-1-138-62873-1 (pbk)
ISBN: 978-1-315-21062-9 (ebk)

Typeset in Times New Roman
by Swales & Willis, Exeter, Devon, UK

Visit the eResources: www.routledge.com/9781138628731

To Julie

Contents

Examples and figure

Examples

Figure

Preface

In this book, I introduce readers to the current state of a range of debates in analytic philosophy of Western music. In my experience, everyone with an interest in music finds the questions addressed in these debates fascinating, but a central challenge to introducing people to the primary literature (e.g., in an undergraduate philosophy class) is that those texts (and other introductions to philosophy of music) are focused primarily on purely instrumental classical music – a kind of music that few are deeply familiar with. I argue, in Chapter 1, that there is a good reason for this focus: To think clearly about song, film music, dance music, and so on, we need a concept of the medium of "pure" music, and the classical tradition is one obvious place to look for works in this medium. But there are bad reasons, too: It is difficult to deny the connections between classical music, class, and race in the English-speaking world during the flourishing of analytic philosophy of music over the past half-century. For instance, jazz is an equally obvious place to look for pure instrumental music, yet it has received a fraction – albeit happily a growing fraction – of the philosophical attention that classical music has. This is surely due in part to jazz being a historically black and popular musical tradition, while analytic philosophy has been dominated by middle-class white men. Anyway, as I hope is demonstrated throughout the book, once we have a conception of the medium of pure music, there is no reason we cannot consider examples of hybrid musical forms (song, film music, etc.) in reflecting on the philosophical puzzles that music raises.

No introduction can do everything, and I should mention what I have not even attempted in this book. First, though I use many examples of hybrid musical works, my focus is on philosophical questions raised by *music*, in a sense that the first and last chapters clarify. Thus, I largely ignore the contributions of the *lyrics* to song, the *pictures* to film, the *dancing* to dance music, and so on. I do not see how one could adequately cover the questions raised by those aspects of these hybrids, or their complex wholes, without essentially writing an introduction to the philosophy of music *and* literature *and* film *and* dance, and so on, not to mention the further puzzles raised by the combination of these media in hybrid works. This focus on music has also led me to merely glance at some central topics in aesthetics and philosophy of the arts more broadly, such as the nature of aesthetic properties and the role of intentions in art.[1] Second, as the title makes clear, this is an introduction to the philosophy of *Western* music. Though I occasionally refer to other musical traditions, most notably in the discussions of basic musical features (Chapter 4) and the definition of music (Chapter 11), I have restricted myself to the musical language with which I am familiar.[2] Third, I have also restricted myself (with a few exceptions), as I have already mentioned, to analytic philosophy of music – the philosophical language with which I am most familiar.[3] Perhaps some would argue that these restrictions damn the book to arcane specialism at best and complete irrelevance at worst. I (unsurprisingly) disagree, but an adequate defense of this approach would exceed the bounds of a mere preface.

I do not wholly subscribe to the now orthodox view among writers of introductions to philosophy that the best way to engage readers critically with a debate is for the author to defend a particular position in that debate. Though my own views and sympathies (not to mention my musical preferences, strengths, and weaknesses) are doubtless evident throughout the book, it seems to me that sometimes it is better to present the range of views and arguments about a topic dispassionately and leave it to the reader to evaluate their relative strength. One application of this approach is that when my own published views come up, I discuss them in the third person, talking of Andrew Kania's view, rather than using the first-person pronoun.

I have endeavored to make each chapter accessible on its own; the chapter overviews and concluding sections should orient you if you proceed cover-to-cover. There are two main sequences of chapters in the book: Chapters 2–5 investigate the most commonly defended sources of musical value: its emotional power and its basic musical features and form. Chapters 6–9 investigate issues arising from different music-making practices, particularly work-performance, improvisation, and recording. Chapter 10 investigates the intersection of music and morality. The book is framed by two chapters (1 and 11) on the nature of music.

Musical examples are extremely helpful, yet not everyone is familiar with the same repertoire and few people read music. My solution has been to supply a few, mostly simple, printed musical examples where I thought they might be helpful, and to supplement the text with Spotify playlists of all the central examples for each chapter (at least, all those available on Spotify – readers may of course turn to Google for the rest). A Spotify account is free (at time of writing!). Direct links to the Spotify playlists can be found on the book's eResources page on the Routledge website: **www.routledge.com/9781138628731** or **www.bit.ly/KaniaPWM**. The QR code below will also take you to that page.[4]

The shortened and full URLs are as follows:

Chapter 1: http://bit.ly/PWM-1 or
https://open.spotify.com/playlist/3TkR9YKdxG5mBt9SBnSS3E?
si=8te2JJ5jR9Ga6AhvM-Arpg
Chapter 2: http://bit.ly/PWM-2 or
https://open.spotify.com/playlist/57KMtTGjmre1Pj8aURYYUC?
si=_DyhH179Q2CB4UlYmvXqRw
Chapter 3: http://bit.ly/PWM-3 or
https://open.spotify.com/playlist/64lTCxZl2FoedEqO5TgHlk?
si=9Bu_0X3wSLS6vMvrZu6cZg
Chapter 4: http://bit.ly/PWM-4 or
https://open.spotify.com/playlist/0hVYiBUlRf9BngcPXoCB7g?
si=6yoJmrtaSumTBVo1O-Xn0g
Chapter 5: http://bit.ly/PWM-5 or
https://open.spotify.com/playlist/5K9vmzh3nt4TYPcteqNvSd?
si=j6c3dg95T-mVZq02jYSDgg
Chapter 6: http://bit.ly/PWM-6 or
https://open.spotify.com/playlist/1IvZe62mwz5OzGEjmdijrm?
si=Yg5jJFncSQChou8mnGodKw
Chapter 7: http://bit.ly/PWM-7 or
https://open.spotify.com/playlist/19a5TudQ88Tw1TIXHCobC6?
si=cyeY6gxlRZSmHBYR2E0S8w
Chapter 8: http://bit.ly/PWM-8 or
https://open.spotify.com/playlist/69uqzOK42UpLprMzxi0AvU?
si=5TBCcmkxSHmJoiOcn7k8fA
Chapter 9: http://bit.ly/PWM-9 or
https://open.spotify.com/playlist/5YRw2IXjMioTFuEUd9Cdih?
si=Bq3SoNECR5e_v8_DwRGKow
Chapter 10: http://bit.ly/PWM-10 or
https://open.spotify.com/playlist/3GIH2qg8Xlf1jcDfhynuFT?
si=TgrRJEQnRGelNiXRvsirLQ
Chapter 11: http://bit.ly/PWM-11 or
https://open.spotify.com/playlist/0zRdj4pZW3rYRedBXIopiM?
si=0JdWUPEtTFehS8xj3qnT2w

I would love to hear from you about your experiences with the book and, of course, your own philosophical thoughts about music, whether you are a student, a fellow academic, or simply someone interested in thinking about music. Please don't hesitate to contact me at akania@trinity.edu.

Andrew Kania

Notes

1 Excellent introductions to aesthetics and the philosophy of art include Stecker 2010 and S. Davies 2016.
2 For a global approach to the philosophy of music and of art more generally, see Higgins 2012 and 2017, respectively.
3 For helpful comparisons between the analytic tradition and others, see Roholt 2017 and D. Davies forthcoming. Andy Hamilton (2007) gives a more historical introduction to philosophy of music, including some continental thought. See also the essays in Parts III and IV of Gracyk and Kania 2011.
4 You may also be able to find the playlists by searching for them on Spotify. Their names are *Philosophy of Western Music: Chapter 1*, etc. However, not all "public" playlists on Spotify are searchable. Unless that changes (or this book goes viral!), you will probably have to access the playlists through the direct links.

Acknowledgements

If I have discussed this book with you, you have probably had an effect on the final product – I thank you. My debt to my former teachers, Stephen Davies and Jerrold Levinson, is obvious throughout the book. Others who have had a significant impact on my music-philosophical education include Lee Brown, David Davies, Julian Dodd, Anne Eaton, Ted Gracyk, and Sherri Irvin. The American Society for Aesthetics has provided a supportive intellectual community for me since the first meeting I attended in 1998. I thank you all. I owe additional thanks to Jerry Levinson for encouraging me to pursue the project at a crucial juncture.

Two models I have kept in mind while writing are Berys Gaut's *Philosophy of Cinematic Art* (2010) and David Davies's *Philosophy of the Performing Arts* (2011). Though I cannot pretend to have attained their seamless blend of introduction, survey, and advancement of a range of interrelated art-philosophical debates – not to mention their philosophical prowess! – I thank them for providing me with an ideal at which to aim.

For reading the entire manuscript (or close to it) and giving me much useful feedback, I thank Vaughn Bryan Baltzly, Stephen Davies, Justine Kingsbury, Julie Post, Matteo Ravasio, David C. Ring, and Daniel Wilson; the students in my Fall 2018 Philosophy of Music course and Fall 2019 Seminar on Music and Values; and an exceptionally helpful anonymous reader for Routledge. For feedback on individual chapters or parts thereof, I thank María José Alcaraz León, Curtis Brown, Julian Dodd, Jeff Garza, Deneese Jones, Amy Mansfield, Jonathan Neufeld, Nina Penner, Nemesio García-Carril Puy, Jenefer Robinson, Bob Stecker, and Paul Vincent, along with audiences at Texas Christian University, Trinity University, the University of Auckland, the University of the Incarnate Word, the University of Waikato, the 2019 Annual Meeting of the American Society for Aesthetics, and the inaugural Jazz and Philosophy Intermodal Conference (2017). Nina Penner was also an invaluable source of help with and advice concerning the musical examples. Why (you might wonder), with so much help from so many wise people, does the book remain riddled with errors and infelicities? I left them in just to make sure you were paying attention.

I drafted over half the book during a sabbatical spent in Auckland. I thank Trinity University for the academic leave and the University of Auckland for appointing me a visiting scholar, as well as Saint Mary's Hall for allowing Julie Post to join me. Thanks to the members of the Auckland aesthetics reading group (especially Stephen Davies, Justine Kingsbury, Matteo Ravasio, and Daniel Wilson) for providing a stimulating philosophical environment and generously devoting several meetings to my work.

My leave would not have been nearly so productive were it not for the generosity of friends and family in setting us up in Auckland, especially Susi and John Kania, Rachel Kania, Mädi Schmidt, Heidi Bowick, Angela Hume, Pauline Faiers, and Amy Mansfield and Hugh Robinson. Less direct, but just as important, support came from Paul, Renée, and Charlie Vincent, David Kelly and Luca Manghi, and Miyo Yoon and Lucas Tomaz de Aquino. Since, I believe, one cannot do good philosophy of music without being actively involved in musical practices, I owe a special debt of gratitude to Amy Mansfield and The Souls for inviting me to lead them in an all-Beatles program(me), including several of my own arrangements.

Back home in San Antonio, Trinity University, and especially the Department of Philosophy, has always provided a stimulating and supportive environment. Special thanks to my colleagues Damian Caluori and Judith Norman, in Philosophy, for help with foreign languages; Tim O'Sullivan and Corinne Pache, in Classical Studies, for discussion of ancient literature and music; and Brian Bondari and Joe Kneer, in Music, for help with some music-theoretic facts and figures. Thanks to Academic Affairs for a summer stipend supporting the completion of the manuscript and faculty-development funds supporting the production of the index. Thanks for Shirley Durst for administrative support in innumerable ways.

At Routledge, Andy Beck has, as always, been a pleasure to work with, as has Marc Stratton, who answered many queries and attended to numerous details. Helen Strain, at Taylor & Francis, and Megan Symons, at Swales & Willis, oversaw the smooth production of the book. Emma Lockley, of EAL Editoral Services, copy-edited the text, saving me from many gaffes. Daphne Lawless, of Metatext, helped prepare the index.

I gratefully acknowledge permission to reprint revised versions of parts of the following publications: "Making Tracks: The Ontology of Rock Music," *Journal of Aesthetics and Art Criticism* 64: 401–14, © 2006 Blackwell Publishing Ltd. "Works, Recordings, Performances: Classical, Rock, Jazz," *Recorded Music: Philosophical and Critical Reflections*, ed. Mine Doğantan-Dack, pp. 3–21, © 2008 Middlesex University Press. "Piece for the End of Time: In Defence of Musical Ontology," *British Journal of Aesthetics* 48.1: 65–79, © 2008 British Society of Aesthetics. "Musical Recordings," *Philosophy Compass* 4: 22–38, © 2009 Blackwell Publishing Ltd. "Silent Music," *Journal of*

Aesthetics and Art Criticism 68: 343–53, © 2010 Blackwell Publishing Ltd. "Performances and Recordings" (co-authored with Theodore Gracyk), *The Routledge Companion to Philosophy and Music*, ed. Theodore Gracyk and Andrew Kania, pp. 80–90, © 2011 Routledge (reproduced with permission of the licensor through PLSclear). "An Imaginative Theory of Musical Space and Movement," *British Journal of Aesthetics* 55.2: 157–72, © 2015 British Society of Aesthetics. "Music and Time," *The Routledge Handbook of Philosophy of Temporal Experience*, ed. Ian Phillips, pp. 349–60, © 2017 Routledge (reproduced with permission of the licensor through PLSclear).

My greatest debt, here as with so many things, is to Julie Post, to whom I dedicate much more than just this book.

1 Song and the Medium of Music

Overview

Prompted by a real-life example, in this chapter we investigate the nature of artistic media, particularly music, language, and their combination in song. Along the way, I make some introductory remarks about what it is to do philosophy of music.

1.1 Are Songs Literature?

On Thursday, October 13, 2016, the Swedish Academy rocked the literary world by awarding the Nobel Prize in Literature to Bob Dylan. The question that exercised many commentators was not whether Dylan's work *merited* such a prestigious prize (most agreed with the academy's judgment of his greatness), but whether it made Dylan *eligible* for the prize.[1] The worry was that the Swedish Academy had made a blundering category error: Bob Dylan is a musician. This prize is for authors of literature. Therefore, however good an artist Dylan may be, he's no more eligible for *this* prize than a painter would be.[2] This reasoning seems to rely on an argument about artistic categories or media something like the following:

1   One is eligible for a literature prize only on the basis of one's works of literature.
2   Songs are works of music, not literature.
3   Therefore, no one is eligible for a literature prize on the basis of their songs.

The obvious response, provided by many commentators, is to reject premise (2), that is, the idea that the categories of music and literature are mutually exclusive. Dylan's songs are music, according to this response, but they are also literature, since they comprise *words* artfully arranged. Like uncontroversial examples of poetry, these arrangements of words have been published in printed volumes, such as *The Lyrics: Since 1962* (Dylan 2014), apparently intended primarily for reading as opposed to singing. Indeed, much of the journalism discussing the prize was illustrated with pictures of just such books, often displayed in bookshops, as if to provide evidence that Dylan is in fact a literary author.[3]

There are at least three ways to take this response. One interpretation is that while a song itself is not literature, it *contains* a literary work – its lyrics – that can be appreciated independently of its musical setting. A second interpretation is that songs are categorially *ambiguous*, that is, they can be properly appreciated in two different ways: as musical *or* literary works. A third interpretation is that *the songs themselves* – words and music together, not the lyrics alone – are unambiguously works of literature. Most commentators, along with the Swedish Academy, endorsed the third interpretation, most obviously in appealing not only to the words of Dylan's songs but also to their musical settings and performances. In this section, I will thus focus on the third interpretation, the claim that a song *taken as a whole* is a work of literature. But first I will briefly consider some issues raised by the first two interpretations of the defense of songs as literature.

We will consider, in §1.3 of this chapter, to what extent (if any) the lyrics of a song can be extracted from its musical setting and still be considered the same text. I will just note here that if we do consider a song's words alone to constitute a work of literature, and thus that the song *contains* a work of literature, it does not automatically follow that the song as a whole is a work of literature. The film *Four Weddings and a Funeral*, for instance, contains a poem – W. H. Auden's "Funeral Blues," recited by one character at the funeral of his partner[4]– but the film as a whole is not thereby a work of literature.[5]

The second interpretation of the claim that songs are literature relies on the idea that songs are categorially ambiguous. Consider *Tarantula* (1971), Dylan's best known uncontroversially literary work. Some call the book a novel; others call it a collection of prose poems. Perhaps one camp is right and the other wrong, or perhaps the book is just a mess of stylistic and genre features. Another possibility, however, is that it can be read rewardingly in two different ways, *either* as a novel *or* as prose poems; perhaps Dylan even intended this. Whatever the truth about *Tarantula*, could *songs* be like this – appropriately appreciated in two different ways, either as music or as literature? It seems unlikely, since appreciating *Tarantula* as a prose poem (rather than a novel) doesn't require ignoring any of it, while appreciating a song as literature requires ignoring much of it – namely, everything that isn't words, what we might intuitively call *the music* of the song.[6] If song does occupy a puzzling middle-ground between music and literature, then, it is not puzzling in the way that the categorization of *Tarantula* is puzzling. Song is an established artistic category; we know what songs are in a way that we aren't quite sure what *Tarantula* is. The question is how we should think of songs in relation to other, similar artistic categories, most notably literature and music.

Let us turn, then, to the most popular defense of Dylan's eligibility for a literature prize – the third interpretation of the response that music and literature are not mutually exclusive – namely, that Dylan's songs, in their entirety, are unambiguously works of literature. According to Horace Engdahl, presenting the prize on behalf of the Swedish Academy, "the straight answer to the question of how Bob Dylan belongs in literature" is that "the beauty of his songs is of the highest rank" (Engdahl 2016, ¶5).[7] Great beauty alone can't qualify something as literature, though, otherwise many sculptures, for instance, would count as literature.[8] But if Engdahl is instead saying that Dylan's songs are in the highest rank of beautiful *literature*, he is of course begging the question in which we are interested (that is, assuming the conclusion for which he is apparently arguing): Beautiful or not, are songs literature *at all*?

As Robert Orr notes in a thoughtful commentary on Dylan's Nobel, the word "poetry" is widely used as an honorific:[9]

> When a person says something like, "That jump shot was pure poetry," the word has nothing to do with the actual practice of reading or writing poems. Rather, the usage implies sublimity, fluidity and technical perfection – you can call anything from a blancmange to a shovel pass "poetry," and people will get what you're saying. This isn't true of opera or badminton or morris dancing, and it can cause confusion about where metaphor ends and reality begins when we talk about "poetry" and "poets."
>
> (2017, ¶7)[10]

Engdahl's comments about the beauty of Dylan's songs, then, might suggest that the Swedish Academy has conflated the idea that Dylan's songs are poetry in the honorific sense with the idea that they're poetry in the descriptive sense. The former idea is widely accepted, but it is the latter that would make Dylan eligible for the Nobel Prize in Literature.

Engdahl also appeals to history and etymology: "In a distant past, all poetry was sung or tunefully recited, poets were rhapsodes, bards, troubadours; 'lyrics' comes from 'lyre'" (2016, ¶2). Now, we might question the validity of etymological arguments for substantive conclusions, but even setting that issue aside, as an argument for the classification of songs as literature, this too is circular. For the past performances to which Engdahl refers appear to be singings of songs. One cannot assume that they were instances of poetry, then, without assuming the very claim at issue.[11] Consider, for example, ancient Greek works such as the *Odyssey* or *Iliad*. We call such works "poetry" in part because we have lost virtually all knowledge – practical and theoretical – of their musical components, and hence have long appreciated only their verbal aspects.[12] Now, suppose that, in the distant future, a few copies of *The Lyrics: Since 1962* survived, but all recordings and notation of Dylan's songs were lost, along with the musical culture within which they would have made sense (roughly the position we are in today with respect to ancient Greek music). In this future, surely something – perhaps much – that is vital to appreciating Bob Dylan's oeuvre has been lost. We should thus, likewise, take even our best understanding of ancient Greek sung "poetry" to be similarly impoverished and acknowledge that its status as literature is just as contestable as that of Dylan's work.[13] Compare this situation with our knowledge of the work of the ancient Roman Catullus. Though few of us speak Latin (and all are at some disadvantage with respect to the cultural context required to fully appreciate Catullus's poetry), we appear to have at least some complete works of his. Since they were intended to be read silently or recited, but not sung, they seem uncontroversially to be works of literature.

Rather confusingly, given the historical argument just considered, Engdahl begins his case for Dylan's oeuvre being literary by suggesting that it marks a "great shift ... in the world of literature," the kind of transformation of a demotic form into high art that changes "our idea of literature" (Engdahl 2016, ¶1). But while it is widely accepted that Dylan transformed rock or popular music (see Chapter 9, §9.3), it is a strikingly original claim that he has transformed our *concept of literature*. As Orr observes, "people don't really think of songs as being poems or of songwriters as being poets," in the descriptive as opposed to honorific sense. "No one plays an album by Chris Stapleton, or downloads the cast recording of 'Hamilton,' or stands in line for a Taylor Swift concert, and says something like, 'I can't wait to listen to these poems!'" (Orr 2017, ¶6). Indeed, if Dylan had transformed our concept of literature, it would be surprising that his eligibility for a literary prize should require defense. So it again looks as though Engdahl is simply assuming that Dylan's work is literature, rather than providing an argument to that end.

It might seem that we haven't yet considered the simplest reason for thinking that Dylan's songs are literature: When printed, at least, "[l]yrics look like poems, or at least a particular kind of poem. They often rhyme. ..." (Orr 2017, ¶3). Of course, the songs also include music – that's why they're called "songs" rather than "poems" – but perhaps they resemble paradigmatic poems enough to be admitted into the literary fold. One challenge raised by such a *resemblance theory* of poetry is that we need to identify the paradigms to which candidate poems are to be compared. But the more serious problem is that resemblance threatens to count *too much* as poetry. Shopping lists resemble paradigmatic poems to a certain extent. The obvious way to exclude them is to say that they don't resemble the paradigms *enough*.[14] The defender of songs as poetry is thus faced with the challenge of coming up with a criterion of sufficient resemblance. But even supposing they meet that challenge, they still face the basic objection just considered: People don't typically think of songs as poems, so why should we think that the proposed criterion is correct? It might be replied that we get to decide what counts as poetry (though precisely who "we" refers to here is a further difficult question), but if this is really to be a *decision* rather than an arbitrary stipulation, we will want to hear a good *reason* for broadening our current conception of poetry to include songs. And it is precisely this reason for which we have been searching in vain.

1.2 Philosophy of Music

We could continue this discussion in a number of ways. For instance, we could pursue more sophisticated resemblance-theories of literature, or theories according to which something's being literature is a matter of its being *intended to be* literature, or standing in a particular *historical relation* to previous literature, or being deemed literature by someone in a position of authority in the *institution* of literature.[15] But since this is, after all, a book on the philosophy of *music*, I will stop here to reflect on why the discussion in the previous section could be described as *philosophy*.

Much of the time we go about our musical and other business without thinking much about it. But occasionally we encounter something puzzling that doesn't seem to fit into our general understanding of the world or some part of it. If trying to solve the puzzle requires answering questions about the most fundamental ways we have of thinking about the world (or the relevant part of it), it is likely a philosophical puzzle. For instance, we all learn things about the world by observing it in one way or another, and scientists have developed extremely fine-tuned and fruitful ways of making such observations and developing wide-ranging and powerful theories on the basis of them. But it occurs to many people, often as adolescents, to wonder whether all this knowledge is ultimately justified: How can we be sure that the basic observations we make, whether in everyday life or the laboratory, are themselves trustworthy? Such questions lead us very quickly into *epistemology* – the study of knowledge and justification. Their enduring interest is manifest in compelling cultural productions from Plato's allegory of the cave (c. 380 BCE) through Descartes's malicious demon (1641) to the Wachowski siblings' film *The Matrix* (1999) and beyond. As with knowledge, so with artistic experience: We go about our business reading novels, watching films, and listening to music, as well as discussing them with friends, reading reviews, and listening to podcasts about them. But when confronted with the Swedish Academy's awarding of the Nobel Prize in Literature to Bob Dylan, many people find themselves puzzled. (What's more, Engdahl's defensive approach makes it clear that the Swedish Academy knew that people would be puzzled.) Everyone sees the poetic aspects of Dylan's songs, yet many feel that it's somehow inappropriate to give Dylan a literary prize. Solving the puzzle requires thinking carefully about the nature of both Dylan's work and artistic categories. The reflections of people such as Engdahl and Orr show that philosophy is not exclusively the domain of trained philosophers, yet the hope is that trained philosophers are better placed to produce and assess philosophical arguments.[16] The point of this book is to introduce you to some of the questions about music that philosophers have found most intriguing, together with the answers that they have found most worthwhile to consider, and – most importantly – some philosophical skills required to continue the discussion.

What makes such topics *philosophical*? I will not offer a definition of philosophy here, but I will point to three features that are characteristic of philosophical enquiry. (Readers familiar with philosophy, especially analytic philosophy, may want to skip to the next section.)

First, philosophical questions are typically *fundamental* in some sense. This isn't to say that they're more important or profound than other questions; they're fundamental in the sense that answers to them are taken for granted by other (less fundamental) disciplines. For instance, physicists are extremely careful about setting up their experiments and interpreting the results. But if you ask your physics professor how she can be sure that she wasn't dreaming when she thought she was doing an experiment, or that we're not all trapped in a Matrix that systematically interferes with our mathematical reasoning, she's likely to roll her eyes and tell you to save such questions for your philosophy professor. Physicists simply *assume* that our perceptual and mathematical faculties are trustworthy. And that's just as well – if humanity had waited for an unassailable epistemological theory before embarking on scientific exploration, there would be no science at all. Another way of putting this point is that in philosophy everything is always – in principle – open to question. Philosophers (ideally) make no assumptions the defense of which they leave to another discipline that is more fundamental.[17] I say that this is a matter of *principle* because *in practice* philosophers have to make assumptions just like everyone else. Someone might have interrupted me in my considerations of Bob Dylan's literary merits, above, to ask how I know any better than the physicist that my reasoning processes are not being interfered with by an all-powerful malicious demon; that is, they might point out that, just like the physicist, I seem to be making some fundamental epistemological assumptions in proceeding with my art-philosophical project. But the point is that *within philosophy* these assumptions are provisional. To turn from physics to epistemology is to turn from doing science to doing philosophy. But to turn from doing philosophy of art to epistemology is to turn from one area of philosophy to another. The philosopher of art might object that these basic epistemological questions are mostly distractions from the topic at hand, but she cannot object that they're not *philosophical*, the way that the physicist can object that they're not scientific.

The second characteristic typical of philosophical questions is that they are substantially *conceptual, non-empirical*, or *a priori*, that is, properly justified independent of any sensory experience.[18] Doing philosophy is, in this respect, more like doing mathematics than it is like doing physics. There are no laboratories in university philosophy or mathematics departments. Researchers in these fields do not proceed by performing experiments; rather they sit quietly thinking (or stride around loudly conversing) about whether or not a certain chain of reasoning is flawless. There's often a temptation, when considering a philosophical question, to think that (despite what I've just claimed) the question could be answered if we were just in possession of the right empirical facts. But this seems to me to be a category error, just like the error – if it is one! – of including songs in the category of literature. If a question can be answered empirically, then it is not philosophical after all, but scientific (or belongs to some other more empirical discipline, such as musicology).[19] Some accept this point and argue that if this is how we are going to classify questions, there are no good philosophical questions – any question that can be answered can be answered empirically. But why should we believe this? A defender of the thesis might give some empirical evidence, but a critic of it might provide a non-empirical objection (e.g., that, for all we can observe empirically, the defender's reasoning may be distorted by his being trapped in the Matrix). To rule the non-empirical objection out of court would be to assume precisely what is at issue. So at the very least there seem to be genuine philosophical questions about what kinds of evidence are *good* evidence for various kinds of claims.[20] Whether or not there are genuine, interesting philosophical questions about music is a matter best settled by engaging with some examples, as we will do throughout this book.

A nice illustration of the conceptual nature of philosophy is given by part of the debate on the problem of freedom, a common topic in introductory philosophy courses. We might present the problem as a paradox, that is, a set of propositions each of which seems initially plausible, but not all of which can be true:

1   *The thesis of freedom*: It is true of some of our actions that we could have acted differently, in a way that gives us moral responsibility for those actions.
2   *The thesis of causalism*: Our actions (like everything else) are ultimately caused by factors outside our control (such as the laws of nature, our genetic inheritance, and our environment).
3   *The thesis of incompatibilism*: At most one of the theses of freedom and causalism is true.

There are at least three ways to try to solve this paradox, each corresponding to the rejection of one of these theses. The solutions that are useful for illustrating the non-empirical nature of philosophy I will call *compatibilism* and *hard causalism*. The compatibilist rejects the thesis of incompatibilism, arguing that some of our actions can still be under our control, in the sense that gives us responsibility for them, even if everything in the world, including ourselves, is entirely constituted by causal processes ultimately beyond our control. The hard causalist accepts the thoroughgoing causal nature of the universe, but argues that this precludes the possibility that our actions are free, thus rejecting the thesis of freedom.[21] What is interesting for our purposes about the debate between these two positions is that the proponents of each agree on the empirical facts – in this case the thesis of causalism. What they disagree about seems to be a matter of the correct *interpretation* or *understanding* of these facts. What constitutes freedom of the sort we are interested in here – the sort that gives us moral responsibility for our actions and the authority to praise and blame, even to punish, others for theirs? Is such freedom compatible with a thoroughly causal universe? These are in some important sense *conceptual* questions, not settled by the empirical evidence. You might think that if philosophy is merely a matter of *interpretation*, then it's not a domain of much importance, perhaps not even a domain of objective truth and falsity. But can it really be that there's no fact of the matter about whether we're justified in punishing someone for murdering someone else in cold blood, that whether he is responsible for his actions is merely a trivial matter of interpretation? That's a position much easier to claim in the philosophy classroom than to defend in "real life." (Imagine trying to defend that line to someone who has lost a loved one to murder.) In considering whether philosophical questions, being significantly conceptual, are "real" questions, I find it also helps to recall the example of mathematics. Most people find it plausible that mathematics is a non-empirical (*a priori*, conceptual) discipline. Yet few think that mathematics is just a matter of interpretation. On the contrary, it is often held up as a paradigm of objective fact and intellectual rigor.

This leads me to the third characteristic of philosophy: Philosophers are particularly concerned with *arguments*, that is, collections of claims (the premises) that are intended to give people good reason to accept some further claim (the conclusion). Of course, people in all sorts of academic disciplines (scientific, humanistic, etc.) and in non-academic life (politics, plumbing, etc.) are concerned with arguments; we make and critically assess arguments all the time. But, perhaps because philosophical questions are fundamental and substantially conceptual, the arguments for and against certain answers to them can often seem much slipperier than those about more immediately practical matters, such as how to fix a leaky faucet. So philosophers spend a lot of time thinking about both the individual concepts that are involved in the arguments that interest them and the structure of those arguments. For instance, is the sense of "freedom" in which our actions are under our causal control the same sense of "freedom" that is relevant to whether an agent is morally responsible for her actions? If not, arguments that use the word may be equivocal and thus fail to establish what they appear to. Some people find this close attention to concepts and arguments exasperating. If you're one of those people, you might not enjoy philosophy very much. But even if you find that philosophy isn't for you, I hope you come to see that philosophical questions are genuine, difficult, and important.

I've drawn examples from outside the philosophy of music to characterize philosophy in general, but to get a sense of the sorts of things we'll be considering in this book, it might help to compare some philosophical questions about music with, on the one hand, similar philosophical questions about non-musical domains and, on the other, related but non-philosophical questions about music. Consider what are often presented as the three main branches of philosophy: metaphysics, epistemology, and ethics. Metaphysics is the study of what exists, in some fundamental sense. The problem of freedom briefly discussed above, for instance, is a metaphysical problem because it is about the kind of being we are and the nature of the world in which we live. Musicologists make various claims about the existence of musical works, such as how many works Brahms composed and then destroyed. But these are empirical questions based on documentary evidence. A philosopher of music might ask, instead, what it is that makes something music rather than mere noise, or what it takes to *create* a musical work and whether it is even possible to *destroy* one.

Epistemology, as already mentioned, is the study of knowledge and justification. These concepts may seem no more related to artistic experience than to any other realm of human life, but philosophers of the arts discuss what it is to *experience*, *understand*, or *interpret* art, relationships between ourselves and the world that bear more than a superficial resemblance to knowledge. (Consider the difference between *truly* understanding a piece of music and mistakenly thinking that one does. The contrast is strikingly similar to that between knowledge and mistaken belief.) While music theorists may discuss the details of a particular work's harmonic structure, say, and formulate general theories of harmony on the basis of many such analyses, a philosopher of music might ask what the relationship between such analyses and our actual experience of the music is or should be, or whether the focus on harmonic structure gives short shrift to equally important aspects of our experience of music, such as timbre and register, not to mention emotional expression.[22]

Ethics – the study of what is morally right and wrong, or how we ought to live our lives – is often taken to be the third major branch of philosophy. But ethics shares its most distinctive feature with other, non-ethical topics and is thus part of a broader area that we might call *value theory*. Consider a classic ethical dilemma: Suppose you are alone on a remote beach and there are two people in the water – your bumbling but loveable child, and a scientist known to be on the brink of finding a cure for all cancers. A sudden storm arises and you realize that while both swimmers are in trouble, they are far enough apart and you are only so strong a swimmer that you will be able to save only one. Whom should you save? One might reasonably respond that most people would save their child. But the ethical question is not the *descriptive*, psychological one of what people *would in fact* do; it is the *normative* or *prescriptive* question of what people *should* or *ought to* do. Normative questions nicely illustrate the non-empirical nature of philosophy, for it is not obvious how we could settle what people *ought* to do by observing what people *actually* do. Value theory is the philosophical study of normativity in all its forms. This branch of philosophy thus includes ethics, but we find normativity whenever we find *evaluative* concepts – concepts such as right and wrong or good and bad (morally or otherwise). Thus value theory includes more than just ethics. Most relevant here is the fact that we evaluate music all the time, encouraging our friends to listen to good music we've just discovered or detailing the flaws of a disappointing album by an artist from whom we'd come to expect great things. Musicologists make claims more formally in favor of one composer or style or school over others. Philosophers of music ask about the nature and basis of such evaluative judgments. Are claims about goodness and badness in the musical realm *subjective*, as many people seem to think? If so, how can this be reconciled with the fact that people give *reasons* for thinking one song or artist is better than another, or the heat with which debates over such matters are often conducted? On the other hand, how could we defend our evaluative claims about music as *objective*, given that knowledgeable people's musical preferences clearly differ?

Having focused on the differences between philosophical and other questions about music, it is worth emphasizing two continuities. First, it is not obvious that there is a sharp division between philosophical and non-philosophical questions about music (or other domains). Claims in non-philosophical domains often rely on apparently non-empirical knowledge, such as what counts as good reasoning, and philosophical claims often draw on extra-philosophical, even empirical facts. (How could one hope to answer a philosophical question about music without appealing at some point to musical experience?) Second, as I have already noted, many people who are not professional, or even trained, philosophers – most notably for our purposes ordinary listeners and musicologists – discuss philosophical questions, just as philosophers of music sometimes engage in musicology, music theory, and music criticism. And just as trained philosophers sometimes get things wrong, untrained philosophers often have valuable philosophical insights. Again, the hope is that philosophical training can, over time and overall, improve our collaborative attempts to understand the fascinating phenomena of musical life.

We now have some sense of what philosophy of music is, but you might still be wondering about its value: Why philosophize about music? There may be some practical value to philosophizing about music, depending on how exactly we demarcate "the practical." Perhaps reflecting on the nature of songs, performances, and recordings, for instance, could lead to better copyright law (e.g., Hick 2017). Closer to home, perhaps reflection on some of the issues discussed in this book will lead you to make different musical decisions, whether it's a matter of buying one recording rather than another, spending some time learning about an unfamiliar musical tradition, or even choosing to make music in a different way. I would not want to neglect, however, the value of the increased *understanding* of music that one gains by philosophizing about music, independent of any effects this has on one's actions, even within the musical sphere. This assessment of the value of philosophy of music relies on the assumption that music itself is valuable. (We will turn in the next few chapters to the question of what that value is.) One philosopher of music has written that if we can do philosophy of music, we can do philosophy of "parking tickets, general elections, the Open Championship, Chardonnay, and fluffy dice" (S. Davies 2003, 30).[23] But presumably we will find philosophical theorizing about these subjects more or less valuable largely to the extent that we find parking tickets, general elections, and so on *themselves* valuable. As with philosophy, so with music: If it leaves you cold, you are unlikely to find this book as interesting as those in whose lives music plays a vital role. (Or perhaps the book will inspire in you a lifelong love of music, philosophy, or both!)

One final clarification about the scope of this book: We might make a distinction between doing philosophy *of* music and doing philosophy *through* music. The subject of this book is the former: philosophical claims and questions about music itself. But it is also possible to use music (particularly songs, with their verbal aspects) as a gateway to considering questions in other areas of philosophy, such as epistemology or political philosophy – thus doing philosophy *through* music. A lot of what might seem to be philosophy of music, published for the popular market, belongs to this category. For instance, of the 18 essays in the collection *Bob Dylan and Philosophy* (Vernezze & Porter 2006), 12 essays are essentially philosophical reflections, inspired by Dylan's lyrics, on topics as varied as love, freedom, personal identity, postmodernism, and Christian philosophy; only three take Dylan's music itself as a philosophical topic, and thus do philosophy *of* music. (The remaining essay offers a critical appreciation of *Tarantula*.)

Having reflected on what it is to do philosophy of music, let's return to the nature of song, this time examining what professional philosophers have recently argued about how we should understand the relationships between song, words, and music.

1.3 Are Songs Music?

1.3.1 What's in a Name? Songs and (Pure) Music

While the claim that songs are *literature* may seem a puzzling one, the claim that songs are *music* is uncontroversial. If Bob Dylan were awarded a prize for being the greatest musician of the twentieth century, people would surely dispute whether the right person had been chosen, but few would seriously challenge the idea that Dylan is *eligible* for the prize, i.e., that he is a musician. Indeed, the way many people use the word these days, "song" is synonymous with "piece of music." But if we're not sure that songs are literature, despite their including artistic words, why are we so certain that they're music just because they include artistic pitches, rhythms, and harmonies?

Before addressing this question, let's pause to figure out what's at stake when we discuss how a given term (e.g., "song") ought to be used. (Note the normative word – "ought" – here.) The word "song" is traditionally used to refer to music with a vocal part. More recently, as just noted, it has become common to refer to any piece of music – with or without a vocal part – as a "song." I suspect that two factors are largely responsible for this recent shift. First, most of the music that most people listen to (hip hop, rock, pop, country, etc.) includes vocal parts, and the Western traditions in which instrumental music without vocal parts plays a central role, namely classical and jazz, command an ever-diminishing share of musical audiences. It is thus unsurprising that many people conflate the general category of music with the kind of music they listen to most often: song (in the traditional sense). Second, many people's listening lives are dominated by iTunes and other similar software, in which the label for the basic unit – the individual track – is "song" (for reasons obviously connected with the first point). Whatever the reasons for the shift in usage (a descriptive matter), is there any justification for the (normative) *criticism* of the new usage? The norms of language use are a complex and politically fraught topic. I will make just one point here that is related to philosophical methodology. *If* one thinks that there should be a shared set of norms governing English usage for the purposes of formal communication among the largest possible group (and this is an assumption that many would question), then one of the principles governing the construction of those norms would surely be something like the following: "A word or phrase is somewhat undesirable if … it blurs a useful distinction" (Garner 2016, xiv).[24] Thus, if one thinks that the distinction between music with sung words and music without them is useful, one has a reason to resist the current semantic creep of "song," reserving the term, at least in its primary, literal uses, for music with sung words.

The relationship between this point about usage and philosophical methodology is straightforward. Since philosophy's job is to help us understand a domain (e.g., music), philosophers will want to develop concepts that reflect the nature of that domain, and of course to have words for those concepts. Thus philosophers, like those in many other disciplines and professions, develop their own specialized concepts and vocabularies, which they think are helpful for understanding their domains. Since music (unlike, say, particle physics) is a cultural domain that is central to many people's lives, philosophers' recommendations for how to use language (e.g., "song") can come across as tyrannical. Who are philosophers to tell you how to use a word? Most philosophers, however, if pressed, would acknowledge two points. First, it makes no difference to them (as philosophers, at least) how people in a non-philosophical setting use language. If, on the other hand, someone wants to understand the fundamental nature of music, then they want to do philosophy of music and will need *some* theoretical vocabulary in order to proceed. Such a person may disagree with others' proposals, but he cannot criticize others for developing such vocabularies, on pain of inconsistency. Second, most philosophers would agree that it makes little difference which particular *words* one uses; what is important for philosophical purposes is the *concepts* that those words stand for. Just as the English word "song" and the German word "Lied" mean the same thing, you can mint a neologism, e.g., "sing-music," or use an already existing word, e.g., "fork," to refer to song.[25] Of course, such choices might make a *practical* difference – it's going to be psychologically difficult to divorce the ordinary meaning of "fork" from the word when you use it to refer to song – which is of course why philosophers and others tend to select terms for their technical vocabulary that approximate in their ordinary use the concept they have in mind. (Consider, for example, the physicist's selection of "weight" or "force" as names for precise theoretical concepts.)

A philosopher who urges a traditional use of the word "song," because she thinks that the concept such usage reflects is useful for understanding music, thus owes us an account of *why* she thinks that concept is useful. This returns us to the question at the beginning of this section: If we're not sure that songs are literature, despite their including artistic words, why are we so certain that they're music just because they include artistic pitches, rhythms, etc.? The obvious place to start in developing a philosophical theory of song is that songs differ from other music (and from literature) in combining two media – words and music. As a result, when we *appreciate* a song – that is, when we understand and evaluate it – we must approach it differently from how we would approach an instrumental jazz piece or a poem, when appreciating them.

Though this might seem unobjectionable, there has recently been philosophical and musicological resistance to the claim that song, along with some other artforms that are apparently combinations of music and other media, is not *simply* music or not *just* music. For instance, Aaron Ridley says that:

> a song is every bit as much a piece of music as a piece of instrumental music is, and so, given that the words are part of what makes a song the song it is, ... the words of a song are part of what makes a song the piece of music it is.
>
> (2004, 79)

Ridley's resistance to treating song as a combination of distinct media is motivated by the idea that philosophers' and musicologists' classification of some music as "pure" or "absolute" is intended to, or effectively does, *privilege* it over other, "hybrid" musical art forms,[26] and that this "autonomania" has insidiously infected the heart of contemporary philosophy of music, perverting theories of song, expressiveness, value, and more, often without the proponents of those theories realizing this source of their distorted views.[27]

This is not the place to consider Ridley's full case against autonomania, but his views provide a useful foil for considering whether, and if so in what sense, song is a composite of music and language. In short, I will suggest, *contra* Ridley, that any adequate theory of song requires a concept of pure music, and that song will not qualify as simply music in this sense.[28] But I do not believe that this in itself has any evaluative implications. From the fact that song is not simply music – not music through and through – it does not follow that song is *inferior* (even musically inferior) to instrumental music. We could just as easily say that song is *more* than simply music, thanks to its comprising both music and words (though, again, I would not want to defend this as an *evaluative* claim).

1.3.2 Artistic Categories and Artistic Media

The basic idea that in order to understand a given artwork, one must understand what *kind* of work it is, that is, *categorize* it correctly, is defended in an influential article by Kendall Walton (1970). Walton's "categories of art" are distinguished by sets of "standard," "contra-standard," and "variable" properties. Take film, for example. *Comprising moving pictures* is a *standard* feature of film: Possessing that feature counts (but not decisively) toward something's being a film. It's not essential (a film may consist entirely of still images[29]) but consisting entirely of still images is *contra-standard* – it counts against something's being a film, even if, all things considered, that thing *is* a film. The kind of plot a film has – whether tragic or comic, say – is irrelevant to whether or not it is a film; such properties are *variable* for the category. Categories of art are often nested. For instance, whether a film is in color or black-and-white is a variable property. But black-and-white images are standard for the narrower category of *silent film*.[30]

Walton gives a number of examples intended to show that correct categorization of a work is essential to its proper appreciation. His most cited example is from the visual arts. Consider Picasso's harrowing Spanish Civil War painting,

"Guernica." Walton asks us to imagine an alien artistic category called (rather confusingly) *guernicas*:[31]

> *Guernicas* are like versions of Picasso's "Guernica" done in various bas-relief dimensions. All of them are surfaces with the colors and shapes of Picasso's "Guernica," but the surfaces are molded to protrude from the wall like relief maps of different kinds of terrain. Some *guernicas* have rolling surfaces, others are sharp and jagged, still others contain several relatively flat planes at various angles to each other, and so forth.
>
> (1970, 347)

It so happens that *guernicas* with sharp, jagged topographies are considered dynamic and vital (by aliens familiar with the tradition), expressive of anger, violence, and so on, while rolling *guernicas* are considered smooth, soft, and gentle. The two-dimensional shapes that we see in Picasso's "Guernica" (the horse, the lightbulb, etc.) do not play any more expressive or representational role in *guernicas* than the flatness of the canvas does in (our) representational paintings. (Don't worry about how the aliens came to have such a strange art-form. Just suppose that the similarity to Picasso's painting is a staggering coincidence.) Clearly, if someone who knew nothing about painting but a lot about *guernicas* saw Picasso's "Guernica," they would (erroneously taking it to be a *guernica*) describe it as "cold, stark, lifeless, or serene and restful, or perhaps bland, dull, boring – but in any case *not* violent, dynamic, and vital" (Walton 1970, 347). The aliens would misdescribe Picasso's work, because they would take it to belong to a category to which it does not in fact belong. This sort of misunderstanding could easily result in a misevaluation. (Perhaps flat *guernicas* were all the rage in the 1960s, but everyone is just so *over* them now.) The idea that we ought to appreciate songs differently from pieces of instrumental music or works of literature is an application of the same ideas to actual artforms.

David Davies (2013a) connects Walton's categories of art with the notion of an *artistic medium*. If, as the name suggests, an artistic medium is the means by which an artist communicates something ("artistic content") to an audience, then the artist and audience must share some understanding of how the artist's use of her materials generates such content. Use of different materials will naturally constitute a different medium, but Davies argues that Walton's examples show that *different uses* of the *same materials* will also constitute a different medium (cf. Lopes 2014, 125–44). Though Picasso's painting and a flat *guernica* might be physically indistinguishable, they must employ different artistic media since they convey radically different content to knowledgeable audiences. Likewise, it is natural to think of song, combining as it does the two different materials of words and music, as a medium distinct from both artistic uses of words alone (e.g., poetry) and artistic uses of music without words (e.g., jazz improvisations).

1.3.3 The Medium, or Media, of Song

We could understand Jerrold Levinson's account of song along these lines. According to Levinson (1987a), appreciating a song typically requires appreciating its three principal elements – the text, the melody to which the text is sung, and the accompaniment – and the various relationships that hold between them. Each element can be appreciated to some extent on its own merits, as if it had been created independently, but these assessments will necessarily be incomplete or even misleading, since the ways in which the elements are related, both in pairs and in the complex whole, are crucial to the success of a song. Levinson observes that there are many different kinds of relationship between these elements that can make for a good song. One is *matching*, as when the expressive tone of the text is matched by the expressiveness of the accompaniment (e.g., "Strange Fruit"), but contrasting expressiveness can be just as effective, with the accompaniment undercutting the text. (I argue below that the jazz song "What's New?" is such an example.)

An issue that arises immediately for Levinson's account is whether he has delineated the three elements of song correctly. There are clearly songs that lack accompaniment (unaccompanied songs for solo voice) and songs that lack a text, such as scat and vocalise, and some rap arguably lacks melody. Perhaps for these cases we can simply modify the account by saying that song appreciation requires appreciating each element *if present* and their interactions. But in other cases, the very idea of separating the elements is challenging. Consider an unaccompanied *polyphonic* choral composition, that is, one in which each voice sings a distinct melodic part, while the notes sung at any given moment constitute the harmony at that moment. (If you're unfamiliar with this style of music, Phillippe Verdelot's "Ultimi miei sospiri" is a good example.) In such songs, each part is equally important, with no single part privileged as *the* melody. However, it is not that such songs have *no* melody; rather they have *multiple* melodies and hence, in a sense, no accompaniment, though in quite a different way from an unaccompanied song for solo voice, since in this case the various melodies supply what must be lacking from the unaccompanied solo song, namely harmony.[32] In *homophonic* unaccompanied choral music, such as many hymns, we can more easily identify the voice that carries the melody while the others provide harmonic accompaniment. Nonetheless, we will surely appreciate such choral accompaniment differently from instrumental accompaniment, precisely because it is sung. However we deal with these examples, there is also choral music (polyphonic and otherwise) that has instrumental accompaniment, complicating Levinson's account further. In light of such examples, it might be better to distinguish, first, between just *music* and *text*, and then allow for a variety of ways in which these elements can be combined.

Even assuming this modification, Levinson's account of song has been criticized by Aaron Ridley (2004, 70–104), David Davies (2013b), and Jeanette
Bicknell (2015, 1–26).[33] Rather than focusing on those criticisms, however, I
will consider the positive views of song that these authors offer, though these
seem to me to be extensions or developments of Levinson's view rather than
alternatives to it.

The heart of Ridley's view is that the words and the music of a song are
much less separable, even in theory or thought, than my discussion so far suggests (Ridley 2004, 78–83; cf. Bicknell 2015, 16–20). What we think of as "the
words" of a song in fact possess musical features, and perhaps vice versa. Ridley argues, for instance, that language – particularly poetry – has musical qualities. We talk quite naturally of the *rhythm* of a line in a poem, a play, or even a
novel, and seem to mean something like what we mean when we talk of musical
rhythm – the duration and timing of the constituent sounds. Similarly, there are
highly developed theories of poetic meter – repetitive structures against which
we hear the rhythms of individual lines – just as there are highly developed
theories of musical meter (e.g., Fabb & Halle 2008 and London 2012). Alliteration, assonance, and rhyme are often considered musical features of poetry, and
rhyme often plays a role similar to that of a musical *cadence* (a point of melodic
or harmonic rest at the end of a short passage). You might wonder whether
there's some equivocation here, however. If theories of poetic meter are distinct
from theories of musical meter, is poetic meter really – strictly speaking – a
musical quality of a poem? Ridley denies that there is "any reason to suspect
this sense of 'musical' of being metaphorical or misleading," giving examples
of poetic effects that are indisputably sonic (2004, 84). But given that not all
artistic sounds count as music (e.g., movie sound-effects), such examples do
not establish the conclusion Ridley draws.[34]

Anyway, more importantly for Ridley's argument, these "musical" qualities
of a text do not simply transfer to a song when the text is sung. Ridley points
out that the rhythm of a sung text is usually quite different from the rhythm of
the same text as spoken. [35] (This is true even of rap, which, as its name suggests,
is one of the forms of music with words that is *closest* to ordinary speech.) And
when a pre-existing poem is set to music, as is often the case in classical music,
the words are sometimes spread out over so long a melodic line that the effects
of alliteration, assonance, and rhyme are either lost or quite different from those
in a recitation of the poem.[36] The musical aspects of the text of a song, concludes
Ridley, are aspects not simply of the text's words, but of those words *as sung*,
and not only that, but as sung *in this particular song*, since different composers
may set the same words to different music with quite different effects.[37] So it is
not as easy to abstract the verbal elements of a song – "the words" – from the
musical elements – "the music" – as Levinson implies. One way of expressing
this point would be to say that the medium of song is not merely the sum of the

media of music and literature, but a new medium in its own right, thanks to the transformation of each individual medium in their combination.

However, there do seem to be limits to the transformation of even the "musical" elements of words when they are sung. Consider the most obvious examples of poor *text setting*, where a weak syllable falls on a strong musical beat. Examples are legion; I'll take one from Orr's piece on Dylan's Nobel. In Fleetwood Mac's "Dreams," the line "when the rain washes you clean, you'll know" is sung so that the second syllable of "washes" falls in a highly salient place in the musical phrase – on a (syncopated) strong beat, on the highest note of the phrase, and at the top of the largest, and only ascending, interval (Example 1.1a). Many people think that the resulting effect ("when the rain wa-SHES you clean, you'll know") is a flaw in the song.[38] (You might disagree with this particular judgment, but surely there are *some* such cases.) It doesn't follow that the simplest adjustment to the line that removes the infelicity would improve the song overall (consider Example 1.1b), but perhaps it shows that the differences between spoken poetry and sung text are not as radical as Ridley suggests.

What is the role of the words *as sung* in Ridley's account of the appreciation of song? He basically thinks that in a *good* song, this new artistic entity – forged from the words and their musical setting – demonstrates an "understanding" of the words alone (as read). Like Levinson, he wants to allow a wide range of relationships between the words and music (congruence, contrast, etc.) to constitute evidence of such understanding, though he emphasizes that congruence or matching is just one among many such relationships and in no way fundamental or primary (Ridley 2004, 97–8; cf. Bicknell 2015, 20–3).

One way of testing the implications of these theories is to consider two puzzling kinds of case: Songs that many people consider exemplary, yet which involve either words or music that when taken by themselves seem lackluster. Examples of the first kind might include the Beach Boys' "Good Vibrations," James Brown's "Get Up," and the "Amen" sections of any excellent mass. Examples of the second kind might include much of Dylan's oeuvre

Example 1.1 Fleetwood Mac, "Dreams," excerpt: (a) original, and (b) altered so that the first syllable of "washes" is more musically salient than the second. (Author's transcription.)

and mediocre settings of great poems, such as August Kestner's "Erlkönig" (famously set excellently by Schubert). Jeanette Bicknell focuses on the first kind of case, arguing that criticizing the words of a song on the basis of their literary qualities has limited value at best, since the words are just one part of an organic whole (2015, 1–5, 20–3).[39] Ridley would, of course, amplify this line of reasoning by arguing that the *text as read* is not the same as the *text as sung*, and thus is not, strictly speaking, even part of the song. He also claims that, surprisingly, philosophers of song typically ignore the counterpart case of a song with exceptionally literary lyrics but music that would be considered poor in the absence of those words. Ridley takes this to be a symptom of the autonomaniac tendency of philosophers of music to favor the music over the text in their theories of song. (Bicknell may be an ironic example of this tendency.)

But Ridley also uses the parallel cases to make a further point. He claims that many philosophers of music implicitly appeal to the following argument:

4a There are excellent songs with texts that are awful when evaluated as literature.
5a Thus, the value of such songs must derive from their purely musical elements.
6a Thus, the value of songs in general must derive from their purely musical elements.

If that argument stands up, he continues, the parallel argument must also:

4b There are excellent songs with music that is awful when evaluated in the absence of the text (i.e., as instrumental music).
5b Thus, the value of such songs must derive from their purely literary elements.
6b Thus, the value of songs in general must derive from their purely literary elements.

As Ridley concludes, this is "silly" – the conclusions of the two arguments are incompatible, so there must be something wrong with at least one of them (2004, 82). The most obvious problem is the generalization from the claim that the value of a given (kind of) song resides in some particular (kind of) element (5a, 5b) to the claim that the value of *all* songs resides in that kind of element (6a, 6b).

It is not obvious, however, that the interim conclusions (5a and 5b in themselves) are silly. Isn't it plausible that some songs (e.g., many of Bob Dylan's) are valuable primarily for their verbal features and others (e.g., the Beach Boys' best work) primarily for their musical features? And though it might not follow necessarily, isn't it also plausible that a song that works as an organic whole, but also has both excellent words and music when those elements are considered separately, would be the best kind of song overall?[40] Of course, if you've been convinced by Ridley's arguments about the musical aspects of words, you will want to gloss "words" and "music" carefully here. But Ridley himself emphasizes that he is "not denying that there are differences between music and words. Nor am I denying that there are differences between vocal and instrumental music" (2004, 79), so he is perhaps open to the possibility of appreciating the various elements of song separately, albeit in the context of the song as a whole.[41]

David Davies (2013b) has proposed a way of thinking about song that, though it draws on his own more general theory of art, implies conclusions similar to Ridley's.[42] Earlier, I mentioned Davies's claim that an artistic medium comprises not just distinctive materials, but also distinctive ways in which those materials are used to generate artistic content. He thus distinguishes between the *vehicular* medium of an artwork – the stuff that gets used in the creation of the work – and its *artistic* medium – the way the vehicular medium is used to convey content or meaning. Language, for instance, is used to write novels and poetry. But, according to Davies, artistic content is generated from language differently in novels and poems. For instance, the sonic properties of language (rhyme, alliteration, etc.) are more significant in the interpretation of poetry than of novels. The two artforms thus share a *vehicular* medium (language), but have different *artistic* media (the different ways in which language generates meaning in the two artforms).[43]

It should be noted, although Davies does not emphasize the point, that language, considered as a *vehicular* medium, already bears meaning or content. It may be true that words generate meaning in different ways in poetry than in prose, but it cannot be that one and the same word has a different basic, literal meaning in these two artforms (e.g., that "sad" names a negative emotional state in one but a positive emotional state in the other), otherwise we would have lost the sense of what it means to say that these different artforms share a *single* language as their vehicular medium. The same is arguably true of "musical languages," e.g., the conventions governing Western music in the "common practice" period (c. 1600–1900 CE). (We will explore the idea of such musical content in Chapter 4.) And there may well be other "contentful" vehicular media. For instance, though there are variations in how things are depicted, all cultures seem to understand *pictures* (or "depictions"), though pictures can be put to a wide range of uses, artistic and otherwise.[44]

On Davies's view, *sung words* are a distinct artistic medium that shares vehicular media with both literature and instrumental music. Just as a great novel broken into separate lines would not make for a great poem, even though both novels and poems are "made of" words, a song's lyrics treated as a poem will be – at least partially – misunderstood. Thus far, Davies's conclusions mirror Ridley's and Bicknell's. But Davies goes further, claiming that this way of thinking about song provides "the beginnings of an explanation" not only of why it is a mistake to attempt to appreciate a set of lyrics as a poem, but also of how "the setting of base verbal materials to music [can] transmute them, … in … songs, into gold" (2013b, 21, 15), that is, how a song with mediocre lyrics (considered as poetry) can nonetheless be an excellent song. Davies's two examples are the jazz standard "What's New?" and the Beatles' classic "Hey Jude" (2013b, 14).[45]

The words of "What's New?" are mostly the banal conversation of someone meeting an ex-lover by chance on the street: "What's new? How is the world treating you? You haven't changed a bit," and so on. The emotional impact of the song comes from two main sources. First, there is a dramatic shift in the singer's topic at the end of the song, from a casual catch-up to a declaration of love (perhaps made only to themselves): "Of course you couldn't know, I haven't changed; I still love you so."[46] This twist is hardly a surprise to the listener because of the other source of the song's emotional power, namely the musical setting of the words. This song is a clear case of the musical elements' *undercutting* the meaning of the text taken alone. No one attending to the song could miss either the banality of the lyrics or the melancholy tone of the music. The obvious interpretation of this contrast is that the music belies the singer's words, revealing the strength of her emotion. This seems less a case of unliterary words being transformed into lyrical gold, then, and more one of dramatic – or musical – irony.[47] The quality of the song as an organic whole (ironically, this time, for Davies's argument) surely depends not on the *transformation* of the words from banality to profundity, but rather on our recognition that the words *are indeed banal* (together, of course, with the excellence of their musical setting).

"Hey Jude" is a different kind of case, since the words in question are arguably not banal but *nonsensical*. Davies quotes the following "semantic infelicities" (2013b, 14): "And don't you know that it's just you, hey Jude, you'll do/ The movement you need is on your shoulder" (2013b, 21 n. 9), but plenty of scorn has also been heaped on the text of the chorus: "Na, na, na, na-na na na, na-na na na, hey Jude." Though reasonable people may differ about just how good a song "Hey Jude" is, one can certainly make the case that the "na na"s of the huge coda that constitutes the second half of the song (foreshadowed between some verses) contribute to the exuberant joy that is the culmination of the song's slow emotional crescendo better than any actual words might have done.[48] It's harder to make a case that the song transmutes into gold the line "the movement you need is on your shoulder" and, indeed, Davies makes no such attempt. Some commentators suggest that the "movement" in question is a *nod*, reinforcing the encouragingly positive message of the song (Spignesi & Lewis 2004, 30), and one might point to its echo of the "shoulders" that appear a couple of verses earlier; but surely the lyricist – Paul McCartney! – might have crafted a more comprehensible line using "shoulder" (or one of the many rhymes unused elsewhere in the song: older, bolder, … told 'er?) that was in keeping with both the song's lyrical indeterminacy and its journey from calm counsel to exuberant joy. It seems to me that, however good the song is, it would clearly have been better, even if only slightly, had such a substitution been made. Even McCartney nods.[49]

In sum, it seems to me that both Ridley's and Davies's suggestions for how to think about song amount to a refinement of Levinson's view rather than a refutation of it. It is when they attempt to go beyond the basic structure of Levinson's view that they overreach, in arguing (in Ridley's case) that song is not a hybrid form but simply music or (in Davies's case) that setting language to music can transmute poor words into great ones. But whether any version of Levinson's view can be defended turns on whether there is *any* sense in which the words can reasonably be separated from the music of a song in the course of its appreciation. Could we use matters considered thus far to more carefully distinguish the elements or aspects of a song, rather than reject the idea that there are such elements or aspects? One way to do so would be to distinguish the *verbal* aspects of a song – something like *the meanings of the words and sentences* that constitute the song's text – from the *musical* aspects of the song, where this would include not just features possessable by instrumental music (melody, harmony, etc.), but also any features of language defensible as musical, and the ways in which both contribute to the artistic medium (in Davies's terms) of sung words. On such a view, song is at least what we might call a *vehicular hybrid* in that it combines, as Davies states, two vehicular media. Developing such a view would require clearly articulating, first, the ways in which meaning or content is generated by the *vehicular media* of music and language and, second, how these media generate meaning or content when combined. (This would certainly include how they generate *artistic* content, though some might argue that the combination effects changes in *vehicular* content, such as the meanings of words, too.)

At times, Ridley seems to suggest that this approach is hopeless. We have already considered his arguments that words may generate content in the same ways that instrumental music does (through rhythm, meter, and so on); he also argues that instrumental music can generate content in much the same way that language can (e.g., by getting us to think of a certain thing in a certain way) (2004, 47–69). But if these are both instances of the generation of *artistic* content, then they leave open the possibility of distinguishing the ways in which music and language generate *vehicular* content.

Davies is more moderate, saying that

> when they are set to music, the contributions of the words and their senses are loosened from the syntactic structures in which they are located, and thereby further removed from the way in which language functions in the artistic ... medium of prose. [Hence,] those things that would strike us as weaknesses in poems do not do so in songs because the artistic medium in song prescinds from these "failings."[50]

(2013b, 21)

But it is not clear how words could be "loosened" from their ordinary (vehicular) meanings merely by being sung.[51] There can of course be ambiguous, vague, or suggestive sentences, such as many of the lines of "Hey Jude," but these lines possess those qualities *in virtue of*, rather than differently from, their ordinary meanings. The selection of these particular words in this particular order seems to give them the (basic, vehicular) meaning they have, rather than their being sung in one way or another (though the latter will undoubtedly affect the artistic content of the song as a whole). And our earlier discussion of poor text-setting suggests that the "musical" (e.g., rhythmic) qualities of sung words cannot successfully stray as far as Ridley suggests from those of ordinary speech.

How music (as opposed to language) generates meaning or content and how we should limn the boundaries of the musical are difficult issues to which we will return throughout this book. But even if Ridley is correct that we can never *practically* separate the verbal and musical *elements* of a song, we may still be able *in principle* to distinguish its verbal and musical *aspects*, that is, the different *ways in which* a song conveys content (e.g., semantically or harmonically). The division between these kinds of content will not match up neatly with the division between, say, the vocal and instrumental elements of a song (how could it, when unaccompanied choral music is a possibility?), but both distinctions will surely be useful in understanding how a song achieves the effects it does – that is, in appreciating the song.

1.4 Review and Looking Ahead

We have considered two claims about the artistic medium of song, or song's correct artistic categorization: the uncontroversial claim that songs are music and the (relatively) controversial claim that songs are literature. I have suggested that both claims are simplistic at best. Songs may contain poems, but they are not *simply* poems.[52] Similarly, songs contain music, but to say that they are *simply* music ignores the complexity of their combination of the two vehicular media of language and music. These more nuanced claims may sound less controversial or interesting than the bold claims they replace, yet working out the reasons for their plausibility requires grappling with some difficult fundamental issues about the nature of the arts.

What do these conclusions imply about the issue that initially prompted our discussion – Bob Dylan's eligibility for the Nobel Prize in Literature? If songs *contain* poems, then it seems reasonable to consider their authors eligible for literary prizes on the basis of those poems. But our discussion suggests that artists are not eligible for literary prizes on the basis of their *songs*, taken as artistic wholes. Though literature and song share a vehicular medium (language), the way in which song combines that vehicular medium with another (music) implies that the way in which the words generate artistic meaning or content cannot be understood independently of the contributions of the music. Thus there is no way to assess the *sung words* of Dylan's songs without taking their musical features and context into account.[53] Does this reasoning imply that songwriters should not be eligible for *music* awards either? This would follow if music awards were understood to be *only* for artists working in *music alone*. There is not space for further consideration of this issue here, however.[54]

Does distinguishing the musical from the verbal aspects of song condemn us as "autonomaniacs" – those who see instrumental music without any accompanying text, dance, images, and so on, as necessarily superior to song, musically accompanied dance, films with musical soundtracks, and the rest? It is well worth keeping the possibility of such distortions in mind as one philosophizes about music. But I have argued only that, in thinking seriously about the nature of music, we cannot do without some concept of *simply* or *purely* musical content or meaning, and that song will not count as simply or purely music in this sense. No *evaluative* conclusions about pure music or hybrids involving music (song, film, etc.) follow from this. As mentioned earlier, why think that the concept of pure music implies that song is *less musical* than instrumental music, rather than *more* than "merely" music?

Whatever your view of the nature of song, a complete theory of song would presumably include large chunks of both a theory of the artistic uses of language and a theory of the artistic uses of music, in addition to a theory of what happens when we *combine* words and music in an artwork. Since this book is an introduction to the philosophy of *music*, I focus in what follows on the medium (or media) of *music*, largely ignoring the complications introduced by the inclusion of words or other media in a work, and sometimes considering purely instrumental music.[55] Over the next three chapters, we will consider two kinds of content that have figured prominently in philosophical theories of music: emotional content and what we might call "purely musical" content, such as melody, harmony, rhythm, and form. We will return to the nature of the medium of music in the final chapter of this book.

Questions

Explain both the best argument, in your view, for Bob Dylan's (or other singer-songwriters') eligibility for literary prizes, and the best argument against such eligibility. Which argument is more successful?

Explain both the best argument (in your view) for the idea that song is *simply music*, and the best argument against that claim. Which argument is more successful?

Which is worse: A song with great lyrics but terrible music, or a song with great music but terrible lyrics?

If you combined a great (pre-existing) poem and a great (pre-existing) piece of instrumental music in a song, it seems unlikely that the result would be a great song. Explain why not. Under what circumstances (if any) *could* such a combination result in a great song?

If one agrees with Ridley that song is *simply music*, is one committed to the idea that other artforms that we might initially have considered hybrids of music and other media are also simply music? Consider such artforms as film, video-games, dance works such as ballets, musical theater, and so on.

Is the correct categorization of an artwork (e.g., as a song, poem, or painting) essential for properly appreciating (i.e., understanding and evaluating) it?

Notes

1 The best criticism of the award on the grounds that Dylan's work *doesn't* merit it is, in my view, Dammann 2016.

2 Strictly speaking, Dylan *is* eligible, since he has produced works that are uncontroversially literature, most notably *Tarantula* (1971). But few seem willing to defend *its* greatness, and the Swedish Academy explicitly based their decision on Dylan's songs, ignoring *Tarantula* completely (Engdahl 2016).

3 There is also published sheet-music for many of Dylan's songs, including both lyrics and musical notation, which is intended to guide singing and playing. It is suggestive that such sheet music was *not* used to illustrate journalism about Dylan's award.

4 Though it doesn't affect the argument here, the case is complicated in that Auden's poem was originally written as a song lyric (!) in the play *The Ascent of F6* (1936). But the poem recited in the film is the version revised for publication in Auden's collection *Another Time* (1940), which replaces the final three stanzas (of five in the play version) with two completely new stanzas.

5 You might think that *all* films are works of literature because, like songs, they comprise words artfully arranged. But this claim stands in need of the same justification as the parallel claim about song that we are currently investigating.

6 Appreciating *Tarantula* as a prose poem may require approaching various aspects of it in different ways, e.g., the significance of its *sounds*. We will return to this idea when we consider David Davies's theory of artistic media in §1.3.3.

7 Calling this the "straight answer" puts the other reasons Engdahl supplies (considered below) in a rather awkward rhetorical position. Are they misleading answers?

8 And once we consider this possibility, we may wonder why *literature* should get all the beautiful art. Why couldn't sculptors, by similar reasoning, argue that Dylan's songs "belong in sculpture" because of their great beauty? Is Engdahl suggesting that literature ranks higher as an art than music? (Thanks to Faith Broddrick and Tyler Herron for suggesting the latter interpretation.)

9 Note the universal assumption that if Dylan's songs are literature, they are *poetry*, rather than, say, short stories, essays, or prose poems. Presumably this is because of their resemblance to paradigmatic poems, to which we will turn below.

10 Philosophers have made the same point about the word "art" (e.g., Weitz 1956, 33–5).

11 Note that I continue to use our conceptual scheme while discussing these ancient examples; the Greeks and Romans may have employed different categories. Thanks to Tim O'Sullivan and Corinne Pache for prompting me to consider this.

12 More is known about ancient Greek *philosophy* of music than about the music itself. For an overview, see Hamilton 2007, 10–39, or Mathisen 2011.

13 One might, of course, argue that such works *contain* literary works, following the first interpretation considered above.

14 Orr implies that even printed lyrics lack the crucial property of *being intended to be read as poems*. Note that this explanation is incomplete without an independent account of what it is to read something "as a poem," rather than "as a song."

15 An excellent introduction to the definition of literature is Stecker (1996).

16 I use the term "trained philosopher" broadly, to include anyone with some philosophical training – students and professors of philosophy, music professors who pursue an interest in philosophy, and so on.

17 To be sure, philosophers often draw heavily on the work of other disciplines, such as physics or biology, that are *less* fundamental in this sense. This is worth remembering if you're ever tempted to think that "fundamental" is an evaluative term here.

18 The very nature and existence of non-empirical knowledge, quite independently of the claim that it is characteristic of philosophy, is a controversial topic within epistemology. For an introduction, see Russell 2017. The emergence of "experimental philosophy" also calls philosophy's non-empirical nature into question. See Knobe and Nichols 2017.

19 For brevity, I often lump all scholars of music under the label "musicologist," even though there are (contested) distinctions between musicologists (in a narrower sense), music theorists, and so on.

20 My consideration of these issues draws on E. J. Lowe's defense of the necessity of metaphysics (2002, 1–13).

21 I am indebted to Elliott Sober (2005, 303–32) for parts of this exposition of the problem and its solutions. For a detailed introduction to the problem and various solutions, see McKenna and Pereboom 2016.

22 Musicologists also consider such questions, but I would argue that in such cases they are doing philosophy.

23 In the context of this quotation, Davies's point is about musical ontology in particular, but I don't think he would object to the broader version of the claim I make here.

24 This is part of a set of ten principles recommended by Bryan Garner and followed in his usage guides. I recommend Garner's discussion of these principles (2016, xiii–xviii) as a thoughtful defense of usage prescriptions based on actual (descriptive) usage.

25 In fact, it is a matter of controversy in the philosophy of language whether words commonly treated as synonyms in translation in fact have the same meaning (or even what that amounts to). But I don't think that affects the basic point I am making here.

26 The history of this view within Western philosophy of music is long and complicated. For a recent account, see Bonds (2014) and the symposium on it in the *British Journal of Aesthetics* 57 (2017): 67–101.

27 Ridley coins the term "autonomania" for this position because of its roots in the idea that music is an "autonomous" art, in the senses of being both *abstract* (or non-representational) and *functionless*. For an overview of the history of these ideas, see Hamilton 2007, 66–94 and 153–91.

28 The term *pure music* has unfortunate moralistic, perhaps even racist, connotations, but I know of no better alternative. It is more awkward to talk of the "absolute" or "instrumental" music of a song, for instance, since those terms typically refer to the *genre* of "music alone" in Peter Kivy's phrase (1990), that is, pieces with no elements or aspects other than the musical.

29 Chris Marker's *La Jetée* (1962) is almost an example of this sort.

30 David Davies (2013a, 230) suggests that, instead of characterizing categories of art in terms of standard, contra-standard, and variable features, we should think of features on a *spectrum of salience* with respect to category membership. The kind of plot something has is at the non-salient end of the spectrum, while consisting entirely of moving images is at the highly salient end. "Dimensionality" might fall in the middle of the spectrum: We accept 3D films as films, but we also think of them as unusual, perhaps implying that their non–two-dimensionality is somewhat salient to their categorization as film.

31 If you find the terminology confusing, imagine instead that the alien artistic category is called "blargs." That is, replace every instance of (lower-case, italicized) "*guernica*" in what follows with the word "blarg."

32 In fact, there are ways for a single voice to produce more than one note at a time, and thus to create polyphony, if of a limited sort. For a scholarly introduction, see (Pegg 2001); for a taste in the context of a gripping documentary film, see *Genghis Blues* (1999).

33 These authors simply assume that words and music are the two basic elements of song, ignoring Levinson's tripartite account.

34 Indeed, in this very paragraph Ridley goes on to put the terms "cadence" and "musical" in quotation marks, suggesting that he does not think these terms apply literally to poetry.

35 French song provides a very clear example of Ridley's point, since there are relatively strict rules about which syllables ought to be sounded when sung – rules that differ from how the same words are typically spoken. Consider the words "frère Jacques" as they are spoken (two syllables) and sung (four syllables). For an overview of empirical studies of the relationship between pitch or frequency patterns of spoken and sung language, see Patel 2007, 216–18.

36 Christopher Ricks gives an example where the musical setting *adds* such features, arguing that in Dylan's "Positively 4th Street," "[m]usically, the unit is of four lines, but verbally (as lyrics) the unit has a rhyme scheme that extends over eight lines. … The effect is of a sequence that both is and is not intensely repetitive. So while musically the song is in twelve verses, rhymingly it is in six" (2003, 58).

37 Classical music furnishes more examples of this sort, since it is much more common in that tradition than in popular music to re-set a song text to entirely different music (as opposed to "cover versions" of popular songs, which invariably retain large swathes of the original's melody, rhythm, harmony, etc.). Consider, for example, Clara Schumann's gentle "Liebst du um Schönheit" with Gustav Mahler's yearning setting of the same text. Cover versions can nonetheless differ radically in meaning from their originals, as we will see in Chapter 9, §9.4.

38 As my choral conductor used to put it, when singing "you have to put the em-PHA-sis on the right syl-LAH-ble."

39 Note that this argument militates against the defense of songs as literature because they *contain* poems.

40 Examples of this last kind are bound to be even more controversial than those of the former kinds, but let me propose Benjamin Britten's settings of poetry widely acknowledged to be great literature (e.g., his *Serenade for Tenor, Horn, and Strings* (1943), which wonderfully sets rich texts by canonical poets such as Tennyson, Blake, and Keats).

41 I must note, however, that this last quotation from Ridley comes from the very page on which he goes on to say, as quoted earlier, that "a song is every bit as much a piece of music as a piece of instrumental music is, and so, given that the words are part of what makes a song the song it is, … the words of a song are part of what makes a song the piece of music it is."

42 Davies unfortunately seems to be unaware of Ridley's work on this topic, since he does not cite Ridley, despite the similarity of their views.

43 This gives us a useful way of thinking about the difference between reading *Tarantula* as a novel or as a collection of prose poems. However, the theory raises some thorny problems. For instance, just as different aspects of words are salient in prose vs. poetry, so are different aspects salient in Romantic vs. modernist poetry, and in Wordsworth's vs. Coleridge's poetry, and in early Wordsworth vs. late Wordsworth, and so on. Won't this result in every work (or even different parts of the same work) being in a different artistic medium? If so, the notion of a medium seems to be stretched very thin, since we typically think that many works may share a given medium.

44 For an introduction to philosophical theories of depiction, see Abell 2013.

45 I leave it to the reader to consider whether Davies would make the parallel claim: that his theory explains how the setting of excellent verbal materials to banal music can transform that music into gold.

46 I say "singer" for simplicity, but it would be more accurate to talk of the fictional persona, protagonist, or narrator of the song, since we take the singer to be using the words she sings not in the ordinary way, but rather to get us to imagine the situation represented by the song. The singer herself may also have a public persona, which may interact with the song's persona in complex ways. We will consider such matters in Chapter 7, §7.5.

47 In dramatic irony, the audience of a play (or other artwork) knows something of great interest to a character but of which the character is (thus *ironically*) unaware. In this case, the musical

elements of the song convey to the audience the singer's feelings about his or her interlocutor, of which the interlocutor is (I presume) unaware.

48 Note that this argument relies on listeners' recognizing that "na" is not a meaningful verbal utterance, i.e., a word.

49 In fact, the historical record suggests that this line is a nonsense placeholder from the demo that, at John Lennon's insistence, was never replaced with a crafted line (as others were) (Gambaccini 1974).

50 Davies's transition from prose to poetry in these quotations is a little puzzling. It may be charitable to replace "prose" with "literature" in the first quotation.

51 I assume that Davies means "semantic" rather than "syntactic." He surely doesn't think, for instance, that "shoulder" is less of a noun (whatever that would mean) when sung in "Hey Jude" than in a recitation of the lyrics as a poem.

52 I say "may" advisedly. Though I think it is more plausible that (some) songs *contain* poems than that they *are* poems, I do not think it is obviously true. Moreover, as is suggested by the popularity of the defense of Dylan's Nobel that his songs – *words and music together* – are literature, it is not clear how well the poems his songs putatively contain stand up in the absence of their musical settings.

53 Several commentators have suggested to me that we can appreciate a text *as lyrics*, that is, with respect to how successfully they *could* be set to music (either ideally, or in a range of different ways), yet without considering them as set in any particular way. It seems to me that this is incoherent. To appreciate how successfully a text could be set requires at least *imagining* its being set in one way or another, though not necessarily in all the detail of an actual musical work or performance.

54 Potentially relevant considerations include (1) how, precisely, categories of art-awards should be (i) individuated and (ii) related to artistic categories or media; (2) the long tradition (in the West, at least) of including songwriters and singers in the musical rather than literary worlds (not to mention artists of other composite or hybrid musical forms, such as ballet, program music, and opera); and (3) the fact that there is no Nobel Prize in Music (or Song).

55 Counterpart textbook introductions to the philosophy of literature include D. Davies 2007 and Lamarque 2009. The only book devoted to the philosophy of song as such is Bicknell 2015.

Further Reading

The only book-length consideration of song by a philosopher, considering a wide range of issues (including the nature and value of singing, and interactions between singing, technology, authenticity, and ethics) is Jeanette Bicknell's *Philosophy of Song and Singing* (2015). The special issue of the *Journal of Aesthetics and Art Criticism* on song, songs, and singing (volume 71, number 1, winter 2013) is a varied collection of philosophical reflections on this undertheorized topic.

A helpful, if slightly dated, discussion of the nature of philosophy is John Passmore's entry on "Philosophy" in the 1967 edition of the Routledge *Encyclopedia of Philosophy*.

Kendall L. Walton's "Categories of Art" (1970) is the *locus classicus* of the view that proper appreciation of an artwork requires its correct categorization. Chapter 9 of Dominic McIver Lopes's *Beyond Art* (2014, 125–44) is a consideration of the relationship between "appreciative" (e.g., art) kinds and media.

2   Emotions in the Music

Overview

In this chapter we consider the major theories of how music can possess emotional qualities, theories that variously locate music's emotional expressiveness in musicians' expression of their emotions, audiences' emotional or imaginative responses, and resemblances between the music and emotions. Along the way, we investigate the nature of emotions themselves, together with theories that deny that music is expressive in the first place.

Many people are passionate about music. We love particular songs, pieces, or genres of music, and can't stand others. We take great care in the selection of music to accompany important life events, such as weddings, funerals, and holidays. Some surround themselves with music at every available moment; others turn to music only at times of high emotion, whether positive – when falling in love or celebrating an achievement – or negative – when grieving or simply down in the dumps. What is it about music that we value so highly? What gives it the importance it has for so many people, or the power it seems to hold over us? Over the next four chapters we will investigate several different aspects of music that consistently appear in attempts to answer these questions, along with various issues that each kind of answer raises.

The subject of this chapter and the next is the emotional power of music. One reason that people are passionate about music is that music can itself be passionate. That is, music often seems to be *emotional* in some way that we value. Listen, for instance, to Radiohead's "We Suck Young Blood" from *Hail to the Thief* or the third movement, "Precipitato," of Prokofiev's Piano Sonata No. 7. Now suppose that someone described the Radiohead song as *upbeat* or the Prokofiev piece as *calm*. These descriptions would surely strike anyone as bizarre. If you don't hear "We Suck Young Blood" as *gloomy* (or something in that vicinity) and the "Precipitato" as *anxious*, you don't seem to be hearing the music at all. Such emotional expressiveness often features in people's evaluations of music. Some might praise the Radiohead song as exquisitely gloomy while others condemn it as self-indulgently maudlin; some might find the Prokofiev movement a masterful exploration of the limits of musical anxiety while others think it is overblown. There is a philosophical problem raised by such commonplace descriptions and evaluations that is thrown into sharp relief by a skeptical challenge to them: Emotions are experienced only by creatures with minds – obviously human beings, but plausibly other animals as well. Whatever music is, it isn't a creature with a mind, so how can we even *attribute* emotions – gloom or anxiety, happiness or sadness – to music, let alone value music for its expressiveness?

It is important to distinguish such questions from the question of the nature and value of music's *arousal* or *elicitation* of emotions in listeners. Even a skeptic about music's *expressiveness* – about the possibility of there being emotions *in the music* – might accept that music arouses emotions *in us* (and, as we shall see, vice versa: Some think that music itself is emotionally expressive, but that it does not arouse emotions in us in any interesting sense). The arousal of emotions in listeners raises its own philosophical puzzles, to which we will turn in the following chapter. In this chapter, I will restrict the discussion as far as possible to the topic of musical expressiveness.

It might seem that my initial examples are quite different in ways that allow for different explanations of their emotional expressiveness. After all, it might be puzzling that one sequence of notes played on the piano is frenzied while another is languid, but is it really surprising that a song called "We Suck Young Blood" turns out to be a little depressing? Since songs have words that can describe situations whose expressiveness is not puzzling (e.g., the sucking of young blood), can't we appeal to those words to explain a song's expressiveness?[1] No one would deny that a song's words can contribute to its emotional content, but it's worth noting that the same puzzle arises from the song's musical aspects as from the purely instrumental piece. One way of seeing this is to consider the complicated interactions between words and music that we discussed in Chapter 1. It will make a huge difference to a song's expressiveness if you sing the words "we suck young blood" to a fast, major-key tune with lots of melodic leaps rather than Radiohead's choice of a slow, minor-key melody that sticks to just a few neighboring notes. The point is that the musical elements seem to be contributing expressiveness to the song independently of the lyrics (even if ultimately one can only account for the song's overall expressiveness by considering the words and music together). Thus, I will focus on instrumental music in considering the problem of musical expressiveness, in the hope that a solution to that problem will constitute a significant portion of the explanation of how songs are musically expressive. I presume that something similar could be said for program music, musically accompanied dance, films with music, and so on.

2.1 Expressionism

If the puzzle of music's emotional expressiveness arises from the apparent absence of a mind experiencing the emotions in question, then one obvious strategy for solving the puzzle is to locate the missing mind. A natural first place to look is to the musicians involved. After all, if anyone is expressing their emotions in a piece of music, wouldn't it be the composer or performer responsible for producing that music? We might summarize this theory – *expressionism* – thus:[2]

> A passage of music, *M*, is expressive of an emotion, *E*, only if *M*'s musician is experiencing *E*.

Though enduringly popular, most philosophers have found expressionism inadequate.[3] For one thing, the list of musicians just given presents the expressionist with an awkward choice for "*M*'s musician" in many cases: Where more than one person is responsible for the music we hear, which person's or persons' emotions are responsible for the music's expressiveness? In some cases we might identify a primary artist. Perhaps in classical music the composer who writes the score is solely responsible for the work's expressiveness, and the performing musicians, though essential for its manifestation, do not contribute to the music's expressiveness. One problem for such an answer is that classical performers often do seem to contribute to the expressiveness of their particular performance of a given work. The conductor of an orchestra or choir is often credited as the source of the performative interpretation of the piece. This interpretation will include many decisions about such matters as *tempo* (how fast to play or sing), *dynamics* (how loudly), *articulation* (how to shape various notes and phrases), and so on, often to expressive ends. Perhaps, as the term suggests, such "interpretations" are attempts to *understand* and thus manifest the expressiveness of the piece, that is, what the composer was *truly* expressing through writing this music.[4] Or perhaps the composer expresses her emotions in a vague way in the work, and the performers add precision by expressing their particular emotions. However plausible these suggestions are for classical practice, they are more difficult to apply to more obviously collaborative practices such as jazz or rock, where the music is often created by joint improvisation, whether in a preliminary compositional phase (as is common in rock) or during the performance itself (as in much jazz). Do the members of such groups somehow get into the same emotional state, as they talk of getting into the groove, which they then express together in their music? Perhaps this sometimes happens, but it seems unlikely that it would *have* to happen for collaborative music to be expressive.

This leads us to one crucial problem with expressionism: It seems implausible that one must be in a given emotional state in order to make music that expresses that state. Consider a typical performance by a singer-songwriter. She may play songs expressive of a range of emotions – tender love songs, passionate political protest songs, songs grieving losses, and so on. But surely she cannot be undergoing the rollercoaster of emotions expressed in this music, and thus required by expressionism, in the course of performing her set list. Indeed, it would seem that the more expressively successful and varied her performance, the more emotionally pathological she would have to be. A mirror-image problem is raised for the extended composition of expressive works of classical music. Samuel Barber's famous "Adagio for Strings"[5] is one of the greatest sustained pieces of sad music (if I may so absurdly reduce the expressiveness of this masterpiece to a three-letter word!). Though the piece runs less than ten minutes in even the most indulgent performances, Barber composed it over the course of several months. Could he really have been in a state of depression extreme enough to match his music throughout that period? Or was it just when he sat down at his desk that misery overtook him? Either way, how could he bring himself to write in such a state?

The expressionist could respond that the emotions expressed by musicians need not be undergone while the music is being made (whether that means composed or performed). Rather, they might say, expression is a matter of "emotion recollected in tranquillity" (Wordsworth 1802, 82).[6] But this raises an even thornier problem for the expressionist: Isn't it possible to create music expressive of emotions that you have *never* experienced? After all, novelists, filmmakers, and game designers all create works that feature situations they themselves have never experienced (murders, childbirth, futuristic utopias). Why shouldn't the same be true of the emotions expressed in musicians' creations? The expressionist might point out that just as a novelist must *imagine* what it would be like to murder someone in order to include such an event in her novel, the musician must imagine what it would be like to experience a given emotion in order to express it in her music. To the extent that the expressionist relies on such a response, he reduces the interest of his theory. As we shall see shortly, those who reject expressionism need not deny that there is often *some* connection between the musician's mental states (such as imagination) and her music; few deny that much expressiveness is intentionally put in the music by musicians. The distinctive characteristic of expressionism was supposed to be that musical expressiveness is precisely literal *expression* by a musician of her actual emotional state, but it is this idea that is abandoned by the "imaginative" response just considered.

In any event, how successful is this response? It would certainly be surprising if it turned out that the novelist responsible for a passage describing a murder had in fact never imagined a situation of the sort she describes in the passage; it might be just as surprising if the writer of a love song had never given a thought to the expressiveness of the musical features of the song. But would it be so surprising if a composer claimed never to have considered emotional matters while composing a piano sonata (or other instrumental work) that most listeners take to be expressive of joy? That is, mightn't expressiveness emerge in music designed solely with an eye to its non-expressive musical features (melody, harmony, rhythm, etc.)?[7] If so, musical expressiveness is more objective – less closely tied to the subjective experiences of musicians – than expressionists claim. Such objectivity is also implied by the possibility that someone might aim to create music expressive of a particular emotion – even an emotion which she is currently experiencing – and *fail*. Thus the second crucial problem with expressionism: Even if experiencing the emotion in question were *necessary* for its musical expression, it is plainly not sufficient. And seeking the further conditions necessary for musical expressiveness return us to the original puzzle.

For the reasons just canvassed, expressionism is extremely unpopular among philosophers. No one now defends the view that expressive music is essentially a matter of the expression of someone's actual emotions. Nonetheless, there has been a resurgence of interest in literal expression independently of the question of musical expressiveness, as we shall see in the next chapter.

2.2 Arousalism

Arousalism locates the actual emotional states expressed in music not in the music's *creator* but in its *audience*.[8] Indeed, before delving into the philosophical literature on musical expressiveness, many people seem to think that what it means to say that a piece of music is, say, joyous – all it *could* mean – is simply that it fills those who listen to it with joy. Nonetheless, arousalism has been almost as widely rejected as a theory of musical expressiveness as expressionism. (It is easy to forget, and thus worth emphasizing, that arousalism is a theory of what musical expressiveness amounts to. *One can thus reject arousalism without rejecting the idea that music arouses emotions in listeners.* One must just have some other theory of musical expressiveness.) We might summarize the view thus:

A passage of music, *M*, expresses an emotion, *E*, if, and only if, *M* arouses *E* in listeners.

The first problem arousalism faces is that the same music may elicit different emotions in different people, which would make music's expressiveness more subjective than it seems to be. (Recall that someone who thinks "We Suck Young Blood" is joyous fails to understand the song on a pretty basic level.) Arousalists can respond to this objection, first, by pointing out that our emotional responses to music fall into at least three categories: associative, broad, and music-specific (Matravers 2011, 212–13).[9] If "We Suck Young Blood" makes you joyous because it was playing when you first fell in love, your response is merely *associative*, and not the kind of arousal appealed to by the arousalist. Similarly, if you are irritated by the song's sentimentality, your response is *broad* and thus irrelevant. For although such a response is more closely connected to the musical features of the song than an associative response, it does not track the music, that is, it does not change as the music changes. If the arousalist can limit the emotional arousal appealed to in her theory to this last, music-tracking kind of response – *music-specific* arousal – she can avoid some of the subjectivity implied by less sophisticated versions of the theory. It is a nice question, however, whether the arousalist can draw the distinction between broad and music-specific emotional responses without making the theory circular. A fan of the song might laugh delightedly at the way in which the sloppy handclaps in "We Suck Young Blood" subvert one of the simplest signifiers of an upbeat mood in pop music – the handclap – in the service of enhancing the song's languid gloominess. The arousalist will not want her theory to imply that this part of the song expresses delight and good humor, so she will presumably want to classify such a response as *broad* rather than music-specific, yet it seems to track specific features of the music. If the arousalist classifies the response as broad rather than music-specific on the grounds that music-specific responses must reflect the expressiveness of the music, however, the theory starts to look circular. If the theory says that a musical passage expressing gloom, for instance, is a matter of it making listeners gloomy *in virtue of its being gloomy*, then the theory has not explained what it is for music to be gloomy after all – it simply takes some music's being gloomy for granted (Mew 1985, 33).

A second strategy the arousalist can employ to reduce the theory's subjectivity is to make music's expressiveness a matter of the emotions it elicits in a particular kind of listener, namely, one who understands the kind of music in question. The threat of circularity lurks in this response, too: We've just said that part of being a competent listener is being able to detect the expressiveness of the music one listens to. If the arousalist then claims that expressiveness is a matter of the elicitation of emotions in the competent listener, she seems to be implying that a musical passage is sad, for instance, just in case it elicits sadness in someone in whom sadness is elicited by sad music. Again, the explanation of what musical sadness *is* appeals to the very concept of musical sadness, and likewise for other emotions expressed by music. But perhaps the arousalist could specify the competent listener in terms of all the relevant knowledge, skills, and capacities required to appreciate music (whatever those are!) *except* one's tendencies to respond to music emotionally (cf. Levinson 1996, 109). The hope would be that one's emotional responses are so tied up with the rest of one's experience of the music that one simply couldn't be a competent listener in all those other respects without responding emotionally in certain ways.

Unfortunately for this suggestion, there are actual, highly competent music lovers who claim to feel no emotions of the relevant sort in response to expressive music. Peter Kivy notoriously maintained for decades that he felt no "garden-variety" emotions (happiness, sadness, etc.) in response to expressive music, and Kivy clearly had a very deep understanding of many features of the music he loved, including its expressive features.[10] Moreover, he was no Vulcan;[11] he often discussed his strong emotional responses to music, but he insisted that these responses were what we've been calling "broad" (for example, joy in the beauty of the music) rather than responses to the emotions expressed in the music. The arousalist might suggest that Kivy and other "dry-eyed listeners" are mistaken about their emotional responses to the music they love – after all, Kivy is asserting just that about arousalists and others. But this will lead to stalemate at best. Jenefer Robinson raises the stakes by appealing to empirical studies that seem to show that people typically respond emotionally, in music-specific ways, to expressive music (2005, 369–76). Such psychological results are of course statistical; they do not establish that there *could not be* a dry-eyed listener. But the arousalist might appeal to the responses of some *proportion* of competent listeners, or even simply exclude by fiat the dry-eyed listener from the class of competent listeners she appeals to in her theory (cf. Levinson 1996, 109 n. 59). While yielding a coherent theory, either of these solutions would make the dry-eyed listener's musical experience rather puzzling. If the music's expressiveness is a matter of its tending to arouse certain emotions in a certain class of listener, then the dry-eyed listener's experience of the music's expressiveness amounts to something like detection of the fact that the music would tend to arouse certain emotions in a certain class of listener – a class to which the dry-eyed listener does not himself belong. That seems implausibly distant from the experience even the dry-eyed listener claims to have of simply hearing the music's expressive content (Kingsbury 2002, 16–17).

We've so far considered the objection that arousalism makes music's expressiveness too subjective. Another objection is that the theory is deeply circular: When we respond emotionally to music (and to other things) we are often responding to the presence of emotions. In non-musical life, these emotions are being experienced by other creatures – a weeping colleague, a wagging dog, and so on. The puzzle of musical expressiveness is precisely the puzzle of how music could "possess" emotions, but the point here is that we often seem to be made gloomy by gloomy music or joyful by happy music *because we are responding to the expressiveness we perceive in the music*. But if our emotional response depends on our prior perception of the expressiveness, the expressiveness cannot depend upon our response, as the arousalist would have it. The simplest response the arousalist can give is simply that we *do not*, in the first instance, respond emotionally to perceived expressiveness in the music.

Rather, we are caused to be in emotional states by aspects of the music that are not in themselves perceived as emotional; we then perceive the music as expressive precisely because it has this emotional effect on us. Moreover, the arousalist need not deny that we respond emotionally to the emotional properties we perceive in the music; she need only deny that *all* emotional responses are to emotional properties. In particular, she must deny that the emotional responses that partly constitute the expressive properties are themselves elicited by expressive properties.

This goes some way to answering a further objection, namely that we sometimes emotionally respond *sympathetically* rather than *empathetically* to music. For instance, rather than being made gloomy by the gloominess of "We Suck Young Blood" (an *empathetic* response, because of the same type of emotion as that expressed), we may experience horror or pity (*sympathetic* responses, because of different types of emotion from that expressed). The problem this raises for arousalism is that it seems to imply that the sympathetic responders will hear the music as expressing horror or pity, when (i) they don't, and (ii) their responses of horror or pity only make sense if they hear the music as warranting such responses (e.g., as gloomy). Following the train of thought of the previous paragraph, the arousalist might claim that even the sympathetic responders are responding empathetically at some prior time or lower level. This is what makes the music gloomy and thus enables the later or higher-level sympathetic responses.

Now, the opponent of arousalism may claim that she feels only horror, no gloom, in response to the music. The arousalist might respond as she does to the dry-eyed listener. But she might alternatively argue that music can express an emotion not only by eliciting a response of the same kind as the emotion expressed, but also by eliciting a response that is appropriate as a *sympathetic* response to the emotion expressed (Matravers 1991; 1998, 162–4). One unfortunate consequence of this strategy, however, is that expression by sympathetic arousal must be a more cognitive process than expression by empathetic arousal. For the latter requires only projecting one's emotional state on to the music, while the former requires making some kind of inference (from one's response to what it would be an appropriate response to) prior to the projection of the inferred state on to the music. We might also worry that there is not a tight enough connection between gloominess and pity (for example) to warrant the required inferences: In ordinary life, gloominess elicits many kinds of responses, and many kinds of emotional expressions elicit pity (S. Davies 1994, 197).

It might seem very strange that the arousalist claims that a subject's *experience* (e.g., one's gloomy response to some music) could, even partly, *constitute a property of the object experienced* (e.g., the gloominess of the music). And yet there is a long history in philosophy of positing such "response-dependent" properties. The classic example is colors (cf. S. Davies 1994, 185–6). (Heads up! Response-dependence will come up repeatedly in the next few chapters, so pay close attention to this discussion, even if you've already given up on arousalism.) What is it for something (e.g., grass) to *be green*? The scientifically inclined might respond that it's grass's tendency to reflect light in a certain band of wavelengths. But suppose that our eyes responded differently to those wavelengths, giving us an experience of what we call *redness* instead.[12] Would we then say that grass is red? Whatever our answer to that question, the response-dependence theorist of color claims that the fact that we can make sense of it shows that *something* about color is essentially phenomenological or experiential – the "what-it's-like-ness" of green visual experience is a necessary component of at least one important concept of greenness. Thus a response-dependence color theorist might claim that greenness is (very roughly) just the tendency to elicit that visual experience in ordinary observers (e.g., those without visual impairments) under normal conditions (e.g., sunlight, not a sealed room at night). The point for our purposes is that the arousalist seems to be arguing that music's expressive properties are similarly response-dependent: A passage of music's being gloomy is (very roughly) just its tendency to elicit that emotional experience in a competent listener (e.g., one familiar with the musical tradition to which this piece belongs) under normal conditions (e.g., not having just won the lottery).

It is difficult to assess how much plausibility the notion of response-dependence can restore to arousalism. The most sophisticated recent defense of the theory is provided by Matravers (1998, 145–224), yet he is less sanguine about the theory's prospects in a recent overview, where he identifies arousalism's most serious problem as follows:

> How can an aroused emotion – even one that is experienced as tracking the music – be heard as an audible feature of the music? There are in fact two problems here. First, according to the theory, expression involves two experiences rather than one: hearing the music and [for example] feeling sad. Second, putting the point crudely, the feeling ends up in the wrong place: not in the music, but in the head of the listener. Expression is a matter of hearing the feeling *in* the music; the theory gives us only having the feeling *and* hearing the music.
>
> (2011, 218)

The claim that expressive properties of music are response-dependent is supposed to go some way toward solving these problems. If colors are response-dependent, then although greenness is "in our heads" in some sense, we still experience the grass as green; we do not have two experiences, one of the grass and another of greenness. However, there are significant differences between our experiences of color and musical expressiveness. We do not have an experience of the "uncolored" causes of our color experiences, that is, we can't ignore the greenness of the grass and focus instead on the wavelengths of light that we "see." But though we may not be able to "unhear" the gloominess of "We Suck Young Blood," we *can* focus instead on what the arousalist claims is ultimately responsible for the music's gloominess, namely, musical features such as its slow tempo and insistently chromatic piano part. To that extent, then, the two experiences are more separate, or separable, than in the case of colors. The problem is that these experiences don't seem so distinct in our experience of music: Just as we see the color "in" the grass – the grass looks green – we hear the expressiveness "in" the music – the music sounds gloomy.

2.3 Eliminativism

If neither expressionism nor arousalism provides a satisfying analysis of what it is for music to express emotions, then we have exhausted the obvious candidates for the source of the emotions in question – the musicians and the audience. Perhaps, then, it is worth taking more seriously the initial skepticism about musical expressiveness that I used to motivate expressionism and arousalism. An *eliminativist* about musical expressiveness claims that *music is not emotionally expressive*, and thus all claims about music's expressiveness can be *eliminated* from our musical theories.

Eliminativists obviously don't need to solve the same puzzle that everyone else does – how music can express emotions – but they face a mirror-image challenge, namely, to explain why it is that so many people seem to think that music *does* express emotion, describe music in emotional terms, and find music's emotional expressiveness to be one of its most valuable aspects. The most popular strategy has been to argue that emotional descriptions of music are *metaphorical*. People use metaphors to communicate something about a target domain by saying something literally false about it, drawing on concepts from a distinct domain. In *As You Like It*, when Jaques says to Duke Senior, "All the world's a stage, and all the men and women merely players ...," we do not take him to have lost his mind, unable to draw the distinction between theater and reality. He (like Shakespeare) is drawing the Duke's (and our) attention to the theatricality of much human behavior and the ephemerality of life (among other things).[13] Getting from the metaphor to what is being communicated about the target requires some interpretation or "paraphrase," since there will always be aspects of the metaphor that don't fit the target. For instance, neither Jaques nor Shakespeare intends his audience to infer that the world is made primarily of wooden boards. Such paraphrases miss the point of the metaphor and thus demonstrate a misunderstanding of what is being communicated, even though they display an understanding of the literal meaning of the metaphor.[14]

An eliminativist, then, owes us an account of how emotion metaphors function in our discourse about music. Different eliminativists offer different accounts, but the basic idea is that emotion terms metaphorically refer to purely sonic, basic dynamic, music-theoretic, or aesthetic features of the music, such as (respectively) loudness, melodic movement, diminished chords, or graceful-ness (Hanslick 1854, 8–27; Sharpe 1982; Urmson 1973; Zangwill 2007).

There are two main reasons that most philosophers reject eliminativism about musical expressiveness. First, if emotional descriptions of music are merely metaphorical, then the eliminativist owes us an account of why we reach for *emotion* metaphors so consistently, rather than any of the huge range of possible metaphors for the features of the target domain. Compare, for instance, the range of metaphors used to describe the beloved in Shakespeare's sonnets, let alone the rest of Western love poetry.

One response that Eduard Hanslick gives, in a short book that is a cornerstone of the debate over the expressiveness of music, is that the dynamic features of music are strikingly similar to the dynamic features of emotional experience (1854, 11). This answer, however, flirts with collapsing eliminativism into a realist (i.e., non-eliminativist) *resemblance theory* of musical expressiveness – to which we will turn shortly. (This danger of collapse into a realist theory is one that any eliminativist must beware of in answering this challenge.)

Nick Zangwill avoids the danger by giving the opposite response. He points out that, on the one hand, we use a wide range of nonliteral terms to describe music, such as "delicate" and "balanced," while, on the other, we use emotion terms to describe non-musical phenomena, talking, for example, of an "angry sky" or "shy flower." He thus rejects that this challenge is peculiar to the elim-inativist: Our use of emotion terms to describe music is just one kind of meta-phorical description of music among many and, moreover, one that we use to describe many non-musical, non-emotional phenomena.

Both parts of this response might be questioned by the opponent of elimi-nativism. It is not obvious that descriptions of a piece of music as "delicate" and "balanced" are metaphorical. It's true, as Zangwill says, that "[s]omething that is aesthetically delicate need not be liable to break, and something that is aesthetically balanced need not have an equal distribution of weight among its parts …" (Zangwill 2007, 392), but to assume that the only literal uses of these terms refer to their most basic or etymologically prior meanings would beg the question. For instance, surely someone might justify their claim that a piece of music is *balanced* by pointing out that the two main sections are of equal length; if anyone were puzzled by this justification, it would seem more likely that they simply don't understand the word "balanced" than that they're hav-ing trouble understanding a metaphor.[15] As for our descriptions of non-musical phenomena in emotion terms, it remains open to an opponent of eliminativism either (i) to appeal to their preferred theory of musical expressiveness to explain these descriptions, or (ii) to point to a relevant difference between the musical and non-musical cases. For instance, (i) an arousalist might argue that we describe the sky as "angry" because that's how it makes us feel, while (ii) an expressionist might point to the fact that musical works are *artifacts*, making it plausible that they are human expressions of emotion, while the flower is only metaphorically shy.

A proponent of musical expressiveness is likely to press the second objection to eliminativism more strongly than the first (Budd 1985, 31–6, S. Davies 1994, 153–4): To the extent that one paraphrases emotional descriptions of music, replacing them with non-emotional descriptions, one fails to describe important features of the music – emotionally expressive features! Imagine a highly trained music theorist with an amazing ear. Suppose she could give an exhaustive description of Barber's "Adagio" or the musical elements of "We Suck Young Blood" in terms of their sonic, dynamic, music-theoretic, and aesthetic properties, but did not hear the pieces as sad or gloomy in any non-metaphorical sense. Opponents of eliminativism will claim that this person has missed a significant aspect of these pieces. Even if the expressiveness of the music can be *explained* in some way in terms of its non-emotional features (we will shortly investigate explanations of this kind), that does not show that the music doesn't *possess* the emotional features thus explained. (To explain is not always to explain away.) And, indeed, few music theorists – those best able to describe music in technical, non-emotional terms – would deny that much music is expressive; the expressiveness of music is just not their primary concern.[16]

2.4 Resemblance Theories

If music is not emotionally expressive in virtue of its relationship to musicians' or audiences' emotional states, how can it be *literally*, rather than metaphorically, gloomy, anxious, and so on? According to *resemblance* theories (also known as "contour" or "appearance" theories), music is sad, say, in the same way in which a basset hound's face or a weeping willow is sad. That is, we hear in the music a resemblance to some aspect or aspects of a person undergoing the emotional experience in question, just as we see in the basset hound's face (regardless of its emotional state) a resemblance to the face of a sad person. The ascription of sadness to the music, then, is connected with human emotional experience, but less directly than in expressionism or arousalism; music's expressiveness is linked not to any particular emotional experience, but to generic aspects of human emotional experience. In short:

> A passage of music, *M*, is expressive of an emotion, *E*, if *M* is heard, by competent listeners, as resembling the phenomenology, or vocal or bodily behavior, typical of someone experiencing *E*.

2.4.1 Interlude on Emotions

So far, I have been talking simply about "emotions," as if we all understand what these are. But though we all have emotional experiences, it turns out that emotions are much more complicated than many people assume, and the variety of kinds and aspects of emotions gives rise to a wide range of possible resemblance theories (among other implications for musical expressiveness). I will thus pause to discuss the nature of emotions themselves.

We commonly use "feelings" as a synonym for "emotions," perhaps because we often assume that emotions are nothing but feelings. But if by "feelings" we mean the *phenomenology* of emotional experience – what it *feels* like, mentally and physically, as we experience an emotion – then a feeling may be neither necessary nor sufficient for an emotion, and a given feeling may not identify which emotional state we are in. Feelings are not necessary for emotional experience if there are emotions, such as pride, that have no characteristic phenomenology. They're not sufficient if you can have a feeling without being in an emotional state – and it's plausible that we're *always* in *some* phenomenological state, yet not always experiencing some emotion. (Your experience reading this book has a certain phenomenological character, even if it's a fairly neutral one.) One might identify a certain subset of feelings (e.g., the non-neutral ones) as the emotions, but we then encounter the problem that our feelings are not fine-grained enough to *individuate* (that is, distinguish between) emotions that we take to be quite different. Consider the fear you might feel on turning the corner on a hiking trail and encountering a mountain lion with her cubs. This could involve a churning, sickening feeling. But you might have the same churning, sickening feeling when highly embarrassed. Surely fear and embarrassment are different emotions. If they involve (or can involve) the same phenomenology, then there must be more to emotions than feelings.

Much the same is true of the *physiological* aspects or components of emotions: One's heart races when one is overjoyed but also when one is terrified, thus we probably can't individuate emotions solely by their physiological aspects. Moreover, one's heart races when one plays tennis, whatever one's emotional state, so no physiological state is likely to guarantee being in a given emotional state. However, Jenefer Robinson argues that physiological states are a *necessary* component of emotions: If one realizes that one is going to fail a course one has been working hard in, and that this will foil one's plans, but the realization has no physiological effect, Robinson maintains that the realization has not given rise to an emotional experience (2005, 1–99; a helpful summary appears at 94–7).

Such a view may seem to contradict many common attributions of emotion to oneself or others. If you ask me at any time, out of the blue, whether I love my spouse, I will say *yes* without hesitation, but perhaps without undergoing any physiological change.[17] Yet love is an emotion if anything is. In light of these considerations, it is common to distinguish between *occurrent* emotions – those mental and bodily processes that involve the physiological components in question, among others – and *dispositional* emotions – on-going psychological states that tend (i.e., are *disposed*) to trigger occurrent emotions under certain circumstances, such as the appearance of one's beloved or a mountain lion. We can ignore dispositional emotions here, since it is occurrent emotions that feature in theories of musical expressiveness.

Suppose that fear and embarrassment have the same phenomenological and physiological components. What then distinguishes one from the other? According to most theorists, many emotions have an essential *cognitive* component – a characteristic suite of beliefs, desires, or evaluations – and an *intentional object* of these cognitive states – what those beliefs, desires, or evaluations are *about*.[18] For instance, your emotional state on encountering the mountain lion on the trail is one of fear, in particular, because you *believe* that the lion (the intentional object of your fear) constitutes a threat to your well-being, you *evaluate* threats to your well-being negatively, and you *desire* to remove the threat, by either attacking the lion or, more likely, slowly backing down the track. If, by contrast, you have just been called on to give a presentation that you have completely forgotten about, your emotional response is one of embarrassment because you believe that you have done something that brings dishonor or shame to you, which you evaluate negatively, and disposes you to make amends or excuses, apologize, or remove yourself from the embarrassing situation.

An intentional object alone is obviously insufficient for emotional experience – we can think about things dispassionately. But it doesn't seem necessary, either. When we say that someone has got up "on the wrong side of bed," the absurdity of the phrase points up the fact that though there is doubtless some *cause* of the person's grumpiness, it has no intentional object; the person is not grumpy *about* anything in particular. (Initially, at least. Their grumpiness may lower the threshold for entering other negative emotional states, and raise the threshold for positive emotions such as joy.) Because of the importance philosophers have recently placed on the rationality of emotions, such states are often classified as *moods* – an important category of affective (i.e., emotion-like) states that fall short of emotion proper.

In light of the fact that emotions have historically been contrasted with reason, it's worth reflecting on the implication of cognitive theories that emotions can be more or less rational. If I react the same way to your new kitten as I do to the mountain lion, even though I know that the kitten poses no threat to me, my fear of the kitten is irrational. (This is one way of understanding what phobias are.) This emotional rationality depends not on the world but on one's perception of it. If some prankster has placed a stuffed mountain lion just around a bend in the trail, my fear of it is rational as long as I (mis)perceive it to be alive – I *believe* it poses a threat to my well-being, even though it does not. The cognitive states characteristic of various emotions don't seem to be sufficient for experiencing those emotions since, as remarked earlier, we can sometimes make a dispassionate judgment about some state of affairs: I believe myself to have been wronged, but my Zen training allows me to make the judgment with equanimity, absent the boiling blood and tendency to take action against my enemy that are characteristic of anger. But there is broad consensus that characteristic cognitive states are *necessary* for many emotions, including such garden-variety emotions as happiness, sadness, fear, and so on. If the concept of a threat plays no role in your cognitive economy at a given time, it is difficult to imagine how you could be experiencing *fear*. Many theorists also distinguish a class of emotions, often called "higher" or "more cognitive" emotions, that are constituted solely by their cognitive characteristics. For instance, it seems impossible to be in a state of *hope* without having some thought of a future state that is better than one's current circumstances, but no particular physiological changes or behaviors seem to be characteristic of that emotion.

At the other end of the cognitive spectrum from the "higher" emotions are what Jenefer Robinson calls "affective appraisals" (2005, 41–7). These are very fast, automatic, *non-cognitive* responses to one's environment that occur "below the threshold of awareness" (41). They are *appraisals* in that they evaluate the environment. They are *affective* in that they involve physiological and phenomenological changes – one's heart begins to race, one's attention is focused on the cause of the response, and so on. Because they are non-cognitive, it is somewhat misleading to characterize them in language, but Robinson approximates their content with exclamations such as **threat!**, **unexpected!**, or **friend!**.

A final component of emotions is characteristic behavior. We've already encountered this in connection with the cognitive aspects of emotion: If I believe the mountain lion poses a threat, and I desire to remove that threat, I will be inclined either to eliminate it (by scaring off or fighting the lion) or avoid it (by fleeing). Behaviors can be extremely varied in a number of respects. They can be automatic, universal, innate, and uncontrollable, as with the startle reflex – a very quick response to "a sudden intense stimulus" that invariably involves blinking and usually other facial and bodily movements, yet can remain below the threshold of awareness (Robinson 1995, 54–5) – or they can be deliberate and culturally specific, such as the Jewish tradition of tearing one's clothes in mourning. Somewhere in the middle may be ways of carrying oneself – the slow carriage and hunched posture of the sad person, or the spring in the step of the cheerful. Often, a characteristic behavior may be a culturally shaped version of a universal response. For instance, sobbing, wailing, or keening are very common behavioral expressions of grief, yet they can take very different forms in different cultures, even though one may think of one's own way of grieving as natural. Even responses at the automatic, universal end of the spectrum may be controllable to some extent, though "there is almost always some 'leakage' of [such] emotion ... even if ... only for a split second" (Robinson 2005, 32).

What, in sum, is an emotion? It seems unlikely that any single characterization will fit everything that we pretheoretically take to be an emotion. This is worth keeping in mind when we return to philosophical questions raised by the relationships between music and emotion. But it is also worth looking at one recent theory of a central class of emotional responses that is more sophisticated than the theories appealed to by many philosophers interested in emotion and the arts. Not only does Jenefer Robinson, like many theorists, convincingly argue that emotions are not simply feelings (or judgments or bodily states) but complex combinations of such elements, she also argues that an emotional experience is a *process* that unfolds over time, in which one element may affect how another develops (2005, 1–99). Even if one disputes some details of Robinson's theory, she is surely right that many paradigmatic emotional experiences are processes rather than static states. This, too, is worth keeping in mind when we return to musical considerations. According to Robinson, an emotional experience begins with an "affective appraisal of the situation that focuses attention on its significance" to the subject, for example **threat!**. This affective appraisal causes physiological changes, most notably in the autonomic nervous system (heart rate, sweating, etc.), facial expressions (e.g., the startle blink), and motor responses (e.g., jumping in fright). At this point enough time has passed (though still only a fraction of a second) to allow for cognition to begin – the subject begins to think about the situation in which she finds herself, her attention focused on what triggered the affective appraisal (Robinson 2005, 59). Such cognitive monitoring may reinforce one's initial appraisal (you see that there really is a disgruntled mountain lion in front of you) or undermine it (you realize that your irrepressible hiking companion has fooled you with a stuffed mountain lion once again), leading to deliberate action (retreating or hiking on). In either case, the initial, non-cognitive changes do not immediately disappear; you may be jumpy for the next quarter hour, that is, have a lowered threshold for subsequent threat responses, even if you know that you have not encountered a mountain lion and that they are extremely rare in this locale (Robinson 2005, 96). Moreover, as you reflect on your companion's prank, you may make a new affective appraisal of the situation you now realize yourself to be in (**anger!**) and cognitively reflect on *that*, perhaps composing a dressing down you intend to give to him when you catch up with him, thus fueling your anger, or recalling that, after all, one of the things you love about him most is his creative tomfoolery, shifting again into a happier frame of mind.

2.4.2 Back to Resemblance Theories

If music is emotionally expressive in virtue of its resemblance to occurrent emotions, some aspects of them are more plausible candidates for such resemblance than others. Most philosophers have agreed with Hanslick (1854, 8–12) that instrumental music lacks the representational resources to resemble a specific intentional object of an emotion (e.g., the beloved), or the characteristic cognitive components of an emotion (e.g., the judgment, essential to fear, that something constitutes a threat). Of course, it is important not to lose sight of the fact that the restriction of our scope of inquiry to instrumental music is temporary: If another aspect of a complex work (a character in a videogame, the text of a song, etc.) can provide the resources that instrumental music lacks, then perhaps music (understood broadly to include multimedia or hybrid works) can achieve such resemblance after all.

The idea that (pure instrumental) "[m]usic sounds the way the emotions feel" (Pratt 1952, 26) is more compelling. After all, the problem for music's resembling "the beloved" or "a threat" is that these seem to be concepts, capturable in language, but incapable of being resembled by the dynamic processes of music. By contrast, the phenomenology, including perhaps some felt aspects of the physiology, of emotional experience, are dynamic and non-conceptual, and thus well-suited to being mirrored in music (Budd 1995, 138–42; Langer 1942, 218–45, 1953, 24–32). For instance, the churning feeling characteristic of fear could be resembled by low, out-of-phase slides on several electric guitars with lots of feedback, while the racing of one's heart could be mirrored in a pounding pulse in octaves on the piano. But resemblance to some aspect of emotion is not enough by itself to ground music's expressiveness. We noted above that the phenomenology and physiology of emotions are not enough to individuate them (e.g., if fear and embarrassment share the same phenomenology). So a musical passage's resemblance to such components will not be enough to make it expressive of particular emotions. Suzanne Langer sometimes seems to embrace this conclusion, arguing that expressive music represents emotional processes in general, rather than specific emotions (1942, 238–45; 1953, 24–32). But to the extent that we take different passages of music to be expressive of different emotional states – joyful music, angry music, and so on – this implication counts against such a theory.[19] (Once more, if we turn to works that involve elements in addition to instrumental music, this objection may lose some of its force.)

More popular among resemblance theorists has been the notion that music is expressive in virtue of its resemblance to behaviors characteristic of various emotions. Some behaviors seem more distinctive of the emotions of which they are characteristic than mere feelings. Sobbing, for instance, is characteristic of sadness, but not of any other emotions. Some such behaviors are nevertheless better candidates than others. Paul Ekman (e.g., 1993) has influentially argued that characteristic facial expressions invariably accompany (perhaps partly constitute) the experience of a set of culturally universal, apparently innate, "basic" emotions. However, since these facial expressions are basically static and two-dimensional, they are easily mimicked in visual arrays (consider how easily we see a colon and parenthesis as a happy or sad face :), but they are not easily, perhaps not possibly, mimicked by music. It is also difficult to mimic the tearing of clothes (as an expression of grief) in music, for much the same reason it is difficult to mimic the cognitive aspects of emotions: Even if one manages to capture the tearing in musical terms, signifying that what is being torn is *clothes* as opposed to weeds, a muscle, or a recalcitrant coupon, seems a sobering challenge. (Again, if the music accompanies a film in which someone is tearing their clothes in grief, this objection may be partly overcome.)

For these reasons, resemblance theorists have favored two types of emotional behavior amenable to mirroring in musical form: (i) vocal behavior, including not only non-verbal weeping, wailing, groaning, etc., but also "prosodic contours" of specific emotions, that is, the distinctive ways in which we tend to talk when experiencing a given emotion, and (ii) bodily behavior, such as "bearing, gait, or deportment," "attitude, air, carriage, posture, and comportment ..." (S. Davies 1994, 239; 2006, 182). So, for instance, "We Suck Young Blood" is gloomy because its tempo resembles the slow pace of a gloomy person (or perhaps merely that of a *sad* person, and the lyrics and other elements sharpen the emotion expressed into gloom); the jumpy melodic lines and asymmetrical meter of Prokofiev's "Precipitato" are anxious because they make the piece sound like the speech of someone in the grips of anxiety; Barber's "Adagio" is melancholy in part because of the falling "sighs" that introduce many of its phrases.

When I introduced resemblance theories, I noted that the link they posit between music and emotion is not to any particular, actual emotional experience, but rather to generic aspects of human emotional experience – the typical contours of emotional phenomenology, vocal expression, or bodily behavior. But how does the resemblance between music and such generic aspects of emotion constitute *expressiveness* on music's part? This question can be divided into a two-part objection to resemblance theories: First, why should resemblance amount to a relation of *significance*? That is, granting the resemblance between some emotional behavior and a passage of music, why should we say that *the music expresses that emotion*, and not that the emotion expresses (or refers to, or signifies) the music? For that matter, why think that the music expresses (or refers to, or signifies) the emotion of which the behavior in question is characteristic, rather than something else it resembles, such as the motion of some distant planets, the structure of a particular organic molecule, or other pieces of music? Second, supposing that we can answer the first objection, does the resemblance theory put too much distance between actual experiences of emotions and the music that resembles them to count as a theory of *expression*? Consider a portrait of the Prime Minister of New Zealand. It seems plausible that the portrait's visual resemblance to the person is closely connected to its being a portrait of her.[20] But although the portrait is *of* the Prime Minister or *depicts* her, it doesn't thereby *express* her.[21] Why shouldn't we say the same of the resemblance theory of musical emotion? Whatever its plausibility, isn't it at best a theory of emotional *depiction* rather than expression?[22]

2.4.3 Expression and Expressiveness

The second part of the objection uncovers complications in the notion of *expression* with which any theory of artistic expressiveness must grapple. The complications are due to the fact that there are several closely related concepts for which we use the term "express" and its cognates, and relatedly different ways in which we use emotion terms, such as "sad" and "happy." The primary uses are surely those referring to an occurrent emotional experience and its outward manifestation. (Even here there are at least two different senses of emotional expression. We might say that both someone's tears and the elegiac sonnet he writes are expressions of his sadness, but the tears may be spontaneous and uncontrollable, while the composition of the sonnet is clearly deliberate.[23])

Resemblance theorists point out that there are standard uses of emotion terms that apply to situations other than those of expression in these primary senses. A popular example is the description of the face of a dog such as a basset hound or Saint Bernard as sad. When we describe the dog's face in this way, we do not imply that the dog is in fact sad. Nor do we think that the dog's face looks the way dogs' faces (of this breed or others) typically look when such dogs are sad. The point of describing the dog's face as sad is that it looks strikingly like the face of a typical *person* experiencing sadness (S. Davies 1994, 227; Kivy 1980, 50). There is clearly no expression in either of the primary senses going on here; no one, human or canine, is expressing their sadness in the dog's face (though one *might* point to a dog's face to indicate one's mood). Resemblance theorists capture this difference by suggesting that we distinguish between things that *express* emotions and things that are *expressive of* emotions through resembling typical human emotional displays (S. Davies 1980, 68–72; 1994, 221–8; Kivy 1980, 12–17; Tormey 1971, 39–60).

Recall that the objection we are considering is that the resemblance theorist has put too much distance between actual, occurrent emotions and expressive music for the music to count as expressive. The resemblance theorist's response is measured. It makes no bones about the fact that music is less directly emotional than primary expressions or attributions of emotion. Stephen Davies, for instance, calls attributions of emotion that are "expressive" rather than "expressions" of emotion *secondary* uses of emotion terms (1994, 173–7). But he emphasizes that

> this secondary use is one of a familiar kind. It is a use established in ordinary, nonmusical contexts in which we attribute emotion characteristics to the appearances of people, or nonhuman animals, or inanimate objects. To that extent, the expressiveness attributed to music is not mysteriously confined to the musical case.
>
> (1994, 228)

In the context of the objection we are considering, this might be taken as an argument that though such uses of emotion terms are secondary, they are well established as indicators of *expressiveness*, as opposed to depiction or some other form of representation.

One might yet push the objection. Since these secondary uses of emotion terms are divorced from primary emotional expression and depend upon perceived resemblance, why think that "expressiveness" is more apt a term for the emotional properties attributed to music than "depiction"? Doesn't that choice of term flirt with begging the question in favor of the resemblance theory of expressiveness? One might respond that philosophers typically consider depiction (and other forms of representation) to be essentially *intentional* (that is, there can be no depiction without a person's intending to depict something) while there can be accidental resemblance. But given that most musical expressiveness is presumably intentional (Young 2014, 97–103) and that there can be *seeming* depiction (as when a cloud looks for all the world like a hippopotamus), this point may not weigh very heavily.

A resemblance theorist could bite the bullet at this point, agreeing that we might just as well say that music "depicts" emotions as that it's "expressive of" them (Young 2014, 87–124). Perhaps it's just a quirk of the English language that we use "express" when the subject of a representation is an emotion. There is this difference between the resemblance of portrait to subject, on the one hand, and of music to characteristic emotional behavior on the other: We use the same perceptual capacities to perceive the portrait as we do to perceive its subject – your visual experience of the portrait is like your visual experience of the Prime Minister. The same *can* be true of music: When you hear the locomotive starting up in Honegger's *Pacific 231* or the bombs bursting in air in Jimi Hendrix's rendition of "The Star-Spangled Banner," your aural experience of the music is like your aural experience of what it represents. But if the music resembles not the *sound* of a sad person (say) but their *gait*, then the resemblance is cross-modal.[24] It is not clear that this distinction helps the resemblance theorist establish music's emotional expressiveness, as opposed to depiction, however. For one thing, some of the resemblances posited by resemblance theorists are not cross-modal, notably the resemblances between expressive music and (non-musical) vocal expressions of emotion, yet the resemblance theorist presumably intends to give a unified account of expressive resemblance. For another, to the extent that cross-modality distinguishes musical expressiveness from depiction, it seems to make music *more* distant from the emotions that it is expressive of than pictures are from their subjects.

2.4.4 Resemblance and Experience

However this issue is resolved, the first part of the objection that we are considering to the resemblance theory asks not whether resemblance is *too far* from primary emotional expressions to count as a theory of musical expressiveness, but the more basic question of whether the resemblance posited between music and emotions is sufficient to ground music's being about the emotions *at all* (and not, say, any of the other things it happens to resemble). Stephen Davies's answer to this question is a clarification of the theory, which might more accurately be called an *experienced-resemblance* theory (2006, 180–4). That is, what grounds music's expressiveness, according to Davies, is not its mere resemblance to characteristic emotional behaviors, etc., but the fact that competent listeners *hear* its resemblance to such emotional behaviors.[25] Thus, while music's mere resemblance to other things (planets in motion, molecules, other pieces of music) may be just as objective as its resemblance to expressive behavior, music does not express or represent those things because competent listeners simply do not hear those resemblances.[26] Similarly, typical emotional behavior does not express or represent pieces of music because we do not tend to perceive that resemblance in the behavior.[27] The *resemblance* between music and expressive behavior may be symmetrical, but the *experienced resemblance* is not.

Is the experience of these resemblances part of our experience of expressive music? The fact that the truth of the theory is not obvious to everyone who hears music as expressive might suggest that it is not. But many features of our experience are not transparent to us (as the illumination of that experience by philosophy and psychology shows). It is a nice question whether and how we could test for the truth of this basic aspect of the theory. But the theory would clearly be much less attractive if it turned out to be false (Ravasio 2019a).

Suppose we do hear the resemblance between music and expressive behavior. One might ask why this should be. Given the existence of all these resemblances, why do we tend to perceptually experience some of them but not others? Peter Kivy speculates that it is plausible from the point of view of evolutionary psychology that we should err on the side of perceiving emotional expression where it might be present, and indeed in "animating" things more generally (1980, 57–9; 2002, 41–3).[28] Better (in terms of evolutionary fitness) to mistake a stick for a venomous snake than a venomous snake for a stick; better to mistakenly hear some sounds as expressing someone's sadness than to miss a fellow human's sad expression. But even such theorists acknowledge that at this point *philosophical* explanation has come to an end.[29]

2.4.5 Conventionalism

Suppose that the resemblance theorist can give adequate responses to the objections we've considered so far. How much of music's expressiveness can be accounted for by such a theory? Perhaps the simplest way to alter the expressiveness of a passage of Western tonal music is to change its "mode" from major to minor or vice versa. Even if you're unfamiliar with these terms, you are doubtless familiar with the phenomenon. Recall the nursery tune "Frère Jacques" (also known as "Brother John" or "Are You Sleeping?"; Example 2.1a). Now listen to the opening of the third movement of Mahler's First Symphony (Example 2.1b). Though there are other small changes to the tune, the starkest difference is that Mahler has transformed the happy children's song into a dirge, simply by transposing it from a major key into a minor key. This is effected by lowering just two of the six notes that appear in the tune a half-step compared to the original, major version. In a sense, this is a change in the "contour" of the tune – it doesn't rise quite as high in a few places – but this change in contour doesn't seem enough to account for the striking difference in expressiveness. After all, one could alter the tune so that it rises even less high, yet leaving it in a major key (Example 2.1c), and its expressiveness would be much closer to that of the original tune than to that of Mahler's version.

Example 2.1 "Frère Jacques": (a) a standard version; (b) as it appears in Mahler's First
Symphony, third movement; and (c) a major variation on Mahler's version.

This suggests that experienced resemblances cannot account for expressive differences due to the major or minor modes. Yet these differences surely account for a significant portion of expressiveness in Western music: Music in minor modes constitutes a significant portion of Western music, and is consistently experienced as darker in emotional tone than music in major modes (though this darkness can take a wide variety of emotional forms).[30] For this kind of reason, resemblance theorists – indeed *most* philosophers of music – acknowledge that a significant portion of music's expressiveness is *conventional*:

> A passage of music, *M*, is expressive of an emotion, *E*, if *M* has feature *f*, and there is a convention in the musical practice to which *M* belongs that passages with *f* are expressive of *E*.

We can think of conventions as shared associations. While idiosyncratic, personal associations are generally considered to be irrelevant to understanding music, when an association is widespread it can become a standard response among competent listeners, and thus part of the intersubjective, response-dependent content of the music. How do such conventions get established? In theory, they might be arbitrary. I might tell all my friends that when we hear an F and G together in any music, we should think of aloha shirts. If I'm extremely popular and persuasive, perhaps this will catch on widely enough to become a convention. But if you think this seems unlikely, you're not alone. Most theorists think that musical conventions develop more organically, from some natural or already established association. For instance, Peter Kivy argues that the expressive darkness of the minor mode is rooted in the historical development of Western tonal music (1980, 80–3). Early in that history (Kivy suggests the seventeenth century and before), minor intervals and chords were more "active" than they are today. One could not, say, end a piece in a minor key because the minor chord would sound unresolved.[31] Even though, over time, the function of minor intervals, chords, and keys changed, their association with "unresolvedness" remained, with the result that minor keys are now conventionally darker, emotionally speaking. Conventions need not be only or simply expressive, since a wide range of things might become associated with some aspect of music. Snare drums, for instance, often have military associations in classical music because of their long use in military bands. This can have an expressive dimension (resoluteness, unyieldingness), but will also bring to mind concepts such as war and death, whose meanings are not essentially emotional.

How much musical expressiveness is due to resemblance and how much to convention? It's surely difficult to answer this question with any precision, but cross-cultural evidence might be useful in arriving at a rough answer.[32] For if characteristic emotional behavior is universal, then we might expect people to be able to detect the expressiveness in music from unfamiliar traditions that is due to resemblance, but not that due to convention. Yet is such behavior universal? Stephen Davies supposes that "Chinese sad-lookingness is much the same as French sad-lookingness" (1994, 243), and asserts that Westerners can hear the basic expressiveness in Javanese music, for instance, and more generally that "I know of no culture that consistently expresses sadness with jaunty, fast, sprightly music, nor of any that expresses happiness with slow, dragging music" (244). On the other hand, while Jenefer Robinson cites empirical evidence that there are consistently cross-cultural behavioral expressions of emotion, particularly in facial expressions, she also notes that such expressions can be heavily culturally constrained.[33] Davies acknowledges two further factors that may confound the cross-cultural recognition of expressiveness (1994, 243–6). First, even if behavioral manifestations of emotions are universal, the conventionalism of musical systems themselves (e.g., the norms of harmonic development in a given musical culture) may make it difficult for novice listeners to hear the contours in the music itself that, if heard, would be readily experienced as resembling expressive behavior. Second, cultural differences may result in different emotions' being considered appropriate to one and the same object. For instance, if funerals are considered happy occasions in one culture, because of the bliss of the departed soul now in heaven, while in another they are sad occasions because of the loss of the departed, the expectations of a listener from the first culture might lead to difficulties for her hearing the sadness in the funeral music of the second. (This will be particularly relevant in music with a program, accompanying drama, and so on.)[34]

There is one little-remarked reason that resemblance theorists should not be so sanguine about appealing to convention to cover the expressiveness left unexplained by resemblance. It is a significant part of the resemblance theorist's case that the experience of musical expressiveness is, as Davies puts it, "more like an encounter with a person radiant with happiness [say] than with a person who dispassionately says that she feels happy" (1994, 173). But if this is a point in favor of resemblance theories, it is a point against conventionalism. Conventional meaning or content is much like linguistic meaning or content. There may be universal, natural cognitive mechanisms underlying the entire linguistic system, but what word stands for what object, say, is mostly arbitrary.[35] There's no natural or essential connection between the sequence of letters "t," "r," "e," "e" (or the corresponding sequence of phonemes) and large arboreal objects, which explains why different cultures may have completely different words for the same concept. Now the resemblance theorist may respond that not *every* experience of expressive music (or every aspect thereof) is like encountering an expressive person; perhaps some are, on the contrary, like hearing someone say that they are sad. Kivy gives an example, which might be interpreted in this way, where the basic expressiveness of a grief-like melody is a matter of resemblance, but the *intensity* of its expressiveness is conventional (1980, 78).

But to the extent that our experience of music's expressiveness is unified, such dichotomous theories should give us pause. The immediacy of the liveliness of a quick, leaping, melody in a major key doesn't seem to reside merely in its speed and contour, but also in its mode. At this point the resemblance theorist might point out that the meanings of words (a paradigm of conventional meaning) strike us immediately – we do not go through a conscious, or perhaps even subconscious, process of "decoding" the conventions by which they get their meanings. But to the extent that the resemblance theorist appeals to such arguments, he will have to abandon the advantages he claims for resemblance accounts *in particular* on the grounds of the immediacy of our apprehension of music's expressiveness.

2.5 Imagination Theories

Some philosophers are sympathetic to the core insights of the resemblance theory, suitably augmented with conventionalism, and yet find insufficient the resemblance theorists' responses to the main objections we have considered. Such philosophers think that there is a way to retain the connection between music's expressiveness and occurrent experiences of emotions – thus making expressive music not merely "expressive of" emotions but closer to genuine expression – without falling into expressionism or arousalism. The heart of this theory is the idea that when we hear expressive music we *imagine* that the music is someone's genuine expression of an occurrent emotion (Levinson 1996, 2006a).[36]

You might think that this theory is easily falsified by many people's experience of instrumental music: You can tell when you're imagining something (e.g., daydreaming delivering your Nobel prize acceptance speech) and when you're not (e.g., working on a crossword puzzle), and your experience of instrumental music falls into the second category (or, at least, it needn't fall into the first category for you to experience the music as expressive). But the imagination theorist will respond with the details of the theory, including some general points about imagination (Trivedi 2011a, 113–15). Though daydreaming may be an instance of imagining, not all imagining is daydreaming. For instance, if daydreams are imaginings, then presumably (night) dreams are imaginings, yet we are rarely in control of our (night) dreams. Indeed, we are typically unaware that we are dreaming while doing so. And just as some imagining is less voluntary than daydreaming, some imagining is less foregrounded or consciously accessible than daydreaming. For instance, there is evidence that when solving certain spatial puzzles, e.g., whether or not two shapes will fit together, people typically imagine the shapes coming together, yet are not aware that they are doing so (Shepard & Metzler 1971). We sometimes tend to equate imagining with *visual* imagining, yet we can clearly imagine sonic and other sensory experiences, whether in combination (as in a daydream) or by themselves (e.g., when you "play back" a piece of music in your mind). Furthermore, not all imagining is sensory imagining. I might imagine a Latina woman to be the President of the United States if I want to figure out how such a state of affairs would affect American foreign policy, but in doing so I need not imagine how anything – not even the President herself – looks or sounds. Finally, in any of these cases, what we imagine need not be wholly determinate. For instance, though every person has a determinate number of hairs on her head, when we imagine Hermione Granger first meeting Harry Potter, we surely don't imagine her having some particular number of hairs, even though we don't imagine that she *doesn't* have a particular number of hairs (nor that she's bald). And this seems to be true whether we imagine Hermione's appearance in great specificity (e.g., as Emma Watson looked as she was filmed for the scene in question for *Harry Potter and the Sorcerer's Stone*), or whether we don't imagine what Hermione looks like at all (as seems to be the case with some people, at least, when reading novels).

The imagination theorist of musical expressiveness, then, argues that Barber's "Adagio" is sad (for instance) because competent listeners tend to imagine – in a backgrounded, possibly not consciously accessible way – that the music is some person's literal expression of their occurrent sadness. "Person" is used here, as elsewhere in philosophy, as a term for a being with the psychological characteristics required for some kind of action – in this case emotional expression. We don't have to imagine that the person in question is a human being or has any particular kind of body (perhaps any body at all), in order to imagine that the music is their literal expression of their sadness; but we must imagine that they are capable of the mental states necessary for emotional experience (e.g., the evaluation of something as regrettable). Nor need we imagine that the person is expressing their sadness in ways that human beings typically do. But that's not to say that we imagine some strange creature expressing their sadness by emanating musical sounds. The details are simply not part of our imagining; the imagining is indeterminate in these respects. (For this reason, imagination theories are sometimes known as "persona" theories, where "persona" simply means "person" in this technical sense.) In sum:

> A passage of music, M, is expressive of an emotion, E, if, and only if, M is imagined by competent listeners as a literal expression of E by a persona experiencing that emotion.
>
> (Cf. Levinson 1996, 107)

If a physiological state (e.g., increased heart rate) is essential to a given emotion (e.g., fear), don't we have to imagine that the expressing persona has a heart and thus a body of some sort? The imagination theorist might reply that we need imagine only the *expression* of the emotion, which is necessarily public, being behavior of some sort. But then it seems that we must imagine that the persona has a body after all. Moreover, isn't it natural to imagine that this being expresses their emotions *sonically*, since the sounds of the music are what we imagine to be their expression of their emotions? And won't that mean that they must have a body of a particular sort – one that can resonate at a wide range of frequencies, and so on? The more detail that is implied by the inelim- inable imagining ascribed to us by the imagination theorist, the less appealing the theory becomes, since the less likely it seems that such detailed imaginings could be so backgrounded or consciously inaccessible as to be surprising to those hearing the theory for the first time. For this reason, imagination theorists such as Jerrold Levinson emphasize that the persona posited by the theory "is almost entirely indefinite, a sort of minimal person, characterized only by the emotion we hear it to be expressing and the musical gesture through which it does so" (2006a, 193–4). Whether the imagination theorist can coherently insist that we imagine this minimal state of affairs is an open question.[37]

2.6 Comparing Resemblance and Imagination Theories

2.6.1 Constraints on Experienced Resemblance and Imagined Expression

The imagination theorist agrees that the resemblances and conventions identi- fied by the resemblance theorist play a crucial *causal* role in musical expres- siveness. That is, it is surely because of the resemblances between music and typical human expressive behavior, in addition to established conventions, that competent listeners are disposed to imagine that some musical passages and not others are expressions of particular emotions. But the imagination theorist insists that expressiveness must amount to more than mere resemblance:

> I can perceive that … a leafy tree resembles a bushy beard, for instance, and not have the experience of seeing the tree as a beard. I can notice the likeness between the two and yet not see the one *in* the other. But surely we cannot speak of a musical passage being *expressive* of an emotion unless listeners are induced to hear … an expressing of the emotion, in the passage, whatever degree of resemblance they might note, in whatever respects, between the pas- sage and the emotion.
>
> (Levinson 2006a, 196)

In a similar vein, Levinson criticizes Davies's version of the resemblance theory by arguing that the only criterion for sufficient resemblance between a musical passage and the typical expressive appearance of a person is our tendency to imagine that the passage is literally a person's emotional expression (Levinson 1996, 196–9). This criticism ignores what Davies has latterly emphasized, namely the dispositional nature of the resemblance theory. He points out that resemblance theorists have typically appealed to the idea of resemblances that we are disposed to hear, as opposed to resemblances that might objectively exist, yet which we are not prone to notice. The dispute then seems to reduce to whether our experience of expressive music is one of experienced resemblance or imagined expression, something that may be difficult to settle by introspection or even empirical study. However, the imagination theorist might claim an advantage over resemblance theorists with respect to the *unity* of our experience of expressive music, considered at the end of the previous section. While resemblances and conventions may be two distinct *causes* of the experience of music as expressive, according to the imagination theorist they give rise to the same basic kind of experience: imagined expression.

Opponents of imagination theories object that music does not constrain our imagining enough to make such imagining the core of musical expressiveness (S. Davies 1997a; Kivy 2009, 101–17). Consider reading a novel. One might imagine how a character looks, including the color of his eyes, for instance, even though the character's appearance is not described at all in the text. Imagining different eye colors might even make the work more engaging for different readers. But it can't be a requirement for understanding the novel that the reader must imagine the character's eye color, certainly not some particular eye color, given the lack of such information in the text. Similarly, the resemblance theorist can acknowledge that imagining personae expressing their emotions in musical passages might help some listeners get into the work, but insist that such imaginings cannot be necessary for appreciating the work since there simply isn't enough information in the work to constrain such imagining. If you're listening to a jazz trio, for instance, how many personae should you imagine? Here are some options: (i) Each instrument gives rise to one persona, and they interact with one another, responding to one another's expressions; (ii) there is just one persona, who expresses the emotions of the performance overall; (iii) there is a persona for each musical theme, who emerges whenever that theme is played. It seems that different listeners could adopt any of these options, or even move from one to another during a single performance. And this will make a difference to the expressiveness one hears in the music: If the personae are linked to themes, they may be more emotionally static than if they are linked to instruments. If we imagine a single persona throughout, the expression may be that of someone's emotional experience developing over time, but if we imagine different personae succeeding one another, there may be emotional contrast, but no development. And so on.

Levinson replies to such objections by claiming that the imagination theorist can remain "agnostic" with respect to when and where particular personae are posited (2006a, 204). But an imagination theorist might just as well turn this objection back upon the resemblance theorist. An individual melody might have one expressive contour while the musical whole to which it contributes has another. A conventional musical expression, such as the association of pipe organs with Christianity, might color the expressive contour of the music played on that instrument. Should we think of the different contours and conventions presented over the course of the work as a mere sequence of emotional appearances or a progression of emotions in the same person? Since the imagination theorist does not dispute the relevance of resemblance or convention, she can adopt whatever solutions the resemblance theorist gives to these problems. She might also point out that there is no reason to choose between the various options we've been considering. We will be able to reject some projections of personae on uncontroversial grounds. If I constantly hear my father in every expressive musical passage, we can safely attribute this to my pathological psychology rather than the music. And it would be equally crazy to posit a different persona every ten notes (or five seconds, or whatever) for every piece of music, because such divisions make no musical or expressive sense. But it surely is often appropriate to appreciate not just the individual musical lines in a performance, but also the musical whole to which they contribute. It may be impossible to attend to all of these at once – perhaps there are limits to our perceptual and cognitive abilities in this regard – but a notional full appreciation of the performance in question may yet have to take account of all such aspects (cf. Maus 1988, 122–3).

2.6.2 The Range of Music's Expressiveness

Another difference between resemblance and imagination theories is the range of emotions they enable music to express. Robinson argues that an imagination theory allows for a wider range of musically expressible emotions than the resemblance theory, and that Davies (perhaps the staunchest defender of the resemblance theory) overstates the resemblance theory's resources in this regard (Robinson 2005, 307–10). The dispute generally turns on whether music can express "higher" or "more cognitive" emotions. The apparent problem for the resemblance theorist is that such emotions have no distinctive characteristic behavioral expressions, and thus nothing for the resemblance theory to latch on to. Such emotions are individuated by their cognitive content rather than any typical behavior. For instance, *hope* requires a conception of some future state better than the present in some respect, but a hopeful person does not typically appear or behave any differently from someone in another positive emotional state, such as happiness. Some resemblance theorists simply embrace the implication, claiming that music can only express garden-variety emotions such as happiness and sadness (e.g., Kivy 1990, 173–201). But others argue that music can express more cognitive emotions, such as hope (e.g., S. Davies 1994, 262–4).[38]

Before we turn to these arguments, it's worth noting that this implies that one constraint on a successful theory of musical expressiveness will be the facts about the range of emotions music can express. Shouldn't we figure that out first, so that we're in a better position to judge the adequacy of theories of musical expressiveness? In principle this sounds great, but in practice it's difficult to get an independent handle on what emotions music can express. If I hear hope in some musical passage and you don't, I may try to get you to hear what I do by asking you to listen to the music again in various ways. If you refuse, philosophical dialogue is at an end. If you accept, you may come to hear the hope in the music and we now agree on (one aspect of) the range of emotions expressible in music. But you may accept and yet fail to hear the hope. Perhaps you think I am projecting the hope on to the music rather than hearing it in the music, and conclude that the ways in which I am asking you to listen to the music are illegitimate. At that point we must return to philosophical dialogue about the nature of expressive music and its proper appreciation. In short, it is unlikely that we will answer the question of the range of emotions music can express independently of investigating arguments for and against its expression of various kinds of emotion, most notably higher emotions such as hope.

How, then, could a resemblance theorist argue that music can be expressive of hope? First, consider the difference, mentioned above, between hearing an extended passage of music as (i) a series of unrelated emotional expressions, and (ii) a development of emotional states in a single agent. Davies argues that the resemblance theory can explain both such experiences (1994, 262–4). Because we hear music as purposive (hearing a chord as a resolution or interruption, hearing a melody as wandering far afield or coming home, etc.), we may hear certain extended passages of complex works as unified emotional progressions, rather than isolated expressive chunks.[39] Robinson agrees that we often hear music this way, but denies that resemblance theories can account for it, arguing that the only way to hear an expressive sequence as a development or progression is to *imagine a single persona* who experiences the various emotions constituting that development or progression.

Second, Davies argues that although the resemblance theory at first seems able to grant music the ability to be expressive only of emotions that have typical behavioral manifestations, other emotions, such as hope, which are more cognitive and arguably lack typical behavioral manifestations, may be expressed by "judicious ordering" of musical passages expressive of emotions that do have such manifestations (S. Davies 1994, 262). For instance, Davies argues, "[w]here deep sadness gives way gradually to joy and abandonment, it may be reasonable to regard the transition as consistent with acceptance and resolution" (2006, 185). Robinson diagnoses two chief difficulties with this view: First, Davies's strategy again relies on the imaginative notion of a series of musical passages' being heard as the emotional progression of a single agent. To the extent that this is illegitimate for the resemblance theorist (for the reasons just covered), the strategy will fail. Second, Robinson argues that there are no sequences of less cognitive emotions that typically lead to a given more cognitive emotion, such as hope:

> Hope requires the expression of desires and thoughts. Merely coming after sadness and before tranquility, for example, isn't enough to distinguish hope from transient joy or a fit of ebullience or from the representation of some non-emotional event such as a break in the clouds or the arrival of a long-lost friend.
>
> (Robinson 2005, 308)

Thus, even if the resemblance theorist can reply to the objection about the musical expression of emotional progressions without collapsing into an imagination theory, he still won't have the resources to grant music the ability to express more cognitive emotions.[40]

At this point it might seem that the imagination theory is no better placed to attribute the expression of more cognitive emotions, such as hope, to instrumental music. After all, if Robinson is right that there are no sequences of emotional expression that typically lead to hope, then gaining the advantage of emotional development in a single agent by shifting to the imagination theory will not enable music to express hope in the way that Davies describes. Indeed, Robinson criticizes Levinson, another imagination theorist, for claiming that imagining a persona expressing itself through the music, together with the resources of resemblance and convention, is enough to secure music's ability to express more cognitive emotions. Levinson argues that although music cannot express or represent the intentional object essential to hope (the happier future state for which one hopes), it can resemble both a general kind of yearning (by means of, say, a series of increasingly wide rising intervals) and the phenomenology of the experience of hope. Together with imagining a person expressing themselves through the music, Levinson suggests, this is enough to enable the music to express hope (Levinson 1990a). Robinson avers that this is not enough to establish hope as the emotion expressed. Yearning is a part or aspect of a wide range of emotional states and there is no pattern of phenomenological or other non-cognitive aspects distinctive of hope in particular (Karl & Robinson 1995a, 1995b, 404–5).[41]

Though Levinson illustrates his general claim with close analysis of a particular example – a passage in Felix Mendelssohn's concert overture "The Hebrides" – Robinson argues that establishing the expression of hope within an instrumental work requires more evidence than Levinson provides, and evidence of additional kinds. Her example of musical hope comes from a very different work, Shostakovich's Tenth Symphony.[42] She points out that "The Hebrides" is program music, the subject of which is explicitly a natural landscape (the island of Staffa or "Fingal's Cave"), which immediately casts doubt on Levinson's psychological interpretation of the piece. She argues that Shostakovich's symphony, by contrast, falls squarely into the historical tradition of the "epic symphony" – a portrait of a (person's) struggle against adversity, resulting in ultimate victory – despite its lack of an explicit program. Like Levinson, she engages in close musical analysis, but argues that various aspects of her target passage (from the middle of the third movement) are reasonably interpreted as expressing several cognitive aspects of hope (Karl & Robinson 1995b, 411–12): (i) a *looking-forward* (represented by the ultimate transformation of the melody of the passage into the main theme of the final movement) to a future (ii) *happy state* (represented by the "languorous and dreamlike" character of the melody (412)), the prospect of which is (iii) *uncertain* (represented by the continual musical resistance that the theme encounters), yet which (iv) the protagonist *desires and strives for* (represented by the persistence of the theme in the face of this resistance).

2.6.3 Expressiveness and the Medium of Music

Even if you accept Robinson's analysis of her chosen passage as expressing hope, you might wonder if we've been guilty of some "mission creep" here. After all, it would be no surprise if a song that competently set Alexander Pope's oft-quoted lines "Hope springs eternal in the human breast ..." expressed hope.[43] But clearly in this case the meanings of the words make a significant contribution to the expressiveness. Indeed, one might turn to the partial aspects of hope that can be musically mirrored according to Levinson and, even accepting Robinson's criticisms of his analysis of "The Hebrides," suggest that the addition of Pope's words are enough to make this music *in the context of this song* express hope. Thus, such an example is beside the point if we are interested in the expressive potential of *pure, instrumental* music. The mission-creep worry is that in taking up Robinson's example we have slipped into the same kind of confusion. If Shostakovich's Tenth Symphony is in the epic-symphony tradition, and this amounts to its being the story of a protagonist who struggles against and finally overcomes adversity, then it is not a piece of pure, instrumental music after all; it's a piece of "program music" – music with an accompanying text or other representational component that must be taken into account in a full appreciation (Kivy 2009, 157–75).[44]

Robinson's reply is that to divide all music into the "absolute" (or "pure") and "programmatic" (or "impure") is simplistic (Karl & Robinson 2015). As the examples of song, music with a specific textual program, and symphonies in the epic tradition suggest, most music (even much instrumental music) falls between two poles of a continuum.[45] To restrict ourselves to music at the very tip of one of the poles of this continuum – music without any element that might be called programmatic – is absurd, especially if our focus is musical expressiveness, which came to the fore as a value of Western classical music during the Romantic period, when most instrumental works can be argued to fall nearer the middle of this continuum.[46] Kivy and other resemblance theorists have to some extent acknowledged this point. At the beginning of his first book on the nature and value of "music alone," Kivy rather disconcertingly admits that:

> I do not even know whether I can say that such "hard core" examples of the instrumental literature as Bach's "Brandenburg" Concertos (written for "social" musicmaking), Handel's *Music for the Royal Fireworks* (written as part of … a "mixed media" event), Mozart's serenades and divertimenti (dinner music), Beethoven's *Egmont* or *Coriolanus* overtures (incidental music for the theatre) really count as music alone, in the full-blown sense, or whether we simply treat them as – as if – music alone. … Perhaps, all things considered …, there is *no* case of pure, unadulterated music alone.
>
> (1990, 26)

What, you might reasonably wonder, is the point of devoting a book to a kind of music of which one isn't even sure there is a single example? Kivy's answer is that even if no piece of music is in itself "absolute" in this sense, we can and do appropriately and rewardingly appreciate much music in the classical tradition (including the examples listed above), *as if it were* absolute, that is, ignoring the elements it contains in addition to the music alone. On the face of it, this stance implies that such appreciations will be *partial*, a bit like a Marxist interpretation of a novel that is compatible with a range of other interpretations. If this is the case, however, then there is no disagreement between Kivy and Robinson, which makes Kivy's vehement objections to Robinson's analysis and theory rather puzzling.

Even if we have achieved a theoretical détente here, have we answered the mission-creep objection? Suppose Robinson is right that all music falls on a continuum between "absolute" music and highly programmatic music. Suppose, even, that it turns out that there is no absolute music (or at least, for our current purposes, no *expressive* absolute music). If we were right to conclude from our discussion of song in the previous chapter that even though one cannot fully appreciate either the words or music of a song independently of one another, one can – indeed must – still distinguish between the two as aspects of the song, then shouldn't we say the same about all instrumental music, even if (*ex hypothesi*) all of it has *some* extra-musical aspect? Indeed, if any sense can be made of the nature and understanding of purely musical features (a question we will return to in Chapter 4), it seems that we *must* distinguish between such aspects of music and others (such as an accompanying program, whether thin or robust). And we can reasonably investigate the expressive capacities of such aspects.

If a Robinsonian were convinced by this reasoning, she might reply that she is indeed guilty of mission creep – if the mission is to understand the expressive potential of music alone. But she might go on to point out that it is far from obvious that this mission is the most important one in a campaign to understand the nature and value of musical expressiveness. As mentioned above, the emotional content of music became a central concern in the Romantic period when most music was not "absolute" but programmatic to a greater or lesser degree. Thus the investigation of the expressiveness of music alone can be at best a preliminary mission in the longer campaign to understand musical expressiveness in general. Indeed, Robinson could be interpreted as arguing in her *magnum opus* (2005) that philosophers have achieved what they can on this preliminary mission, and that it is time to move on with the campaign. In doing so, she argues that although simple expressionism of the sort considered at the beginning of this chapter may fail as a theory of the expressiveness of music alone, a sophisticated expressionism is in fact the correct theory of the expressiveness of much actual (non-absolute) expressive music, namely much Western music since the dawn of Romanticism at the turn of the nineteenth century.

To understand Robinson's theory, however, we must turn from the focus of this chapter – the expression of emotions in music – to a closely related topic: listeners' emotional responses to music. In fact, this topic, as we will see, is another that has been used to argue for and against different theories of musical expressiveness, especially resemblance and imagination theories.

Questions

What is the puzzle that philosophical theories of music's emotional expressiveness are supposed to solve?

What are the two most promising theories of music's expressiveness, in your view? Explain them in your own words. Then argue for the superiority of one over the other.

Which, if any, theories of musical expressiveness fail to account for *any* of music's apparent expressiveness? Explain those theories in your own words. Then explain why they fail.

Is there one correct theory of music's expressiveness, or should we accept more than one theory? Could more than one theory correctly explain the same instance of musical expressiveness? Are any two of the theories mutually exclusive (i.e., one must be false if the other is true)?

Notes

1 In fact, it's not obvious how *literature* achieves its emotional expressiveness. After all, a poem might depict a scene likely to *make us* sad, but as we've just seen that's a different thing from a poem's *being sad itself*, i.e., expressing sadness. And the apparently simplest way in which words might be emotionally expressive – by *naming* the emotions expressed (e.g., "heavy sadness, doom and gloom") – is not a strategy often employed by the best writers. For an introduction to expressiveness in music *and* literature, see Stecker 2010, 201–20.

2 My use of the term *expressionism* here for one theory of musical expressiveness should not be confused with the same term's more common use in connection with the artistic movement of the early twentieth century.

3 Perhaps because most philosophers find simple expressionism inadequate, it is difficult to find uncontroversial examples of adherents to the view. Commonly cited figures include Tolstoy (1898), Dewey (1934), and Collingwood (1938).

4 We will consider some questions about interpretation in Chapter 4.

5 This is Barber's arrangement for string orchestra of the middle movement of his string quartet.

6 A little learning is a dangerous thing. Wordsworth's very next words potentially return us to the initial problem: "the emotion is contemplated till by a species of reaction the tranquillity gradually disappears, and an emotion, kindred to that which was before the subject of contemplation, is gradually produced, and does itself actually exist in the mind" (1802, 82).

7 Igor Stravinsky infamously claims that "music is, by its very nature, essentially powerless to *express* anything at all ..." (1936, 53), so presumably he did not aim to create expressive music. But many would insist that he did so nonetheless.

8 Throughout my consideration of arousalism, I am indebted to Matravers's lucid discussion of the theory (2011).

9 Matravers uses the term "affective" where I say "broad." I find that use confusing, since "affective" is widely used (in philosophy and elsewhere) to mean "of, or related to, emotions and emotion-like states."

10 For two examples, see Kivy 1980 and 2009. The notion of "garden-variety" emotions will be fully explained in Chapter 3; for now you can just think of them as paradigmatic or typical emotions.

11 I here refer to the fictional Vulcans of the *Star Trek* universe: creatures with psychologies much like ours, perhaps superior to ours in rationality, but who feel no emotions. Unfortunately, checking this reference on Wikipedia reveals that things are more complicated than I supposed: https://en.wikipedia.org/wiki/Vulcan_(Star_Trek)#Emotion (accessed September 16, 2018).

12 This is not a difficult supposition given the existence of "color blind" people, and evidence that different animals visually perceive different ranges of the electromagnetic spectrum and perceive it as divided into different bands.

13 Of course, there's also an almost postmodern irony in a dramatic character's voicing these sentiments. His world really *is* a stage and the people upon it merely players.

14 Metaphor itself is a rich philosophical topic. For a general introduction, see Hills 2017; for an introduction focused around artistic metaphors, see Hagberg 2013.

15 To be fair, Zangwill has a sophisticated theory of such "aesthetic properties" (2001), consideration of which would take us too far afield.

16 Some philosophers argue that it is not our *descriptions* of music that are metaphorical, but the music's *possession* of expressive properties (Goodman 1968, 45–95) or our *experience* of music as expressive (Peacocke 2009, 257–75). Consideration of these views would take us too far afield, though we will consider a related theory of musical space and movement in Chapter 4, §4.1. For criticism of Goodman, see S. Davies 1994, 137–50; for criticism of Peacocke, see Boghossian 2010 and S. Davies 2011c.

17 One might say this only shows that my ongoing love involves a constant physiological state, initiated when I fell in love and to end only when death do us part. But it seems implausible

that, as I go about my daily routine, not thinking about my spouse at all, I am in a different physiological state than when I did so before I met her.

18 Both "cognitive" and "intentional" have more than one meaning in philosophy. Here, "cognitive" means roughly *to do with articulate thoughts*, as opposed to phenomenology or physiology, for instance, while "intentionality" means roughly *aboutness*, in the sense that your thoughts are *about* some object. (This is related to "intentional" in the sense of "on purpose," but is an importantly distinct sense.) Some theorists of emotion and music, however, use "cognitive" more narrowly to mean *to do with beliefs* (as opposed to other articulate thoughts, such as desires or imaginings).

19 For exposition and discussion of Langer's theory, see Higgins 1991, 100–8 and S. Davies 1994, 123–37.

20 For an introduction to the complexities of pictorial representation, see Abell 2013.

21 Of course the portrait may, in virtue of *how* it depicts the Prime Minister (including divergences from perceptual resemblance), express various things about her, including emotional things. What visual expressiveness amounts to is, of course, a question for philosophers of the visual arts parallel to the one we are grappling with in this chapter.

22 In the literature on musical expressiveness, the term "representation" is sometimes used to mean "depiction" (e.g., S. Davies 1994, 51–2). I follow more general philosophical practice in using "representation" as a general term, allowing for specific kinds of representation such as depiction (representation by pictures) and semantics (representation by language). I ignore the unpopular view that music represents emotions semantically. For discussion, see S. Davies 1994, 1–49. We will consider the more general proposal that music is a language in Chapter 4.

23 Though some nineteenth-century Romantic theorists may have claimed that expressive music and other artworks are spontaneous betrayals of their creators' emotional states, most philosophers – including contemporary expressionists – now agree that the deliberation required for the creation of any artwork implies that artistic expression should be understood in the second, deliberate way (cf. Robinson 2005, 237–8, 246, 261–4).

24 "Modal" here refers to "modes" of perception: vision, hearing, etc.

25 The resemblance theory thus makes music's expressiveness *response-dependent*, as with arousalism. What distinguishes the theories is the different responses appealed to.

26 Don't we hear the resemblance between one piece of music and other, for example, when a jazz musician quotes a classical tune, or when we realize that the piece we're listening to is in sonata form? The resemblance theorist can probably allow the first case as a kind of representation – quotations represent their sources. He may explain away the second by arguing that one's experience of a piece as in a particular form is *inferential*, not immediately perceptual as is one's experience of the resemblance between music's dynamic contour and expressive behavior (though see Chapter 4, §4.6 for complications raised by this response).

27 But, for example, the basset hound's face *is* expressive of sadness since we *do* tend to experience its resemblance to a sad person. There are still important differences between the dog's face and music, however. For instance, since the music is an artifact, it (unlike the dog's face) can be *about* the emotions it's expressive of.

28 For second thoughts, see Kivy 2002, 46–7. For critical discussion of evolutionary explanations, see Ravasio 2018.

29 It would indeed be devastating to the theory if psychologists discovered that competent listeners *do not* tend to hear resemblances between expressive music and typical emotional characteristics, but all philosophical theories of musical expressiveness are likely hostage to empirical claims in this way.

30 An instructive example is Schubert's String Quartet No. 14, "Death and the Maiden." All the movements are in minor keys (i.e., they begin and end in minor keys, though there are many major-mode passages throughout the work), yet the expressiveness of the minor-mode passages is extremely varied.

31 For an example of musical failure to resolve, try singing "Happy Birthday," but ending on the penultimate note. The unsatisfyingness of ending here is due to the lack of musical resolution. (If you think the words are to blame, sing "Sue" instead of "to" on the note in question. The difference is negligible.) We will consider such matters at greater length in Chapter 4, §4.3.

32 Very few scholars have defended conventionalism as a theory of *all* musical expressiveness. Such a view approaches the idea (considered briefly below and in Chapter 4, §4.4) that music is a language.

33 Robinson discusses one study in which the presence of an authority figure (an observing scientist) led Japanese, but not American, students to repress their expression of disgust in response to a "gory and unpleasant film" (2005, 32).

34 For further discussion of empirical evidence, see Young 2014, 22–6, and S. Davies 2011a.

35 The exceptions include onomatopoeic words (e.g., "plop") and general constraints. (For instance, it's not just coincidence that there are no 50-syllable exclamations meaning "look out!".)

36 Other imagination theorists of musical expressiveness include Bruce Vermazen (1986), Kendall Walton (1988a), Jenefer Robinson (2005), and Saam Trivedi (2017). I focus on Jerrold Levinson's account as the most comprehensive and highly developed, with the possible exceptions of Jenefer Robinson's complex theory, to which I turn in the next chapter, and Saam Trivedi's, which appeared too late in the writing of this chapter to allow extended discussion.

37 We will consider these imaginative issues further in Chapter 3.

38 Davies does not defend a particular example of hopeful music. Two examples we will discuss below are passages from Felix Mendelssohn's concert overture "The Hebrides" and Shostakovich's Tenth Symphony.

39 We will investigate musical movement and purposiveness in Chapter 4.

40 Recall that Davies presses this same kind of objection against arousalism.

41 I will continue to talk of "Robinson" although I cite work that Robinson co-authored with Gregory Karl. I do so not to downplay Karl's contributions, which Robinson acknowledges even in her sole-authored work (especially Robinson 2005), but merely to avoid further complicating my prose.

42 There is unfortunately no space here to go into the details of Levinson's or Robinson's analyses of these pieces, which make for a fascinating pair of philosophical arguments rooted in a deep appreciation for instrumental classical music.

43 For a real example, albeit one that does not include the *word* "hope," listen to the opening of Crowded House's "How Will You Go": "Escape is on my mind again … ." Note the melody's use of increasingly wide rising intervals – Levinson's example of a promising musical correlate of hope.

44 The slip (if such it be) is easy to make in this case because there is no actual text or other artifact that must be consulted in appreciating the symphony. Rather, the epic-symphony tradition is a kind of convention; one must only keep the general idea of the triumph-over-adversity plot in mind when appreciating a work in this tradition.

45 I take the conclusions I defended in Chapter 1 about the necessity of the concept of pure music to any adequate philosophy of music to be compatible with Karl and Robinson's idea that such a concept defines one pole of a continuum.

46 Similarly, Robinson criticizes Levinson's imagination theory of musical expressiveness as being too monolithic, ignoring music that is expressive simply in virtue of resemblance (Robinson 2005, 453–4 n. 9).

Further Reading

Though published over 20 years ago, Stephen Davies's *Musical Meaning and Expression* (1994) remains an excellent overview of the issues raised by, and theories of, musical meaning and expression. A more recent, magisterial attempt to synthesize empirical and philosophical work into a comprehensive theory of emotion and the arts is Jenefer Robinson's *Deeper than Reason: Emotion and its Role in Literature, Music, and Art* (2005).

In "Hearing and Seeing Musical Expression," Vincent Bergeron and Dominic McIver Lopes (2009) draw on psychological research to argue that our attributions of expressiveness to music in live performance depend not just on our aural but also our *visual* experience of the performers, raising the question of whether music and its expressiveness are purely sonic.

3 Emotions in the Listener

Overview

In this chapter, we investigate various ways in which listeners respond emotionally to music, with an emphasis on those that are both relevant to appreciating music and philosophically puzzling. We end with a consideration of Jenefer Robinson's sophisticated expressionism.

No one – not even a single philosopher, as far as I am aware – denies that people regularly respond emotionally to music. To do so, one would pretty much have to deny that people have emotional capacities at all, since we regularly respond emotionally to anything that affects our interests in some way. If you can be annoyed by an advertisement interrupting your viewing pleasure, you can be annoyed by the thumping music of a passing car while you're trying to get to sleep. If you can be thrilled by the sight of your beloved walking through the door, you can be thrilled to hear her latest song played on the radio. Philosophers' interest in our emotional responses to music, then, has largely been restricted to certain kinds of emotional responses – those that are philosophically puzzling in some way – and our emotional responses' relevance to the appreciation of music.[1]

3.1 Uncontroversial Emotional Responses to Music

We can begin by considering emotions that are responses "to the music" only in a tangential sense. Recall Derek Matravers's distinction between associative, broad, and music-specific emotional responses (2011, 212–13). If you feel sad every time you hear Joni Mitchell's "Big Yellow Taxi" only because it was your recently deceased sibling's favorite song, then your response is associative and idiosyncratic. This may be an important and valuable kind of emotional response to music, but it is not philosophically puzzling, nor would we expect anyone else who appreciates Mitchell's song to share it. After all, this seems primarily to be an emotional reaction to the loss of your sibling, rather than to the song, which merely triggers it.

If you are a tone-deaf literary critic responding emotionally as you read the text in the program during a performance of Benjamin Britten's "Rejoice in the Lamb," we might suspect that you are responding solely to the text (excerpts from Christopher Smart's poem "Jubilate Agno"), and not to any musical aspects of the work. Emotional responses to literary works can be philosophically puzzling, but the point of this example is to remind us that many musical works (broadly construed) comprise more than one medium and that our focus is on emotional responses to the *musical* aspects of such works.

You might be as startled by a cymbal crash in the middle of an otherwise quiet song as you would be by someone dropping a tray of glasses at the back of the venue. As the comparison illustrates, this is a rapid, non-cognitive response to a mere sonic stimulus, as opposed to a fully-fledged emotional response to the music (though it might give rise to a fully-fledged emotional response to something, such as annoyance at the band or the server).[2] Sometimes it is not easy to tell whether a response is non-cognitive in this way. For instance, Haydn's "Surprise" symphony (no. 94) is so called because halfway through the opening theme of the second movement, for the most part played quietly by the strings, comes a sudden fortissimo chord played by the entire orchestra. However, though unexpectedly loud, this chord is not cacophonous – it fits entirely predictably within the harmonic structure of the theme. Indeed, this was one of Haydn's musical jokes, understood as such by his original audiences (and not, as is sometimes claimed, the composer's revenge on a dozy audience). Thus, though one's response may begin with a startle, one's ultimate emotional response (if one gets the joke) is a highly cognitive one.

Less musically tangential are what we've called *broad* responses to music. If you are irritated by a song because the performer didn't tune his guitar before beginning, then in some sense it is the music to which you are responding. But to the extent that the object of your ire is the performer's negligence rather than the resulting music, it is not a response to the music itself. Similarly, if you are filled with pride at your child's performance of Beethoven's "Moonlight Sonata" because you know what hard work she has put into practicing it, your response seems to be to the performer rather than to the music itself. Nonetheless, as we saw in our discussion of arousalism in the previous chapter, it is not always easy to distinguish broad from music-specific responses. Your irritation at the guitarist is essentially tied up with some kind of negative evaluative response to the out-of-tune chords he plays, as your pride at your child's performance is tied up with a positive evaluative response to its (as opposed to her) perfection. Those responses may not be irritation and pride, exactly, but they are arguably emotional and music-specific.

Uncontroversially music-specific affective responses include a family that I will call "Meyer-style" responses because they were extensively discussed by Leonard Meyer (1956).[3] Almost all music is patterned in some way. There are larger-scale patterns, such as the alternation between verse and chorus in a pop song; at a smaller scale, the structure of melodies, harmonies, and rhythms tend to follow predictable patterns. We will investigate some of these patterns in the next chapter. Their relevance here is that we respond affectively to having our expectations satisfied or frustrated – when listening to music as in any other activity. Lullabies, for instance, tend to be relatively predictable. Their melodies are constructed of small intervals and their harmonies and rhythms are stable and unsurprising. As a result they literally *lull* us into a sense of security. Dropping a beat from a measure late in a song that is consistently in a single meter, as the Beatles do near the end of "Good Day Sunshine," may delight us with surprise, but the way it makes us sit up and take notice would obviously be counterproductive in a lullaby. We will return later in this chapter to the role of this kind of response in our appreciation of music; the point here is that the fact that we respond in such ways to music is not philosophically puzzling.

Emotional responses to aesthetic or artistic properties of music raise no philosophical problems for music in particular.[4] Just as some people are moved to tears by a beautiful sunset or bored by the monotonous scenery of a long train journey, some people are moved to tears by the beauty of a musical passage or bored by the derivative nature of an uninspired song. Peter Kivy has emphasized this kind of emotional response to music in particular, because he thinks that it contrasts sharply with another kind of response, one that many theorists take to be an important component of the value of music, yet which, according to Kivy, makes no sense, namely, listeners' emotional responses to the emotional content of music, that is, to music's expressiveness.

3.2 Emotional Responses to Music's Expressiveness

3.2.1 The Puzzle

We have just considered some different kinds of emotional responses to music. While there is disagreement about their importance and role in the appreciation of music, everyone admits that they are possible and indeed occur regularly. What is different about emotional responses to music's expressiveness? Kivy points out that in all the cases considered above there is an easily identifiable intentional object of the emotional response in question, one that satisfies the conditions of that emotion's "formal object" – the characterization that any object of the emotion must meet, such as the *threatening* nature of objects of fear. For instance, the dropped beat in "Good Day Sunshine" is *surprising* in light of the metrical regularity of the song up until that point. That we react *with surprise* to this metrical irregularity is thus not puzzling in the slightest. Similarly, the delight we take in that moment of the song depends on our judging that the dropped beat here "works" in the context of the song as a whole, as opposed to the dismay we might feel in response to someone's unintentionally missing a beat in a live performance. Compare this with feeling sad or even pitying in response to Barber's "Adagio for Strings," or anxious in response to Prokofiev's "Precipitato." Sadness, pity, and anxiety each require that the person experiencing them evaluate their objects negatively in some way. One is made sad by, or pities people in, situations that one takes to be regrettable, while one is made anxious by the possibility that things will turn out to be regrettable. But if one thinks that the music to which one is responding, including its expressiveness, is not regrettable but *wonderful*, then a response of sadness, pity, or anxiety seems at best irrational. Note that the same is true of positive emotional responses to music. It may not be puzzling that one is delighted by the beauty of the third movement of Brahms's First Symphony, but how could one (rationally) be moved to serene happiness by that emotion's *expression* in the music if such expression involves no one's actually being in such a happy state (Kivy 1999, 3–4)?

Kivy's response to such questions is simply: One couldn't. While few contemporary philosophers of music agree with Kivy on this point, Eduard Hanslick also thought that people do not respond emotionally to music's expressiveness.[5] Hanslick's argument was simpler, however, since he denied that music *has* any expressive content. If music has no expressive content, people cannot be responding emotionally to such content. Thus, Hanslick defended eliminativism about emotional responses to music's expressiveness: Our emotional responses to music are associative (among other things) but we often mistake such responses for responses to emotions in the music (Hanslick 1854, especially Chapters 2 and 5). Kivy's argument cannot be quite the same, since he acknowledges the existence and importance of the emotional *content* of music, but he similarly offers an eliminativist theory of emotional *responses* to that content: Though music can be expressive, because that expressiveness is a matter of resemblance and convention it is not the right kind of object for "garden-variety" emotional responses, such as happiness or sadness, in listeners.[6] People's claims that they experience such emotional responses to music is the result of their confusedly taking their rational emotional responses to the music (such as delight in its expressiveness) to be empathetic or sympathetic emotional responses to the emotions expressed in it (Kivy 1999, 4–6).

You might think that Kivy's eliminativism is more plausible for our positive emotional responses to music (e.g., happiness) than our negative ones (e.g., sadness). We might confuse our delight in good (expressively upbeat) music with happiness, but how could we confuse our delight in good (expressively downbeat) music with sadness? Delight is similar to happiness, but quite different from sadness. Kivy's response is that we are confusing the nature of the emotion we feel with its object. Because the emotions in question are necessarily directed at some object, we think of the object as essential to the emotion. For instance, the delight we take in a joke on *Girls* we think of as *Girls*-joke delight, while the delight we take in our puppy's antics in the meadow we think of as puppy-meadow-antics delight. In one sense, these emotional states feel different, indeed *are* different, because of their different objects; yet in another sense they are the *same*, since they are both delight. The confusion in the musical case arises, according to Kivy, because the *object* of our emotional state, namely music's emotional expressiveness, is itself closely tied to emotion. So when we feel happy-music delight we sometimes mistakenly think we're feeling happiness, indeed a happiness as distinctive as the music that expresses it, while when we feel sad-music delight we mistakenly think we're feeling sadness, and again, a sadness as distinctive as the music in question (Kivy 1999, 10). It is worth noting that although Kivy's theory allows for emotional responses to expressive music, these are emotional responses not exactly to the music's *expressiveness*, but rather to the *excellence* of the music. Kivy, for instance, could not argue that we delight in mediocre sad music. If such music seems to make us sad, then, it will count against Kivy's theory.

However plausible you find Kivy's defense of his eliminativism about emotional responses to music's expressiveness, most philosophers, including other resemblance theorists, have attempted instead to defend the possibility, rationality, and value of emotional – or at least affective – responses to music's expressiveness.

3.2.2 Emotional Contagion

Stephen Davies argues that in listening to expressive music we often experience a "mirroring" response. The process is one of emotional "contagion" wherein the listener is "infected" with the emotions expressed in the music (1994, 279–307; 2011b). As the medical terminology suggests, this process is something that *happens to* the listener rather than something she *does*. But Davies is at pains to emphasize that a listener's being emotionally affected by music she is *appreciating* is different from the case of, say, a shopper's being emotionally influenced by background music of which he may not even be aware. The appreciative listener pays attention to the music, including its expressiveness, and is likely aware that the music is affecting her. Nonetheless, it is a crucial aspect of the contagion theory of music's emotional effects on listeners that, as Kivy points out, the listener's emotion has no appropriate formal object (e.g., something regrettable, in the case of sadness). When a sad piece of music infects a listener with sadness, the music *causes* the listener's sadness, but she is not sad *about* the music, because there is nothing regrettable about it (S. Davies 2011b, 46–8, 53).

If one holds fast to a simple cognitive theory of the emotions, then one might conclude that none of this implies that Kivy is wrong about the impossibility of emotional responses to music.[7] If an intentional object characterized as regrettable is essential to sadness, then the listener infected by the sadness of a piece of music cannot be experiencing sadness, for there is no such intentional object for the appreciative listener. However, as we saw in the previous chapter, a cognitive view that has this implication is probably too simplistic as an account of human emotional experience. In a recent defense of contagion theory, Davies points out that there are many apparent counterexamples to such a view: We respond emotionally to fictional characters, such as Frodo Baggins, without believing there is such a hobbit braving dangers to return a piece of jewelry; people fear house spiders that they know to be harmless; and we are sometimes in a bad mood without thinking there is anything around us that justifies our ill temper (S. Davies 2011b, 48–51).[8] Can the contagion theory of our emotional responses to music be assimilated to any of these cases? Since resemblance theorists reject the notion of an imagined agent in expressive instrumental music, they reject the idea (which we will investigate in more detail soon) that our emotional responses to such music are like our responses to fictional characters. Most are also reluctant to liken such responses to phobias, since we typically think of phobias as pathological, something to be ameliorated or cured, if possible, rather than a valuable feature of our lives to be understood and even celebrated. *Moods*, then, are the most attractive to the resemblance theorist of these three models for our emotional response to expressive music. Recall that a mood, in this technical sense, is an affective state related to a garden-variety cognitive emotion, but which lacks the intentional object typical of (or essential to) that emotion. Perhaps a mood has no intentional object at all, or perhaps it has an extremely vague or attenuated intentional object, with the subject thinking that there is *something* regrettable out there somewhere, even if he doesn't know what or where.

Even if moods are the best model for the emotional states with which we respond to expressive music, Davies still wants to distinguish the kind of emotional contagion provided by music from other mood processes.[9] In particular, as we saw above, he emphasizes that the appreciative listener *attends to* the music's expressiveness and is thus aware of its role in her emotional experience, unlike the case of the person who wakes up in a foul mood, who may be unaware of the crucial role played in that mood by his fourth martini of the night before. Nevertheless, Davies does not think that this kind of process is unique to music. He lists other people's emotional expressions, the weather, and even décor (such as the color of a room) as examples of things that can initiate a similar process of contagion (S. Davies 2011b, 55). This distinction between different ways in which we enter mood states is important to Davies because it is the source of a reply to a further objection to his view. An emotional cognitivist who accepts the counterexamples given above to the simple version of the theory (responses to fictions, phobias, and moods) may point out that although these cases show that the relevant belief (e.g., that something is threatening) is not essential to the *occurrence* of an affective state (e.g., fear), it may be essential to such states' *rationality*. As already noted, a phobia is usually something to be cured, and someone may be talked out of the bad mood they wake up in by cogent arguments that this *is* just a bad mood, since their life is in fact a bowl of cherries. (If they cannot be talked out of their mood in this way, we may, as with the phobic person, start to think of their emotional state as pathological – depression, for instance.) Why not think that our contagion-induced emotional responses to music are similarly irrational and thus something to be avoided or mitigated rather than celebrated?

Davies admits that this objection "has some force" (2011b, 55). Because there is no appropriate intentional object for the moods induced by music, he acknowledges that we cannot criticize someone who is *not* moved by expressive music on grounds of irrationality or even impoverished emotional capacity. But he suggests that our contagion-induced responses to music are better characterized as *non*-rational than as *ir*rational. They are still apt, appropriate, or normal in the sense that, first, they have a place in our extra-musical emotional lives (the same place as our contagion-induced responses to weather, décor, and other people) and, second, they contrast with other, inappropriate, inapt, and abnormal responses to expressive music. A person's being made sad by the sadness of Barber's "Adagio" is puzzling for the reasons we have been considering, but a person's being made *joyful* by that piece's sadness would be downright bizarre (S. Davies 2011b, 55–6).[10]

We might question both parts of this response. First, we don't typically pay attention to the weather or décor for the emotional states they induce in us; in fact, Jenefer Robinson argues that such attention tends to *diminish* the effects of contagion, since we recognize the non-rational nature of such responses (2005, 387, 394). This makes Davies's appeal to the attentional nature of the contagion response a double-edged sword: Our paying attention to music's expressiveness makes the response more relevant to appreciation (contrasting it with our response to shopping-mall Muzak), but it also makes the response unusual. Davies responds that Robinson gets the empirical facts wrong: Psychologists observe that people are *more* likely to experience contagion when they recognize others' expressiveness (2011b, 56–7). However, there is another objection in the vicinity, namely, that emotional contagion usually occurs without our *awareness* – of the contagion itself, rather than the expressiveness that gives rise to it – and when we do become aware of it, its effects are typically diminished (precisely because we recognize the irrationality of the response). If this is right, it suggests that we may be less likely to experience emotional contagion on the basis of resemblance than Davies implies.

Second, locating contagion responses to musical expressiveness in a broad psychological theory does not amount to a rational *justification* of them, as Davies claims. It is more like a value-neutral *explanation* of them. Any normativity such responses have (as appropriate, apt, or normal) is statistical rather than rational. To the extent that this is true, it seems bound to limit the value of such responses to music.

Why should rationality matter to the value of a response to an artwork? Because rationality is itself a value: If someone is being irrational, then it seems …, well, *reasonable* to criticize them for it. Of course, rationality is not the only value. If someone has just learned that their spouse has died, it may be unwise to point out that they are acting irrationally in obsessively devoting themselves to cleaning the house. This may be part of their grieving process, which is more important than their current rationality, and may be essential to their future rationality. On the other hand, if they are threatening to kill themselves from grief, reasoning with them seems more defensible, since the value of their life is greater than the offence or interference with their grieving that one might cause by one's intervention. The case of our emotional responses to artworks is less extreme, but it conforms to the same basic pattern. There may be value in some irrational affective responses (a point we will return to in Chapter 5) but, other things being equal, a theory that renders our affective responses to music rational will be preferable to one that makes them non-rational or (worse) irrational.

3.2.3 Emotional Responses to Imaginings

The imagination theorist's solution to the puzzle of our emotional response to music's expressiveness is in some ways simpler, and in others more complex, than the contagion theory. The solution is simpler in that it classifies our emotional responses to musical expressiveness with other, widely acknowledged emotional responses to artworks, namely, our emotional responses to *fictions*, such as novels, films, and videogames, the idea being that the persona we imagine expressing their emotions through the music is a kind of fictional character. The solution is more complex in that our emotional responses to fictions themselves present a philosophical puzzle, widely known as *the paradox of fiction*, that has generated a large literature including many different solutions. One way to evaluate this solution to the puzzle of our emotional responses to music's expressiveness, then, is to ask, on the one hand, how plausible a given solution to the paradox of fiction is and, on the other, to what extent it is applicable to our experience of music.

Like the problem of freedom introduced in Chapter 1, the paradox of fiction can be introduced as three propositions, each of which seems plausible by itself, but which cannot all be true:

1   We feel emotions (e.g., pity or fear) for fictional characters (e.g., Hermione Granger).
2   We only feel emotions (e.g., pity or fear) for things that we believe exist.
3   We know that fictional characters (e.g., Hermione Granger) don't exist.

The first proposition is supposed to be plausible given our experience with fictions. Just as with music, many people seem to feel a wide range of emotions while reading a novel or watching a film, including what we might call, following Matravers's terminology, "character-specific" emotions, such as fear for what might happen to Hermione next, or pity for her suffering. The second proposition relies on the plausibility of the cognitive theory of emotions. We might respond with fear to a creak of the floorboards, but only if we believe (or at least suspect) that the creak was caused by an intruder. The third proposition, like the first, is supposed to be fairly obvious given our experience of fictions. Perhaps children are sometimes confused about the status as fact or fiction of what they hear or see. To the extent that they think that Barney (the purple dinosaur) exists, there is no paradox of fiction regarding their emotional responses to him. But few adults have any doubt about the non-existence of Hermione Granger.

As with the problem of freedom, one can eliminate the paradox by disputing the truth of any one of the three propositions, but not just any such rejection constitutes a satisfactory solution to the paradox. For instance, one might argue that fictional characters do in fact exist, citing some of the extensive literature on the metaphysics of fiction (see Kroon & Voltolini 2016). After all, J. K. Rowling created Hermione Granger, didn't she? Hermione didn't exist before Rowling had the idea for the books, and then came into existence at some point as she wrote them. But even if this is correct, it doesn't solve the ultimate problem. Whatever Hermione, the fictional character, is "she" (better: *it*) is not a person. Hermione might have been created by Rowling, but not in the same way that Rowling created her daughter Jessica! If fictional characters are, say, sets of words (for Rowling certainly created a lot of those, which seems intimately related to her creation of Hermione), then they don't seem to be the kind of thing to which we would respond in the way we do to Hermione's travails. For sets of words, unlike people, don't suffer; yet we weep for Hermione (if we do) in a way at least analogous to the way in which we would weep for a person undergoing the events that Hermione (fictionally) undergoes.

Theorists have proposed more satisfactory solutions to the paradox by rejecting each of the three theses. One of the most famous solutions, though one currently unpopular with most philosophers, is that our interaction with fictions involves a "suspension of disbelief" (Coleridge 1817, 179). According to this theory, we literally believe, while interacting with a fiction, that it is fact. Thus, believing (temporarily) that Hermione exists and undergoes the travails we read about or see on screen, it is no surprise that we feel strong emotions for her. This solution is rejected by most philosophers because they find it implausible that we truly believe, even temporarily, that the events of a fiction actually transpire.[11]

3.2.3.1 Waltonian Theories

The most influential solution to the paradox of fiction in recent years has been Kendall Walton's (1978; 1990, 195–289; 1997a). Strictly speaking, Walton rejects the first proposition of the paradox, denying that we feel emotions for fictional characters. But his view is more complex and subtle than this categorization suggests. It might be better thought of as a modification of the first and second propositions so that they cohere rather than clash with one another and the third proposition. The first thing to point out is that Walton's rejection of the first proposition is quite unlike Kivy's rejection of music-specific emotional responses.[12] Walton does believe that we respond affectively to fictions, but in a way that does not quite rise to the level of fully-fledged, garden-variety emotions. He begins by labeling our undeniable affective responses to fictions – pounding hearts, sweaty palms, etc. – *quasi-emotions* (1978, 6–7). Their close relationship to ordinary emotions is indicated, according to Walton, by the phenomena that give rise to the paradox in the first place, e.g., the fact that, as one reads a passage in a novel describing Hermione in mortal danger, one's heart races and one tends to say things such as that one *fears for* Hermione.

Walton next develops a theory of fiction, the central notion of which is *imagination* (1978, 10–12). He asks us to consider daydreams, children's games of make-believe, and fictions such as novels or films. In a daydream we can imagine whatever we like – there are no rules. In children's games of make-believe, however, Walton points out that there often *are* rules, although these are rarely formulated explicitly. For instance, in a game of mud pies, it seems to be a rule that any lump of mud manipulated by a participant in the game is (imagined to be) a pie. Now, it may take some explicit verbal behavior to get the game going. ("What are you doing?" "I'm making pies!" "Why did you put your pie in that crate?" "That's the oven!" And so on.) But Walton notes that we can infer some rules from how the game proceeds, rules that no participant may even have formulated to herself. For instance, children (and the rest of us) seem naturally to assume that the bigger a lump of mud, the bigger the (imagined) pie, even though we could in principle just as easily have a rule according to which the *smaller* the lump the *bigger* the (imagined) pie. On the other hand, we seem naturally to assume that the (imagined) *taste* of the pies is unrelated to the taste of the mud. Conventions may also develop, for instance that the tallest participant is (imagined to be) the chef.[13]

Walton's theory is basically that works of fiction, such as novels and films, are *props* designed for grown-ups to use in games of make-believe, just as the lumps of mud and the crate are props in the mud-pie game. Even though we have not explicitly formulated the rules of fiction, we can tell that there are such rules by carefully observing people's interactions with fictions, just as we can tell what the rules of the mud-pie game are by carefully observing children playing it. For instance, the following sentences seem roughly to capture a rule of the mud-pie game and the "novel game," respectively.

If there is a mud-lump of size x, then you should imagine it's a pie of size x.

If the novel says that p, then you should imagine that p.

Walton points out that these rules allow for what we might call "fictional facts," that is, things that are fictional independently of anyone's actually imagining them. He gives the example of a lump of mud that, unbeknownst to everyone, was left in the crate. It would not be at all surprising if the children took this state of affairs to imply that (everyone should imagine) there was a pie in the oven all along without anyone realizing it. Similarly, the fact that no one has read some obscure novel makes no difference to what is fictional in that work (i.e., what one ought to imagine when one reads the work).

Returning to our emotional responses to fictions, Walton argues that a range of observable facts about our affective interactions with fictions (e.g., that one's heart races and one says that one *fears* for Hermione) suggests that one implicit rule in the game of fiction is:

If you have a *quasi-E* experience in response to a fictional character or event (where E names an garden-variety emotion), then you should imagine it is a fully-fledged E experience.

That is, just as we imagine *of this lump of mud* that it is a pie, we imagine *of our quasi-fear experience* that it is a (genuine, ordinary) fear experience (1978, 21–2). It is unsurprising that we might confuse this experience with an ordinary experience of fear, since (i) it shares many features with fear (e.g., the racing heart), (ii) we *imagine* that it is an experience of fear, and, relatedly, (iii) it is caused by our imagining states of affairs that, were they real, would elicit an ordinary fear experience.

Sometimes this view is summarized as the idea that our emotional responses to fictions are themselves fictional or imaginary. That is fair enough, but it can lead to confusion. Our fear experience is fictional in the sense that it's not a fully-fledged experience of garden-variety fear. But it's a genuine affective – if not strictly *emotional* – experience. And it is imaginary, but not in the sense that the content of a daydream is imaginary. We are not in complete control of the experience (as with much ordinary emotional experience) and, again, an affective experience of *quasi-fear* is as real as the lump of mud in a game of mud pies. It is imaginary only insofar as fear differs from quasi-fear, just as the pie is only imaginary insofar as it differs from the mud lump.

My summary of Walton's solution to the paradox of fiction requires one final clarification. If it turns out that your emotional response to Hermione is fictional, in the sense just explained, then doesn't it turn out that you are a character in the world of Harry Potter? After all, Hermione's and Ron's actions are part of the same fictional world in part because their actions are interrelated. (E.g., Hermione talks to Ron, who hears her.) By the same reasoning, shouldn't we say that *you* are a character in the world of Harry Potter, on Walton's theory, since it is fictional that you react (emotionally, at least) to Hermione's predicament? The idea of being a character in one of the most popular and successful fictional franchises of all time might not seem so bad, but philosophically it would come at a heavy cost. If *you* are part of the world of Harry Potter, then so is Jo Blow (a person living in Tasmania whom neither you nor I have ever met),[14] along with all the other people who have read the books (and perhaps seen the films).[15] But now it turns out that you are only familiar with a tiny fraction of the inhabitants of the Harry Potter world. That seems to preclude your appreciating much of the fiction, since you are unaware of most of the (admittedly rather repetitive and boring) characters that make it up.

Walton understandably does not want to go down this road. Instead, he distinguishes between *work worlds* and *game worlds* (1978, 17–19). The work world of a fiction is what we usually think of as its fictional world. This includes all the characters and events described and implied by the work. Because the work is independent of any experience of it, this world is relatively objective, determined by whatever it is that determines the content of works of fiction.[16] In sharp contrast to this, there is a distinct game world for every individual experience of the work. Just as when you play solitaire and I play solitaire there are two different experiences of one and the same game, when you and I "play the Harry Potter game" (e.g., read the books), there are two different "game worlds" – the world of your experience of the work and the world of my experience of the work. These two worlds will be largely similar (both will include Harry's training to become a wizard, and so on) but they will differ with respect to two "characters" that are not part of the work, namely, you and me. And part of what will be fictional in these worlds will be our emotional responses to its events.

Though Walton's solution to the paradox of fiction is not simple, once one has grasped it, it is relatively easy to apply to our emotional responses to expressive music – on the assumption that the imagination theorist is correct about the nature of musical expressiveness. In hearing music as expressive, according to the imagination theorist, we imaginatively hear it as the literal expression of some persona's actual emotions. Imagining such genuine emotional expression causes us (for psychological reasons, the details of which are not part of Walton's theory) to be in various quasi-emotional states that include, say, physiological and phenomenological elements of the garden-variety emotions we would feel were we to encounter such expression in real life. Then, just as in our interactions with narrative fictions such as novels and films, we imagine of these quasi-emotions that they are genuine emotions of the relevant kind.

Walton himself does not think that his theory of our emotional responses to narrative fictions applies very well to our experience of instrumental music, in part because he is skeptical of the imagined-persona theory of musical expressiveness.[17] Walton argues that our experience of music is quite different from our experience of representational fictions such as novels and films in at least two respects. First, we do not *imagine hearing* the content of music the way that we *imagine seeing* the characters and events of a film or *imagine being told* the events of a novel. So we lack an external perspective on the content of a piece of music. Second, though Walton believes that music has content, including emotional content, and is thus representational in some sense, whatever we imagine of the music is so "radically indeterminate" (1994, 52) that it does not cohere into a unified fictional world. Think of the indeterminacies we discussed when considering the imagination theory of musical expressiveness: How many personae are there in a given piece? What musical features do they correspond to? What are they like? How are they related? Walton thinks that the fact that these questions are unanswerable suggests that there is no fictional "work world" corresponding to an instrumental musical work, only a "game world" involving our imaginative engagement with the work. Walton's alternative hypothesis to the imagined-persona theory of expressiveness is that we imagine, not *of the music* that it is someone else's expression of emotion, but *of our experience of the music* that it is *an experience of our own emotional state* (1988a). In a sense, *you* are the musical persona, according to Walton (though he does not put the point this way). Walton thus, to some extent, collapses the notions of emotional expressiveness in, and arousal by, music, but in a different way from the arousalist.

I have just emphasized what is distinctive of Walton's theory of music and emotion, but there are also significant similarities between it and imagined-persona theories. Walton does think that we "project" actual and imagined affective states induced by the music back on to the music,[18] attributing expressiveness to the music itself, and he acknowledges that this implies

> an experience as of there being something or someone or other, or several such, that/who is/are in this state – the state I am in. … [But this] is a far cry from recognizing a *persona*, a fictitious … person [in this state], in the music.
>
> (1999, 147)

Whether Walton is right about this, and whether it amounts to a significant distinction between Walton's theory and the kind of imaginative theory we considered in the previous chapter, are questions I leave you to answer for yourself.

3.2.3.2 Realist Theories

Though Walton's solution to the paradox of fiction has been highly influential, some philosophers argue that the benefits of the theory can be gained without its costs, including both its complexity and its denial of the claim that we respond to fictions with fully-fledged, garden-variety emotions. One way of attempting this is by denying the second proposition in our original formulation of the paradox, that is, by arguing that we do not only feel emotions for things that we believe to exist. Such theories are sometimes called *realist* because they argue that our affective responses to fictions are not merely quasi-emotions or imagined emotions, but *real* (genuine, fully-fledged) emotions.[19]

Like the contagion theorist, the realist might begin by pointing out that we sometimes feel fully-fledged emotions without the beliefs that the cognitivist (including the Waltonian) implies are necessary for such emotions.[20] Phobias are one kind of example. Berys Gaut also mentions fear in response to (i) the mere appearance of danger that we realize is not actual (e.g., walking out on to the glass-floored observation deck of Auckland's Sky Tower), (ii) consideration of counterfactual situations (e.g., entertaining the idea that the creak you heard last night was caused by an intruder, even though you know it was not), and (iii) imagined states of affairs (e.g., daydreaming that you encounter a mountain lion on a hiking trail) (2007, 210–12).

The Waltonian may object to all of these examples on various grounds: Is our feeling when we walk on the glass floor fully-fledged fear or just a repeated, non-cognitive startle response? Doesn't considering a counterfactual situation require *imagining* it and thus collapse into the third category? And doesn't proposing that our affective responses to imagined situations are fully-fledged emotions amount to begging the question? The realist might turn the charge of question-begging back on the Waltonian. Not all the claims in the original paradox can be true – that's why it's a paradox. So it might seem to an impartial observer that the assumption that the beliefs in question are essential to emotions is also question-begging in the absence of further considerations. (We will turn to some such considerations below.)

A related consideration that Gaut brings to bear on the paradox is the *range* of emotions typically considered in the philosophical literature (2007, 209). He points out that however puzzling it is that we seem to feel fear or pity in response to fictions, it is less puzzling that we should *admire* Moana's courage in *Moana* or be appalled by the behavior of David Brent in *The Office*. Moana's actions are as obviously admirable as Brent's are appalling. Thus the historical focus on pity and fear (due to their consideration by Aristotle in the *Poetics*) may have skewed the debate against the realists.

What of the absence in our responses to fiction of the *behavior* that is characteristic of fully-fledged emotions?[21] If one genuinely feared for Hermione, wouldn't one try to do something about the danger she is in? The realist might respond that this question implicitly assumes anti-realism. One's lack of behavior would perhaps be puzzling if one *believed* a young witch were in mortal danger, but the lynchpin of realism is that one can feel fully-fledged emotions in response to fiction-inspired (and other) *imaginings*. Since one knows that one cannot do anything to change what happens in the fictional world of Harry Potter, behavioral attempts to do so would be irrational (Gaut 2007, 212–14). The Waltonian might press the point, arguing that to claim that such a behaviorless affective state *is* a fully-fledged emotion is similarly to beg the question. But this won't work, since we often respond with genuine emotion to events that, because of our powerlessness or distance in space or time, we don't attempt to affect. We can pity the soldiers in the trenches of World War I without attempting in any way to ease their suffering, since we know that their suffering is now over.[22] Perhaps such emotion is genuine but not fully-fledged in that it lacks characteristic behavior but, if so, the Waltonian will have to admit that genuine emotional states sometimes lack such characteristic behavior. Alternatively, the realist can argue that it is not the *behavior* that is part of the fully-fledged emotion, but the *desire* to act in a certain way. One can have that desire and yet never act on it because one realizes that nothing one could do would have any effect on the state of affairs in question.

Suppose you are convinced of the *possibility* of feeling genuine emotions in response to imagined objects and events. What of the *rationality* of such emotions? Gaut rejects realist theories according to which our emotional responses to fiction are irrational (e.g., Radford 1975), arguing instead that the criteria for an emotional response's being rational are more complex than we might at first have thought. He offers three criteria, each addressing a different aspect of emotion:

> (C1) The rationality of fear of objects believed to exist requires one to believe that they are dangerous; and the rationality of fear of objects merely imagined to exist requires one (correctly) to imagine that they are dangerous.
>
> (2007, 220)

(C2) An emotion is irrational if it motivates [goal-directed] action, though its subject lacks motivation-relevant beliefs [about the object or the possibility of action].

(2007, 223)

(C3) An occurrence of an emotion is irrational if experiencing it involves suffering to no point.

(2007, 225)

I postpone consideration of Gaut's affective criterion (C3) until Chapter 5, where we will consider the puzzle of negative emotional responses to music. We have just seen how the behavioral criterion (C2) works: The lack of behavior we observe in people responding emotionally to fictions is no less rational than that we observe in people responding to real events over which they have no control. Gaut points out that the cognitive criterion (C1) can be generalized: "for each emotion, one should substitute in the formula the evaluative property that individuates that emotion – for pity, suffering; for anger, having been wronged, and so on" (2007, 220 n. 32). What is striking about this criterion in contrast to the other two, however, is that it is disjunctive; that is, it seems to be two independent criteria yoked together as alternatives.[23] This raises two matters worth discussing: the content of the controversial disjunct, and the fact that the criterion is disjunctive at all.

The controversial disjunct, of course, is the second one, according to which it is rational to fear merely imagined entities that (fictionally) meet the relevant conditions on an object of fear. Why should we accept this part of the criterion? In part, Gaut would surely respond that it must be assessed as part of the realist's entire theory. It is plausible to the extent that the entire theory hangs together as a convincing account of a wide range of our emotional responses. Still, the basic puzzle here is how or why one might rationally *fear* something that one knows not to exist. Gaut attempts to reduce the distance between Waltonianism and realism here by pointing out that both entail that our fully-fledged emotional responses are directed to "thought contents," the difference being that the Waltonian insists that the thought must be a belief, while the realist allows for emotions in response to imaginings (Gaut 2007, 212).[24] But, says Gaut, if we're already allowing that our response is to a thought content, it's not a great leap to allow the same response to the same content in a different kind of thought:

Judgmentalism [i.e., the theory that one can only fear what one *believes* to exist] holds that asserted thoughts (beliefs) are necessary for emotions; and that the intentional object of the fear is the belief-content – that is, what the belief is about. Anti-judgmentalism [e.g., realism] holds that unasserted thoughts [e.g., imaginings] are all that may be required for an emotion, and should relatedly hold that the object of fear is the thought-content – that is, what the thought is about.

(2007, 212)

These sentences raise some thorny issues in the philosophy of mind and language, which we are in no position to settle, but the basic worry is that when we talk of the object of a thought – what a thought is "about" – as a "thought content," we might mean one of two things: (i) the actual thing out there in the world (e.g., the mountain lion ten feet away from you), or (ii) the mental representation of that thing – what makes it possible for you, unlike a rock or a mirror, to have a thought about that thing (e.g., some pattern of neuron activity in your brain). In the sentence about judgmentalism, above, the natural reading seems to be the first: It is the lion you fear, not your own neurons. But in the sentence about realism, this reading is problematic. There is no Lord Voldemort outside your head, nor is there an evil wizard *inside* your head. (Voldemort wouldn't fit into your cranial cavity.) Thus the only reasonable reading of the second sentence is that by "thought content" Gaut means a mental representation. But then the attempt to reduce the distance between the two theories seems to turn on an equivocation: "Thought content" means one thing in the first sentence and something quite different in the second. If this criticism is sound, then the puzzle remains, and Gaut must fall back on the response that realism must be evaluated as a whole.

The concern about C1's disjunctiveness in itself is that it could be a sign that there are, as the Waltonian insists, two different kinds of emotional response covered here: Emotional responses to fictions are different from emotional responses to real things after all. Gaut replies that two mental states' having different criteria of rationality is not sufficient for their being two distinct kinds of mental state. He gives the example of *a priori* beliefs (those properly justified independently of any sensory experience) and *a posteriori* beliefs (those properly justified, at least in part, on the basis of sensory experience). It's rational to believe things on *a priori* grounds about mathematics (e.g., the Pythagorean theorem), but not about chemistry (e.g., how water molecules are structured). But that doesn't mean that these beliefs are two different kinds of mental state. There are just two different ways of (rationally) acquiring beliefs, each appropriate to distinct subject matters. Similarly, there are two different ways of (rationally) getting into a single kind of emotional state (e.g., fear), according to Gaut, each appropriate to a distinct "mode of cognition" (i.e., belief and imagination) of the emotion's intentional object (Gaut 2007, 222–3).

Even if this response works, it gives the Waltonian some recourse in the face of the objection that her theory's complexity is not justified by its benefits. For the realist theory now looks a little more complicated than it seemed at first.

And Walton himself points out that his theory is much more than just a theory of emotional responses to fictions and thus that it, too, should be judged as a whole (1997a, 284–5).

Walton finally notes that even if it turns out that we experience genuine, fully-fledged emotions in response to fiction, it doesn't follow that we *don't imagine* having such experiences. He gives the analogy of a child making-believe that she is riding a stagecoach (1997a, 285). She might do this while sitting on the roof of a barn, but she might just as well do it sitting on an old stagecoach inside the barn. The fact that she really is sitting on a genuine stagecoach does nothing to impugn the fact that she is imagining sitting on a stagecoach (in the course of riding it). So perhaps realism and Waltonianism about our emotional responses are complementary rather than rivals.[25]

3.2.4 Comparing the Theories

Whether one adopts a Waltonian or realist solution to the paradox of fiction makes little difference to the range of either the *kinds* of emotions we can feel in response to expressive music, or the *intensity* of our emotional responses, since on either account we are responding to a fictional persona and the theories differ only in how that phenomenon is to be explained. (The difference between the Waltonian and realist theories will be of greater consequence when we turn, in Chapter 5, to the *value* of these responses.) The bigger contrast here is between the resemblance theorist's contagion account and imagination theorists' more cognitive accounts of our emotional responses to music.

A resemblance theory of expressiveness combined with a contagion theory of emotional responses to music restricts the range of emotions listeners can feel in response to musical expressiveness in two ways. First, as we saw in the last chapter, the resemblance theory allows for the expression of a narrower range of emotions than imagination theories of musical expressiveness. Fewer emotions expressed means fewer emotions that might be transferred to the listener by contagion. Second, recall the distinction between *empathetic* emotional responses, in which the listener experiences the same emotion as that expressed by the music, and *sympathetic* emotional responses, in which the listener experiences an emotion different from, but related to, that expressed in the music. The nature of contagion rules out the possibility of sympathetic responses, which, to extend the biological terminology, are more like the production of antibodies.[26]

In comparison, an imagination theory of musical expressiveness coupled with a Waltonian or realist solution to the paradox of fiction arguably allows for a wider range of emotions to be expressed by music – notably the more cognitive emotions discussed at the end of the last chapter – and for sympathetic responses to the emotions expressed by the fictional persona. Moreover, just as the imagination theorist can incorporate much of the resemblance theory into her theory of expressiveness as one mechanism by which we tend to imagine a musical persona expressing their emotions, so she can allow the possibility of contagion responses to musical expressiveness, in addition to our more cognitive responses to our musical imaginings.

Recall that the contagion theory implies that our affective responses to music lack the "formal object" characteristic of the relevant emotion (e.g., something regrettable, in the case of sadness). Even if, as Davies emphasizes, the response may be attentionally focused *on* the music, it is not directed *at* the music in the sense that sadness, say, is characteristically directed at something that the emoter considers regrettable. This makes the emotion felt by the listener less than fully-fledged. A similar point applies to Waltonian solutions to the paradox of fiction. To call our affective responses to fictions *quasi*-emotions, as the Waltonian does, is precisely to indicate that they are less than fully-fledged because they lack the belief characteristic of the emotion in question. The Waltonian goes on to argue that we *imagine* of this response that it is a fully-fledged emotion, but of course an imagined fully-fledged emotion is no more a fully-fledged emotion than an imagined wizard is a fully-fledged wizard. According to the realist, by contrast, our emotional responses to fictions are as fully-fledged as those to actual events over which we have no control.

Walton points out, however, that to say that an affective response is not fully-fledged in this way is not to say that it is any less *intensely felt* than a fully-fledged emotion. Watching a good horror movie, one's heart might race and one might involuntarily clutch one's seat and shriek. On the other hand, our emotional responses to fictions seem to be less intense, on average, than our emotional responses to events in our own life. But perhaps that's simply because fictional events do not affect our real lives and we are similarly incapable of affecting them. There's no reason *in principle* that the contagion theorist could not say the same thing as the Waltonian about the intensity of the emotional responses he posits, but though this is ultimately an empirical matter, it seems likely that the less directly cognitive nature of a contagion response would make it less intense than even a quasi-emotional response to a fictional character's emotional expression.

What is the upshot of this comparison? As with the question of the range of emotions expressible by music, whether this discussion favors one theory of emotional response over the others depends on the range, kinds, and intensity of emotional responses that we in fact experience in response to music's expressiveness. For instance, if we do not experience sympathetic responses to music's expressiveness, the resemblance theory's "restriction" of our emotional responses to empathetic responses is not a cost but a benefit of the theory. Unfortunately, as with that previous question, there is unlikely to be dependable pre-theoretical consensus on this matter. Once more, though psychological research and reflection on our own experiences may help to some extent, which theory we end up endorsing may depend on how we see the entire domain of music and emotion hanging together.

3.3 Robinson's Sophisticated Expressionism

Having explored various theories of our emotional response to music, we are in a better position to consider Jenefer Robinson's sophisticated expressionism, which is in part a theory of music's expressiveness, but one which accords significant roles to our emotional responses to music without qualifying as an arousalist theory. Recall that Robinson argues that emotions are processes. Each process begins with a non-cognitive affective appraisal – a fast and loose response, such as **threat!**, that focuses the subject's attention on the object of the appraisal and gives rise to physiological changes (e.g., increased heart rate and sweating), facial expressions (e.g., the widened eyes and open mouth of surprise), and motor responses (e.g., jumping in fright). Cognition then kicks in as the subject considers the object of her affective appraisal. Such cognition may reinforce or undermine the initial appraisal, depending on existing beliefs, on-going perception, and so on, and often leads to deliberate action (e.g., an attempt to eliminate the threat or remove oneself from the situation). Our control over our physiology is limited, however. You may be able to close your mouth once the initial surprise has passed, but you cannot simply dial down your heartrate as if it were a metronome or siphon adrenaline from your system, even if you know full well that you are hiking in New Zealand and thus that the movement you saw in the bushes couldn't possibly be a mountain lion. A further cognitive process, unique to human emotional experience, is reflection on, including labeling of, current or previous emotional experiences. Because such reflection and labeling is conscious and linguistic, it is affected by the rest of your cognitive economy, including what you believe about emotions, which for most people includes much "folk theory," that is, what is commonly accepted about emotions. As a result, such reflection and labeling can be inaccurate and unreliable. But, as in many other domains of cognition, that does not prevent it affecting further thoughts and behavior. If you think of your response as one of *fear*, you may hesitate before proceeding with your hike; if, on the other hand, you think of it as one of *excitement* at the stimulating unpredictability of the natural world, you may be emboldened to hike on even more enthusiastically (Robinson 2005, 79–86).

Robinson emphasizes three ways in which emotional processes are even more complicated than the description above suggests. First, there can be a kind of feedback loop, whereby the development of one emotional process initiates a new emotional process (Robinson 2005, 61–70). For instance, you could be surprised by your being so forgetful of your surroundings that you thought, even subconsciously, that there might be a mountain lion nearby, the beginning of a process that leads to your being embarrassed by your obliviousness. Second, one emotional process may affect (without initiating) another, as when your startled fear lowers the threshold for your entering other emotional states (2005, 96). Third, even if the processes do not affect one another in either of these ways, you may experience multiple emotional processes or "streams" at the same time, making your overall on-going affective state an intricate tapestry (2005, 79, 81).

Robinson applies this theory of emotion in two broad ways to our experience of music. First, she notes its power to explain how various elements and aspects of our emotional response to music work together to help us appreciate the music, including its expressive and structural features. Second, she points out that music resembles emotion in being a temporal process that involves various "streams" (the temporal tapestry of various melodies, harmonic progressions, rhythms, and so on), and thus that her theory of emotion is well placed to explain music's aptness for genuine, Romantic expression of emotion. I will address these applications in turn.

3.3.1 Emotional Response and Appreciation

Near the beginning of this chapter, I introduced Meyer-style responses to music: surprise when a chord progression does not continue as expected, bewilderment when new material is introduced late in a song, anxiety about whether a melody will reach its goal, and so on. Robinson points out that her theory of emotion coheres well with such responses. Surprise, bewilderment, and the rest plausibly begin with a non-cognitive appraisal, a quick realization that something is not right (and *mutatis mutandis* for their counterparts such as satisfaction or relief). This often results in focusing on, and cognizing about, the aspect of the music that was unexpected: What exactly was surprising there? How can it be made sense of in the context of the rest of the piece? And so on. Thus, Meyer-style emotional responses to music not only show that we are already following the music's patterns at some level, but also aid us in understanding it better, by drawing our attention to salient features (2005, 360–5). Robinson also uses her theory of emotions to extend Meyer's theory in two ways. First, where Meyer focuses on our emotional responses' ability to alert us to non-emotional features of the music, such as harmonic progressions, Robinson points out that the same explanation can be given of how our emotional responses alert us to *expressive* features of the music. In her example from Shostakovich's Tenth Symphony, for instance (see Chapter 2, §2.6.2), our *surprise* at the appearance of a loud horn call of a different harmonic character from the accompanying material draws our attention to its *resolute character* in contrast to the anxiousness of its surroundings (2005,

366–9). Second, she argues that her theory of emotions can answer a question that puzzled Meyer himself: If expectations and their fulfillment or frustration play a significant role in our experience of music, how is it that we still find experiences of music that we know very well rewarding? If the surprise of a modulation is an important part of why we value it, shouldn't we value it less the more familiar it becomes? Robinson's answer to these questions is that since our emotional responses begin with an affective appraisal that is *non-cognitive*, it is impervious to our knowledge of the piece. Just as you still jump when the killer suddenly appears reflected in the bathroom mirror during a horror film you've seen many times before, you are still surprised by the unprepared dissonance in your favorite song (2005, 365).[27]

This application of Robinson's theory of emotions is not without its limitations and problems. As Robinson acknowledges, our Meyer-style responses to musical features such as cadences and melodic progressions are fairly coarse-grained compared to our experience of the music (2005, 364, 377, 460 n. 52). For example, though the theory might be able to explain how the *intensity* of my surprise at various musical events correlates to their degree of unexpectedness, it lacks the resources to say anything about differences in the *kind* of unexpectedness that I may well notice. For instance, even someone completely untrained in music theory can tell the difference between unexpected *rhythms* and *harmonies* (though he may not describe it in such terms). But he may be equally surprised by each. Of course, Robinson does not think that Meyer-style responses are the *only* kind of response relevant to musical understanding, but the less they contribute to our musical understanding, the less significant they are.

There also seems to be a tension between Robinson's solution to Meyer's puzzle about the persistence of our surprise in response to familiar music, and part of her theory essential to that solution. The relevant part of the theory is a proposed solution to yet another puzzling aspect of our Meyer-style responses to music. We typically respond emotionally to things that affect our interests, but how the harmony of a given piece of music progresses, for instance, doesn't affect my interests at all.[28] Robinson's response draws on empirical psychology to argue that we generally respond emotionally to the surprising, bewildering, and so on, because (as with our startle responses to loud noises), it's better to be safe than sorry when it comes to responding to things that *may* affect our interests. As we learn, typically from mere exposure, the conventions of the musical system of our culture, our responses of surprise, bewilderment, and so on, come along for the ride (2005, 384–6). The tension is between this theory of our ability to learn what counts as, say, *surprising* in a musical system and the persistence of our non-cognitive responses to familiar music (e.g., continued surprise at a sudden change of key). After all, if there is a particular rock that resembles a mountain lion around a corner of a hiking trail, we may be startled when we first hike the trail. But if we hike the same trail every weekend, we surely come to expect the rock and cease to be startled by it. Shouldn't the same be true of our emotional responses to surprising (etc.) musical events in pieces we are familiar with? Perhaps Robinson can admit that our surprise wanes on repeated listening, but that the attention it has drawn to the key change now allows us to have a deeper, more cognitive response to the emotional expression constituted in part by that change.

In addition to Meyer-style responses, Robinson thinks that we respond affectively to music in ways that are *caused by* the music, but do not take the music as their intentional object. This might sound quite similar to contagion theory, yet Robinson criticizes Davies's version of that theory on two counts and suggests replacing it with what she calls "the Jazzercise effect" (2005, 387–405).[29] First, as we have already seen, she says that Davies's theory is implausible because it requires the listener's *recognition* of the music's expressiveness, while contagion typically occurs without recognition of its source and, indeed, recognition of the source may *reduce* the effects of contagion (2005, 387, 394). Second, she argues that it is implausible that we typically respond in this way to *mere appearances* of expression. "After all, if living with a basset hound were like living with a depressed person, would normal folk choose a basset hound as their life's companion?" (2005, 388). Davies has responded to these objections (2011b, 56–8), but at this point the debate may turn on empirical questions about how exactly contagion works. More useful here is a comparison between contagion theory and Robinson's proposed replacement for it.

The main difference between the Jazzercise effect and contagion seems to be that where contagion is a response to *recognized, expressive* features of the music, the Jazzercise effect is a *less cognitive* response to *non-expressive* features, such as timbre, loudness, or pitch.[30] Indeed, it is less cognitive precisely because it does not require the recognition of similarities between the music's dynamic contours and typical behavioral expressions (i.e., resemblance-theory expressiveness), or even attention to the music. And Robinson willingly accepts what Davies resists, namely, the characterization of the induced affective responses as *moods* rather than emotions (2005, 392). Robinson even argues that Jazzercise responses do not begin with an affective appraisal; they are simply caused by music's impact on "our motor and other bodily systems" (2005, 392). However, these moods often *become* emotions, in two related ways. First, we constantly cognitively monitor our own affective states. Thus, puzzled by a change in one's affective state (the result, unbeknownst to one, of the Jazzercise effect), one may cast about for a suitable characterization of it. If one "labels" it with an emotion term, it may *become* that emotion (2005, 400–5). In a sense, one *decides* that one is fearful (say), though one is unsure of what, exactly. Second, whether or not one labels one's affective state, since moods affect the way one perceives the world, once one is in a particular mood, one's threshold for entering into related fully-fledged emotional states is lowered. (If you are in an objectless sad mood, you are more likely to be saddened by things than if you are in an objectless happy mood.) Thus the Jazzercise effect primes us for further emotional responses to music (2005, 393).

Even if the empirical evidence turns out to favor the Jazzercise effect over contagion, the victory may be somewhat Pyrrhic.[31] Davies counts as an advantage of contagion theory that it requires close attention to the music, particularly its expressiveness, since that makes it easier to integrate such emotional responses into a theory of music appreciation. Thus, if it turns out that the Jazzercise effect is a more accurate account of (some of) our affective responses to music, it may make such responses more difficult to integrate into a theory that places value on such responses to music, as Robinson clearly wants to do (S. Davies 2011b, 58–60). Similarly, since the labeling of our Jazzercise responses to music is somewhat non-rational (since it attempts to classify our non-cognitive mood responses as cognitive emotions), it results in different labeling of the same affective state by different listeners (Robinson 2005, 401–5). Thus, as Robinson admits, "the *labelling* of Jazzercise effects is probably not a particularly insightful way of responding to music and may ... be positively misleading" (2005, 466 n. 70). On the other hand, Robinson argues that this process may at least contribute to attention to the music and our responses to it, which is likely to enhance appreciation in other ways (2005, 466 n. 70).

3.3.2 Music as Romantic Expression

However one assesses Robinson's account of the role of affective responses in the appreciation of music, it is largely independent of the second major application of her theory of emotion to our experience of music, namely, her account of the genuine, Romantic expression of emotions in music (2005, 229–347). It is important to keep in mind that in reviving a Romantic theory of expression, Robinson does not intend to defend a simple expressionist theory of musical expressiveness, according to which such expressiveness is necessarily a matter of an artist expressing their emotions. As we saw at the end of the previous chapter, Robinson can rather be seen as returning philosophers of music, after decades of focus on one particular question – how it is that instrumental music can be expressive of emotions – to broader issues concerning the role of emotion in art. In particular, Robinson aims to see what of the Romantic theory of expression can be defended in light of work that has been done in the psychology and philosophy of music and emotion since Romanticism's heyday (the early nineteenth century).

What, then, *is* "the Romantic theory of expression"? A satisfactory answer would require an in-depth historical essay, but for our purposes we can focus on three central claims. First, the sense of expression involved is not one of the "betrayal" of emotions, such as the uncontrollable tears running down someone's face, but one of thoughtful, reflective expression, as when one tries to explain what one is feeling to a sympathetic listener. Second, as in this non-artistic example, the process of reflecting on one's emotional state may lead not only to a clearer *understanding of* that state, but to that state's actually *becoming* more specific or precise, in the way captured by the expression. Third, it is generally taken to be essential to Romanticism that such expression is (i) essential to art, and (ii) what is of central value in art. Robinson points out that simple expressionism about musical expressiveness is no part of, nor implied by, Romanticism thus understood. She is also very clear that she rejects the third part of Romanticism; she agrees with critics of the Romantics that there are valuable artworks unconcerned with emotional expression. But she defends versions of the first and second claims.

As in her discussion of Meyer-style responses to music, Robinson observes that the Romantic theory of expression aligns rather neatly with the theory of emotion she defends. Recall that, according to Robinson, cognitive reflection on and labeling of our affective states is part and parcel of the process that is human emotional experience. Artistic expression of our emotions is thus not something separate from emotional experiences, but a refined, sophisticated version of part of those experiences (2005, 273–4). Note that both the cultural and causal aspects of such reflection and labeling find their place in the Romantic theory. First, artistic productions are undeniably cultural, and thus often reflect the artist's context, just as the way one thinks about and labels one's everyday affective states is affected by how one thinks about the emotions, including assumptions drawn from one's culture. Second, the articulation of an emotional state in the creation of an artwork might affect the emotional state the artist is in, just as labeling an everyday emotion one way or another can affect how that emotional state develops.

Robinson summarizes her "new Romantic theory of expression" in a list of necessary conditions:

If an artist expresses an emotion in a work of art, then

1   the work is evidence that a persona (which could but need not be the artist) is experiencing [or] has experienced this emotion;
2   the artist intentionally puts the evidence in the work and intends it to be perceived *as* evidence of the emotion in the persona;
3   the persona's emotion is perceptible in the character of the work;
4   the work articulates and individuates the persona's emotion; and
5   through the articulation and elucidation of the emotion in the work, both artist and audience can become clear about it and bring it to consciousness.

(2005, 270)

In a sense, all but condition 2 are "success conditions" on Romantic expression. Condition 2 merely requires that the artist *attempt* Romantic expression; the others provide ways in which the artist might fail in her attempt.[32] For instance, if you create a work "expressing" an emotion that you (or the relevant persona) have (or has) not experienced, the work fails to meet condition 1, and is thus not a true Romantic expression. You also fail if you have experienced the emotion in question, but don't manage to make that emotion perceptible to the relevant audience (condition 3). If the emotion is perceptible, but doesn't individuate the emotion finely enough (for instance, by being no more expressive than a smiley face, or an utterance such as "I am sad") once more this will not count as true Romantic expression (condition 4). Finally, the expression must be such that both artist and audience can learn something about the emotion expressed (condition 5). It is not clear to me whether an attempted Romantic expression could meet conditions 1–4 yet fail to meet this final condition (Robinson provides no such examples), but we can read condition 5 as an explication of a central *value* of Romantic expression, the value of gaining a deeper understanding of our emotional capacities.[33]

The biggest difference between this theory and traditional Romantic theories of expression is the inclusion of the possibility that the emotion expressed is experienced not by the artist but by a (non-existent, imaginary, fictional) persona.[34] At first glance, this raises problems for the view. For instance, if no one has actually experienced the emotion in question, how could anything count as *evidence* of someone's having experienced it? But Robinson can wheel in machinery from her preferred theory of fiction to deal with such a problem. Perhaps she would say that the evidence in question is evidence of what we are supposed to *imagine* of the persona's emotional experience, rather than of what any actual person's emotional experience really was. However, if the notion of *sincerity* is central to Romanticism – in the idea that one can commune with the Romantic artist, who expresses her genuine emotions in her work, for instance – then the inclusion of the possibility of a fictional persona in a theory of Romantic expression may seem like a betrayal of its heart. After all, a non-Romantic imagination theory of musical expressiveness (such as Jerrold Levinson's, considered in the previous chapter) can account for emotional expression of the sort characterized by Robinson's necessary conditions. Indeed, such a theory will be more general than Robinson's, since it will count expressions that meet Robinson's conditions as a specific, perhaps more satisfying and rewarding, kind of expressiveness, but will also count cases that fail to meet some of her conditions as expressive (e.g., cases where the emotion expressed is general rather than specific and thus the expressiveness is relatively weak).

Now, Robinson can still distinguish between cases of sincere Romantic expression and what we might call imagined Romantic expression, but if she includes the latter in the central concept she valorizes (because such expressions can be just as valuable as sincere ones), then it's not clear that sincerity bears any weight in the theory. Perhaps it is the other features of Romantic expression – the articulation and elucidation of quite specific emotional experiences – that she is most concerned to reintroduce to philosophical considerations of emotion in the arts. In any case, none of this amounts to an objection to the truth or usefulness of the theory; these are more matters of how we should assess the relationship between Robinson's and others' work on emotion and the arts.

So far, my discussion of Robinson's theory of Romantic expression has been quite general. Let me end by examining how it applies to music in particular. First, Robinson points out that understanding a piece of music as a Romantic expression of the artist's or a persona's emotional experience can provide the work with a unity that would otherwise be lacking. For instance, in the example from Shostakovich's Tenth Symphony (see Chapter 2, §2.6.2), perhaps the sudden appearance and insistent repetition of a theme musically unrelated to what has come before only makes sense when considered as an expression of the protagonist's hope for a happier future. Second, resemblances between a passage of music and some aspect of emotional experience that are by themselves insufficient to qualify the music as expressive of the emotion in question get a boost in that direction, as it were, from our knowledge that the piece in which the passage occurs is intended as a Romantic expression of the emotional experience of the artist or persona. Third, music, as an art of temporal process, is perhaps uniquely well-suited to mirror various aspects of emotional experience. In addition to the typical behavioral manifestations of emotion appealed to by resemblance theorists, the dynamic nature of melodies, harmonies, and rhythms – separately and in combination – can resemble the phenomenological and physiological aspects of emotional experience. And, as we saw in the previous chapter, the presence of a persona in the work allows for the expression of more cognitive emotions, such as hope. Furthermore, since music, like emotion, comprises multiple "streams" – different melodies, harmonies, rhythms, and timbres all occurring at the same time – it can mirror that complex aspect of our emotional experience. Finally, Robinson would remind us that music's ability to arouse emotions in us, in the various ways considered earlier in this chapter, often helps us to discern and understand the emotions expressed in the music as well as our own emotional capacities.

Perhaps most importantly for Robinson, understanding much music (especially Romantic and post-Romantic music, not to mention most songs and musical theater) as the Romantic expression of someone's emotional experience explains the great value we place on such music. As she puts it at one point, after a close analysis of Brahms's Intermezzo for solo piano, op. 117, no. 2:

> Without paying attention to the piece as a psychological drama I would suggest that we cannot appreciate its poignancy or its profundity. Why is this music

poignant, and why profound? The answer is that it records and expresses a poignant and profound psychological experience. Music in A-B-A' form is not poignant and profound just because it is in that form. It is, in [Anthony] Newcomb's words, the "metaphorical resonances" of the music, in particular what it means psychologically, that makes it poignant and profound.

(2005, 346; internal quotation from Newcomb 1984, 625)

In order to assess these claims we need to investigate competing theories of music's value – the topic of Chapter 5. But in order to make a fair comparison, we must investigate the musical features that Robinson dismisses in her negative claim here. So we turn in the next chapter to the nature and understanding of music's form and more basic musical properties.

Questions

What emotional responses to music are philosophically puzzling? What distinguishes them from emotional responses to music that are *not* philosophically puzzling?

Why do resemblance and imagination theorists tend to offer different accounts of our emotional responses to music? Include an explanation of each kind of account in your answer.

How plausible is the contagion theory of our emotional responses to music? How important are such responses to our appreciation of music?

How plausible are imagination theorists' accounts of our emotional responses to music? How important are such responses to our appreciation of music?

Which theory of our emotional responses to imaginings is more plausible – a Waltonian theory or realism?

Explain Jenefer Robinson's sophisticated expressionism as a theory of musical expressiveness. How does it fare in comparison to the theories we encountered in Chapter 2?

Notes

1 I focus, naturally, on philosophical as opposed to empirical work on emotional responses to music. For philosophical overviews of the latter, see Robinson 2005, 369–76; S. Davies 2010; and Young 2014, 44–66.

2 Since these terms come up repeatedly below, let me be clear that by "fully-fledged" emotions I mean emotional responses that include all of the typical parts or aspects of paradigmatic emotions (fear, joy, etc.), including physiological, phenomenological, cognitive, and behavioral components. By "garden-variety" emotions, I follow Peter Kivy in meaning just such paradigmatic emotions (fear, joy, etc.) as opposed to affective states that typically lack some

such aspect, for instance non-cognitive affective responses (e.g., startle), moods, and more-cognitive emotions (e.g., hope).

3 Recall that "affective" means "of, or related to, emotions and emotion-like states." The relevance here is that the responses Meyer discusses may be only physiological and phenomenological components of fully-fledged emotions.

4 We will consider these kinds of properties in Chapter 6, §6.3.3.

5 For a contemporary defense of Hanslick's views, see Zangwill 2004.

6 On "garden-variety" emotions, see note 2, above.

7 Recall that, according to a cognitive theory, an emotion requires a characteristic suite of beliefs, desires, or evaluations, and an intentional object of these cognitive states.

8 Whether or not such cases imply the falsity of the cognitive theory of emotions depends on (i) what precisely we take that theory to comprise, and (ii) how a cognitivist might respond to these alleged counterexamples. For our purposes it is enough to recognize that they are robust counterexamples to a *simple* emotional cognitivism.

9 In fact, Davies rejects the label of "moods" for the affective states we enter through contagion by music's expressiveness, precisely because of these differences. Nonetheless, I will continue to call them moods, since they seem to fit a consensus view about moods. (See, for example, Carroll 2003.)

10 Of course, they might rationally be made joyful by the piece because it's beautiful, because it was playing when they met their spouse, because their recording of it has sold a million copies, or because it's the perfect example of expressive music for their textbook. But none of these is a music-specific response to the piece's expressiveness.

11 For a methodical investigation and rejection of a variety of interpretations of this solution, see Walton 1978, 6–10.

12 Another way of rejecting the first proposition is by claiming that we feel the emotions in question, but not toward fictional characters. One might argue, for instance, that the fiction reminds us of real people in similar situations, and we thus respond emotionally to these people who do exist. Most philosophers consider this theory at best incomplete, since it seems undeniable that we feel *something* for fictional characters themselves.

13 The clunkiness of my repeated reminders that the pies are imagined points up how naturally we talk of fictions *as if* they were real. However, for that very reason, when theorizing about fiction it is surprisingly easy to become confused, hence my inclusion of the parenthetical reminders.

14 Apologies to readers in or from Tasmania, which I'm sure seems much less remote when you're there.

15 In talking of "the world of Harry Potter," I pass over some difficult questions for any account of fictional work-worlds raised by serial and interactive fictions. For an introduction to some, see McGonigal 2013; Robson and Meskin 2016; and Wildman and Woodward 2018.

16 I here pass over a number of difficult questions concerning what these "worlds" are, and how they are generated by works of fiction. See Walton 1990, especially 138–87.

17 In fact, given its widespread acceptance as a theory of our emotional responses to fictions, and the large literature on music and emotion, it is surprisingly difficult to find explicit applications of Walton's theory to the musical case. But see Levinson 1982, 334.

18 Walton speculates that one reason music induces feelings (and encourages imagining experiencing them) is that sounds are like feelings in ways that sights (e.g., the visual appearance of a painting) and words (e.g., in a novel) are not: We are less in control of what we hear than what we see or read; we separate sounds from their sources more easily than sights; and we are more disposed to react bodily to sounds than sights (1994, 57–8).

19 My discussion of realism is indebted to Berys Gaut's (2007, 203–26), which I highly recommend for more detail.

20 Walton himself has changed his mind on the question of whether such beliefs are essential to emotions (Walton 1997a, 280, n. 11).

21 I refer here to voluntary behavior. We often exhibit involuntary bodily reactions to fiction, such as jumping and shrieking at horror films.
22 One might, of course, be inspired by such pity to do something about current wars.
23 Grammatically, Gaut's formulation of (C1) is *conjunctive*. But the criterion is disjunctive in the sense that it implies your fear is rational as a result of meeting one *or* another of two distinct criteria; it doesn't (and arguably can't) meet both.
24 Gaut addresses this issue in the context of the possibility, not rationality, of emotional responses to fiction, but it seems to me just as relevant here.
25 I doubt Gaut or Walton would endorse this conciliatory conclusion. Each seems to think that his own theory renders the other's otiose.
26 Jenefer Robinson points out that although contagion cannot cause sympathetic responses, there may be other relatively automatic, sympathetic affective responses to the appearance of emotional expression, such as a response of "tenderness and love" to something that sounds like a baby's cry (2005, 388–9).
27 Walton proposes a different solution to a related puzzle about fictions. How can we be so gripped by the plot of a Harry Potter novel when we know exactly what is going to happen, having read it many times before? Walton argues that though we *know* what is going to happen we *imagine* that we do not. Whether or not this solution can be applied to our experience of music, and to what extent it is compatible with Robinson's views, are questions I leave the reader to answer.
28 Of course, I might care about music, but *that* interest in music won't explain the variation in my emotional response that Meyer is concerned with. (For example, my interest in good music is *continuously* satisfied by a piece that involves much tension, relief, surprise, and so on.)
29 The effect is named for a fitness franchise founded in 1969.
30 It is unclear to me whether Robinson also allows for Jazzercise responses to perceived expressive properties.
31 For competing assessments of the empirical evidence, see Robinson 2005, 395–400 and S. Davies 2011b, 56–64.
32 Robinson provides a derivative definition allowing for the unintended expression of emotion in, for example, pre-Romantic artworks (2005, 271).
33 We will consider such value claims in more depth in Chapter 5, §5.2.
34 Robinson used to be a traditional Romantic in this respect. She critically discusses her earlier theory in Robinson 2005, 266–70.

Further Reading

Peter Kivy expounds the position of the dry-eyed listener in "Feeling the Musical Emotions" (1999). Stephen Davies defends the contagion theory in "Emotional Contagion from Music to Listener" (2011b). Kendall Walton's solution to the paradox of fiction is explained in his classic "Fearing Fictions" (1978), developed in *Mimesis as Make-Believe* (1990, 195–289), and defended in "Spelunking, Simulation, and Slime" (1997a). Berys Gaut defends a realist solution in Chapter 9 of *Art, Emotion, and Ethics* (2007, 203–26). Jenefer Robinson develops her sophisticated expressionism in the second half of *Deeper than Reason* (2005, 229–412).

4 Musical Understanding

Overview

In this chapter, we investigate philosophical issues raised by our experience of some basic elements of music: pitch, rhythm, and harmony. We then turn to our experience of large-scale form and its relationship to music analysis. Along the way, I introduce some basic concepts of music theory and consider whether they justify calling music a language.

In the opening chapter, we considered what it is to understand a song as a song (rather than, say, a poem). The central topic of Chapter 2 was what it is to understand music as expressive of emotions, while in Chapter 3 we discussed the extent to which our affective states when listening to a piece of music contribute to our understanding of it. We have, then, been thinking about musical understanding throughout the book so far. This chapter is titled "Musical Understanding," however, because we now turn to aspects of music that are, first, uncontroversially essential to what must be understood when one appreciates a piece of music and, second, more fundamental than emotional expressiveness. The aspects I have in mind are things like pitch, rhythm, and harmony. Understanding these is uncontroversially essential to the appreciation of music because even if, like Hanslick, you think that music has no emotional content to be appreciated, you couldn't possibly reject the idea that to understand a piece of music one must hear its notes and how they are combined into rhythms, melodies, and harmonies. These aspects are more fundamental than emotional content because everyone agrees that emotional content must somehow depend upon them. After consideration of these fundamental aspects of music, we will turn to the higher-order feature of music that is the principal rival of emotional expressiveness in theories of musical value – *form* – asking what it is and what role it plays in musical understanding.

Once more, our focus will be on the medium of music alone – instrumental music and the musical aspects of hybrid musical artforms – since these features seem to distinguish the medium of music from others.[1] To address the understanding of song lyrics, for instance, would be more or less to address *literary* understanding – a topic that is beyond the scope of this book.[2]

The topic of "literary understanding" raises a terminological issue worth addressing at the outset. It is more common to label this topic "literary interpretation." Should we then be talking of musical *interpretation* rather than *understanding*? The two literary concepts amount to much the same thing. To *interpret* a literary work is to attempt to *understand* it – to figure out its meaning or content. So our choice between the two words is largely terminological. But the word "interpretation" comes with a lot of baggage. People often have strong pre-theoretical views about interpretation (for instance, that no one can be wrong about their interpretation of a poem, since it is "only their interpretation"). The notion of understanding does not seem quite so freighted, though we can motivate the same debates that we have over literary interpretation using the concept of understanding. (For instance, is there only one complete and correct way of understanding a given poem?) With respect to music in particular, the word "interpretation" is ambiguous.[3] It is common, at least in the classical-music world, to talk of the way that a musician plays a piece as her *interpretation* of it. But this is clearly not the same kind of thing as a verbal analysis of the piece (of the sort that a music theorist might give), which is the musical equivalent of an interpretation of a poem given by a scholar of literature, for instance (though it is an interesting question how the "performative" and "critical" interpretation of a musical work might be related).[4]

A final reason to prefer the term "musical understanding" to "musical interpretation" for our purposes in this chapter, is that "interpretations" of artworks are often aimed at higher-level meaning or content, while we will also consider lower-level phenomena in some detail. For example, Alan Goldman (2002) points out that Ernest Hemingway's novel *The Sun Also Rises* can be interpreted as an optimistic story of progress in the lives of the two main characters or as a pessimistic story of those characters repeating their mistakes. The optimism or pessimism of the work is "higher-level" in the sense that it depends on facts or hypotheses about what happens in the novel (e.g., how the characters feel about one another at various points). And these facts or hypotheses in turn depend on more fundamental facts or hypotheses about what individual sentences in the novel mean. Now, one's interpretation of a given sentence may depend upon one's overall (higher-level) interpretation of the novel, or the two may be interdependent. But some aspects of the lowest levels of interpretation (e.g., the grammatical structure of a simple sentence) are not seriously disputed. Nonetheless, there are difficult and fascinating questions about how we understand even simple sentences, though these are now typically considered the domain of scholars of linguistics rather than literature, since we presumably use largely the same cognitive faculties to understand the language of literary and non-literary texts. Understanding aspects of music such as pitch, rhythm, and harmony seems more like understanding lower-level aspects of literary works such as words and sentences than like figuring out whether a novel is, all things considered, optimistic or pessimistic. Musical "form" resides at a higher level than pitch, rhythm, and harmony, since it depends on those lower-level aspects, just as the feelings of a novel's characters for one another depend on the meanings of the sentences in the novel. But what the perception of musical form is, and what role it plays in understanding a piece of music are surprisingly controversial, given the central role that form has occupied in the scholarly study of music over the past century and more.

4.1 Pitch

4.1.1 Frequency and Pitch

Some sounds are music and some sounds aren't. What makes the difference? A full answer to this question would require something like a definition of music, a task to which we will turn in Chapter 11. Here, we will just consider some aspects of the experience of hearing a sound as music. One such aspect central to Western (and much other) music is hearing a sound as *pitched* – as a *note* or a *tone*, as opposed to a mere sound. It might seem at first that this feature does not distinguish musical from non-musical sounds. If "pitch" is just another word for "frequency," then many – perhaps all – sounds are pitched. For instance, you may begin tuning your flute by listening to the "A 440" produced by your tuner app. The app makes the molecules in the air vibrate 440 times per second (by vibrating a tiny speaker-cone at the same rate). It seems, then, that anything that causes an audible medium to vibrate 440 times per second emits an A. But to call a sound "an A" in the musical sense is to locate it within a musical system, the system in which the A is nine semitones above "middle C," the notes closest to the A are the G-sharp (or A-flat) below it and the B-flat (or A-sharp) above it, and so on. Notice that there are many *frequencies* closer to the A than these neighboring notes. Indeed, frequency is a continuum, just like the color spectrum of visible light, so there is an *infinite* number of frequencies between an A and the B-flat above it. But when we listen to music, we do not hear notes as simply falling on a continuum. As with our perception of visible light as falling into colored bands (red, yellow, etc.), we hear musical sounds as falling into pitch *categories* (A, B-flat, etc.). This *categorical perception* of pitch is unlike color perception in that we perceive the boundaries of pitch categories as quite precise. Whereas we have difficulty telling (and, relatedly, there is no fact of the matter regarding) when precisely a leaf has changed from yellow to orange or red, even though we are quite capable of distinguishing these three colors, we tend, in a musical context, to hear a pitch as (say) a sharper and sharper A-natural until there is a "flip" in our perception of it and we suddenly hear it as a very flat A-sharp (Stainsby & Cross 2009, 54–5).

Notice two features of categorical pitch perception. First, there is no objective fact about the frequency continuum that corresponds to our pitch categories. If we consider that different musical cultures divide the frequency continuum into pitch categories in different ways (i.e., they have different scales), this lack of objectivity should be obvious. Second, the qualitative differences between sounds perceived as pitched do not neatly match up with differences in frequency. For instance, a very sharp A-natural (x in Figure 4.1) and a very flat A-sharp (y) may sound more different (with respect to pitch) than the same very flat A-sharp and a perfectly-in-tune A-sharp (z), even though the difference in frequency is greater between y and z than between x and y. Our categorical perception of the frequency of musical sounds suggests that pitch is a distinct property from frequency, and I will respect this difference in my use of the terms "frequency" (for the wholly objective, scientific feature) and "pitch" (for the musical feature).

A second feature of our perception of musical sounds that bolsters this distinction is *octave equivalence* (Deutsch 2013, 249–50). We hear music as containing a relatively small number of different *kinds* of pitches (what music theorists call "pitch classes") – A, B-flat, C-sharp, and so on – which repeat at different "heights." Sing or listen to the first two notes of "Somewhere Over the Rainbow" (the lyric "Some-where").[5] These are two different notes in one sense – the second is higher than the first – but in another sense they are the same *kind* of note – they are both A-naturals (if, like Judy Garland, you're singing the song in A major).[6] Interestingly enough, octave equivalence roughly corresponds to differences in frequency of a factor of two.[7] That is, the note an octave above "A 440" is "A 880." This again may give the impression that octave equivalence is objectively present in the frequency continuum. But, of course, we could group frequencies according to any mathematical function (all the odd-numbered frequencies, frequencies related in a Fibonacci series, etc.), yet we would hear almost none of these as grouping pitches in a musically relevant way.[8]

A-flat	A-natural	A-sharp	B-natural
	x | y	z	

frequency ——————▶

Figure 4.1 Representation of the categorical perception of frequencies as pitches.

Putting these two features together, we might say that to hear a note as pitched is to hear it as *occupying a place in a scale*, where a *scale* is simply a division of the octave into pitch categories. In Western music, there are typically seven distinct pitch classes in a scale; that is why the repetition of the first pitch class is called the *oct*ave – the eighth note of a scale belongs to the same pitch class as the first. But many different scales have been, and are still, used in Western music and other musical cultures around the world. You may be familiar with the *blues scale*, while *pentatonic scales* (consisting of five pitch classes) are extremely common across the globe.[9] The fact that octave equivalence and categorical pitch perception are apparently universal in traditional (as opposed to self-consciously avant-garde) musical systems suggests that our experience of pitch is rooted in cognitive resources common to all people, though, as with language, the cultural variation allowed for within the common framework is so broad that we can be quite at sea when exposed to music from an unfamiliar culture (Stevens & Byron 2009, 15–16).[10]

4.1.2 Pitch Space and Movement

I have spoken above – indeed, throughout the book so far – as we commonly do, of notes as *neighboring* one another, being *higher* or *lower* than one another, of a scale as *ascending* or *descending*, and so on. Such terms imply that musical pitches bear spatial relations to one another and that there is often some kind of movement within that space. Notice that this implication is taken for granted in any appeal to a resemblance theory of musical expressiveness, to the extent that it relies on resemblances between musical movement and human behavior. If a sequence of notes resembles tears because the notes themselves constitute a falling cascade, then the notes must be *moving downward* in some sense. If a melody is joyous in part because it leaps like a joyful person, there must be something *moving swiftly upward* in the music. Musical space and movement also seem to be taken for granted in many music-theoretic descriptions. The members of a barbershop quartet are said to sing in *close harmony* not because they're standing next to one another but because the notes of the chords they sing are closer to one another than in traditional classical choral music. A modulation *up* a step has a very different effect from a modulation *down* a step. And so on.

The philosophical puzzle raised by all this talk of pitch *space* and *movement* is that, fundamental though the phenomenon seems to be to our experience of music, it can be quite baffling to consider what we could be hearing moving in the music, and what space such movement could be located in. All sorts of things move when music is made, of course. Every musical sound depends on some physical movement (e.g., the vibration of a string or a speaker cone), and people typically move their bodies when making music, both internally (e.g., the singer's vibrating vocal cords) and externally (e.g., the pianist's dancing fingers). But none of these movements necessarily correlates with the movement we hear *in the music*. We will consider four philosophical theories of musical space and movement below. But first it is worth considering two theories that no philosopher (as far as I know) has defended in print, yet which seem to be initially appealing when people are first introduced to the puzzle. I call these theories *scientistic* and *conventionalist*.

According to scientistic theories, pitches are higher or lower than one another in a quite literal, unproblematic sense: They have higher or lower frequencies. Now, it is certainly true that the air vibrates at a greater rate for a higher pitch than a lower one, and that this causes a cascade of effects, including our perception of the relative height of the pitches. But none of vibrational rates, the differences between them, or the numbers used to represent them, need represent spatial differences. On the basis of these factors alone, we might think of pitches with greater frequencies as *hotter* and those with smaller frequencies as *colder*. Even if we do take these factors to represent spatial difference, there is no reason they would have to represent the particular spatial properties we hear in the sounds. For instance, why should we not hear the greater frequencies as a measure of *depth* rather than height? So, by themselves, the frequencies of the sounds and the way we represent these frequencies no more suggest we would hear the pitch with the greater frequency as higher than as hotter or lower.

Another problem is the status of the theory. You don't need to know anything about the physics of sound to hear a melody as rising and then falling. In what sense, then, can the non-obvious details of the physics (or its theoretical representation) explain our experience? This leads us to the heart of the problem with the scientistic approach: Musical space and movement are puzzling precisely because of the apparent mismatch between the nature of their objects (sounds that are non-spatial in the relevant respects) and our experience of them (as musical entities capable of occupying spatial locations and moving between them). Scientistic theories ignore the experience that gives rise to the puzzle.[11]

Conventionalist theories do not ignore the apparent divide between musical experience and its objects, but their explanation of the bridge across it is equally implausible. As the name suggests, these theories posit that the reason we describe or experience musical notes as higher or lower than one another is that we associate the differences in our perception of various frequencies with differences in (literal) height in some other domain.[12] For instance, it is sometimes suggested that modern Western musicians and audiences think of notes as higher and lower only because that is how they are represented in musical notation.[13] Singers sometimes suggest that it is because we naturally stretch upward when trying to sing notes at the top of our range, and force our faces into a downward grimace at the other end of our range, that we think of notes as high and low.[14]

There are both conceptual and empirical reasons to reject conventionalist views. Conceptually, it seems at least as plausible in each of these cases that the association goes the other way. For instance, it is arguably because we *hear* pitches of greater frequency as higher that we conventionally *represent* them higher on the page. A compelling parallel situation is our tendency to describe our physical interactions with musical instruments in spatial terms that correlate with musical rather than physical space (S. Davies 1994, 233). For instance, we talk equally naturally of violinists and cellists as moving *higher up* the fingerboard, when their hands are moving horizontally or downwards in physical space. It seems plausible that amateur singers' physical stretching for their high notes is similarly a consequence of their thinking of them as high, given that such stretching (the bane of vocal instructors) in fact hinders one's ability to reach the notes.

Empirically, conventionalism implies that describing or experiencing pitch in terms of spatial concepts is culturally specific. It would count as evidence against the notation theory, for instance, if most oral musical cultures describe pitch in the same spatial terms that contemporary Westerners use. There is also cross-cultural evidence suggesting that the experience of music in spatial terms is more consistent than conventionalism would suggest. Stephen Davies summarizes several cross-cultural studies, concluding that music's being "heard in spatial terms would appear to be more or less universal" (1994, 232). The terms vary somewhat. The notes Westerners would call "high" some other cultures call equivalents of "small," "weak," "sharp," and "white" (the latter from an *upward* notational stroke), while terms that parallel "low" or "deep" include equivalents of "big," "strong," "flat," "heavy," and "black" (from a downward notational stroke). But Davies claims that these are all terms for spatial concepts and that there is no evidence of a culture in which these "synaesthetic equations" are reversed, that is, in which what Westerners would call high notes are called low, big, heavy, or the like (1994, 232).

In sum, conceptual problems with conventionalism and the cross-cultural evidence suggest that our perception of music as spatial and mobile is more deeply rooted than that theory implies. Let's turn, then, to the more sophisticated theories that have been developed and defended by philosophers.

Roger Scruton (1983, 80–8; 1997, 1–96) argues that our experience of musical space and movement is *essentially metaphorical*. By this he means not that our *linguistic descriptions* of music as spatial and mobile are metaphors (such a view would be closer to eliminativism, to be considered next) but that our *experience* of music as spatial and mobile is metaphorical. The basic idea is that, as in a linguistic metaphor (see Chapter 2, §2.3), in our experience of music we apply concepts to the music under which we know it does not literally fall. For instance, when we say that someone is a weasel, we know that our claim is not literally true, though it might convey a truth. So, Scruton suggests, when we hear the music as moving, we know it does not literally do so (and do not experience it as literally doing so), yet there is something right about perceiving it as moving. The invocation of metaphor is also supposed to explain the partial and sometimes paradoxical way in which we apply such concepts. When Alex describes Sam as a weasel, we rightly infer that she thinks he is devious and cunning, but not that he is genetically more similar to a polecat than an ape. Similarly, Scruton says,

> [w]e must concede that hearing movement in auditory space is very different from seeing or hearing movement in physical space. It does not involve an act of re-identification: it does not require the perception of the same thing at different places, and the consequent inference of a movement from one place to the other.
>
> (1983, 84)

Malcolm Budd objects that this theory makes our experience of music mysterious (1985, 237–45). What is it to hear something as moving without hearing one and the same thing (i.e., "re-identifying" something) as being at different places at different times? Budd argues that, as illustrated by our weasel example, a metaphor only has meaning to the extent that one can interpret it, that is, say something about which aspects of the metaphorical domain (weaselhood or space) apply to the literal domain (Sam or musical sounds). He allows that one might utter a metaphor without having thought about how it should be interpreted, but claims that it's implausible that whenever we experience music as spatial or mobile we apply a metaphor in this way.

Budd's alternative proposal is that these spatial and mobile metaphors *are* interpretable. We *can* say which aspects of musical sound are like which aspects of space and movement, just as we can say which aspects of Sam are like which aspects of a weasel. As a result, however, the metaphor is not, as Scruton would have it, essential to musical experience; on the contrary, it – along with the concepts of space and movement – is eliminable from a theory of musical experience. In arguing for such *eliminativism*, Budd draws an analogy with timbral properties, that is, the "tone color" or "quality" that allows us to distinguish between two sounds of the same pitch and loudness (2003, 213–14).[15] He points out that we commonly refer to such properties using terms from other sensory modalities – the *piercing* wail of an electric guitar, say, or the *chocolatey richness* of a cello – but that no one suggests *these* metaphors are essential to the experience of timbre. (For example, there is no reason to think that someone who had never heard of, much less tasted, chocolate would be missing something in her experience of hearing the cello.) Most of us are unfamiliar with any technical vocabulary for referring to timbral features, but that does not prevent us from recognizing the inessentiality of the metaphors on which we thus rely in describing them. Budd believes that pitch is no different from timbre in this respect. He claims that "sounds have a character, *pitch*, that can be heard, recognized, discriminated, without this character being brought under spatial concepts" (2003, 251).

It may be telling that Budd makes this point about *sounds* as opposed to musical *notes* or *tones*. Of course, he's right that we distinguish between ordinary sounds on the basis of their frequencies. But this is different from hearing a sound as *occupying a place in a scale*, that is, as having a *pitch* in the musical sense, which raises two problems for eliminativism. First, even if we can discriminate between ordinary sounds on the basis of their frequencies without using spatial concepts, it doesn't follow that we can do so with respect to musical notes. One dog's bark may be adequately described as *gruffer* than another's, but to describe one B-flat as gruffer (rather than as *lower*) than one at a different octave seems to leave something essential out of the musical picture. This problem may be even worse for musical movement. Though we may hear some ordinary sounds as moving in the sense in which a melody moves (e.g., a siren sliding up and down), perhaps we need not do so. But wouldn't someone who failed to hear the beginning of "Somewhere Over the Rainbow" as *leaping up* be missing something of importance in that song? Second, the cross-cultural evidence surveyed in our discussion of conventionalism should give us pause. If spatial concepts are eliminable from our experience of music, then we might expect different cultures to have developed different extended metaphors to describe differences in musical pitch. Perhaps one culture would describe pitch differences with color terminology (different pitches as different hues, octave differences as different saturations of those hues, etc.), another with taste terminology, a third with tactile terminology, and so on. Thus, the extent to which all cultures describe musical pitch in spatial terms defines the size of the coincidence implied by eliminativism.

Davies appeals to this cross-cultural evidence to argue that spatial concepts are ineliminable from our experience and descriptions of music (1994, 231–2). But he agrees with Budd's criticisms of metaphorical theories of musical space and movement (S. Davies 2011c, 27–30). Davies argues instead that music is *literally* spatial and mobile. Such *literalism* escapes the obvious problems that give rise to the puzzle of musical space and movement in the first place by appealing to the idea that the meanings of spatial terms as they apply to music are *secondary*, just as Davies argues that emotion terms (e.g., "sad") apply literally, but in a secondary sense, to music (see Chapter 2, §2.4.3) Davies thinks that our perception and description of musical notes as higher or lower than one another, and melodies as rising and falling, are as natural and literal as our description of other temporal processes in such terms. He points out that

> [n]ot all processes are constituted by elements that have a location in space ....
> There may be political moves toward war in the Middle East; the Dow Jones
> Index responds by dropping; as a result, the government lurches to the right;

this causes my spirits to plunge; the peace movement attains new standing. In these cases, no identifiable individual changes its location in space and nothing moves from place to place.

(1994, 235)

Literalism thus treads a middle way between metaphorical and eliminativist theories of musical space and movement.

It is worth noting that Scruton's and Budd's more recent views appear to be converging on Davies's literalism. Scruton (2004) seems to have demoted the role of metaphor in his theory from essential concept to mere analogy, while Budd (2003, 220) has backed off his eliminativism, citing Davies on secondary literal senses of words. If literalism leaves one anti-eliminativist doubt to nag at us, however, it is that we seem to experience music as spatial and mobile in the *primary* senses of those terms. We hear the beginning of "Somewhere Over the Rainbow" as leaping *up*, not simply as moving in the way the Dow Jones Index does (a process that might just as well be represented with a table of numbers as with a graph). Such controversial phenomenological considerations may be too tenuous or tendentious to justify rejecting literalism outright, but perhaps they are reason enough to investigate one final theory that also attempts to steer a course between the Scylla of metaphorical theories and the Charybdis of eliminativism.

Just as imagination theories of music's emotional expressiveness posit that we imagine of music that it is someone's emotional expression, according to the *imagination* theory of musical space and movement, our experience of music involves imagining that something in the music is spatially located and able to move within that space.[16] Budd argues that the most obvious candidate for the "something" – musical notes or tones – is a non-starter, since the identity of a musical note is determined in part by its pitch (2003, 216). What makes the first note of "Somewhere Over the Rainbow" the note that it is, and distinct from the note that follows it, is that it is the *A below middle-C*. It would thus be incoherent to imagine *that* note leaping *above* middle-C.

This is a little quick, however, since although impossible things cannot *occur*, we seem able to *imagine* them. For instance, we have no trouble becoming immersed in incoherent time-travel stories, such as those in the *Back to the Future* movies, which depend on the notion (widely rejected by philosophers and physicists) that the past could be changed. Nor does being a committed physicalist prevent you from enjoying a good ghost story (Kania 2015, 165). Nonetheless, it behooves theorists appealing to imagination to reduce the amount of incoherence implied or allowed by their theories, lest imagination start to seem like a get-out-of-jail-free card to be waved in the face of any objection, lending the theories an air of unearned unfalsifiability. An alternative, then, to the idea that we imagine a musical tone, identified in part by its pitch, moving from one place in pitch space to another, is the idea that we imagine *something indeterminate* (but definitely *not* identified even in part by its pitch) so moving.[17] Consider a circle of lights of different colors turned on and off so as to generate an illusion of movement around the circle (cf. De Clercq 2007, 162–3). We seem to perceive a re-identifiable thing moving around the circle, which has a different color property in each position, yet there is no such object. This might take some of the mystery out of the idea that we imagine something moving from one position on the pitch continuum to another. We can, of course, generate questions about the imagined moving thing in either case: How big is it? Does it have mass? What shape is it? In some cases there may be answers to these questions – the thing we seem to see moving around the circle of lights may clearly be circular or spherical, for instance – but most of them are "silly" in the sense that, though they have no answers, we do not *need* answers to them in order to experience movement in the lights or the music (Kania 2015, 167–8; Walton 1990, 174–83).

As with imagination theories of musical expressiveness, though imagination theories of musical space and movement make use of Walton's theoretical machinery, Walton himself does not subscribe to such a theory.[18] One reason for his hesitation is that our experience of musical space is unlike our experience of *pictorial* space in that it is not (typically) perspectival. We do not hear a melody rising at any particular distance, or in any particular direction, relative to us: "The music appears to have its own separate space, one unrelated to the listener's space" (Walton 1994, 53–4). Correlatively, according to Walton, we do not imagine hearing sounds when we listen to music, which contrasts sharply with our imagining seeing the represented contents of a picture, on his view. For if our experience were one of imagined hearing, we would perforce imagine hearing the objects of that experience from some perspective (e.g., from above, nearby, etc.); yet we do not have such an experience.

4.2 Rhythm

Another aspect of musical sounds that seems as basic as pitch is *rhythm*. Interestingly enough, given that they seem equally fundamental to music, while pitch could plausibly be argued to be *exclusively* musical (if a sound is pitched, then it is a musical sound), rhythm is more ubiquitous in human life. In Chapter 1, we briefly considered whether the "rhythms" of music and literature (to say nothing of those of dance, cinema, or other artforms) are the same kind of thing. But rhythmic activity is common even outside artistic practices. Much of what we do in the kitchen, for instance, from chopping herbs to beating egg whites, we do rhythmically. Sometimes these practices rise to a rhythmically complex – perhaps quasi-musical – level, as with the pounding of rice in Bali (Hamilton 2007, 144–5).

What *is* this ubiquitous feature of human activity, so salient in music, that we call "rhythm"? Those familiar with Western musical notation might think that it is an objective feature of music – the feature represented by the different kinds of "notes" (the stemless, hollow whole-note or semibreve; the eighth-note or quaver, filled in and with a single-flagged stem; and so on), as opposed to their vertical placement on the musical staff, representing pitch. But this, like much other musical notation, is a practical simplification of what actually goes on when one plays from the score. If one played a score with mathematical rhythmic precision, it would sound lifeless, as do the sounds produced by much music-notation software. An alternative view might be that the rhythm of a musical passage is its objective temporal structure *in performance*, that is, the temporal detail (perhaps at some level of "grain") that could be captured by processing a digital sound file of the performance. But this, too, would miss something essentially phenomenological about rhythm. The missing aspect can be helpfully illustrated with examples of rhythmically ambiguous music. Consider the opening of The La's "There She Goes" or Radiohead's "Pyramid Song." In each case, exactly the same sounds can be heard in two different ways. In "There She Goes," the difference depends on whether one hears the first note as a single, short upbeat to the second note (the downbeat), or the beginning of an extended upbeat to a downbeat on the lowest note of the phrase.[19] Example 4.1 represents the two ways of hearing this example in musical notation.

Understanding the rhythmic ambiguity of "Pyramid Song" requires introducing a distinction between rhythm (in a narrower sense than I have thus far been using) and meter. In this narrower sense, *rhythm* is the temporal structure and patterning of the musical surface – the perceptible temporal properties of, and relationships between, various musical events – while *meter* is a more abstract hierarchical structure that emerges in our perception of the musical surface, allowing us to make sense of the rhythm (and other musical features) by, say, anticipating when certain musical events will occur. For instance, if we hear "There She Goes" in the first way, the entrance of the drums is very natural, reinforcing the meter, but if we hear it in the second way, the drums seem to enter in the wrong place and, as they continue, they redefine how we hear the meter, locking us in to hearing it in the first way.

Example 4.1 The La's, "There She Goes," opening: (a) as ultimately heard, and (b) an alternative way of hearing the opening (before the drums enter). Upbeats marked "u"; downbeats "d." (Author's transcription.)

This example demonstrates two things about rhythm and meter. First, both are ineliminably phenomenological. There is no way to describe a rhythmic ambiguity without referring to the different ways in which people can *hear* the music. Note also that the possibilities for how to hear the music are tightly constrained. There is no reason *in principle* why we shouldn't be able to hear the downbeat as falling on any one of the first sixteen notes of "There She Goes" – or anywhere between any two notes for that matter. But it's practically impossible to hear many of these possibilities, presumably because our ways of hearing are constrained by both our psychological make-up and cultural background. For instance, there seem to be quite general psychological constraints on basic factors such as how fast or slow a rhythmic pulse can be and still be heard as such by human beings (London 2012, 25–64), while the "additive rhythms" of some classical Indian music are inaudible to most people unfamiliar with those traditions, even though they can hear all of the sounds that constitute those rhythms.

Second, though we typically think of rhythm and meter as *temporal* phenomena, the perceived *organization* essential to rhythm is not exclusively a matter of temporal features. For to hear the opening of "There She Goes" in one way rather than the other is not to hear any of the notes as occurring at different points in time, or as longer or shorter, nor to hear a different *periodicity* in the temporal organization; it is to hear the notes as *grouped* differently, to hear the "period" or group as beginning at one point or another in the musical manifold. And such grouping is often heavily influenced, if not determined, by nontemporal features. Perhaps most obviously, merely by *accenting* every third note (e.g., playing it more loudly), we can "group" a string of otherwise identical notes into threes beginning with the accented note. But harmonic and melodic features also give rise to such grouping, as when the harmony begins to change at a rate at odds with the meter established up to that point (as in Example 4.2).

Example 4.2 Bach, "Jesu, Joy of Man's Desiring," excerpt. A well-established meter of three groups of three notes is disrupted (in the second measure) by a repeated melodic shape with a periodicity of two groups of three notes (indicated by brackets), reinforced by harmonic change with the same periodicity. The original meter is restored with the return of the main theme (in the last measure). This passage begins near the end of the final choral entry, around 1:55 on the recording on the Spotify playlist for this chapter.

The rhythmic ambiguity of "Pyramid Song" is of a different kind than that of "There She Goes," in that the two ways of hearing it depend not only on hearing its rhythmic events under two different metrical groupings (e.g., hearing the downbeat as falling in two different places), but also – perhaps more importantly – on hearing those rhythmic events as related in different ways to the underlying metrical structure. On first hearing, it is difficult to figure out the meter of the music – one of many elements that give the song its unsettled feel – but by the end of the first two sung verses (the first two minutes of the track), it's relatively easy to hear the song as in the standard rock meter of 4/4. Since the piano chords are relatively (but not precisely) evenly spaced, one natural way of hearing them is as being played in a "rubato" style. That is, the temporal distance between successive notes is stretched or shrunk, but in such a way that the underlying (metrical) tempo is unchanged (e.g., the music overall would not get ahead of, or fall behind, a metronome set to the basic tempo). Again, this lends an off-kilter feel to the music. But when the drums finally enter, as with "There She Goes," they organize the rhythm quite differently. With the help of the drums' subdivisions of the four beats in each bar, we now hear the piano chords as falling precisely on various beats and subdivisions of beats (see Example 4.3).[20] In one way this makes the music sound much more regimented, since the piano chords are clearly being played in a very precise rhythm, rather than with rubato; but the rhythm itself is highly syncopated,[21] which continues the sense of unsettledness. The more one listens to the song, the easier it becomes to hear the opening two minutes in the second way, since one can "fit" the surface rhythmic events to the underlying meter with more precision.[22]

Example 4.3 Radiohead, "Pyramid Song," opening (slightly simplified): (a) as, perhaps, initially heard, and (b) as ultimately heard. (Adapted from "Pyramid Song." Words and music by Thomas Yorke, Jonathan Greenwood, Colin Greenwood, Edward O'Brien and Philip Selway. Copyright © 2001 Warner/ Chappell Music Ltd. All rights in the U.S. and Canada administered by WB Music Corp. All rights reserved. Used by permission of Alfred Music.)

What do these rhythmic phenomena imply for philosophical theories of rhythm and meter? To some extent, philosophical questions about these features recapitulate those about pitch space and movement. Roger Scruton, for instance, argues that our experience of rhythm is a metaphorical one in which we apply concepts of *dancing* to the sounds we hear – concepts that we know do not literally apply to those sounds (1983, 88–91, cf. 1997, 35–6). Malcolm Budd and others, as we have already seen, criticize Scruton's notion of metaphorical perceptual experience. In the case of rhythm, Budd adds that to appeal to the concept of *dance* in one's explanation of the experience of rhythm is circular, since the notion of rhythmic action is implicit in the concept of dance (1985, 242–3). Budd offers an eliminativist account of our experience of rhythm, that is, one that does not appeal to concepts of dancing or any kind of life or action:

> The experience of rhythm in a sequence of sounds and rests ... (i) ... does not require that the sounds should be heard as differing in pitch, timbre, duration or loudness, and (ii) the sequence must be heard as grouped into units in which one element is heard as accented (prominent, salient) relative to the others.
>
> (1985, 243; cf. 2003, 221–2)

No one has defended a literalist theory of our experience of rhythm, along the lines of Stephen Davies's literalism about musical space and movement. Perhaps this is a sign that the phenomenon of rhythm is not as puzzling as that of pitch. Even Scruton seems unsure of exactly what concepts are essential to the experience of rhythm, appealing at different points to candidates as varied as dance, life, action, and causality. But Andy Hamilton argues for an even stronger connection between rhythm and movement, claiming that musical rhythm is just one among many manifestations of bodily movement (2007, 142–8). Hamilton points to other examples of rhythmic activity (dancing, marching, physical work, etc.), but it is unclear how these are supposed to illuminate our experience of music. What exactly does a "manifestation" of bodily movement amount to, particularly if it is present when we experience the rhythm of a piece of music while sitting immobile? One possibility is suggested by Tiger Roholt, who argues that the experience of musical *grooves* requires moving one's body in sympathy with the groove's temporal nuances (2014, especially 105–39). Think of the way you might move your body when the drums arrive halfway through "Pyramid Song" and you finally "get" what the piano is doing rhythmically. In nodding your head and swaying back and forth, you are quite literally getting into the groove, according to Roholt. The obvious problem with using this theory to explain rhythmic perception in general is that, as just mentioned, though it may be natural to move with rhythmic music, we seem able to perceive musical rhythm even when stock still, or moving in a way that is unrelated to the music (e.g., when driving a car), not to mention the capacity of people with various forms of bodily paralysis to appreciate music.[23] Justin London argues that empirical research into rhythm perception suggests that Roholt has gone a step too far. Perhaps actual bodily movement is necessary for *acquiring* the ability to perceive grooves and other rhythmic phenomena but, once acquired, the mere mental representation of such movement is sufficient for experiencing rhythm (London 2016, 102–3).[24]

4.3 Harmony

The word "harmony" is used in a variety of ways in connection with music. The sense that is most important for our concerns is that of "functional harmony" – the understanding shared by musicians and audiences in a wide range of Western music of the *roles* or *functions* of various kinds of chords that constitutes a system of norms governing musical progression, somewhat like a musical grammar or syntax. In this section, I offer a brief introduction to functional harmony, which will be most immediately relevant to the upcoming sections on musical form and analysis. (Readers familiar with Western music theory may want to skip this section.)

The Western system of functional harmony developed during the "common practice" era, roughly the Baroque to Romantic periods (c. 1600–1900 CE). The system is based on major and minor scales. The distribution of successive *intervals* (the distance between two notes) in these scales is asymmetrical, with the result that we can more easily keep track of which note of the scale we are hearing. One consequence is that different notes (in a melody, say) can have different saliences. For instance, as mentioned several times already, we typically anticipate that a melody will end on the *tonic* or "home" note of the piece, that is, the first note or *degree* of the scale (C in C major, G in G minor, and so on). Try singing "Happy Birthday" and ending on the penultimate note. The experience is unsatisfying, even frustrating. Of course, ending here doesn't just upset the pitch-structure of the melody; it also leaves the melody rhythmically and textually incomplete. But if you sing the last word of the song on the same pitch as the penultimate note (the second scale degree) the unsatisfyingness is not removed.[25] Psychologists of music have established the existence of a large number of such expectations, which give rise (among other things) to the Meyer-style responses discussed in Chapter 3.[26]

As for individual notes in a melody, so for chords.[27] Just as we hear a melody as wanting to return to the *tonic* scale degree, we hear the harmony as wanting to return to the *tonic chord* (i.e., a C-major chord in the key of C major, a G-minor chord in the key of G minor, and so on). The tonic chord is typically preceded by a major chord built on the fifth note of the scale (a G-major chord in C major, a D-major chord in G minor, and so on.)[28] When a chord functions in this way (i.e., preparing you for the tonic), it is called a *dominant* chord.

(It is often represented by the Roman numeral V because it is built on the fifth note of the scale, just as the tonic chord is often represented by the Roman numeral I.) Likewise, the dominant chord is typically preceded by one built on the second or fourth note of the scale (a D-minor or F-major chord in C major, an A-diminished or C-minor chord in G minor, and so on, represented by the Roman numerals ii, IV, ii°, and iv respectively).[29] Any chord with this function is a *pre-dominant* chord.

When people talk about country or rock music as "three chords and the truth," the three chords they're talking about are not built on three particular pitches; they're the chord *functions* of predominant, dominant, and tonic.[30] A given chord has no function outside a particular musical context. A C-major chord is the tonic in a passage in the key of C major, but in a passage in the key of F major it is (i.e., *functions as*) the dominant chord, while it is a pre-dominant (IV) in G major. This phenomenon is a little like a word that has more than one grammatical function. The word "bank" is, in itself, neither a noun nor a verb. In the sentence "You can bank on it" any competent English speaker knows from its place in the sentence that it is functioning as a verb (even if one is unfamiliar with the term "verb"), while in the sentence "You'll be laughing all the way to the bank" one knows that "bank" is functioning as a noun. Similarly, even if you knew no music theory before reading this section, you still heard the first two notes of "Happy Birthday" as implying a dominant harmony and the piece as ending on the tonic (otherwise my explanations would have been much more mysterious). A substantial part of Western music theory is the theory of functional harmony – of what goes on when we listen to music with harmonic understanding – just as the grammar of a language is a substantial part of the theory of what goes on when we listen to the language with understanding.

I may have given the impression that the system of functional harmony I've been describing constitutes the fixed rules of a universal musical grammar. Brief consideration of music from other cultures, however, quickly demonstrates that musical systems are highly culturally-contingent. Even within Western music the functions of chords vary across time and between musical traditions. I mentioned in Chapter 2 (§2.4.5) that just a few hundred years ago, minor chords were considered too dissonant to end a piece of music. Similarly, chords that are dissonant in Western classical music from 150 years ago can function as "colorful" tonics in rock music (e.g., the final "added sixth" chord of the Beatles' "She Loves You"). The harmonic language of much jazz is even freer.[31] Nonetheless, there appear to be some basic psychological constraints on traditional (as opposed to self-consciously revolutionary) harmonic systems. For instance, all musical cultures seem to include the phenomena of octave equivalence, a tonic, and a kind of dominant, i.e., a pitch about the same distance from the tonic as the Western fifth that functions as a strong contrast with the tonic (Stevens & Byron 2009).

4.4 Music as Language

I have used terms such as "language," "syntax," and "grammar" to describe functional harmony. This seems natural enough given the similarities between language and music. For instance, in both cases there seem to be some universal features (i.e., features common to all musics or languages) rooted in our shared human psychology, but which are clothed in such culturally diverse specifics that we must devote considerable time and effort to learning the music or language of another culture. And, of course, we often experience music, like language, as deeply meaningful. Could it be that music just *is* a kind of language? There is broad consensus among philosophers, psychologists, and linguists that, despite the similarities, music is not language.[32] Two kinds of argument lead to this conclusion.

First, there are several essential aspects or components of language that are absent from music.[33] The grammar of a language is a set of rules for combining words of various grammatical classes (noun, verb, etc.) into sentences whose meanings are a function of the meanings of their individual words.[34] Now, consider *words*. These are the smallest units of meaning in language. The word "tree," for instance, is meaningful – but not in virtue of the meanings of its individual letters (e.g., "t") or phonemes (e.g., "ee"), since these elements have no meaning. Rather, the meaning of "tree" is completely arbitrary and conventional. To the extent that a note has meaning, by contrast, its parts also have meaning. The first half of a long note, for instance is crucial to how a competent listener understands it. So there appears to be no smallest unit of meaning in music, i.e., no words. The meaning of a word is also *fixed*, in the sense that it is independent of its context (e.g., the other words in the sentence). But whatever meaning an individual note has seems to depend heavily on its context (e.g., the key of the passage in which it occurs). Is it more plausible that short motifs, melodies, or chords are the "words" of music? These candidates still typically lack the conventional, fixed meanings of words.[35] And as the size of the candidate musical entity increases, we face the problem of distinguishing musical words from musical sentences.

Turning to grammar, whatever the status of the "rules" of functional harmony, they are a far cry from linguistic grammar. Obviously, if there are no musical words or word meanings, there can be no musical grammar in the sense of a function from word-meanings to sentence-meanings. But even if we could identify musical units corresponding to words, these would not belong to different grammatical classes; there is no distinction between a musical noun and a musical verb. It might seem tempting to classify musical elements into grammatical classes on the basis of their dynamic character. Perhaps the more-active musical elements are verbs and the less-active ones nouns, for instance. But, despite the first-pass characterization of verbs as "action" or "doing" words, this bears little resemblance to grammatical class. After all, "stagnate" is just as much a verb as "run," while "explosion" is no less a noun than "lump." Perhaps all musical "words" could belong to the same grammatical class (cf. Higgins 2012, 79), but this would result in the "sentences" of music being very strange indeed (if the notion of a grammatical class even makes sense without there being at least two such classes). Anyway, there are no musical equivalents of other crucial parts of language such as logical connectives ("and," "but," "or," etc.) or quantifiers ("all," "some," "none," etc.).

Second, similarities between music and language only imply that music is a language if those similarities are not also shared by further, non-linguistic phenomena. For instance, if music "has meaning" in a sense that is shared not only by language but also by pictures and winks (for instance, it is *about* something, in a general sense) then this is insufficient to show that music is language. It might rather show that music and language both belong to some larger class, such as intentional human behavior.[36] Ray Jackendoff surveys seven cognitive capacities central to musical and linguistic behavior, and concludes that none are exclusive to these two domains (2011, 103–4). Though he concurs with the kinds of arguments given above that music has no grammar of the sort possessed by language, he has developed (with Fred Lerdahl) a sophisticated theory of tonal music that marries recent linguistic theory with a well-known theory of musical form known as Schenkerian analysis (Lerdahl & Jackendoff 1983). The theory posits that music, like language, has "prolongational structure," a kind of recursive hierarchical structure that can be represented by a tree diagram.[37] But Jackendoff is at pains to point out (i) that musical and linguistic prolongational structures are of quite different kinds (corresponding to some of the differences between music and language canvassed above), and (ii) that prolongational structure itself may be common to a wide range of complex human behaviors, including "actions as ordinary as shaking hands or making coffee" (2011, 110).

So, music is not a language in any robust sense, though the metaphor remains popular. This might seem harmless as long as one understands the metaphor's limits. But Kathleen Higgins argues that critical investigation of the metaphor reveals an unjustified valorization of language over music (2012, 78–105). She pursues one stimulating strategy for uncovering and questioning that valorization: Rather than asking whether music is a language, she asks whether "language is a music." The result is not only a defense of the value of music, but the disclosure of avenues of inquiry that help us to understand language better by revealing ways in which it is musical.

4.5 Form

We have thus far been considering the fundamental building blocks of music – pitch, rhythm, and harmony. You might have thought that higher-level musical entities, such as melodies, can be understood simply as collections of such features. But it turns out that things are more complicated. For instance, we hear the same melody recurring even if it is now made up of different notes (because embellished, reduced, or transposed into a different key), different intervals (because now appearing in the minor rather than major mode), different rhythms (because now twice as slow or transformed from a waltz into a march), or is harmonized differently. Yet not just anything goes. Change enough features and you have a distinct, if derivative, melody; change more and you have an entirely new tune. Moreover, such matters are highly contextual. What counts as the reappearance of a melody in a different guise in one context might be considered a distinct melody in another. The same kind of complexity can be found in rhythmic and harmonic structures (S. Davies 2001, 45–58; Scruton 1997, 19–79, 239–308). Rather than investigate all of these intermediate levels of musical organization, we will now leap straight to one of the highest – one which has been of particular interest to musical theorists and philosophers – namely, large-scale form.

The word "form" here refers, as you might expect, to the *shape* or *structure* of a piece of music.[38] An extremely common form in rock music, for instance, is the *verse-chorus* structure, in which one chunk of music is used repeatedly to set a number of different stanzas of text (the verses), alternating with another chunk of music used repeatedly to set the same text (the chorus). This basic form admits of a number of common variations, such as (i) beginning with an introduction comprising additional musical material, (ii) beginning with a chorus instead of the first verse, or (iii) presenting two verses before the first chorus. Common as they are, these variations have reliable effects on the listener's experience. For instance, delaying the arrival of the chorus results in tension and anticipation (e.g., Coldplay's "Yellow"), while leaping straight in to the chorus can provide a sense of exuberance or other driving force (e.g., the Beatles' "She Loves You"). As these examples suggest, there may be some interest in a form shared by a large number of pieces. Presumably one reason the verse-chorus form has proven so enduring is that it strikes a nice balance between unity and variety, but of more interest are (a) the way in which an individual piece (or pieces in a particular genre) *instances* the form (the way that the melodies, phrase structures, harmonies, and so on, embody the form), and (b) ways in which an individual piece (or a particular genre) *departs from* the form. As an example of the former, consider the quiet-verse–loud-chorus pattern common to many grunge songs (e.g., Hole's "Violet"). In comparison to the equalized dynamics and expressive tone across verse and chorus common to both "alternative" rock and punk (both central influences on grunge), this high-contrast approach gives the music an emotional charge, suggesting moody brooding that erupts in rage. As an example of the latter (departures from the form), consider The Beach Boys' "Good Vibrations." The song begins with two iterations of a verse-chorus pair but then this structure is virtually abandoned for three distinct episodes, each introducing new musical material (instrumentation, melodies, rhythms, even meters).

The disorientation of the sudden and extended departure from the established verse-chorus form contributes to the "psychedelic" feel of the song, though the reappearance of chorus material in the third and final episode provides a dose of unity that prevents the song from dissipating into chaos.[39]

The fact that songs have a significant verbal component – the lyrics – doubtless explains in part the formal simplicity of much song. Jeanette Bicknell argues that, as with poetry, the repetition and redundancy in common song forms have their roots in song's history as a kind of oral communication (2015, 1–5). But, as we saw in Chapter 1, the inclusion of words also provides an additional realm of artistic content for song, with the result that a simple musical form can provide a foil for complex lyrics. (Bob Dylan is an obvious example. The reverse might also occur, as "Good Vibrations" perhaps illustrates.) In instrumental music, much more common in classical music than in the popular tradition, we might thus expect more formal complexity.[40] And, indeed, formal analysis of classical music has been at the heart of the theory of Western music since the middle of the nineteenth century. Most people who have played classical music with others, whether in an orchestra or chamber groups, will be familiar with common classical instrumental forms such as *rondo, minuet and trio*, or *theme and variations*. To give a taste to those unfamiliar with it of how form is treated in classical music, however, I will take an example in perhaps the most widely used and highly esteemed single-movement form in the classical tradition: *sonata form* (also known as sonata-allegro form or first-movement form).[41]

Sonata form is a three-part structure comprising (1) an *exposition* (which is often repeated), (2) a *development* section, and (3) the *recapitulation*. The exposition has two main parts: (i) a primary theme (or group of themes) is presented in the tonic key (e.g., G major), and (ii) a secondary, contrasting theme (or group of themes) is presented in another key – paradigmatically the dominant (e.g., D major), though there is often significant interest in (a) an introduction, (b) transitions between the main parts, and (c) a *coda* or tailpiece, which can also serve as a transition to what comes next. In the development, themes from the exposition reappear in various guises (altered melodically and rhythmically) and in different keys or tonal centers, typically ranging further afield than the original tonic and dominant. The recapitulation parallels the exposition in having two main parts: Both themes (or theme groups) are presented once more (along with transition and codas), but this time all the material is presented in the original tonic key.

A well-known example of sonata form is the first movement of Mozart's *Eine kleine Nachtmusik* (*A Little Night-Music*). If you play an instrument, you can, while listening to this piece, play a G-major chord (or just a G) as it begins.[42] When this no longer sounds like the tonic, or home chord, of the melodies you hear, start playing a D-major chord (or a D). Notice that when this begins to sound like the tonic, new melodies are being introduced (the secondary theme-group). When the music returns to G, the exposition is being repeated (unless the repeat is skipped on the recording you're listening to!).[43] When the exposition is over, you'll notice that the music starts to move all over the place harmonically – you'd have to play many different chords to keep up with the key changes through this development section. After less than half the length of the exposition, however, you'll hear the confident return of the opening material in the original tonic – G major – signaling the beginning of the recapitulation. It's even easier to play the tonic along with the recapitulation than with the exposition – you can play a G-major chord (or G) the whole way through, since both groups of themes are now in the home key.

The interest of sonata form itself is often defended in terms of harmonic tension and resolution. The secondary theme-group introduces tension in the exposition by moving away from the home key; the development presents the threat of losing sight of the home key altogether; the recapitulation resolves these tensions by not only returning us to the home key but also bringing the secondary theme-group into the fold of that home key. However, as with verse-chorus form in song, the very fact that the form is repeated in a huge number of different musical works suggests that most of the form's value is not in its standard features but rather in the variation it makes possible, both as a foil (for presenting novel melodic, rhythmic, and harmonic material) and in departures from the textbook version of the form. To give some sense of this I will discuss one small example that draws on the notions of functional harmony and sonata form introduced so far.

Edward Cone (1960) and Joseph Dubiel (2011) both discuss an intriguing feature of the second movement of Beethoven's Piano Sonata no. 30 (op. 109). This short, sonata-form movement alternates between vigor and tentativeness. Though it is in E minor and modulates in the exposition, as is standard, to the dominant (B minor), there is no secondary theme-group to speak of, only a short variation on the primary theme. After a brief development section in which the music seems almost to lose its way, the beginning of the recapitulation is unmistakable. Cone points out that this is partly because the recapitulation "bursts in upon the development" (1960, 42). He argues that one explanation of this abruptness is that Beethoven violates the "rules" of functional harmony in this transition (see Example 4.4). The first chord of the recapitulation (m. 105) is, as one would expect, the tonic (E minor), but the chord that precedes it (m. 104) is not the dominant (B major) that one would expect but rather a *pre-dominant* chord (F-sharp major).[44] It is as if the recapitulation can't wait for the dominant chord for which the pre-dominant prepares us and bursts in a measure early.

Cone points out that this violation of the harmonic grammar is tempered by the fact that the expected dominant does soon show up (at the end of the first phrase of the recapitulation (m. 108)), and that this dominant prepares us for the tonic E-minor chord at the end of the second, "consequent" phrase (m. 112). So one can hear the recapitulation as "catching up" after having briefly got ahead of itself. Dubiel demonstrates that Cone's observations open a treasure

Example 4.4 Beethoven, Piano Sonata no. 30 (op. 109), second movement, mm. 97–113. My interpolation – the grayed-out measure between mm. 104 and 105 – "corrects" the harmonic progression by inserting the dominant chord between the pre-dominant and tonic. This passage begins around 1:22 on the recording on the Spotify playlist for this chapter.

trove of new ways of hearing various aspects of this passage, other parts of the movement and sonata as a whole, and even other works that may be similar in these ways or contrast with them (Dubiel 2011, 527–32). For example, one of the many unusual features of this sonata is that the first movement runs into the second without a break. (Beethoven indicates that the pianist should hold the last chord of the first movement with the sustaining pedal until she begins the second movement.) Dubiel points out that the recapitulation thus recapitulates not just the melodic, rhythmic, and harmonic materials of the primary theme (as with any standard recapitulation), but also the abruptness with which the second movement "bursts in upon" the gentle ending of the first.

4.6 Analysis

4.6.1 The Nature of Analysis

Observations such as those of Cone and Dubiel that I've just reported come from the realm of *music analysis* – a musical analogue of literary interpretation. They are attempts to "explain" the music in some sense, so that readers of the analysis might better understand and evaluate it. Dubiel claims that:

> [t]he ineliminable music-analytic activity … is the drawing of a connection between the structure found by an analysis and someone's experience – actual

or potential – of the music. If we find that we cannot relate a pattern in the music to *a way of hearing the music*, then it is not clear that we should consider the pattern to be part of musical structure.

(2011, 526)

This raises a number of questions. First of all, is the claim true? Stephen Davies argues that music theorists (those who produce analyses) can reasonably be interested in "forms of organization in the musical background that produce no effects on the surface of the music," that is, that are not hearable by any listener (2011d, 126). Davies seems to have in mind the methods by which a composer might create a piece of music, methods that can thus be discovered by, say, studying the score closely, but that cannot be experienced in listening to performances of the piece. Perhaps the order of the notes has been generated by some mathematical formula, for example, or the notes were chosen in part for how the resulting score appears visually rather than how the music sounds when performed. Davies is surely right that such matters can be of interest, but Dubiel also seems right to suggest that the criterion of hearability is so crucial to our conception of music that we should consider the explanation of features that affect our aural experience of the music to be *central* to music analysis. After all, our interest in the non-hearable structures that Davies discusses is presumably parasitic on our interest in all that we can hear in music.

A second question raised by Dubiel's characterization of music analysis is what the nature of the "connection" between musical structure and musical experience is. Mark DeBellis (1991) argues that there are two quite different kinds of connection that music theorists are properly interested in. A *phenomenological* musical structure is one that is heard by the listener.[45] For instance, if you hear the violation of the conventions of functional harmony while listening to the Beethoven example discussed above, that violation is a phenomenological structure (or part of one). At first glance this seems to imply that musical structure (and thus analysis) is subjective, but DeBellis points out that one could develop a dispositional theory, according to which phenomenological musical structures are those hearable by *a certain kind of* (e.g., a competent) *listener*, or hearable in a sense derived from a theory of *musical capacities* (in the same way that we might consider a sentence of a thousand words grammatical, even if no one could actually understand it because of its length). Such a dispositional conception is implicit in much music analysis.[46]

A *causal* musical structure, by contrast, is one that has an effect on a listener's experience, yet is not itself hearable – perhaps by anyone. For instance, according to the highly influential system of music analysis established by Heinrich Schenker, the greatness of works in the classical canon is to be explained in part by their having a deep structure. In a nutshell, Schenker argues that such works have, at the deepest level, a harmonic structure of I–V–I (tonic, dominant, tonic) and a melodic structure descending from the third, fifth, or eighth scale-degree to the first. Schenker's theory, and other theories of deep musical structure, have been criticized for a number of reasons.[47] The criticism relevant to understanding DeBellis's notion of a causal structure is that these deep structures *cannot be heard* – by anyone – while listening to the music. DeBellis's reply is that if this deep structure affects our listening experience in some way – for instance, causing us to experience the music as unified (in a way we would not if it did not have that deep structure) – it is still relevant to an analysis of the piece, in Dubiel's sense of uncovering a connection between the music's structure and the listener's experience, even if we do not, or even cannot, hear that structure.

One significant difference between analyses that posit phenomenological and causal structures is the way in which one might test them. The test of a phenomenological structure must primarily be phenomenological: If no one can hear the posited phenomenological structure, it isn't there. One could carry out an "external" such test by performing a psychological experiment, but for the most part this is not how music theorists have operated. Rather, they have tested "internally," by examining their own experiences of music. The test of a causal structure, by contrast, cannot be internal, precisely because what makes the structure causal is that it has its effect independently of whether or not it is perceived;[48] one must instead perform a psychological experiment (S. Davies 2011d, 124–6; cf. DeBellis 1991, 389). DeBellis, for instance, cites an experiment in which people displayed no preference for music that begins and ends in the same key over music that begins and ends in different keys. He concludes that this is evidence against the idea that large-scale harmonic form plays a causal (let alone phenomenological) structural role (1991, 388).

Kendall Walton (1993) defends a conception of music analysis that DeBellis cites approvingly (1991, 389). Walton draws an extended analogy between understanding humor (e.g., jokes) and music. He points out that though there is doubtless (at least in principle) a science of humor – anthropological or neuropsychological explanations of why people laugh at certain kinds of things – this is not what we're interested in when we want to "get" a joke, that is, to understand why people find it funny. The science of humor takes the joke as a *cause* of the audience's laughter, while someone who wants to understand the joke takes it as the *intentional object* of the audience's laughter – something that the audience experiences in a certain way. To understand a joke you don't get requires employing your "sense of humor" empathetically, putting yourself in the audience's shoes (Walton 1993, 32–5). An analysis of a piece of music is like an explanation of a joke; it attempts to make explicit how the features of one's experience (e.g., the harmonic progressions in the music, or the recounting of what happens when the horse walks into the bar) have the results they do (e.g., surprise without bewilderment, or amusement). This may result in an experience of *recognition*, when you come to see why you react as you do to a piece of music or a joke you already "get," or *realization*, when you come to understand (some aspect of) a piece of music or a joke that previously mystified you (Walton 1993, 35–42).

Both Walton (1993, 42) and DeBellis (1991, 389) argue that our perceptual experience of music – what we hear in it – is quite malleable and conceptually informed (e.g., by what we believe about how the music is structured). Thus a structure that *was* merely causal can *become* phenomenological when it is drawn to our attention by a music theorist. But if, as both DeBellis and Davies suggest, there are causal structures in music that *cannot* be experienced, they will not be amenable to this process.

4.6.2 The Necessity of Analysis

Dubiel, following DeBellis, identifies this process of "conceptualizing what we hear" – the shaping of our perception by concepts – as one of the primary benefits of music analysis (2011, 527–8). While such sentiments are widely accepted by philosophers of music, more contentious is the question of whether such application of concepts is *essential* for musical understanding. The debate is usually framed in terms of whether "formal musical education" – such as instruction in music theory (functional harmony, formal analysis, etc.) or "ear training" (learning how to aurally identify scale degrees, chords, etc.) – is essential for some sort of baseline musical understanding.[49] One problem with the debate is a lack of clarity about what this baseline is. Everyone agrees that musical understanding comes in degrees and that formal musical education deepens one's understanding of music. Though he doesn't put it in these terms, DeBellis could be interpreted as arguing that someone without a formal musical education lacks baseline musical understanding because he is incapable of having a certain kind of musical experience, namely one in which a music-theoretic concept becomes "fused" with his perceptual experience of music to which that concept applies (1995, 126–9).[50] Consider our Beethoven example once more (Example 4.4). Alex, enculturated in Western music, recognizes the Beethoven piece as music and would know that something was wrong if the music stopped at the end of measure 104 or 105. Blair, who is more familiar with classical music in particular, notices that there's something sudden about the way the music moves from measure 104 to 105. Casey also hears this and, having studied the piece in a music-theory class, knows that the suddenness is due to the chord in measure 104's being a pre-dominant that is followed by the tonic rather than the dominant; however, Casey can't *hear* the chord in 104 *as* a pre-dominant. Drew has taken more music theory, along with ear training, and hears the suddenness of the transition from measure 104 to 105 as a pre-dominant followed immediately by a tonic. It is only Drew's experience that is one of "fusion," in DeBellis's terminology, since only she both *possesses* the concept of a pre-dominant (like Casey) and (unlike Casey) is able to *apply* it in perception.

Stephen Davies argues that DeBellis does not give enough credit to "ordinary" listeners, that is, those who have no formal musical education. He claims that such listeners can develop the relevant concepts through immersion in a given musical tradition. They will not develop the same theoretical vocabulary, of course, but they may develop their own "folk" terminology or identify the relevant musical objects and events in other ways, such as "the chords that sound like 'Amen' at the end of a hymn" (what a music theorist might call a "plagal cadence") or "here the tune is turned upside down" ("melodic inversion" to a theorist) (S. Davies 2011d, 103, 104). The same applies to large-scale musical forms, according to Davies:

> More extended or complex forms, such as ... sonata form, may be harder to grasp, but I see no reason to assume they will be beyond the command of the serious but untutored listener, who becomes conscious of them as patterns common to (movements of) a number of works.
>
> (2011d, 105)

Note that this dispute between DeBellis and Davies is not over whether or not the application of concepts such as *plagal cadence* is essential to some given level of musical understanding, but rather over whether formal musical education is essential for acquiring such abilities. Both parties to the dispute would surely agree that whether we use the same *term* to stand for this concept is beside the point. Moreover, Davies acknowledges that formal musical education "might be the fastest method" for acquiring such skills (2011d, 105). The dispute, then, is really over whether formal education is (at least practically) *essential* for such skill acquisition.[51]

Erkki Huovinen thinks that it is. He gives a relatively simple example – a melody in C major that later appears in D-flat major an octave lower – and then outlines how four different listeners might describe the music:

> Listener A understands [only] that he is hearing the "same melody" as before. ... Listener B understands that he is hearing the "same melody" as before, but now "lower." ... Listener C understands that he is hearing the "same melody" as before, but now "higher." ... Listener D understands that he is hearing the "same melody" as before, but now "transposed down a major seventh."
>
> (2008, 324–5)

Huovinen argues that there are three different levels of musical understanding on display here, with listeners B and C at the same level. Both B and C describe the music accurately; the music is lower in the sense that the melody has been transposed *down* a major seventh, but it is higher in the sense that the key of D-flat major is a semitone (half-step) *above* the key of C major. But understanding this, according to Huovinen, requires acquiring distinct concepts such as *pitch* and *key* (whatever terms we might label them with) that are highly unlikely to be acquired without formal musical education.

Davies might reply that Huovinen is simply wrong about the abilities of listeners to acquire sophisticated music-theoretic concepts in the absence of formal education, but at this point it is difficult to see how we could advance the debate without turning from philosophy to psychology. Alternatively (though it seems unlikely that Davies himself would make this move) one might reply that the kinds of concepts that could not be acquired by an untutored listener are simply not part of baseline musical understanding, but belong to the rarefied experience of a music connoisseur (cf. Huovinen 2008, 327–8). Developing this reply would require not only establishing the range of concepts typically acquirable without musical education, but also getting clear on the vague matter, identified earlier, of what exactly is to be included in "baseline" musical understanding. We cannot pursue this issue any further here, but note that figuring out what counts as "baseline musical understanding" seems likely to involve determining what is ultimately *valuable* about our experience of music, since if someone's experience of the music excludes what is most or centrally valuable about music, she could fairly be charged with lacking baseline musical understanding. It is to the topic of the value of music that we turn next.

Questions

What is the difference between *frequency* and *pitch*?

Explain the two most promising theories of musical (pitch) space and movement, in your view. Then argue for the superiority of one over the other.

What does it mean to say that rhythm and meter are "ineliminably phenomenological"? Is this claim correct?

Explain the harmonic terms "tonic," "dominant," and "pre-dominant." Why are these called terms in *functional* harmony?

What difference does it make whether we call music (or some aspect of it) "a language"? Is music (or some aspect of it) a language?

What is "large-scale musical form"? What, if anything, plays the role of *content* in such form?

What is an *analysis* of a piece of music, and what is the point of such analyses?

What kinds of musical experience (if any) is formal musical education essential for? How important are these kinds of experience in the context of musical experience as a whole?

Notes

1 We will consider the claim that *rhythm* is not exclusively musical in §4.2, below.

2 See Chapter 1 for a fuller version of this argument. It bears repeating, because of the concerns of philosophers such as Aaron Ridley discussed in that chapter, that nothing evaluative is implied by this. Good essay-length philosophical introductions to literary interpretation include Currie 2003 and Stecker 2013. An excellent book devoted to the philosophy of literary and legal interpretation is Stecker 2003a. The first part of Gracyk 2001 (13–80) is devoted to developing a theory of interpretation for rock music that takes both music and lyrics into account.

3 In fact, there are *many* senses in which one can "interpret" a musical piece or performance. For discussion of five such senses, see S. Davies 2002a; for even broader application of the term, see Thom 2007.

4 Jerrold Levinson (1993) discusses these two different senses of musical "interpretation" and the relationships that might hold between them.

5 The recent popularity of Israel Kamakawiwoʻoleʼs ukulele-accompanied performance of this song demands that I specify that I'm talking about the original version, sung by Judy Garland in *The Wizard of Oz*. We will consider issues raised by the puzzle of how two performances with different notes (and hence different higher-level properties) could be performances of the same piece in Chapters 6–9.

6 There's nothing deeply mysterious about these different senses of sameness. Consider how many letters there are in the name "Anna." There are (i) four different letters if you're counting each individual (or "token") letter, (ii) two different letters if you're counting each kind (or "type") of letter (i.e., each "letter of the alphabet"), and (iii) three different letters if you're distinguishing between lower- and upper-case letter types.

7 The psycho-physical details are complicated. See Thompson 2013, 123–7.

8 I do not mean to deny that there is some connection between the simplicity of the mathematical relationship between octaves and the perceptual phenomenon of octave equivalence. My point is only that the mathematical relationship alone cannot explain the phenomenon.

9 If you have a piano keyboard to hand, a simple way to generate a pentatonic scale is to play six consecutive black keys.

10 As with octave equivalence, patterns of similarities and differences between scales from various cultures suggest connections between quite general features of sound, our perception of it, and the phenomenon of pitch (Stevens & Byron 2009, 14–17; Stainsby & Cross 2009, 54–6; Thompson 2013, 127–31).

11 This is why I dub the theory scient*istic*, rather than scient*ific*. None of this implies that science has nothing to offer in understanding the phenomena of musical space and movement. For a respectable theory of pitch space that draws heavily on the cognitive science of pitch, see Nussbaum 2015, 502–13.

12 A conventionalist theory could perhaps be developed in the direction of a metaphorical, eliminativist, or imaginative theory (all to be introduced shortly), depending on the role the association is supposed to play in a broader theory of our experience of musical space and movement.

13 Stephen Davies (1994, 232) attributes this view to Robin Maconie, though I can't find Maconie's endorsement of it. In his typically enigmatic and elliptical way, Maconie says only that "[t]here are acoustical reasons for such associations" between musical and "real world" space terms (1990, 21). Carroll C. Pratt (1931, 48) attributes something like this view (or perhaps an eliminativist version of it) to the composer Hector Berlioz.

14 Roger Scruton (1983, 81 n. 7) attributes something like this view to Carroll C. Pratt, though it seems to me that Pratt (1931, 47–52) rejects this view as simplistic.

15 Timbre has its physical basis in the complexity of the sound wave along with its attack and decay profiles. For an overview, see Taylor and Campbell 2001, §6.

16 Imaginative theories of musical space and movement have been floated by Rafael de Clercq (2007), Saam Trivedi (2011b), and Andrew Kania (2015).

17 Compare this thin notion with that of the "persona" imagined to be expressing its emotions through the music according to the imagination theory of musical expressiveness (Chapter 2, §2.5).

18 As far as I can tell, Walton does not defend *any* particular theory of musical space and movement. The views I attribute to him in what follows come from his discussion of the issue in the context of considering instrumental music's "abstractness" (Walton 1988a and 1994, especially 53–4).

19 The *downbeat* is the first, or strongest, or most salient beat in a measure or bar. (A measure, for our purposes, is roughly the shortest metrical structure that repeats – the division of the music represented by the repetition of the sequence of numbers when you count along to a piece (e.g., "1, 2, 3" for a waltz or "1, 2, 3, 4" for a march). Measures are typically represented in scores, but since scores are primarily practical tools for performers, the notated rhythm and meter does not always match the meter or rhythm as we perceive it, as illustrated by the examples in the main text.) The *upbeat* (or *pick-up* or *anacrusis*) is a rhythmic element that occurs just before the downbeat and is heard as "leading to" the downbeat. The first two notes of "Happy Birthday" (sung to the word "Happy") constitute an upbeat, while the first syllable of "birthday" is the downbeat. Note that a kind of suspense is created when you sing "Happy" slowly, since our knowledge that these notes are an upbeat leads us to anticipate the downbeat. (Slowing down the notes of "birthday" has a very different effect.)

20 The *subdivisions* of a beat are the more frequent "mini-beats" that we hear in a meter. For instance, if you count "one and, two and, three and, four and" to a typical rock song, the numbers you count are beats and the "ands" are subdivisions of those beats. Beats can be subdivided in different ways. For instance, in example 4.2 each beat is subdivided into three ("one-and-a, two-and-a, three-and-a").

21 *Syncopation* is a phenomenon in which metrically weak beats (e.g., the second and third beats in 3/4 or waltz time) are emphasized and strong beats (e.g., the first beat of a measure) are de-emphasized in a systematic fashion. In the case of "Pyramid Song" the emphasis is simply a matter of a chord being played on the weak beat (or subdivision) in question, and the de-emphasis a matter of no chord being played.

22 Note that, since the opening phrase of "Pyramid Song" is repeated many times, although I have notated the "rubato" version as ending with a single 2/4 measure, one could notate it either entirely in 2/4, or entirely in 4/4 with every second phrase beginning on the third beat of the measure.

23 Roholt offers only a theory of grooves in particular, not rhythm in general, but the criticism here applies to his theory of groove perception as well as a generalization of it to other rhythmic phenomena.

24 This hypothesis still seems to rule out rhythmic understanding for people with various forms of lifelong paralysis. The musical experiences of people with paralysis is little discussed, even in the disability-studies literature. For example, it is largely absent from Howe et al. 2016; but see Straus 2011, 116–22.

25 One tricky thing about this illustration is that, if you are singing unaccompanied, you may yet hear "in your head" the accompaniment resolving harmonically, reducing the unsatisfyingness (though not completely!).

26 Bigand and Poulin-Charronnat 2009 provides a partial overview.

27 For our purposes, a chord is simply a collection of simultaneous pitches that plays a functional harmonic role.

28 This is not the place to explain all the music-theoretic details, such as how to "build" a chord on a given note in a certain key. For more, see any good music-theory textbook, e.g., Kostka, Payne, and Almén 2018.

29 In the widely used Roman-numeral notation I'm using, upper-case letters represent *major* chords, lower-case letters *minor* chords, and the "degree" symbol *diminished* chords.

30 It doesn't matter how much truth you've got to share; if the only three chords you know how to play are B major, C major, and C-sharp major, you're not going to be writing a country-music hit anytime soon. Your music career is equally unpromising if you can play C-, F-, and G-major chords flawlessly, but you never know which one you should end your songs on.

31 These are gross simplifications of very complex musical developments. Two large complications for discussing such developments over the last hundred years or so are (i) the self-conscious rule-breaking of much avant-garde classical music, e.g., Schoenberg's deliberate and highly influential "emancipation of the dissonance," and (ii) the splintering of most musical traditions into a huge variety of subcultures.

32 I am particularly indebted, in the following discussion, to S. Davies 1994, 1–49; Jackendoff 2011; and Higgins 2012, 78–105. See also Scruton 1997, 171–210.

33 For helpful parallel considerations of film as language, see Currie 1993 and Gaut 2010, 51–60.

34 Note that "function" here has a meaning quite different from that in "functional harmony." The meaning of a sentence is a *function* of the meanings of its words in the same sense that the output of a mathematical formula is a function of its input. Harmonic functions, recall, are more like *roles* that chords play.

35 The best known attempt to provide a theory of such a musical "vocabulary" is in Cooke 1959. For critical discussion, see S. Davies 1994, 25–7.

36 Of course, you might draw the conclusion that pictures and winks are languages, too, but this would destroy the theoretical usefulness of the concept of *language*; the point of the original claim that music is language was that music and language are significantly similar *in ways that are not shared by other phenomena.*

37 I briefly consider Schenkerian analysis again in §4.6.1.

38 The target of a "formal analysis" is typically a single, continuous piece of music, such as a single song or symphonic movement, rather than collections of such pieces, such as albums, concerts, or symphonies, though such formal analyses often play a role in an interpretation of these larger musical entities, and one can analyze just part of a song or movement.

39 For more about the structure of "Good Vibrations," see Covach and Flory 2015, 253–5; for a deeper music-theoretic analysis, see Harrison 1997, 41–5.

40 Similar considerations might explain the complexity of vocal works with extremely well-known texts, such as choral settings of the Christian mass. The centrality of improvisation to instrumental jazz complicates application of this argument to that music. See Chapter 8.

41 Despite its names, this form (i) is no more common in sonatas (multi-movement works typically for one or two instruments) than in other kinds of works; (ii) is commonly found in movements of multi-movement works other than the first; and (iii) has nothing to do with the music's tempo. It is surprising that the form has not become known as something like "standard" or "common" form, but the name "sonata form" is firmly entrenched, and I will follow this usage.

42 If you read music, two useful schematic diagrams appear as examples 2 and 3 in Webster 2001, which is a more detailed introduction to sonata form.

43 The beginning of each theme group is notated in Chapter 10, Example 10.1.

44 Those familiar with more music theory than I've had the chance to introduce here will recognize this chord as a *secondary dominant* – the dominant (F-sharp major) of the dominant (B major) of E minor.

45 DeBellis uses the term "intentional" rather than "phenomenological."

46 Dubiel, by contrast, argues that music analysis is more "subjective and relative" than most practitioners suppose, and thus music theorists ought to pay greater attention to the variety of people's experience of music (2011, 533–4).

47 A reasonably accessible introduction to Schenkerian analysis is in Bent and Pople 2018, §II.4. For philosophical discussion of Schenker's and similar theories, see Kivy 1990, 124–45; Scruton 1997, 309–42, 392–437; and S. Davies 2011d, 120–6.

48 Of course, the phenomenological *effect* of a causal structure is perceived, but we may be unable to tell whether it is caused by the posited unperceived structure.

49 The "formal" in "formal education" refers to *formality*, not musical form.

50 Evidence against this interpretation is the fact that DeBellis characterizes a listener who does experience fusion as "expert" rather than, say, "competent." But he seems to imply that the less-than-expert listener misses much that is valuable in music (cf. S. Davies 2011d, 103 n. 19).

51 By "practically essential" here, I mean something like the essentiality of formal mathematical education to understanding calculus. Calculus was developed by people. It thus seems that *in principle* a very smart person with no mathematical education might independently develop mathematics, up to and including the calculus, from scratch. But, let's face it, this is never in fact going to happen. If *that's* the kind of possibility Davies is appealing to, he's debating a straw man.

Further Reading

Chapter 2 of Roger Scruton's *Aesthetics of Music* (1997, 19–79), is a detailed discussion of many musical elements, including pitch, rhythm, melody, harmony, and timbre, amply illustrated with musical examples. Stephen Davies considers a range of philosophical issues raised by elements of musical works, including pitches, melodies, harmonies, rhythms, and meters, in Chapter 2 of *Musical Works and Performances* (2001, 45–58). *The Philosophy of Rhythm* (Cheyne, Hamilton, & Paddison 2019) is a collection of new philosophical essays on rhythm.

Jerrold Levinson (1997) has influentially questioned the value of large-scale formal structure in works of classical music, arguing instead for "concatenationism" – the view that baseline musical understanding consists in following the musical and emotional qualities of passages of music (and transitions between them) that are short enough to be apprehended in a momentary experience. Peter Kivy (2001), in response, has been the staunchest defender of "architectonicism." Levinson replies in 2006b. Other notable discussions include a symposium in the journal *Music Perception* (vol. 16, 1999, 463–94); S. Davies 2011d, 95–9; and Huovinen 2013.

5   The Value of Music

Overview

We've spent the last three chapters considering the form and content of music because it is in those features that many philosophers locate music's value. In this chapter, after addressing some general questions about musical value, we turn to squarely confront the question of whether and, if so, how these features make music so important to us.

What is the value of music? This question can be interpreted in many different ways. For one thing, there is ambiguity in what "music" refers to. Most philosophers have discussed the value of *pieces* of music – compositions, performances, and recordings. But we might equally well ask about the value of *taking an interest in music in general* or the value of *having a vibrant musical community* (S. Davies 1987, 207–12). Perhaps the former is valuable because it makes a substantial contribution to flourishing as a person; the latter might be valuable for society in general. These values may be more or less distinctively musical. Perhaps you would flourish just as well by taking an interest in crochet; perhaps societies with vibrant theatrical communities but no music are just as well off as those with vibrant musical communities but no theater. But suppose for the sake of argument that this is *not* the case, that music is essential to some of these benefits. It might still be that the *quality* of the music that one listens to, or that one's community produces, is independent of these benefits. That is, perhaps these musical values are independent of the value of the particular pieces of music appreciated by the individual or produced within the community. Perhaps a vibrant community of talentless death-metal enthusiasts is just as beneficial to society as a vibrant community of top-notch jazz players. Or perhaps some middle-ground position is correct, for instance, that striving for (if not necessarily attaining) musical excellence is essential to the benefits of a vibrant musical community. Despite the interest and difficulty of these questions, in this chapter I will focus on the value of pieces of music.

So much for what "music" means in *What is the value of music?* What about the "value" part? If you ask someone to assess the value of your coffee table, say, they are likely to assume that you are enquiring about its economic value. And pieces of music obviously have such value: You might pay 99 cents for a track on iTunes but not 99 dollars. I am not concerned here with this kind of value; my focus, rather, is on the values that underwrite such economic value. For instance, you might be willing to *pay more* to hear *really good* musicians play live. This kind of relationship also seems to hold between some other kinds of less and more fundamental or distinctively musical value. Other ways in which music is valuable include that it can alert you that someone is calling you (when your ringtone sounds), wake you up (via your phone's alarm), or help put your baby to sleep (when you sing a lullaby). Some of these functions could be performed by things other than music. The sound of a gunshot might be an even more effective way for your phone to get your attention. But presumably you prefer your chosen ringtone to the sound of a gunshot in part because you enjoy hearing music more than you enjoy hearing gunshots. Moreover, you presumably prefer hearing the particular piece of music you've selected for these functions more than the thousands of others you might have chosen. So these values that music shares with other things (the capacity to wake you up, etc.) seem to be more or less closely linked, as is its economic value, with something more distinctively or fundamentally musical, something to do with the appreciation of the music *for its own sake*.

5.1   General Issues about Musical Value

5.1.1   Intrinsic, Instrumental, and Inherent Value

What does it mean to value something "for its own sake" or "in itself"? The comparison of money with music is helpful here. Money is clearly valuable for what it can get us. A twenty-dollar bill is only valuable (as money)[1] because other people agree that it has a certain exchange value; you are willing to accept twenty-dollar bills as payment for your labor because you are confident that they will be accepted in turn at the supermarket, say, in exchange for food. The value of money thus resides not in the money itself, but rather in what one can get with it. We are unconcerned for our financial well-being when the government decides to redesign the twenty-dollar bill, but may become concerned when it adopts policies that result in our twenty-dollar bill buying four loaves of bread instead of five. The standard philosophical terms for this kind of value are *instrumental* or *extrinsic* value, since money is valuable as a *means* to some further end, outside itself. But if money is instrumentally valuable,

valuable in virtue of the value of the bread (etc.) we can get with it, where does the value of the bread reside? Well, it helps keep us alive, for one thing. But what is the value of being alive? Since this isn't a book about the meaning of life, let me just observe that this buck-passing chain of value can't plausibly go on forever. Nor does the chain seem likely to be finite but circular. Suppose someone claimed that the value of being alive is that it allows you to eat more bread, and the value of bread is that it keeps you alive. We could fairly object that this person has not, after all, identified where the value of bread or life ultimately comes from or resides. So not all value can be instrumental or extrinsic; the buck-passing chain of value must stop at some ultimate source of value.[2] Suppose, for the sake of argument, that we decide that the value-buck stops with *being alive*. Then, unlike everything else in the chain (money, bread, etc.), the value of being alive would not reside in something else. Being alive would thus be not extrinsically or instrumentally valuable, but *intrinsically* valuable, valuable *in itself* or *for its own sake*.[3]

One might thus suppose that music's distinctive, fundamental value is its *intrinsic* value (as opposed to money's fundamentally *instrumental* value). A piece of music *may* be instrumentally valuable (e.g., as a way to wake you up) but its distinctive or fundamental value is the value it has in itself. One problem with this idea is that the value of music we are getting at seems to reside in our *experiences* of it (or its potential for such experiences). The music and our experience of it are two different things, thus the value of music turns out to be instrumental after all; its value is *as a means* to valuable experiences (which may in turn be valuable instrumentally or intrinsically).[4] On the other hand, this way of cashing out music's value doesn't seem to make it *as* instrumental as, say, the economic value of money. We have no trouble imagining a coin replacing the twenty-dollar bill; anything will do to play the role of this unit of exchange. But it is harder, if not impossible, to imagine what could replace Billie Holiday's 1939 recording of "Strange Fruit" as a means to the experience of listening to that recording with understanding.[5] For this reason, we might appeal to the intermediate category of *inherent* value (Stecker 1997, 251–8, following C.I. Lewis 1946, 390–2). The value of Holiday's recording is in the experiences it affords, so the value is not intrinsic to the recording, yet those experiences essentially involve this particular means – the valuable experience is one *of this particular performance*. In this respect, the recording's value, albeit instrumental, is unlike the instrumental value of money, medications, and mousetraps, each of which we would be happy to replace with something else quite different, provided it achieved the same ends.[6]

Even if we agree that music is inherently valuable as a means to certain experiences, we might yet ask about the value of those experiences: Are they valuable for their own sakes or as means to further things of value? Historically, a lot of importance has been claimed for a certain kind of experience, particularly of artworks and nature, that is valuable for its own sake: *aesthetic experience*. There is little agreement about what, beyond being intrinsically valuable, makes an experience aesthetic; yet such an account is essential if, as is plausible, other kinds of experiences (e.g., bodily pleasure) are intrinsically valuable. According to the traditional, Kantian theory, an aesthetic experience is a *perceptual* experience of the *formal features* of an object, in which one takes *disinterested pleasure*, that is, pleasure independent of the object's further, instrumental value to the perceiver.[7] Each of these aspects of the theory is questionable, however. Most glaringly, our experience of some artforms, notably literature, is not perceptual.[8] And many theorists have argued that we can have aesthetic experiences of non-formal features, such as the colors and representational content of a painting or the timbres and expressiveness of a song. Finally, there seem to be clear examples of aesthetic experiences that are neither disinterested nor pleasurable. For instance, a critic may aim to experience a work aesthetically precisely so that he can report on the work's aesthetic value and thus get paid – and the work may be excellent, yet painfully discordant. There is no need to pursue the nature of aesthetic experience any further here. For our purposes, we can proceed on the assumption that, at the very least, an aesthetic experience must be an intrinsically valuable experience of some external object's features – not just basic perceptual features (e.g., color, shape, timbre, and loudness), but also higher-level perceptual features (e.g., pitches, melodies, and expressive or representational content), and non-perceptual features (e.g., linguistic meaning) (Stecker 2010, 39–64, 225–6).

As we will see below, many philosophers attribute not just aesthetic or other intrinsic value to the experience of music, but also *instrumental* value (because the experience adds to our knowledge, for instance). To sum up this subsection: To the extent that music is valuable solely for the experiences it affords, it is not intrinsically, but instrumentally valuable. Nonetheless, because the value of those experiences is closely tied to the particular features of individual works, performances, and recordings, we may classify it as *inherent* value. But this raises the question of the value of the experiences themselves. We have seen that such experiences may, but need not, be intrinsically valuable. Thus music's value could be inherent, but in virtue of an experience that is itself instrumentally valuable.

5.1.2 Monism and Pluralism about Musical Value

For much of the history of philosophy of art, philosophers offered *monistic* theories of musical (and artistic) value. That is, they argued that there was a *single* value that all music (or art) embodied or properly strove to embody. For instance, an *aesthetic theorist* might argue that music's (and art's) sole value is in the aesthetic experiences it affords. Such theories are now widely rejected. Most philosophers of music and the other arts are *pluralists* about musical and artistic value; they think that music and art may properly aim for, and possess, not just aesthetic value but many different values.[9] (This is one reason we need not pursue the nature of aesthetic experience any further for our purposes: If we are not limiting music's value to the aesthetic, it is less important that we precisely delimit such value.)

Stephen Davies defends what we might call a *weak* pluralism. He argues that the inherent value of the particular experiences a piece of music makes possible must be the *primary* (if not *sole*) value of music, because otherwise musicians wouldn't bother putting so much time and effort into creating music that affords such experiences (1987, 198–9).[10] But while this is plausible for both the pop songs sampled for ringtones and classical music written for concert performance, it's not as plausible for *functional* music such as lullabies, work songs, and religious music, nor perhaps for music that contributes to hybrid artforms such as film, musical theater, and ballet. Consider Noël Carroll's theory that much film music functions as "modifying music," that is, music that inflects what else we see and hear in the film (1988, 213–25). A simple kind of example is where the music shows us, through its expressive properties, what a character is feeling. As Carroll observes, the music and other elements of the film often bolster one another in such cases – the images provide intentional objects for the emotions, which the music itself lacks, while the music supplies emotional specificity to the images. It is plausible that the primary value of such music is its (non-inherent) *instrumental* value, as a means to providing a good overall cinematic experience, rather than the inherent value of the experience the music alone affords. The same kinds of consideration suggest that the primary value of music in other hybrid forms is instrumental. Still, such music is often *also* inherently valuable (for the sake of the particular experiences it affords by itself), and even if it isn't, to the extent that it contributes to a hybrid artistic experience that is inherently valuable, it may be ultimately amenable to the kind of theory of value that Davies defends.

Functional music such as lullabies, work songs, and religious music is not so amenable to Davies's theory. For such music is not created primarily to contribute to a more comprehensive artistic experience, but rather for some other end – to help put babies to sleep, coordinate action and distract people from tedious work, or glorify god (Wolterstorff 2015, 255–72). We should expect, then, that people put time and effort into making such music not (primarily) for the value of the experiences its appreciation affords, but for its effectiveness in fulfilling these various functions. Moreover, it is possible that such functions might promote the creation of music that is *less* inherently valuable. Effective lullabies, for instance, are not harmonically inventive; effective work songs, like much music written for dancing to, are typically monotonous in their length and rhythmic repetitiveness (when appreciated independently of their function); and so on.

The problem here seems to arise from Davies's assumption that *all music is art.* Consider this summary of his argument:

> it is my contention that an aesthetic interest taken in a musical work *qua* music has a *special* importance among the interests that might be taken in musical works, for, were such an interest never exercised, music would be neither written nor performed, or it would be subsumed under some concept other than that of art.

> (S. Davies 1987, 198)

Elsewhere in this essay, Davies makes clear that by "an aesthetic interest taken in a musical work *qua* music" he means an interest taken in it for the experiences it affords (1987, 199–207). The last sentence of this quotation, then, could be read as implying that music *not* intended primarily for appreciation of the experiences it affords is not art (and possibly not, strictly speaking, *music*). Now, one might simply embrace this implication. Though few would be willing to deny that lullabies and so on are *music*, one might defend a narrow definition of *art* that restricts it to things primarily valuable for the experiences they afford. But that would still fail to establish the conclusion Davies argues for, since now the conclusion would be not that the primary value of *music*, but only that the primary value of *art music*, is the inherent value of the experiences it affords. (And, given the way art music is defined according to this strategy, that conclusion is unsurprising, not to say question-begging.) Davies would thus require a different argument if he wanted to show that this is the primary value of *all* music. Alternatively, he could drop the idea that there is a single, primary value of all music and investigate instead the different values of different kinds of music, thus retreating from weak to strong pluralism.

Most philosophers of art these days, including Davies himself, have a more capacious conception of art.[11] That is, they prefer to include things such as lullabies, work songs, and religious music under the umbrella of art, despite such music's having primary functions other than the provision of inherently valuable appreciative experiences. For instance, in his introduction to the philosophy of art, Davies proposes that something whose primary function is not aesthetic "is a work of art if its artistic and aesthetic features contribute significantly to its primary function" (2016, 192). Such a view might provide the beginnings of a different argument that the primary value of art music is its aesthetic value, since such value is connected to the primary function of such works. But note that, first, Davies's proposed condition is only sufficient, not necessary, for something's being art. Thus it leaves open the possibility of completely non-aesthetic art music. And, second, though this casts the net of art music more widely, it still allows for music that is not art at all. Perhaps some doorbells, work chants, and so on, are music, yet have no aesthetic function or value at all. One might still argue for aesthetic value as the single primary value of art, but that would now require showing why the values of these non-aesthetic musics (and the functions they serve) are subsidiary to, or outweighed by, music's aesthetic value.

Despite the room left open in the above discussion for a plurality of uses for – and thus values of – music, for the remainder of this chapter I restrict the discussion to the inherent value of music, that is, the value of our experiences of pieces of music in all their individuality. (Recall that inherent value allows for such experiences to be intrinsically or instrumentally valuable.) I impose this restriction in part because that is where the lion's share of the philosophical work on music's value has been done. But it is also undeniable that almost all music that has a primary function other than rewarding appreciation is also imbued with *some* properties that reward appreciation. I will consider such value the value of music *as art*.[12]

Implicit in this last formulation (and the above discussion more generally) is the idea that to evaluate something is to evaluate it *from some perspective* or *as some kind of thing*.[13] For instance, the later Harry Potter books are better *as doorstops* than the earlier ones. That's a true, objective evaluation of them but it's irrelevant to most discussions of how good the Harry Potter books are, since those discussions are clearly (if implicitly) about how good the books are *as literature* (i.e., as art). In what follows, I will usually talk simply of "the value of music"; the qualification that I am talking of music's value *as art* (as glossed above) should be taken as read.

5.1.3 Subjective, Objective, and Intersubjective Value

Different people may value their experiences of music for all sorts of different reasons, and some take this to be evidence that matters of musical value are subjective, that is, that the value of music for a given person is simply what that person values in their experience of the music, which may be quite independent of what anyone else values in their experience – even of the same music. If this is right, then the question of music's value *period*, without relativizing it to some particular person or people, doesn't really make sense. It would be like asking whether people – in general – should drink lemon or peppermint tea. How could we expect an answer to this question in the absence of information about a particular (kind of) drinker – for example, whether they prefer lemon or peppermint, are allergic to either substance, and so on?

Like other foundational issues about values, the question of whether musical value is subjective is a difficult one. Because many people assume, on the contrary, that it is *simple* – the obvious answer being that the value of music is subjective – my aim in this subsection is to suggest, first, that the reasons many people take musical value to be subjective are not decisive and, second, that there are some good reasons for thinking that musical value is not simply subjective.[14]

We've already seen one reason why the fact that people value music for a variety of reasons doesn't imply that music's value is subjective. People might value mousetraps for all sorts of different reasons (as engineering marvels, as mementos of their childhood, as metaphors for the dangers of eating too much cheese), but that doesn't show that the value of mousetraps *as mousetraps* is anything other than their potential for trapping mice. If some of the ways in which people value music are not valuings of music *as art*, then, they are irrelevant to our current enquiry.

Another reason one might think that the value of music is subjective is that people "have different values" when it comes to music, as when it comes to many other things. But people have different beliefs about whether New Zealand is part of Australia or whether Barack Obama was born in the United States of America; that doesn't show that these matters are subjective. We all have true beliefs and false beliefs, and often we disagree with one another about which are which. There's a fact of the matter about New Zealand's political status and about the former President's birthplace. Thus, when we say that people have different values, if all we mean is that they have different *beliefs* about what's valuable, then this is no evidence that musical, or any other, value is subjective. Some people might simply be wrong about music's value.

So much for a couple of bad arguments for the subjectivity of music's value. A more compelling reason for thinking that music's value is subjective returns to the basic idea that its value resides in people's experiences of it. It seems obvious that different people find different musical experiences rewarding or, to put the same point another way, that one person might find the experience of a given piece of music – as art – rewarding while another person might find it unrewarding or downright unpleasant. It's one thing to disagree with someone's *belief* or *theory* of the value of music; it's quite another to deny their claims that the *experience* they have while listening to a particular piece of music is rewarding or unrewarding.

Those who resist the idea that musical value is subjective may respond to this kind of argument by pointing to the equally undeniable fact that people often give *reasons* for their value claims about music (and much else). If a friend doesn't understand why you like a certain piece or kind of music, you might draw your friend's attention to the aspects of the music that you think make listening to it worthwhile – the surrealism of the lyrics of Bob Dylan's "Ballad of a Thin Man," the way the expressive longing of Billie Holiday's singing invests the banal lyrics of "What's New?" with deep emotion, or the way the complex meter of Radiohead's "2+2=5" contributes to its sense of unease. This kind of dialogue suggests that when we evaluate music we implicitly assume that other people ought to evaluate the same music in the same way, just as when we evaluate an action for its morality.[15] And our provision of the reasons that we find the music good or bad suggests that we think our interlocutor may be missing some relevant information – perhaps they haven't realized that the Radiohead song is in an unusual meter. (Of course, we might always turn out to be wrong about some purported fact we offer in defense of our evaluation, but the assumption is that that would affect our commitment to the evaluation in question.) A different illustration of the same point is that we typically hesitate to offer an evaluation of a kind of music with which we are deeply unfamiliar. If you've grown up with Western music, you are likely to be flummoxed by Balinese gamelan music. But although you may thus prefer to listen to Justin Bieber rather than an excellent gamelan performance – even though you judge Bieber's music to be quite poor – you will (hopefully!) not judge the former to be *better* than the latter, since you're aware of your ignorance about Balinese music.

This example illustrates one further helpful distinction for thinking about musical value – that between preference and evaluation. Even when we understand two artworks equally well, we may prefer to experience the one that we judge to be inferior. You may be well aware that the worst Radiohead song is better than Justin Bieber's greatest hit, but sometimes you just can't take another depressing Radiohead song. All this shows is that *preference is not the same thing as evaluative judgment*. This is important to remember in disputes about which artworks or artists are better than which others, and in disputes about value more generally. We tend to focus on the hard cases: Who's the greater singer – Adele or Beyoncé? Pursuing such questions, we may come to think that there's no fact of the matter here – that we are ultimately stating our subjective preferences rather than defending objective evaluations. But, even if this is correct, it doesn't show that there aren't *easy* cases. Few ask: "Who's the better singer – Beyoncé or me?" The answer (in most cases) is obvious, and obviously not subjective. Moreover, our difficulty in answering the hard question could be due to our ignorance or other shortcomings, or to the fact that neither Adele nor Beyoncé is, objectively speaking, the better singer. (Perhaps they are equally good, or perhaps there is no fact of the matter about which is better.)[16]

But *why* do we think that (putting ignorance and preference aside) other people ought, at least sometimes, to evaluate the same music in the same way we do? Surely someone could come to hear the meter of the Radiohead song and yet be unmoved with respect to its value? If this is true in general of artistic evaluation, then such evaluation is indeed subjective. But our willingness to engage in rational debate over artistic evaluation, to consider the opinion of experienced critics, and to learn more about music that many people seem to find rewarding, suggests that (we think that) we share capacities that will ultimately or ideally lead to agreement with respect to at least large swathes of musical evaluation, even if there is some remainder that can only be explained as individual preference. Compare this situation with less controversially subjective matters, such as whether lemon or peppermint tea is more delicious. It might be fun to engage in an absurd debate over this question, but such conversations get old quickly since, in this case, we don't expect our "reasons" to have any weight with respect to the pleasure our interlocutor takes in the experience of the two flavors.[17]

If the evaluation of music as art is essentially tied to experiences of music, it cannot be wholly objective in the strongest sense of that term. But recall our consideration of the "response-dependence" of colors in Chapter 2, §2.2. If greenness is something like the tendency to elicit a particular kind of visual experience in ordinary observers under normal conditions, then it is not wholly objective – it essentially involves visual experiences, and experiences are essentially subjective (they necessarily belong to experiencing *subjects*). But because these experiences are widely shared in response to the same stimuli, they are not *wholly* subjective, in the way that the comparative deliciousness of teas is. We might say instead that they are *intersubjective*. David Hume famously draws the analogy with colors on the way to his theory of the "standard of taste" (by which he means something like the objective measure of judgments of artistic value):

> Strong sense, united to delicate sentiment, improved by practice, perfected by comparison, and cleared of all prejudice, can alone entitle critics to [be true judges of art]; and the joint verdict of such [true judges], wherever they are to be found, is the true standard of taste ....
>
> (Hume 1757a, 109)[18]

Hume's summary touches on many of the points we have considered: the importance of knowledge of the kind of art being evaluated and the distinction between preference (Hume's "prejudice") and evaluation proper. But it also makes clear some *differences* between color perception and judgments of artistic value. We agree fairly quickly on color judgments, and can begin to work out what's going on when there's persistent disagreement (e.g., that someone's "color blind"). Artistic evaluation seems much more difficult, apparently requiring "strong sense, united to delicate sentiment" (as opposed to ordinary perceptual and affective capacities), which have furthermore been "improved by practice and perfected by comparison" of many different examples of art. Thus, while the "response" on which color properties "depend" is that of an ordinary observer, the response on which artistic-value properties depend is that of an expert.[19]

5.2 The Value of Musical Emotions

In Chapters 2 and 3, we investigated the relationships between music and emotion at some length, since many have located a significant portion of music's (artistic) value in its emotional capacities. Just as we divided our discussion of musical emotions into two parts – emotions in the music and emotions in the listener – we can consider the value of these two affective aspects of music separately.

5.2.1 The Value of Emotions in the Music

Given the large literature devoted to explaining how music can be expressive of emotions, surprisingly little has been said about the value of such expressiveness; much more has been said about the value of the emotions that music arouses in listeners. This asymmetry is understandable if music's expressiveness is necessary for emotional arousal, yet philosophically puzzling in itself. But it is worth noting that if the value of music's expressiveness resides solely in the arousal it enables, then its value is more instrumental than if that expressiveness were inherently valuable.

Sometimes it seems to be suggested that one value of the expressiveness of a piece of music is that one cannot fully understand the piece if one fails to detect its expressive qualities. The claim about understanding is undoubtedly true, but it leaves unanswered the question of why it should be valuable to understand such qualities. Peter Kivy argues that *any* perceptible property that admits of qualitative degrees (i.e., that can be possessed to a greater or lesser degree) is an artistically valuable feature of a work if it is (i) possessed to a great degree, and (ii) not necessarily a defect (e.g., ugliness) (1980, 122–31). It follows that some works will be valuable in part for their intense expressiveness. As Kivy admits, some expressive properties *may* count as necessarily defective. He gives the examples of despondency and brutality. It is questionable whether the latter is in fact an emotionally expressive property, and we may be able to defend despondency and the like by arguing that even if *actual* despondency must be a defect in a work, the mere *appearance* of, or *expressive*, despondency is not necessarily a defect in an artwork. Anyway, as Kivy also admits, this explanation says nothing about the distinctive value of music's *expressive* properties in particular.

Kivy also argues that "[s]ome expressive properties serve to highlight musical structure, as color might be used by a painter to emphasize contour or mass. Other expressive properties serve as structural properties in their own right" (1990, 196). An example of the first kind of case might be an emotional climax that coincides with the recapitulation of a sonata form movement; an example of the second might be the constitution of a piece's ABA structure by its sad–happy–sad expressive profile. In both cases, however, note that the value of the expressiveness seems to be purely instrumental – as a means to the appreciation of musical form. In the first case, a climax in loudness might have served just as well to highlight the recapitulation while, in the second, non-expressive musical features might have been used to constitute the same ABA structure. Thus this explanation, too, says nothing about the distinctive value of the music's *expressiveness*.

One simple defense of the value of musical expressiveness is that we just do value (experiences of) expressive properties (S. Davies 1994, 271; Kivy 2002, 91–2; Levinson 1996, 124–5; Young 2014, 175–6). Just as we value a short story for being "true to life" or the realism of a glistening fish in an oil painting, we value vivid presentations of emotional properties in sound. As Jerrold Levinson puts it, the value of musical expressiveness is, in part, "the value of confronting images of human experience, ... but ... woven out of the substance of music," which enables a peculiarly intimate experience of the emotions expressed (1996, 125). This may not seem very informative, but perhaps defenses of intrinsic value claims necessarily face this problem. In John Stuart Mill's formulation: "Questions of ultimate ends are not amenable to direct proof. Whatever can be proved to be good, must be so by being shown to be a means to something admitted to be good without proof" (1863, 4–5). Malcolm Budd, however, simply denies that the mere experience of expressiveness is valuable:

> The basic and minimal sense of the musical expression of emotion does not in itself constitute an aesthetic value: it does not automatically endow music that accords with it an aesthetic value; the aesthetically sensitive listener can perceive an emotion in music ... and yet be aesthetically unaffected by the perception.
>
> (1995, 154)

More widely touted than any discussed so far is the argument that music's expressiveness is instrumentally valuable in providing us with *knowledge* of the emotions. We will encounter the same justification of music's arousal of emotions in listeners below, but it is worth noting that expressiveness in itself is sometimes claimed to have such "cognitive" value.[20] This is most obvious for an expression theorist. In her summary of the heart of the expression theory, Jenefer Robinson notes that "artists in expressing themselves and audiences in recreating those expressions for themselves are acquiring a special kind of knowledge: expression is a *cognitive* process" (2005, 257; cf. S. Davies 1994, 271–2; Young 2014, 177–8). (To the extent that this process involves emotional arousal, it will be difficult to separate the value of the expressiveness from that of the arousal.) But resemblance theorists also defend the cognitive value of expressiveness. Stephen Davies claims that "[t]he expression of emotions in music ... conveys knowledge of the natures of emotions (either by reflecting or, more directly, by arousing them) ..." (1994, 271), where the first disjunct in the parenthesis presumably refers to the music's resembling some aspect of an emotion. But in his wider discussion of the value of expressiveness (1994, 267–77), Davies clearly locates the lion's share of the value of music's expressiveness in its arousal of emotional states in the listener.

Though he does not always clearly distinguish the cognitive value of expressiveness from that of arousal, James Young seems to make even greater claims for the value of expressiveness, arguing that expressive music can give us insight into the nature of the various emotions it expresses, patterns of emotional experience, and thus human character (2014, 179).[21] He further argues that by presenting appearances of emotions in a certain light (e.g., a sadness as *noble*), music can convey insight about the *moral* aspects or capacities of emotional states (179–82). Some of these claims may stand or fall on the outcome of debates over musical expressiveness itself, of the sort we investigated in Chapter 2 (e.g., whether music can represent a pattern of emotions in a single agent, rather than a mere succession of emotion appearances). But they also raise difficult questions about the cognitive value of art more generally. Suppose Young is right that a piece of music can represent sadness as noble. Can we learn from experiencing this nobly sad music that sadness really is, or even can be, noble? Perhaps the music is misleading, much as someone might tell us that "sadness is noble," yet be lying. Young points out that the possibility of lies doesn't prevent us from learning lots of things from other people, and argues that music is in no worse a position than language as a source of knowledge in this respect. This raises further questions about the similarities and differences between music and language, however. We're usually fairly clear about whether someone is using language to *assert* something (e.g., that the chemical structure of water is H_2O) as opposed to doing something else (e.g., *asking* us to drink some water). But it isn't so clear that expressive pieces of music are, or contain, assertions about the emotions.[22]

A second defense Young gives of the cognitive value of music's expressiveness is that, even if the music does not *assert* that sadness may be noble, it may nonetheless give us that idea, which we can then test against our ordinary experience (e.g., seeing whether people's sadness is in fact sometimes noble). The cognitive value of having this idea confirmed or disconfirmed would seem to come largely from the extra-musical experience, but the music nonetheless plays a crucial role if the idea would not have occurred to us without it.

A final worry regarding cognitivism about musical expressiveness is that other things, such as philosophical and psychological books about emotion, might seem to be much better sources of knowledge about them. If so, this may show the cognitive value of musical expressiveness to be rather slight, in the same way that the value of butterfly nets for catching mice is shown to be slight by comparison with the effectiveness of mousetraps.

5.2.2 The Value of Emotions in the Listener

I have already mentioned that most philosophers locate the main value of musical expressiveness not in the expressiveness itself, but rather in the emotional experience that it elicits in listeners. As you might expect, the value of such experiences depends on one's theory of the nature of our emotional responses to music. Those, such as imagination theorists, for whom our emotional experience of music is a more intimate one – more like interacting with an actual person who is expressing her emotions – tend to place greater value on our emotional responses, while those, such as resemblance theorists, for whom our emotional experience of music is less like such interpersonal interactions, tend to place less value on such responses.

We can see all of these points illustrated in the question of the (instrumental) cognitive value of our emotional responses to expressive music. The cognitive value of such responses is more secure than that of the experience of expressiveness because the question of accuracy does not arise so forcefully. If we are learning about an emotional experience by *having* it, as opposed to perceiving its expression in the music, then it seems much more likely that the beliefs about it that we acquire, say, are accurate.[23] But now recall, from Chapter 3, §3.2, some of the differences between resemblance and imagination theorists' accounts of our emotional responses to expressiveness: The resemblance theorist believes that we are "infected" with the mood associated with the emotion expressed by the music, while the imagination theorist thinks either that we imagine of such a response to the music that it is one of fully-fledged emotion (if a Waltonian), or that we simply respond with a fully-fledged emotion (if a realist). Since the imagination theorist can allow for contagion responses in addition to any further emotional responses to which our musical imaginings give rise, her theory likely allows for a wider range of emotional responses in at least three respects. First, her theory allows for sympathetic responses, while the resemblance theorist can sanction only empathetic responses. Second, while our affective responses, according to the resemblance theorist, are restricted to *moods*, the imagination theorist can allow more-cognitive affective responses, such as imagined or actual fully-fledged emotions (depending on whether she is a Waltonian or realist). Third, the fact that the range of emotions *expressed* by music is wider, according to the imagination theorist – including, for instance, higher-order emotions such as hope – may result in a wider range of emotional responses to music's expressiveness. Since imagination theories allow us a wider range of emotional experiences, we can presumably learn more about the emotions from music if such a theory is correct. Thus the imagination theorist can make a greater appeal to the value of emotional responses to music than the resemblance theorist. (Similarly, perhaps the realist can claim greater cognitive value for our emotional responses than the Waltonian, since, according to the realist, these responses are actual emotional states, while for the Waltonian they are "merely" imagined.) Of course, as we noted in a similar connection in Chapters 2 and 3, this is no independent reason to favor imagination over resemblance theories; it is a mere consequence of the difference between the theories, which must be taken into account in an overall evaluation of them.

The most obvious cognitive benefit of affective responses to music, appealed to by everyone who touts the value of emotional responses to music, is that we can come to know (or be vividly reminded of) what it is like to experience the affective state in question (Budd 1995, 154–5; S. Davies 1994, 271–4; Levinson 1982, 339–40; Young 2014, 165, 174–8). If the music is being used to communicate an emotional state (e.g., in a case of Romantic expression), then one might learn by one's empathetic response what the expressive artist has felt (Budd 1995, 155; S. Davies 1994, 198; Robinson 2005, 289–92). Closely related to such cognitive benefits is the value of entering (or feeling as if one is entering) into a kind of emotional communion with the expressive artist or other audiences of the same music – the feeling that one is not alone in one's emotional experience (Budd 1995, 155; S. Davies 1994, 271–2; Levinson 1982, 342). This might be a source of simple pleasure, but more likely it connects to our deeply rooted sense of ourselves as social beings.

A different kind of cognitive value of our emotional responses to music, already discussed at some length in Chapter 3, is the understanding they give us, not of emotional experience in general, but of *the music* to which we are responding. The more common argument is that our emotional responses help us to perceive and understand the expressive content of the music. Most obviously, both empathetic and sympathetic emotional responses can alert us to the causes or (real or imagined) intentional objects of those responses, which in many cases will be expressive properties of the music (Goodman 1968, 250; Levinson 1982, 337; Robinson 2005, 348–78; Ridley 1995a, 120–45). Less common is the argument, defended in greatest detail by Jenefer Robinson, that our emotional responses alert us not only to expressive but also to *structural* features of the music (Robinson 2005, 260–5). The cognitive value of such responses will, of course, turn on the plausibility of the argument, which we considered in Chapter 3, §3.3.1.

Most philosophers also allow that there can be therapeutic benefits to emotional responses to music. The purported benefit with the oldest pedigree is "catharsis," either a kind of purgation of negative emotions or a training of our emotional dispositions (Aristotle 2018, 9 (1449b); S. Davies 1994, 271; Levinson 1982, 338). We may also be reassured of our capacity to respond emotionally in ordinary life (Levinson 1982, 340; cf. Feagin 1983). Levinson adds two further psychological benefits of different kinds of empathetic imagined emotional experiences (1982, 340–2): First, we may take solace from the fact that our negative emotional experiences can be satisfyingly resolved (as they are in the music, and thus our empathetic responses to it). Second, if one imagines oneself to be the persona expressing itself through the music, one may get a sense of oneself as being effortlessly expressively powerful. To the extent that it is an empirical question whether any of these psychological benefits in fact accrue to one who responds emotionally to music, some skepticism may be warranted. Stephen Davies further points out that not all emotional progressions in music end happily (1994, 309). Two responses are available to the defender of the benefits: Levinson argues, with respect to the second benefit, that we are not *deceived* into *actually believing* that we are effortlessly powerful musical expressers of our emotions, but the imagined experience is no less satisfying for being purely imaginary (1982, 238–9). Alternatively, one might argue that even if listeners *do* mistakenly believe that they are accruing these (in fact illusory) benefits, the assurance they receive from such beliefs is no less valuable for being false. The degree to which such responses are acceptable may turn on broader issues, for instance, the comparative value of knowledge and happiness. (Is it better to be deceived into happily thinking you are an exquisitely emotionally responsive person, or to realize the depressing truth about your limited emotional capacities?)

Finally, some defend the intrinsic value of experiencing emotional responses to music. Davies puts the point simply in terms of pleasure, while Levinson argues that because our emotional responses to music are not entangled with our practical affairs, we can savor their affective components in a way that is often impossible, and may be morally objectionable, in emotional responses to other people and ordinary events (S. Davies 1994, 271; Levinson 1982, 323–5).

5.2.3 The Puzzle of Negative Emotional Responses to Music

One value-related puzzle raised by our emotional responses to music is why we should choose to listen to music that we know will elicit "negative" emotional responses in us, such as sadness or fear. Though formulating the puzzle as a paradox is a little artificial, it can help us isolate its central elements and various solutions to it:[24]

1   Some music elicits negative emotional responses in us (e.g., sadness or fear).
2   We avoid negative emotional experiences.
3   We don't avoid music that elicits negative emotional responses in us.

Some might solve the paradox by retorting that they do not belong to the "we" referred to in (3). It is true that the paradox as formulated does not apply to those who avoid music that elicits negative emotions in them, but as long as there are some people to whom it does apply, the paradox requires a solution. (Perhaps one could even argue that it is some sort of failing to avoid such music.)

One simple solution to the paradox would be to reject (1), arguing, as Peter Kivy does, that we do not respond with anything like garden-variety emotions to the expressiveness of music. But the cost of such simplicity, as we saw in Chapter 3, §3.2, is an implausible theory of our affective responses to music.

Another simple solution is to reject (2), pointing out that we often embrace negative emotional experiences as the inevitable cost of some compensatory benefit.[25] Perhaps the cliché that it is "better to have loved and lost than never to have loved at all" is an example of such a view: Though no one would choose to experience the pain of heartbreak for no reason, many are willing to take the chance of such an experience for the rewards that love brings.[26] It may be that our sadness in response to sad music, say, is even more certain than heartbreak's following upon love, but we often choose certain pain (e.g., the prick of the anesthetic needle) over certain greater pain (e.g., the excruciation of enduring dental work while unanaesthetized or the agony of having one's teeth rot away in one's head).[27]

In the previous section, we saw a slew of proposals for the value of emotional responses to music, all of which seem to apply just as well to negative emotional responses (e.g., sadness) as to positive ones (e.g., joy). To recap, responding emotionally to music has been claimed to let us (i) understand expressive and structural features of the music, (ii) better understand emotions and our emotional capacities, (iii) train our emotional dispositions, (iv) purge our negative emotions, (v) savor our affective responses in the absence of a practical context for them, (vi) emotionally commune with expressive artists and sympathetic audiences, and (vii) be reassured (accurately or otherwise) that (a) we have such emotional capacities, (b) we have great *expressive* capacities, and (c) our negative emotions can be satisfactorily resolved (cf. Levinson 1982, 337–42). If those benefits require negative emotional responses to music, then perhaps they outweigh the emotional cost. Though most philosophers accept this reasoning, some argue that it cannot fully explain our seeking out music that we know will make us sad. For one thing, the solution makes the value of our negative emotional responses purely instrumental, when some believe that such experiences have at least inherent value.

A different kind of response to the paradox is to resist the characterization of the affective responses to music in question as "negative" in a way that makes (2) unproblematic with respect to music. (Depending on how one recasts the claims, this might amount to a rejection of (1), (2), or both.) David Hume (1757b) argues that in our appreciation of great tragedies, ordinarily negative emotions such as pity and fear are subsumed and transformed in our experience of the artistic presentation of the objects of those emotions into pleasurable (non-negative) experiences. Many philosophers have found the posited process of transformation more puzzling than the original paradox. The differences between tragedy and instrumental music also raise the question of the extent to which Hume's theory applies to the latter.

Philosophers have more recently argued that it is a mistake to characterize the sadness, and so on, that we feel in response to expressive art as *negative*.[28] Kendall Walton argues that what is "negative" about ordinary instances of sadness is not their phenomenology but the regrettable situation (absent in the musical case) that is the object of the emotion. As a result, when the response is appropriate, as when a loved one has died, we "welcome" the sorrow we feel (Walton 1990, 257). Similarly, given the expressive qualities of a piece of music, we welcome our affective response as appropriate. Also, according to a Waltonian theory of emotional response to expressive music, what we feel is not fully-fledged sadness, but a quasi-sadness that we imagine to be fully-fledged (Chapter 3, §3.2.3.1). This aspect of the theory helps solve the puzzle of sad music in denying the presence of a regrettable object of one's affective response, though we might further enquire whether it is rational to choose to imagine, rather than experience, fully-fledged sadness.

Realists, such as Berys Gaut, maintain that our emotional responses to fictions *are* fully-fledged (Chapter 3, §3.2.3.2). Assuming that the same applies to our emotional responses to music, we could adapt Gaut's account of negative emotional responses to fiction to our puzzle. Gaut argues that it is not the nature of the *object* of one's emotion, but rather one's *evaluation* of that object that makes it appropriate to label the emotion "negative." Though such negative evaluations *typically* lead us to avoid their targets (and are thus *typically* unpleasant), they don't *necessarily* do so, as the rational pursuit of rollercoaster rides, mountain climbing, and demolition derbies illustrates for fear. In such cases, among which some musical experiences may number, we may enjoy the phenomenological components of such emotional responses (Gaut 1993).

Stephen Davies suggests that the kinds of solution to the puzzle of sad music we have considered so far inherit a narrowness of vision from the way in which the problem is formulated, which seems to assume that we move about the world considering what to do on the basis of a kind of cost–benefit analysis of the individual experiences that our actions will give rise to (1994, 311–20). Davies avers that this is not how the typical person approaches music or much else (cf. Matravers 1998, 157–8). Rather, someone who is interested in music primarily values understanding it for its own sake, not for the pleasure it results in (though it does often result in pleasure). Compare the decision to raise a child. The reasons for doing so are doubtless complex and vary from person to person, but surely many people (reasonably) choose to raise children because they believe it is a valuable, worthwhile activity in itself. If someone points out to such a person that, given the demands of parenting (financial, emotional, etc.), they would be happier overall if they did not raise a child, the prospective parent may well respond that that's irrelevant. It is crucial to this analogy that raising a child is being compared to the appreciation not of a single piece of music, but rather of music in general (or some particular musical tradition). One might then object that the cases are not suitably analogous, since when it comes to parenting one must take the pleasant experiences along with the unpleasant, while when it comes to appreciating music, one can easily pick and choose which pieces to appreciate. Davies may respond that appreciating a musical tradition requires appreciating the full *range* of pieces written in that tradition. But this seems to return us to cost–benefit reasoning after all: In order to appreciate a musical tradition, we must take the good emotional responses with the bad.

5.2.4 Resistance to the Affective Value of Music

Before turning to the other major purported source of musical value – music's formal and basic-musical features – it is worth recalling that most philosophers of music are pluralists about musical value, and thus deny that we must choose between these different sources. Nonetheless, while only a few philosophers have objected to *any* link between emotions and music's artistic value (typically on the grounds that music does not express or arouse emotions in any artistically relevant way (Zangwill 2004)), some have argued that the value of music's emotional expressiveness and arousal can account for only a *small portion* of music's overall artistic value.

One cause for complaint is that many defenses of music's affective value make our experiences of it quite instrumentally valuable, where some philosophers were hoping they would be intrinsically valuable. Such defenses thus run the risk of making music dispensable, given other avenues to the benefits of music's affective powers. Indeed, Alan Goldman points out that whatever music's capacity to express emotions, other arts – most obviously those that are uncontroversially representational – have a much greater capacity, since they can easily represent the *objects* of a wide range, perhaps the complete panoply, of emotions (1992, 36–7). Literature, moreover, has an unparalleled capacity for describing nuances of the contexts in which emotions arise and perhaps even fine distinctions between phenomenological states. One might further argue that, since the arousal of emotions by music is frequently tied to its expressiveness, music must be less powerful in its ability to arouse emotions than other arts, precisely because of its more limited expressiveness. But this may be too fast if music arouses emotions in a particularly direct or powerful way, as Jenefer Robinson argues (2005, 375–6).

After a careful and sympathetic assessment of music's expressive capacities (1995, 133–55), Malcolm Budd comes to the somewhat surprising conclusion that

> music's capacity to express emotion, even when harnessed to other valuable musical qualities, is insufficient to explain the artistic value of music, for it plays no role in the explanation of the value of many musically impressive passages, and no or only a minimal role in the explanation of the value of many musical works.
>
> (1995, 157)

It is a little difficult to tell how strong this conclusion is supposed to be. The immediately following sentence, which concludes Budd's assessment of the value of musical expressiveness, states merely that "the expression of feeling is only part of the explanation of music's value as an abstract art" (157). This is logically compatible with the view that music's expressiveness is of great value, perhaps even the primary value of music. Yet it seems clear from Budd's discussion as a whole that he thinks that the affective value of music has been grossly overrated. The reasons he gives include that (i) not much music is expressive of emotion (and that which isn't expressive for any length of time); (ii) there's no correlation between expressiveness and musical value (e.g., there are both extremely valuable musical works that are not at all expressive and extremely expressive works of little value); and (iii) what's valuable in expressive music is not the expressiveness itself but how the expressiveness is realized in the music (i.e., the value is ultimately located in more basic-musical features) (155–7). The first point is open to debate. The second and third seem to depend on an account of further values music possesses, in particular the value of purely musical and formal features of the sort discussed in Chapter 4. It is to the value of such features that we now turn.

5.3 The Value of Formal and Basic-Musical Features

Arguments for linking the (artistic) value of music to emotions, particularly to our emotional responses to music, have a *prima facie* benefit and a related *prima facie* drawback. The benefit is that, since it is widely taken for granted that emotional experience is an important part of human life, an account of musical value that draws on emotional experience stands to inherit some of its value from that importance. The related drawback is that, since the importance of our emotional experience is independent of music, the affective value of music seems in danger of being more extrinsic or instrumental than we might have hoped. This *prima facie* benefit and drawback have a kind of mirror image in the other source of musical value that has been widely defended – the value of purely musical features such as the melodies, harmonies, rhythms, and forms of instrumental music. The benefit is that, as the term suggests, *purely musical* features would seem to be the best place to look for an intrinsically valuable musical experience. The related drawback of this idea is that it is unclear why we should find such musical features valuable at all, if (unlike music's affective qualities) they are unconnected with our extra-musical lives. We will look at two kinds of response to this drawback. The first defends the value of purely musical features *despite* their disconnection from our extra-musical lives, while the second defends the value of purely musical features *in virtue of* their disconnection from our extra-musical lives.

5.3.1 The Value of Musical Content and Form

The simplest defense of the value of melodies, harmonies, rhythms, and musical forms is the brute claim that we just do value (the experience of) such things. As we saw when discussing the value of expressive properties, there is a fundamental difficulty with defending claims about what is ultimately valuable that suggests we shouldn't expect too much from such defenses. To start with lower-level musical features, such as individual notes, melodies, harmonies, and rhythms, the defense of the value of such things must to some extent rest with appealing to others' experiences of these things as valuable. Perhaps we could also re-employ Peter Kivy's argument that the possession of any "non-defective" perceptible property to a great degree is a source of artistic value (1980, 122–31) to defend the value of some basic properties of musical sound, such as loudness and softness, harmoniousness and rhythmic drive, even timbral qualities.

Much more has been said about the value of musical form than about the value of lower-level musical features. Two ways in which philosophers have attempted to bolster the basic appeal to others' experiences of musical form are to point, first, to other areas in which we value formal complexity and, second, to ways in which music can be an even richer source of these valuable properties than those other areas.

In the first way, for instance, Peter Kivy points to the Alhambra in Granada, Spain, one of the most popular tourist sites in the world for the awe-inspiring formal complexity of its architectural decorations. He also suggests that the beauty of mathematics and (borrowing an example from Stephen Davies) chess strategies are non-sensory examples of the same kind of valuable formal complexity (Kivy 2009, 202–3, 244–8). If we value the experience of such things for their own sake, says Kivy, why wouldn't we expect to value the experience of formal complexity in music? Davies introduces the example of chess strategies to make a different point. Relying on the fact we noted in Chapter 4, §4.5, that the interest of formal properties is not so much in the music's adherence to a formal pattern as in how it fills in or departs from that pattern, Davies argues that music, like chess strategies, can be profound (and thus valuable) in virtue of its exemplification of the capacities of the human mind, notably "imagination, originality, and a deep ... understanding of the principles and potentialities of" some domain (2002b, 351).[29]

As for the second way, Malcolm Budd points out that music presents its audience with *pure* formal properties (because it lacks representational content), making it easier for us to focus on those properties alone, whereas when it comes to, say, literature, we must pay attention to the fictional world presented by the work (1995, 165; cf. S. Davies 2002b, 351). Of course, the same benefits may accrue to other non-representational arts, such as architectural decoration, but Kivy floats the possibility that hearing is the sense "by far the most amenable to being pleased and intrigued by pure formal structure" (2002, 262).[30] More problematic for this line of reasoning is the sense in which music *does* have content. Just as we cannot understand the form of a novel without understanding its individual sentences and the fictional situations that they collectively represent, we cannot understand the form of a piece of music without understanding its more basic musical features, such as melodies, and (if Kivy, Robinson, and others are right) the expressive properties that partly constitute that form. But perhaps the basic point is defensible on the grounds that such content falls short of being representational in the sense of presenting a fictional world of ordinary people, places, and things.

Budd and Kivy also point to ways in which the abstract forms of music differ from those of other arts. First, music is *temporal*, unlike architectural decoration or abstract painting (Budd 1995, 166–8), and typically features a number of distinct musical lines pleasing in themselves and in combination (Kivy 1993, 354–5). Again, this may not make music unique, since temporal formal complexity arises from the interplay of various individual components in abstract dance or film. A basic feature of musical form that may be unique to music among the non-representational arts is the quasi-syntactic nature of functional harmony (Kivy 1993, 355–6). In Chapter 4, we saw how the functions of scale-degrees, chords, and keys give musical forms a kind of systematic dynamism and purposiveness that can generate expectation and satisfaction, tension and release, in a peculiarly compelling manner.

Budd makes a final point that music's non-representational nature does not prevent its being *about music* in various ways (1995, 169–71). To return to the Beethoven piano sonata that we discussed in Chapter 4 (Example 4.4), recall Joseph Dubiel's observation that the way the recapitulation bursts in upon the development reflects the way the opening of the second movement bursts in upon the first movement. If correct, this seems to make the passage in question *about* the transition from the first to the second movement, in some sense. Budd argues further that music can "exemplify" in this way not only specifically musical features (e.g., a variation's being about its subject theme), but also features that music shares with non-musical things (e.g., an imitative passage's being *about imitation*, or a beautiful passage's being *about beauty*).

How far do these defenses of the value of musical form and content go in replying to Jenefer Robinson's criticism of musical formalism that we encountered at the end of Chapter 3?

> Why is ... music [such as Brahms's Intermezzo, op. 117, no. 2 for solo piano] poignant, and why profound? The answer is that it records and expresses a poignant and profound psychological experience. Music in A-B-A' form is not poignant and profound just because it is in that form.
>
> (2005, 346)

Of course, our earlier consideration of claims for music's affective value is relevant here, as is the point that we need not choose between affective and formal values – we've seen no reason to deny that music can have both. There is also arguably some tension between this criticism and Robinson's defense of the value of our affective responses to music on the basis of how they draw our attention to structural (i.e., formal) features. Those responses can only be valuable in this way if the formal features are themselves valuable. Finally, it might seem a little disingenuous of Robinson to characterize the form of this piece as simply A-B-A'. After all, this summary comes after seven pages of a perceptive close analysis of this short piece, in which Robinson avails herself of a wide range of formal music-analytic tools (in addition to many insightful observations about the piece's affective properties and effects). The formal values of the piece, as with any formally rewarding piece of music, are for the most part located not in the coarsest template that might be applied to the piece, but rather in the details of its particular structure that this form makes possible and its similarities to and differences from other pieces exhibiting the same basic form. Thus, the defender of the value of musical form may charge that "A-B-A'" no more accurately captures the formal structure of the piece than "sad–happy–sad-ish" captures its expressive structure.

Now, Robinson might respond that her point was not to deny the formal interest of the piece in question, or music more generally, but rather to observe that the pleasure, however great, that we take in such abstractions cannot account for the *poignancy* or *profundity* of the most valuable musical experiences, precisely because they are divorced or "abstracted" from the things most important in our extra-musical lives, such as our emotional experience. We have already seen one response to this objection: Since we know that the Intermezzo, like all musical works, is a human creation, we can be awed by the jaw-dropping skill with which Brahms has constructed it (S. Davies 2002b). Others, however, have argued that music's value *depends* in a crucial way on its distance from our extra-musical lives. It is to such a theory that we now turn.

5.3.2 The Value of Music's Abstractness

Alan Goldman (1992) argues that music's purely musical content and form, even together with its affective value, cannot explain the *distinctive* value of music that leads some music lovers to favor it over the other arts, since all arts can be appreciated for their basic and formal features. He locates music's distinctive value in the fact that it presents us with a (sound) world separated from our practical lives, but in which we can use our cognitive, affective, and perceptual capacities to their fullest, interacting with something possessing pleasing formal features, in which all tension (unlike in the real world) is perfectly resolved. This distinguishes music from literature and painting, for instance, and perhaps even abstract dance, since these other arts don't remove us so far from the world of everyday struggle (cf. Kivy 1997, 202–17).[31] He further argues that music may grant the listener the experience of a pure meeting of her mind with those of the composer and her fellow listeners that is impossible in the real world.

There are two main challenges that such a view must overcome. First, the abstractness touted as a central source of musical value becomes attenuated as the argument develops. Not only does Goldman allow for whatever affective values music may have, he locates the value of the experience of its abstractness partly in an affective experience – that of experiencing the satisfying resolution of emotional and other tensions. It is unclear whether this argument will apply to pieces of music that end in a formally satisfying, yet emotionally dark, way (cf. S. Davies 1994, 309). Also, to the extent that the rewards of such experience are predicated on comparison with everyday experiences, it might seem that music cannot be lifting us as far out of the stream of everyday existence as was at first suggested. Goldman's response is that the expressive features of the work make it more accessible to us, making us more at home in the otherwise alien world of musical sound (1992, 42). Even if this response works, though, it is less obvious how the value of communion with musicians and other listeners divorces us from, rather than connects us more intimately to, the world we share with others. (Moreover, as we saw in §5.2.2, the value of such "communion" may turn on whether it is accurate or illusory.)

The second challenge Goldman's view faces is in its integration with the value of music more broadly. Though I have focused, like many philosophers, on the value of instrumental music, there is no great mystery about how accounts of music's affective, purely musical, and formal values could be used in a theory of the value of hybrid musical artforms, such as song, film, musically accompanied dance, and so on. The non-musical aspects of these artforms plausibly have affective and formal value, in addition to other medium-specific values (the value of verbal arts in the case of song, moving pictures in the case of film, and so on). So although the details may be difficult to work out (as we saw with respect to song in Chapter 1), it is not puzzling that, for example, the formal value of their purely musical elements contributes in some way to the value of these hybrid artforms. But if a central value of music is due to its detachment from the everyday world reflected in representational arts such as literature, it is difficult to see how that value could contribute to the value of, say, song, the lyrics of which typically reintroduce the everyday world. To be fair, Goldman does not claim that the sole value of music resides in its abstractness, but he does isolate it as a value that "makes music, as opposed to other artforms, so important to its more ardent devotees" (1992, 37). To the extent that these devotees ardently love not just instrumental music but also song, musical theater, musically accompanied representational dance, and other hybrid musical forms, the integration of this value of pure music into a theory of musical value more generally remains puzzling.

5.4 Review and Looking Ahead

Music's value is perhaps the most difficult issue raised by philosophical reflection on music. It is also arguably the deepest, in the sense that other philosophical questions about music are largely compelling to the extent that they arise from valuable aspects of music. In this chapter we have focused on the artistic value of pure music, in part because that is what most extant work on the value of music is about, and in part because, as with the issue of music's expressiveness, considering music alone simplifies the task. As this restriction suggests, however, future philosophers of music will have to grapple more directly with both music's non-artistic values as well as the artistic value of works, such as songs, films, and dances, that combine music with other media.

Over the next four chapters, we turn from the nature of music itself to various ways in which music is *made* – performance, improvisation, and recording – before returning to questions of value in Chapter 10, this time investigating music's relation to moral value, and, finally, in Chapter 11, to the definition of music, where the relations between music, art, and value arise once more.

Questions

Is music intrinsically, inherently, or instrumentally valuable? What implications does your answer to this question have?

What does it mean to talk about the value of music *as art*, rather than some other aspect of music's value? Is music's artistic value its *primary* value?

Is the artistic value of music subjective, objective, or something in between? What is the most serious challenge to your answer, and how would you respond to it?

What is the artistic value of music's emotional expressiveness? How big a portion of music's total artistic value would you say this constitutes?

What is the artistic value of music's tendency to evoke emotional responses in listeners? How big a portion of music's total artistic value would you say this constitutes?

Why do people willingly listen to sad music, given that many think it makes them sad?

What is the artistic value of music's non-expressive content and form? How big a portion of music's total artistic value would you say this constitutes?

Notes

1 This parenthetical qualification is usually implicit, but note that we might think that some twenty-dollar bills are more valuable than others because of their visual beauty, ease of handling, and so on.
2 Perhaps there are interdependent complexes of ultimate value, but it seems unlikely that *all* value constitutes such a complex (or that bread and life constitute one).
3 Some, following Christine Korsgaard (1983), argue that we should make two separate distinctions here, that between *extrinsic* and *intrinsic* value, on the one hand, and that between valuing something *instrumentally* and *for its own sake*, on the other. The idea is that the first distinction is about the *source* of something's value and the second distinction is about *how* the thing is valued. Robert Stecker (2003b, 307–10) critically surveys the arguments for this distinction in the context of artistic value.
4 For dissent, see Shelley 2010.
5 So, is it just hard, or actually impossible? Answering this question raises many difficult issues about value in general, and aesthetic and artistic value in particular. A good introduction is Stecker 2010, 229–32.
6 You might be unwilling to replace your father's old mousetrap because you are sentimentally attached to it, but then you are valuing it *as a memento of your father* rather than *as a mousetrap*.
7 There is wide agreement that this theory derives from, at best, a partial interpretation of the views Kant expresses in his *Critique of Judgment* (1790). For a helpful introduction, to which I am indebted here, see Stecker 2010, 40–5.
8 Of course, we must *access* literature using our senses. But if we can equally well access a literary work by reading a bound volume or listening to an audiobook version, our experience of the work is plausibly not perceptual but linguistic or cognitive.
9 I am indebted here to Robert Stecker's fine discussion of monism and pluralism about artistic value (2010, 221–46).
10 Davies does not use the term "inherent," but he clearly has something similar in mind (1987, 199–201).
11 Davies defends a definition of art in his 2015d. Moreover, he now thinks that "[t]here appear to be few limits to the functions music has been put to and I doubt that any single function stands out as the primary one" (2012d, 451).
12 In doing so, I pass over many difficult issues regarding the nature of art and its value. Good introductions to such issues include S. Davies 2016p, 24–79, 193–224 and Stecker 2010, 1–122, 221–46. Some of these issues will emerge prominently again when we turn, in the final chapter, to the definition of music.
13 Compare the discussion of categories of art in Chapter 1, §1.3.2.

14 For a more detailed introduction to this issue, see Stecker 2003b, 318–23.
15 The most influential statement of this kind of argument is Kant's (1790, 96–8, 121–4 (§§6–7, 18–22)).
16 For discussion of the relationship between preference and value, see Levinson 2010.
17 Perhaps the deliciousness of teas is not wholly subjective, either, but that doesn't affect the point I'm making here.
18 Another historically influential account of the objectivity of artistic-value judgments is that of Immanuel Kant (1790), discussed in Stecker 2010, 40–5. For a comparison of Hume's and Kant's views on disputes about artistic value, see the first two chapters of Kivy 2015 (1–21). Though beyond the purview of this book, Theodor Adorno and Pierre Bourdieu influentially argue that the apparent objectivity of artistic judgments is a pernicious façade caused by socio-cultural forces. For introductions and further reading, see Hamilton 2011 and Roholt 2011, 287–90, respectively.
19 The "expertise" here may not be that of a professional or formally trained listener. Recall our discussion of the role of formal education in the appreciation of musical form in Chapter 4, §4.6.2.
20 Although related (via the concept of belief), this is a distinct sense of "cognitive" from that in the "cognitive theory of the emotions" introduced in Chapter 2. I should also note that many authors do not treat the value of music's emotional expressiveness and arousal separately, and thus my attributions of certain views here may be controversial.
21 Relatedly, Jerrold Levinson notes that we can gain further, non-cognitive, rewards from such emotional knowledge, such as being relieved on learning that negative emotions, such as despair, can be overcome (1982, 327).
22 Compare the discussion of music as language in Chapter 4, §4.4.
23 Of course, most philosophers believe it is possible to be wrong about the nature of one's own experience in various ways. The security of the cognitive value of emotional responses also depends on precisely what cognitive benefit is being considered. For instance, it is one thing to believe that you are capable of a certain emotional experience, quite another to believe that you respond with that emotion appropriately in ordinary life.
24 This puzzle is analogous to the more famous *paradox of tragedy* (and its recent offspring, the paradoxes of horror and disgust), which asks why we seek out fictions (e.g., tragedies or horror films) that elicit negative emotional responses in us (Neill 2013, 415–18; Carroll 1990, 158–95; Korsmeyer 2011, 113–35). How close the analogy is may turn on the differences between works, such as tragedies and horror films, with robust fictional worlds, and the comparatively abstract art of instrumental music.
25 Recall from Chapter 3, §3.2.3.2, Berys Gaut's third criterion of emotional rationality: "An occurrence of an emotion is irrational if experiencing it involves suffering *to no point*" (2007, 225, italics added).
26 Though the words of this cliché are from Alfred, Lord Tennyson's poem "In Memoriam A. H. H.," the popular understanding of them as about romantic love ignores their original subject: the death of a friend.
27 Of course, we sometimes avoid going to the dentist even as we realize that that's crazy. But, for the reasons covered in Chapter 3, §3.2.2 philosophers want to avoid a theory that would make our appreciation of music irrational.
28 The views I attribute here to Walton and Gaut are developed as part of accounts of our emotional responses to fictions rather than music. Neither theorist should thus be held accountable for the ways in which I have extended their views to the musical case.
29 Davies mentions that music's expressiveness can be similarly profound (2002, 355–6).
30 Compare Robinson's claim, mentioned above, that music is particularly emotionally powerful (2005, 375–6).
31 Charles Nussbaum's theory that music provides a quasi-religious experience that helps assuage our "horror of the contingent" (2007, 259–300) may be classified with Goldman's and Kivy's theories, but its complexity places it beyond the scope of this chapter. Though it is also beyond

the purview of this book, no full account of this kind of theory of musical value is complete without a tracing of its roots in the work of Arthur Schopenhauer (1819, 191–295 (Book III); 1844, 464–74 (Chapter 39)) and theories of aesthetic experience more broadly (for discussion of which, see Stecker 2010, 39–64, especially 45–8).

Further Reading

In the final chapter of *Music Alone* (1990, 202–18), Peter Kivy proposes the puzzle of how instrumental music can be profound, given that it is non-representational. Several philosophers have offered solutions to the puzzle (all of which raise issues connected to music's value), including David A. White (1992), Jerrold Levinson (1992), Aaron Ridley (1995b; 2004, 132–65), Stephen Davies (2002b), Julian Dodd (2014a), and (arguably) Jenefer Robinson (2005, 405–10). Kivy responds in a couple of places (1997, 140–78; 2003).

Charles Nussbaum's *The Musical Representation* (2007) considers many of the issues covered in Chapters 2–5 of this book. Though it is well worth exploring, I found Nussbaum's theory too difficult to integrate into discussion of the more widely held views covered here.

There has been some debate over the comparative value of Western classical music and other musical traditions, particularly rock. One informative exchange is between Bruce Baugh (1993; 1995), James O. Young (1995), and Stephen Davies (1999). Another is between Roger Scruton and Theodore Gracyk. Though their positions are expansively defended in their books *The Aesthetics of Music* (Scruton 1997) and *Listening to Popular Music* (Gracyk 2007), a condensed version of their debate, with a helpful introduction by the editors, can be found in the third edition of the anthology *Arguing about Art* (Neill & Ridley 2008, 115–50).

6   Performance

Overview

We have thus far investigated the medium of music itself. In this chapter, we investigate the making of music, especially in performance. We then turn to one central kind of musical performance – the performance of a musical work – and ask what that entails, raising in turn the question of what kind of thing a musical work is.

6.1 What Is a Musical Performance?

Music, along with dance, theater, and perhaps some other art forms, is commonly referred to as one of "the performing arts." This term presumably indicates that what we appreciate in these artforms is a *performance* – a particular kind of *event*, the making of music before an audience – as opposed to the finished *objects* we appreciate in art forms such as painting, sculpture, and literature. What makes a performance *musical* is a matter of what music is, a topic we will take up in Chapter 11. In the next four chapters, assuming that we can distinguish musical performances from dance performances, theater performances, and so on, we investigate some puzzling questions raised by musical performances of various kinds.

On the Grateful Dead collection, *So Many Roads*, there is a track called "Whiskey in the Jar" (an Irish folk song). But the track doesn't record a live show by the Dead, or even an attempt to lay down a track for the studio album they were recording. Rather, it records part of a rehearsal by the band. Though it's difficult to tell exactly what's going on, Jerry Garcia seems to be reintroducing the band to the song, playing it for them as they play along with him – though with a few breaks, and passages where Garcia sings nonsense syllables when he forgets the words. Do we hear a performance of "Whiskey in the Jar" on this recording? If not, what do we hear?

In an insightful exploration of the performing arts, David Davies points out that the notion of an artistic performance essentially involves notions of evaluation, intentional action, and audience (2011, 4–7; cf. Thom 1993, 2–6). The evaluative aspect of performance can be illustrated by certain uses of the concept in non-artistic settings. For instance, feeling a little warmer than usual, I might have a technician come to my house to assess the "performance" of my air-conditioner. What I hope is that the technician will accurately *evaluate* how well the air-conditioner is performing its function – to cool warm air. We might similarly discuss someone's performance on a physics test, wondering how he did so well considering his study habits. But when we say that someone is "a real performer" – perhaps ostentatiously laughing as she looks over the physics test when it's first handed out, slapping her pen down halfway through the allotted time, and sauntering out of the room with a knowing wink at the poor saps still struggling with their equations – part of what we seem to mean is not just that we might evaluate her actions, but that she *intends* us to do so. Indeed, she presumably hopes for a particular kind of evaluation, perhaps that we assess her as a cool customer in the face of advanced mathematics. My air-conditioner clearly cannot perform in this more full-blooded sense, since it's not capable of intentional action, that is, guiding its behavior in light of some purpose or result. It might be performing well, but not in order to impress me (indeed, not even in order to cool the house); air-conditioners don't intentionally do anything.[1] Musical performances are performances in the more full-blooded sense: A musical performer "*intends* for her [musical] actions to be appreciated and evaluated, and thus is consciously *guided* in what she does" by how she expects some audience will understand and evaluate her actions (D. Davies 2011, 6). An audience, then, is just anyone who plays the role of appreciating a performance. Because appreciation involves understanding and evaluation, the audience role, like that of the performer, can thus be played only by intentional agents. You cannot perform for your toaster (unless you have some rather unusual beliefs about toasters), since you know it is incapable of understanding or assessing your actions in any way whatsoever.

Paul Thom encapsulates this general conception of artistic performance in the title of his book, *For an Audience* (1993). But is the requirement that a performance be *for an audience* merely intentional, or is it a success condition? That is, does performance require only the *intention* to play for an audience, or must there actually *be* an audience for there to be a performance?[2] Both Thom (1993, 190–3) and Stan Godlovitch (1998, 41–9) argue for the stronger claim: An actual audience is necessary for there to be a performance. They argue that performance is essentially *communicative*, and thus requires two parties – performer and audience. Godlovitch describes two situations that, he suggests, we would call "performances" only in some secondary sense. In the first, a musician decides to go ahead with the show even though no one has turned up to hear him. In the second, a musician plays a politically incendiary work in defiance of the government officials who have locked the audience out of the hall (Godlovitch 1998, 43). These thought experiments do not quite show what they are intended to, however. For in both these cases there is neither an actual audience nor an intended audience in the relevant sense. These performers "intended" to perform for others, but the past tense of the verb is telling. The relevant sense of a performance's being *intentionally* for an audience is the sense in which one's actions (playing, singing, and so on) are guided in part by the belief that one is playing for people who are capable, at the very least, of listening to the sounds one is making. The musicians in Godlovitch's cases do not have this belief, since they know no one else is present. One can have the relevant belief mistakenly, though. Imagine a musician who comes on stage and plays for the audience in the hall, only realizing after she's stopped, when the blinding stage lights are dimmed and the house lights come up, that there is no such audience. Such a musician's actions are intentional in the relevant sense *despite* the absence of an audience, and thus might be said to constitute a performance. This view does not undermine the analogy with ordinary communication. When a child leaves a note for Santa Claus, it is as much a communication as when she writes a note to her father. If one is convinced there is a burglar in the house, one might utter a warning, such as "Who goes there?" This action is intentionally directed at whoever else is in the house, even if it turns out that one is mistaken and there is no such person. Indeed, one might utter such a warning even if one suspects, but is unsure, whether there were someone else in the house. This kind of thing may happen regularly in cultures where musical works are performed exclusively for the gods. If there are two such cultures, each with beliefs in incompatible deities, then if Godlovitch and Thom are right, at most one is actually engaged in musical performance. This seems wrong.

Thom gives another argument for the necessity of an actual audience, namely, that performers address their audiences in a different way from non-performance artists, such as painters or novelists. The latter make a "hypothetical" address, according to Thom, "to whoever happens to be the addressee," while as a performer, "I make a categorical address to the audience, whom I assume to exist. In performing I believe myself to be referring to present persons, to whom I am in effect saying, 'You, attend to me'" (1993, 192). To the extent that Thom refers here only to a belief or assumption that the audience exists, it does not establish the need for an actual, as opposed to an intended, audience any more than the arguments considered above. But Thom perhaps also implies that a performer must have some sense of who the people are for whom she performs – not just "whoever happens" to hear her music, but some particular person or persons. However, there are clear cases where a musician performs for many people about whom she knows nothing other than that they showed up to hear her play – stadium rock shows are one example. It is difficult to see how such a performer's conception of her audience (e.g., these 10,000 people in Cleveland) differs from a painter's conception of his audience (i.e., whoever happens to see his work).

What remains of Thom's argument is the idea that a performer must at least believe that an audience is *present*. This condition is also too strong, if it implies immediate physical or spatial presence, since a musician can perform a live broadcast for "the folks at home" without any audience present where she plays. The situation is more complicated when we enter the recording studio, since what ends up on the final recording is often not a simple "record" of a single, continuous musical event. Much more material is recorded than is typically released, and different musical events may be spliced together and overlaid.[3] Nonetheless, if we focus just on the attitude of the recording musicians, there is no obvious reason to deny that they intend what they do to be appreciated by whoever eventually hears the recording, should what they do end up on the final cut. It seems, then, that the attitudes of performing artists are not at base so different from those of other artists. They present their efforts to whoever is in a position to appreciate them, even if occasionally no one occupies that position.

You might wonder whether we need to worry about cases where there is no audience present, since in those cases the performer herself might play the audience role. This may indeed be *possible*, but it doesn't follow that musicians do in fact perform for themselves on any given occasion. Performing is often so mentally taxing that the performer is in no position to play the role of both creator and appreciator of the performance. One may also be aurally or acoustically in the wrong place. If the rock band hears its performance through monitors, it may have no sense of how it sounds out in the stadium, relying on its sound crew to get the balance right; the harpist, sitting near a wall at the side of the stage may be poorly positioned to hear the orchestral performance to which he contributes (Godlovitch 1998, 42–3; Gracyk 1997, 149 n. 6; cf. Thom 1993, 172).

I have so far suggested that performing requires that the musician believe there to be some audience for whom she plays, though that belief may turn out, in unusual circumstances, to be false. But Davies argues that the concept of an intended audience does not imply even belief in an actual audience. Rather, the crucial feature of an intended audience is that their anticipated responses guide the performer's actions. As Davies puts it, the "audience must be in some way identifiable by the performer – either by acquaintance or under some description – and she must have certain beliefs or expectations as to how this audience will respond to various things that she might do" (2011, 176).[4] He uses this characterization to explain how we might distinguish between cases where someone is merely playing or singing, say, and cases where one is performing for oneself. It is only when one's actions are guided by one's own anticipated responses that one is performing for oneself. When, by contrast, one is playing merely for the sheer joy of playing, or singing only to improve one's vocal projection, one is not performing for oneself (or anyone else).

More controversially, however, Davies argues that the intended-audience condition might be met in cases where the performer is fully aware that her intended audience does not exist (2011, 177). He gives the example of a dancer performing for her recently deceased tutor, dancing in just the way he would have liked. But, as Davies realizes, this conception of the intended-audience condition classifies many musical events as performance that we normally think of in other terms, most notably practicing and rehearsal. For in those situations, one is typically guided in one's actions by how one thinks one's ultimate (or ideal) audience will (or would) respond to one's "ultimate performance." I put this final phrase in scare quotes because, of course, we will still want to make a distinction between what we ordinarily call rehearsal and performance, even if we want to classify both kinds of events under a more general concept of performance. Davies suggests that we distinguish between *performing*, taken to include rehearsal and performance in the ordinary sense of the term, and *giving a performance*, taken to require "the establishment of a performance setting and performance location in Thom's sense" (2011, 177). "Thom's sense" of a performance setting is quasi-institutional, something like a time and place publicly understood to be the setting for a performance. Unfortunately for Davies, this conception appeals explicitly to the concept of a performance,[5] and is thus of little help in distinguishing rehearsal from performance without some further explanation (which neither Thom nor Davies provides). Davies thus cannot appeal to Thom's sense of a performance setting and location to distinguish between rehearsals and performances.

There is a further problem for Davies's understanding of the intended-audience condition on performance. For if, as seems necessary, we interpret the condition hypothetically, as requiring the performer to have beliefs about how some audience *would* respond to what she does, many ordinary actions will qualify as performances. Consider one of Davies's own examples: "Ben's mother may comment that he is getting better at brushing his teeth properly, but we would resist saying, on these grounds, that Ben's tooth-brushing behavior is a performance in the full sense" (2011, 6). That is, Ben may be "performing" in the merely evaluative sense, but not in the intentional sense. But suppose that Ben, now a strapping young man, continues to hold himself to high standards of dental hygiene. Perhaps once in a while he chastises himself for brushing lackadaisically and, recognizing that his now sadly deceased mother would not approve of such weak scrubbing, redoubles his efforts in a way he knows would make mummy proud. We would presumably still not want to call Ben's brushing a performance in the intentional sense; nothing has changed in that regard as he's grown up. But it seems that Davies may have committed himself to this unintuitive classification of Ben's actions in both cases. After all, Ben knows exactly who his mother is, has "certain beliefs or expectations as to how [she would] respond" to his brushing technique, and these expectations guide his actions.

It may be, then, that Davies has gone too far in responding to those who argue that performance requires an actual audience. But even if we return to the idea that performance requires only *belief* in an actual audience, we may face objections similar to those just raised against Davies's less demanding conception. Consider, for example, a band playing for a record-label talent scout. Suppose the scout has not come to a regular show, but wants the band to play for her alone. As they do so, they are clearly playing *for* the scout, and it's plausible that they are guided in their playing by their expectations regarding the scout's responses, particularly those that might have an effect on whether she offers them an album contract. (Perhaps, knowing of the scout's love of punk, they crank the feedback up just a touch more than usual.) Is the band really *performing* in this situation, or are they just *playing* for the scout? We might be similarly puzzled by the case of a classical masterclass, where student musicians play or sing for an expert who then, more or less witheringly, critiques their performance – or would it be more accurate to say *their playing*? One reason we might pause in according these events the status of a performance is that the kind of attention the musicians expect from their audiences in these situations is somewhat different from that of an audience in an ordinary performance. For the talent scout is not merely attending to the band's music-making in order to appreciate what they are doing *as artists*, but rather (or perhaps also) in order to assess whether they are capable of making an album that will sell. Similarly, the "master" of the masterclass listens with a view to advice he might give to help the musicians improve. So we might yet distinguish between situations where musicians' actions are guided by expectations regarding the responses of a "performance audience" and those where their actions are guided by expectations regarding other kinds of responses, such as "commercial-viability" or "educational" audiences' responses. To be fully satisfying, this theory would require developing an account of what counts as a "performance audience." Perhaps that could be done on the basis of a theory of what it is to appreciate music *as art* or *as music*, questions addressed in Chapters 5 and 11.

Though I have tried to clarify conceptual distinctions important for thinking about musical performance, it is worth acknowledging that actual music-making is rarely as clear cut as even the roughest such distinctions. That does not, however, prevent these distinctions from being valuable or even necessary for understanding actual music-making in all its messiness. For example, perhaps the band playing for the talent scout is *both* performing *and* playing in a way that they think will maximize their commercial viability. This might even explain why they don't play as well in this situation as they usually do. But another band might simply perform for the talent scout, and a third merely play in ways they calculate will be most likely to get them a contract – without performing. In the case from the beginning of this chapter, Jerry Garcia seems to be not so much *performing* "Whiskey in the Jar" as communicating its basic structure to the rest of the band, since he would regard as misguided any critical attention they might pay to the details of *how* he is playing the song. The band, in turn, seem to be playing along with Garcia largely in an attempt to pick up how the song goes, rather than performing for anyone.

Some philosophers would argue that the search for sharply delineated concepts of cultural activities such as performance is misguided. Perhaps it is better to think of such concepts as having a "prototype" structure. Where, like Davies, I have argued that an actual audience is not necessary for a musical performance, such philosophers might respond that this is not as important as the fact that a *paradigmatic* or *prototypical* performance would have an audience.[6] We can then understand the various puzzle cases we have been considering as greater or lesser departures from the prototype. For instance, the musician who realizes that the hall is empty only after he has finished playing would perhaps be closer to a prototypical performer than one who intentionally plays for her dead teacher. Or perhaps not. By exchanging the task of giving necessary and sufficient conditions on performance for that of outlining the concept's prototype structure, the prototype theorist accepts the task of giving an account of both what determines something's distance from the prototype and when something is so far from the prototype that it doesn't count as a performance at all.[7]

6.2 Music-Making without Performance

However we ultimately understand the intended-audience condition on performance, we often make music without playing for anyone, that is, without performing at all. One interesting case is the singing of a lullaby to a baby. Here one certainly sings for another person in some sense, yet one does not intend, let alone expect, that the child will understand, much less evaluate, the lullaby one sings. It is unlikely that a baby understands even *that* one is singing a lullaby.[8] To some extent, one is merely attempting to have a certain effect on the baby – to ease it into sleep. Of course, one may also be expressing one's love for the child, warming up one's voice, trying to remember a particular tune, and so on. But none of this implies that one is performing for the baby or anyone else.[9]

Different kinds of non-performance music-making can be distinguished by their various functions. For instance, one practices scales or a particular part of a song to develop one's general facility on one's instrument or one's ability to sing that particular work. When one *noodles*, one plays an instrument or sings without playing or singing anything in particular (producing no recognizable melodies or lyrics, say), perhaps trying things out for future use, perhaps just messing around for the hell of it. *Jamming*, in one sense at least, is collective noodling. Each person participating in the jam is making music, perhaps without playing any particular pre-existing musical material, but, unlike when noodling alone, each attempts to make her music mesh with that of the others in the group.[10]

Communal singing is a different kind of group music-making that serves various social functions (Bicknell 2015, 28–9). When the congregation sings a hymn in church, they sing together, but not for any audience, including themselves – perhaps not even for God (Wolterstorff 1987, 119). Similarly, when campers sing folk songs together around the campfire, they make music together, but perhaps not *for* anyone. A third example is the singing of a national or other kind of anthem, such as a school song. In each of these cases, unlike in a jam, everyone tries to sing the same thing, and this seems connected to the social purpose of such singing.[11] We sing this hymn together to publicly express our worship of the same god, or this folk song to affirm our shared values. A slightly different kind of example is the work song, for instance, sea shanties or the field songs of enslaved African Americans. These function in part to coordinate the actions of a group, perhaps because the work requires it (e.g., a group of sailors pulling on a rope all at the same time), perhaps to keep people going at a task that is tiring or repetitive. But everywhere that a tradition of work songs arises, it becomes (or is perhaps from the very beginning) communal singing, in which the workers express their shared attitudes toward their labor, such as the sailor's love–hate relationship with the sea, or the enslaved person's anger at and rejection of his bondage and his yearning for rebellion, freedom, and rest.[12]

Some of the kinds of non-performance music-making we've considered thus far often *serve* performances in some way. For instance, one's noodling may help one improve skills that will be helpful when one performs for others. Jamming is a common way of developing musical material for a new song that may eventually be performed. Practicing and rehearsal are perhaps the most obvious performance-directed, non-performance activities. When such activities derive their purpose from some future performance, that performance is often not only directed *to* or *for* something (namely, an audience) but is also *of* something – a particular piece of music, what philosophers and musicologists typically call a musical *work*.[13] In such cases, the audience appreciates not only a fleeting event – the performance – but also an enduring object – the work.

6.3 Performances of Musical Works

What makes a performance a performance of a particular musical work?[14] For instance, what would you have to do in order to perform a particular song, such as Neil Finn's "Don't Dream It's Over"?[15] A plausible first suggestion is that you would have to perform all the parts of the song – not just from beginning to end, but all the elements of the song (the lyrics, melodies, and chords, for instance) with their constituent elements (pitches, rhythms, etc.). But for this account to work, we'd need to figure out what is essential to the song. This is a puzzling task because, on the one hand, we do this all the time. (People have no trouble playing songs at home by themselves, at parties with others, and professionally, on stage or in a recording studio – and we usually have no trouble identifying when someone has made a mistake in performing a song.) But, on the other hand, it is difficult to specify, even for a quite simple song, what is essential to it. Let's begin with just the lyrics. You could find these on the internet or learn them by listening to the song. But what if you made a mistake in singing these lyrics? Suppose that where Neil Finn originally sang " … but you'll never see the end of the road while you're traveling with me," you omit the initial "but," or sing "reach" instead of "see." It would be odd to say that you have thereby failed to sing this song. Indeed, Leigh Nash substitutes "reach" for "see" in this line on Sixpence None the Richer's 2002 cover of the song (and I doubt Neil Finn waived his songwriting royalties on the grounds that the band wasn't playing his song!). But we can imagine a range of performances that depart further and further from the original lyrics until we get to a performance that has entirely different lyrics from the original recording of "Don't Dream It's Over" (cf. Goodman 1968, 186–7). It seems clear that this would not be a performance of "Don't Dream It's Over." But in that case, where do we draw the line between the lyrics that are essential to the song and those that are not?

The answer to this question is not obvious. Perhaps the fact that the *music*, including the melody to which the new lyrics are sung, is the same is enough to preserve the identity of the song. Even ignoring the complications, considered in Chapter 1, raised by the ways in which words and music affect one another in song, the implication that lyrics have nothing to do with a song's identity would be controversial, to say the least. The reputations of some highly respected songwriters, such as Bob Dylan and Leonard Cohen, are arguably based almost entirely on their lyrical, rather than musical, compositional abilities (cf. Bruno 2013, 67). But even if we decide that singing entirely different words to the same music is sufficient for performing the same song, the original problem resurfaces when we consider what is required to perform "the same music." For just as one can omit or substitute a word and still sing the same song, one can omit or substitute a note, motif, chord, or rhythm – indeed, apparently any musical element of a song – without failing to perform that very song. (For instance, Sixpence None the Richer disappointingly omits the catchy, sinuous bass riff that appears near the beginning of the original recording of "Don't Dream It's Over.") Yet, as we imagine substituting more and more musical elements, we can imagine arriving at a performance that, while it preserves the original lyrics, has none of the same music as the original recording or, combining these two thought experiments, a performance that preserves nothing of the original recording's music or words. (Following the same path with omission, rather than substitution, might lead to a performance consisting of a single note or chord – or perhaps none at all!) Again, without any similarity between one's performance and the original song, we would surely deny that we have a performance of "Don't Dream It's Over." So we again face the question of where to draw the line between what is essential and inessential to a given musical work.

To answer this question, we need to distinguish clearly between what is essential to *a work* and what is essential to *a performance of* the work. It is easy to conflate these two notions because if we think of a performance as simply an instance of the work, then it might seem that whatever the work has, its performances must have (otherwise they *wouldn't* be instances of the work after all). For instance, a square, by definition, has four sides. Thus, anything that fails to have four sides can't be a square (though it might be square*ish*); what's essential to a square, considered as a kind or type of thing, is essential to every particular square. But perhaps there are different kinds or types of kinds or types. Perhaps musical works, despite being, like squares, "ontologically multiple" entities (i.e., admitting of multiple different particular instances) are unlike squares in the relation that holds between the kind or type and its instances. Biological species, for instance, seem to be more forgiving than squares in this respect. Whether we think the essential characteristics of being a dog are its anatomical features, such as having four legs, or more arcane biological features, such as a particular set of genes, we want to allow that there are dogs that depart from these essential characteristics (e.g., by having only three legs or a genetic mutation).[16] This example points up another distinction between species and geometrical shapes: Whether something is a square is simply a matter of its intrinsic features.[17] If it's two-dimensional, has four straight linear sides of equal length and four internal right angles, it's a square. Whether something is a dog may be *partly* a matter of its intrinsic features (if it has no body or genes *at all*, it probably isn't a dog), but it is also a matter of its *causal history*, more specifically of its place in a chain of biological reproduction. To reach for a rather fanciful philosopher's example: If there is a creature on a distant planet that is just like my dog in every intrinsic respect, but which was created in the laboratory by a mad alien scientist who had never seen or heard of a dog, that creature would not be a dog.[18]

The point for our purposes is that it's plausible that musical works are *norm kinds*, like species, rather than *strict kinds*, like geometrical shapes. That is, what is essential to the work characterizes a "properly formed" instance of it, but there can also be flawed instances (Wolterstorff 1975, 126–9).[19] Maybe a performance with *no* right notes fails to be a performance of the work in question. But that doesn't show that a performance with *one* wrong note fails to be a performance of the work. What is essential to the work is a matter of what the "right" notes are, but something may be a *performance of* the work without comprising *all* (or only) the right notes, just as a particular genetic sequence may be essential to a species, yet something may belong to that species without containing exactly that genetic sequence.

The distinction between what's essential to a work and what's essential to a performance of it may help us to solve the puzzles raised earlier in this section. As we have already seen, a performance is a kind of action. It follows that, even if a storm on Jupiter produces sounds exactly like those of Björk's "Venus as a Boy," those sounds are not thereby a *performance* of that song, since it is not an action. Moreover, not all actions that result in such sounds count as performances in the usual sense. If someone intentionally drops a bunch of marbles randomly on a sound-generating machine and what emerges sounds exactly like Björk's "Venus as a Boy," we would not think that he has thereby performed the song. It seems plausible that, just as a performance must be intended for an audience, a performance of a work must be intended to be of that work. That is, for a sound event to count as a *performance of* a given work requires that the performers intend to produce all the right notes (Wolterstorff 1975, 131–3). Since intentions (like genetic replication) can fail, one can succeed in performing a work, by *acting intentionally* to play all the right notes, yet fail to play all the right notes (just as there can be a dog without all the "right" dog genes). A more forgiving version of the theory would require that the performer intend to produce *most* – but not *all* – of the right notes (S. Davies 2001, 165–6).[20]

This way of understanding work-performance allows us to sidestep the question of how many wrong notes a performance may contain and still count as a performance of the work in question. For if a work-performance is an *attempt* to do something (e.g., play all or most of the right notes), then it is no less a performance for containing errors. You might be concerned that this makes it too easy to perform musical works. If all I need do is *attempt* the work in question, then can't I perform Beethoven's Fifth Symphony by shouting "Dum-dum-dum *dum!*" a couple of times and then trailing off when things get trickier? If so, the theory would indeed be a failure. But the theory may appeal to a notion of *reasonable* intentions (Predelli 1995, 347–8). If you know that many different instruments are essential to Beethoven's Fifth Symphony, then you cannot reasonably attempt to perform it by yourself, let alone with no instruments on hand. It's true that this account includes a promissory note – it appeals to an account of intentional action that has not been spelled out. But an account of any area of human activity will require some theory of intentional action, so at least what is being appealed to is not a parochial concern of philosophers of music.

Finally, the theory may require some notion of *successful* intentions: Impeccable intentions won't result in a work-performance if circumstances beyond the musicians' foresight and control stymie their actions. We might again appeal to a general theory of action for such a notion, or we could define the intentions' success in terms of the recognizability of the work in the resulting performance by a competent audience (S. Davies 2001, 166–75; Levinson 1980, 26–7 n. 33).

Even if this intentional account of work-performance means that we don't have to decide how many wrong notes a work-performance can contain, it doesn't release us from the obligation to give an account of the work itself – that is, the thing that performers of the work must aim to produce an instance of. We will consider various attempts to give such an account in the remainder of this chapter and the next.

6.3.1 Sonicism vs. Contextualism I: An Introduction

Suppose that in 1970, Empty Flat (a reclusive band from the north of England) were playing around with some recent ideas and ended up producing a set of sounds that are indistinguishable from Crowded House's original 1986 recording of "Don't Dream It's Over." Would Empty Flat have played the song on that track?[21] A *sonicist* would say *yes*: She believes that the identity of a musical work is exhausted by the (kinds of) sounds essential to it (Dodd 2007, 201–4). If you produce the right (kinds of) sounds, then you have produced an instance of the work.[22] There's something odd about the idea that a song written in the 1980s could be performed in 1970, but a sonicist would say that that's the wrong way to think about the scenario we're imagining. If "Don't Dream It's Over" is really just a particular kind of sonic event, then in the hypothetical scenario we're imagining it was *not* written – in the sense of *created*, at least – in the 1980s. Perhaps it was created in 1970, when Empty Flat produced the first instance of it, or perhaps it has always existed. After all, if it is just a kind of sonic event, an instance *could* have occurred at any point, as an accident of nature on a distant planet long before human beings evolved. If sonicism is correct, "Don't Dream It's Over" is no more Neil Finn's creation than radioactivity is Marie Curie's invention. Finn *discovered* the song, just as Curie discovered certain facts about the physical world (Dodd 2007, 112–21; Kivy 1983, 112–20).

Contextualists disagree with sonicists about the nature of musical works. For one thing, many believe that songs and other musical works are the genuine creations of the people to whom we typically attribute them. For instance, according to a contextualist, "Don't Dream It's Over" might be not just a kind of sound event, but that kind of sound event *as penned by Neil Finn in the 1980s*. Different contextualists will disagree about which elements of the context of a work's creation are essential to it, but in this case the suggestion is that a particular person (Finn) and art-historical context (the 1980s) are no less essential to the identity of a musical work than the notes are (cf. Levinson 1980, 19–26). Thus, simply producing the kinds of sounds that constitute *part* of what's essential to the work (as we have been imagining Empty Flat did with respect to "Don't Dream It's Over" in 1970) is not *sufficient* for producing an instance of that particular musical work.

But if Neil Finn is essential to "Don't Dream It's Over," how can anyone else perform it without having Neil join the band? Recall the distinction between works and their performances. Just as a performance need not include all the work's constitutive notes, but only be intended to, it need only be related in "the right way" to the work's author. Different contextualists spell out the relation in different ways but, again, both causal and intentional conditions are popular. For instance, one might argue that a performance of "Don't Dream It's Over" must be causally connected in some way to Finn's composition of the song back in the 1980s. Specifying the causal connection is not easy, but the basic idea would be that *the performers intend* the sounds they make to match the essential elements of the song that Finn composed. The causal chain might run from Finn's writing of the song through his recording it with Crowded House in 1986, which resulted, among other things, in Sixpence None the Richer's covering the song, which our contemporary performers hear, which affects what they try to do when they perform this song (their intentional actions). If their intentions are successful – if they understand what's essential to the song and their performance is more or less the way they intend it to be – then they have performed the song (S. Davies 2001, 163–75).

So what were Empty Flat doing, according to the contextualist? He might say that they created their own musical work, distinct from Neil Finn's: Both works share some essential features (e.g., their sonic features), but differ in other essential features (e.g., their creators and historical contexts). Thus they are different works. The contextualist may argue that this is no stranger than (though perhaps as unlikely as) a situation in which two painters, working independently, produce canvases that are visually, indeed physically, indistinguishable. Clearly two works of art have been produced in this case, though they share many important features (S. Davies 2001, 72–86; Levinson 1980, 10–14).

6.3.2 Platonism vs. Materialism

The sonicist may reply that there is a clear difference between the case of the two paintings and the case of the "two songs." For it seems obvious that a painting is, at least in part, a physical object – some paint distributed on a piece of stretched canvas. We clearly have two paintings in our hypothetical scenario because we have two distinct physical objects. But musical works seem to be different in this regard. Because there can be many performances of one and the same work, it is not obvious that a musical work is a physical object or event.[23] Some sonicists and contextualists alike have concluded that musical works are not physical things at all, but rather *abstract objects*. Traditionally, abstract objects have been posited to account for things that appear to be ontologically multiple in much the same way that musical works appear to be.[24] For instance, all electrons have negative charge. But what does it mean to say that they are "the same" in this way, given that the individual electrons are distant from one another in space and time? *Platonists*, as those who posit abstract objects are sometimes known (after Plato's theory of the Forms, which may be considered the first developed theory of abstract objects), might say that the property of negative charge – *negative-chargedness* – is an abstract object, something that exists outside space and time, which individual electrons "instantiate." If musical works are abstract objects, and abstract objects exist outside space and time, then sonicism may look more appealing. How could Neil Finn or the 1980s – clearly things enmeshed in space and time – be part of, or essentially tied to, an abstract object? Some Platonists have attempted to answer this question, but pursuing their answers would take us too far afield from musical concerns, into the rarefied air of metaphysics.[25]

Materialists, in contrast to Platonists, balk at positing abstract objects of any kind. They believe that everything there is exists in the spatio-temporal realm. How, then, can they explain the idea that two electrons are "the same" in some respect or that two performances are "of" the same song? There are several options open to materialists. Appealing to similarity or resemblance has long been a popular materialist strategy: To say that all electrons have negative charge is to say that they resemble one another in a certain respect.[26] This response may be easier to defend for electrons than for performances of musical works, because of the wide variation between different performances of the same song. But there are other strategies available to the materialist, including the one just considered in connection with contextualism: Perhaps a performance is of a given work just in case the right kind of causal and intentional relations connect it to the act of composing that work.

But what is "the work," according to this materialist theory? One possibility would be to identify it with the *act of composition* at the beginning of the intentional-causal chain that results in a performance of the work (D. Davies 2004; cf. Currie 1989). Another would be to identify the work with the collection of some or all of the physical things that manifest it in some way, such as performances, recordings, and sheet music (Caplan & Matheson 2006; Tillman 2011; cf. Rohrbaugh 2003). Both of these suggestions have unintuitive consequences. According to the first, a songwriter's compositional act doesn't bring a song into being, but rather *is* that song. As a result, when we talk about how great a song is, we are really evaluating a compositional act. According to the second, there is no song independent of its instances: Each performance is but a small part of the song, with the result that we cannot evaluate the song independently of its performances (something we often appear to do). Deciding between Platonism and materialism will in part depend on how we assess the costs and benefits of our metaphysics' matching our intuitions or facts about musical practice, but it may also depend on quite general metaphysical concerns, such as arguments about the possibility that abstract objects exist *at all* (Dodd 2007, 1–200; Mag Uidhir 2012). Obviously, if someone has a knockdown argument that no abstract objects exist, Platonism about musical works is a non-starter. But such arguments are notoriously difficult to come by (Szabó 2003) and, indeed, some Platonists argue that materialism is less appealing in general once we consider the existence and nature of musical works and other complex cultural items (Thomasson 2004, 90).

It is worth noting that, at least on the face of it, the debate between Platonists and materialists is independent of the debate between sonicists and contextualists. Sonicist Sam might hold that a performance's being of a given work is a matter of its instantiating a particular abstract object – the structure of sounds to be identified with the work, say – making her a Platonist (cf. Dodd 2007). But sonicist Sue might argue that a performance's being of a work is a matter of sonic similarity between various sound events – most obviously musical performances, but perhaps including natural sound events, too – making her a materialist (cf. Tillman 2011).[27] Similarly, contextualist Chris might hold that certain kinds of abstract objects can be created, and thus that a performance of a given work (an instance of that kind of abstract object) is essentially linked to its context of creation – making him a Platonist (cf. Levinson 1980) – while contextualist Carl might maintain that work-performance requires only an intentional-causal connection between the performance and some material, work-determinative event, such as the completion of a score or track – making him a materialist (cf. D. Davies 2011, 42–4). However, appearances may be deceiving here. For instance, perhaps it is more difficult to defend a Platonist contextualism than a materialist one, simply because it is obvious that material objects and events are enmeshed in space and time, but not obvious how abstract objects could be.

6.3.3 Sonicism vs. Contextualism II: Aesthetic and Artistic Properties

I introduced the distinction between sonicism and contextualism to help us think about what we should say when faced with the possibility of two performances that sound exactly the same but where one predates what we ordinarily think of as the creation of the work that both performances seem to be performances *of*. But there is another issue – of even greater importance for our understanding of musical works – that similarly leads to a divide between sonicists and contextualists:[28] Contextualists argue that sonicism cannot account for *aesthetic and artistic properties* of musical works, appreciation of which is essential to the proper appreciation of those works. Now, the existence and nature of aesthetic properties, their relation to aesthetic experience (discussed in Chapter 5, §5.1.1), and what distinguishes them from artistic properties are all highly controversial topics. For our purposes, we can assume that (i) aesthetic properties are response-dependent properties, such that (ii) aesthetic experience is a crucial part of the response in question;[29] and (iii) artistic properties differ from aesthetic properties in that aesthetic properties are more directly experienced. For example, aesthetic properties of music (e.g., propulsion or gentleness) are simply *heard* by competent listeners, while artistic properties (e.g., originality or retro-ness) are perceived in a more cognitive fashion.[30]

Consider some purportedly aesthetic properties. The Beatles' "Helter Skelter" (1968) is *powerful* in part because of the rough, heavy sound of the distorted guitars and constant crash cymbal. Arnold Schoenberg's *Pierrot Lunaire* is an *eerie*, even *creepy* cycle of 21 pieces, in part because of the vocalist's use of "Sprechstimme" – vocal production halfway between speech and song – to deliver a set of Symbolist poems, accompanied by various combinations of instruments (Levinson 1980, 11). Contextualists argue that the power and eerie-ness, which are crucial to properly appreciating these works, depend on their historical contexts. Had the Beatles never created "Helter Skelter," but instead a different band had released a track that sounded just like it in 2018, the new track would not sound as powerful, according to the contextualist, since we would properly hear such contemporary works in light of the musical developments of the intervening half-century, including much heavier genres such as death metal. It might be difficult to imagine a context in which the techniques of *Pierrot Lunaire* failed to sound eerie (perhaps one in which all songs are written in this style?), but Levinson claims that if a different composer had set the same texts in exactly the same way 15 years earlier, that earlier work would have been *even eerier* than Schoenberg's. Levinson's conclusion, again, is that there is more to a musical work than its sounds. Since two musical works could be identical in their sonic features (notes, instrumentation, etc.), yet different in their aesthetic properties (more vs. less powerful, somewhat vs. very eerie), there must be more to a musical work than its sonic features: Some features of the art-historical context of the work's composition are essential to its identity.

Now consider some artistic properties: Radiohead's *OK Computer* (1997) is widely regarded as one of the greatest rock albums of all time. Clearly rooted in 1990s Britpop, electronica, and earlier "concept albums," *OK Computer* was nonetheless an original musical synthesis, in addition to a powerful expression of millennial angst and alienation. By contrast, we might criticize Sixpence None The Richer's cover of "Don't Dream It's Over" as unoriginal. Though 15 years had passed since Crowded House's release, the Sixpence version could have been recorded the same year. If anything, their version seems to have *removed* valuable features of the original, such as the bass line mentioned earlier. In short, one wonders why they bothered to record the song at all. Whether or not you agree with these particular assessments, it seems clear that they make essential reference to the art-historical context of these recordings: You can't understand a style as an *original* synthesis without understanding that the synthesis had *not previously been achieved* (or, for that matter, that the styles it synthesizes *preceded* it historically). You can't understand a cover as *unoriginal* without recognizing that it was made *after* the track it so closely resembles. Other essentially historical features of musical works and performances include influence and allusion: To hear Tom Petty's vocal style as influenced by Bob Dylan's requires placing the development of the former *after* the establishment of the latter. To understand Dire Straits's "Romeo and Juliet," one obviously has to compare it with Shakespeare's play.

Sonicists cannot plausibly deny that artistic features such as originality, influence, and allusion are essentially historical. But they can deny that these are features of musical works. They might say instead that it was original of *the members of Radiohead* to produce the music of *OK Computer* when they did, and unoriginal of Sixpence None The Richer to produce their cover of "Don't Dream It's Over" when they did, but that in neither case is *the music itself* original or unoriginal. The music is a certain sequence of sounds, and is just as good (or bad) whenever it is produced. Similarly, it may be of *historical* interest that Tom Petty's singing style is related to Bob Dylan's, but that has nothing to do with the *musical* appreciation of Petty's performances. Finally, *Mark Knopfler* was clearly using the words he sang in "Romeo and Juliet" to allude to Shakespeare's play, but the words themselves contain no such allusion – Ben Jonson *might* have jotted just those words down slightly earlier than Shakespeare wrote his play, but Jonson couldn't possibly have thereby alluded to a play that did not yet exist.[31] Whether you find these responses compelling will depend on whether you think the features under discussion are "merely historical" matters or whether they are in fact features of the music that are central to its appreciation.

The sonicist's reply to putative examples of essentially contextual *aesthetic* properties is similar: "Helter Skelter" is powerful to a particular extent. Though audiences in the 1960s may have found the track more powerful than we do today, that is plausibly attributable to its novelty in that historical context (i.e., they overrated it). That we find contemporary use of the same sonic features less powerful perhaps reveals more about our musical jadedness than about the character of the feature itself (i.e., we underrate it). Similarly, it would have been more surprising had someone penned the music of *Pierrot Lunaire* 15 years earlier than Schoenberg did, which might have contributed to its *seeming* even eerier to its first audiences, but perhaps this shows nothing more than the commonplace that first audiences – unfamiliar as they are with the music in question – are not in the best position to judge music's aesthetic features.

There is a problem for this sonicist reply, however: It's manifestly true that a musical work's aesthetic features are not simply there for the appreciation of anyone with ears. As we saw in Chapter 4, if you don't know anything about classical music, you're unlikely to appreciate certain features of classical works, such as the length of the coda of a sonata-form movement. The problem needn't be that you can't evaluate the feature accurately; it could be more simply that you can't even hear it. The problem is thrown into even sharper relief if we consider the music of cultures unfamiliar to us. I know next to nothing about Chinese opera. The fact that it sounds shrill and monotonous to me doesn't reveal these as aesthetic features of the music; it merely reveals my ignorance. This suggests that we must know *a lot* about the historical context of a musical work in order even to *perceive* the aesthetic properties relevant to its appreciation, for we must at least be familiar with the "rules" of the musical tradition to which the work belongs, and that surely requires experience with a wide range of other works in that tradition. *Sophisticated sonicists* accept this point, but they argue that the kind of knowledge required for proper appreciation of a work can be limited in ways that clearly distinguish the view from contextualism.[32]

In short, sophisticated sonicists argue that a musical work's aesthetic features depend on not just the work's sounds but also the *category of art* to which the work belongs, in the sense discussed in Chapter 1, §1.3.2. The idea is that as long as one perceives the musical work in question in the correct category, the aesthetic features are there to be heard in the sounds of the work. For instance, Julian Dodd, following Kendall Walton's lead, gives the example of an alien category of art called "chaconnes" (Dodd 2007, 210–11).[33] These are film-like works all of which have the same sonic features (they all sound like a particular recording of the last movement of Bach's Partita No. 2 for solo violin), but each of which includes different visual elements. (Some display purely abstract patterns of lines and shapes, while others present visual narratives of people falling in love, and so on.) Dodd then asks us to imagine a "chaconne" whose visual component consists entirely of a blank screen. He claims that this minimalist "chaconne" would be "boring and dull" due to the lack of interest in its visual features, while Bach's musical work is a beautiful and dynamic masterpiece, even though the two works have exactly the same features.[34] This is mysterious if we think that aesthetic features such as dullness or dynamism depend solely on sonic features, but understandable if we think that they depend on both sonic features and correct categorization: The blank-screen "chaconne" is correctly categorized as a "chaconne," and is thus dull, while Bach's piece is correctly categorized as *music*, and is thus dynamic.

However, Dodd does not consider a more difficult case for sonicism, suggested by Walton himself (Walton 1988b, 238–9). Walton asks us to imagine a Martian tradition wherein composers specify not pitches, rhythms, and instrumentation, as in the Western classical tradition (such features are left to the discretion of the Martian performers) but rather details "concerning dynamics, tempos, articulation, vibrato, nuances of accent and timbre, etc."

(1988b, 238). He points out that the Martian Philharmonic might give a performance of Ludwig van Marthoven's Sixth Symphony that just happens to sound exactly like a particular Earth performance of Beethoven's Sixth Symphony. But, of course, the Martian performance will likely have entirely different aesthetic properties from the Earth performance because of differences in what is standard, contra-standard, and variable in the two categories of art – two categories of *musical art* – to which these two works belong. If, as seems plausible, correctly categorizing works requires understanding their art-historical contexts, then sophisticated sonicism threatens to collapse into contextualism after all.[35]

6.4 Looking Ahead

In this chapter we have considered a range of questions raised by musical performances, including performances of musical works. In the next three chapters we look at three issues that further complicate any answers to these questions, and that arise most prominently in three different Western musical traditions. The first issue (Chapter 7) is that of whether particular instrumentation is essential to musical works – an issue that arises particularly for performers of historical works of classical music. The second issue (Chapter 8) is that of how to understand improvisation in terms of musical works and performances – an issue impossible to ignore when considering jazz music. The third issue (Chapter 9) is that of how recordings are related to musical works and performances – an issue that has featured prominently in recent philosophical theories of rock and other popular music.

Questions

What do the purely evaluative concept of "performance" (which applies to air-conditioners) and the full-blooded, intentional concept of "performance" (which applies to musicians) have in common? How does the second sense of "performance" differ from the first?

Is an audience necessary for there to be a performance?

If a musical work is constituted, at least in part, by a sequence of notes, how (if at all) can there be a performance of the work missing some notes or including some wrong notes?

Explain both sonicism and contextualism with respect to musical works. Then defend the superiority of one view over the other.

Explain both Platonism and materialism with respect to musical works. Then defend the superiority of one view over the other.

Notes

1 For general introductions to intentional action and agency, see Wilson and Shpall 2016 and Schlosser 2015. For an introduction to the notion of intentions in an artistic context, see Livingston 2005, 1–61.

2 Throughout, I often use "play" as short for "play or sing."

3 We will consider recordings in more depth in Chapter 9.

4 Given the discussion below, it might have been more accurate had Davies said that the performer must have beliefs about how her audience *would* (as opposed to "will") respond to what she does. I am given pause, however, by the fact that Davies repeats this phrasing on the next page: "What is crucial is that an agent be … guided in how she … executes … actions by her expectations as to how these actions will affect an intended audience" (2011, 177).

5 "The concept of a performance space is simply the concept of a space for performance" (Thom 1993, 175).

6 For a detailed cluster of features that might form the basis of such a prototype, see Godlovitch 1998, 50, and the preceding discussion (11–49).

7 I am unaware of any published prototype theory of performance in particular. For a defense of prototype theory with respect to the concept of art, see Dean 2003; for critical discussion, see Adajian 2005.

8 What makes all this the case is also what leads many philosophers to deny that babies are indeed "persons" in the sense of fully-fledged moral agents. The same lack of capacities for performing intentional actions and understanding those of others that prevents babies from being able to fulfill the role of an audience also precludes the moral evaluation of babies' behavior.

9 As with some of the other non-performance kinds of music-making to follow, depending on the situation and one's theory of performance, one *might* perform *for oneself* while singing a lullaby. But I will henceforth assume that it is at least possible to do these things without performing for oneself or anyone else.

10 For apparent noodling or jamming in performance, I will use the term *improvisation* – the topic of Chapter 8.

11 There may be different parts to, say, the hymn – soprano, alto, tenor, and bass lines – but everyone is attempting to play their part in singing the one hymn.

12 For an in-depth study of a wide range of work songs, see Gioia 2006; for philosophical consideration, see Wolterstorff 2015, 255–72.

13 Whether all musical performances are performances of works is a question we will consider in Chapter 8, devoted to consideration of the most plausible counterexamples: improvisations. There may also be a thinner sense of "performance" according to which any complete instance of a work (e.g., the singing of a particular lullaby) counts as a performance, whether or not the kinds of conditions considered in §6.1 are met.

14 The questions addressed in the remainder of this chapter, and many of those in Chapters 7–9, are often referred to as questions in *musical ontology*. Ontology is the branch of metaphysics devoted to the enumeration and characterization of the basic categories of existence and the relations that hold between them. (For example, are there both material entities, such as bodies, and immaterial entities, such as souls? Are biological organisms fundamentally different kinds of things from their physical constituents? And so on.) Much of what is called musical ontology seems not to fit into this specific branch of metaphysics and thus would perhaps be better labelled simply musical *metaphysics*.

15 Throughout Chapters 6–8, I treat recordings as one kind of performance. Whether this is reasonable is a question we will tackle in Chapter 9.

16 In fact, the metaphysical nature of biological species (not to mention squares!) is as hotly disputed as that of musical works. (See, for example, Ereshefsky 2017.) What I say here should be taken only as a heuristic to help us think about musical works.

17 *Intrinsic* features are those that an object has *in itself*, specifiable without reference to any other thing (e.g., weighing five pounds). *Relational* features, by contrast, essentially involve some other object (e.g., being a parent).

18 Of course, as in other philosophical debates, we can use the term "dog" in any way we like. The point here is that the identity of biological species is presumably not simply a matter of intrinsic features but has something to do with the way in which organisms are reproductively related to one another.

19 Philosophers sometimes draw distinctions between different kinds of "generic entities," such as types, kinds, universals, and so on. These distinctions are beyond the scope of our discussion. Anyway, not much seems to turn on them (S. Davies 2001, 42).

20 It is unlikely that we could eliminate the vagueness of the "most" in this version. For criticism of the notion that aiming at producing the right notes is necessary for a work performance, at least in the classical tradition, see Dyck 2014.

21 Assume that this is a massive coincidence, not an instance of Crowded House's plagiarizing Empty Flat.

22 Sonicists might say that any instance of those sounds is an instance – if not a *performance* – of the work. I ignore the distinction between instance and performance in this subsection. For discussion, see S. Davies 2001, 159; D. Davies 2011, 57–67; Levinson 1980, 26–7.

23 Such reasoning applies not just to performance arts. Literature, photography, and cast sculpture are among the ontologically multiple artforms.

24 Some philosophers, following this line of reasoning and then returning to the case of the two paintings, have concluded that even paintings, hewn sculptures, and other artworks that appear to be ontologically singular are in fact, like musical works, ontologically multiple, albeit having only one actual instance in most cases (e.g., Currie 1989).

25 The classic statement of contextualist Platonism is Levinson 1980. Good entry points to these more metaphysical debates include Caplan and Matheson 2011 and D. Davies 2011, 23–70.

26 Resemblance is a metaphysical "primitive" on such theories, not further explicable in terms of, say, the possession of the same properties (since resemblance was posited to explain sameness of properties).

27 As far as I am aware, Tillman takes no stand on sonicism vs. contextualism, but I think his view is consistent with sonicism.

28 In the primary literature, the position I attribute to the sonicist in what follows is known as *empiricism* rather than sonicism to reflect its epistemological rather than metaphysical focus. But the two views tend to go together.

29 On the notion of response-dependence, see Chapter 2, §2.2.

30 For a detailed introduction, see Stecker 2010, 65–92.

31 You might wonder (a) whether Ben Jonson could possibly have written down "you know the movie song" (one of the lines from the Dire Straits song); (b) if he could, what he possibly could have *meant* by it; and (c) whether whatever he meant by it would truly count as writing down *the same words*. Pursuing these concerns would lead us to a debate in the philosophy of literature parallel to that between sonicists and contextualists in the philosophy of music. For a helpful introduction, see D. Davies 2007, 17–31.

32 Sophisticated sonicism is known as "moderate empiricism" in the primary literature.

33 As with Walton's "*guernicas*" in Chapter 1, if you find this terminology confusing, rename the alien works "blargs."

34 This isn't quite right, since the "chaconne" has a visual element while Bach's musical work does not, but we can ignore this complication.

35 You might wonder whether the Martian tradition described is really a *musical* tradition. Consideration of such matters must wait until Chapter 11. However, the same argument could be made with an uncontroversially musical hypothetical tradition (though I leave that as an exercise for the reader).

Further Reading

In Chapters 2 and 3 of *Philosophy of the Performing Arts* (2011, 23–70), David Davies provides a much more detailed introduction to metaphysical theories of musical works for performance. Recent theories of musical works that there was no space to discuss here suggest that works are acts of composition (D. Davies 2004), ideas (Cray & Matheson 2017), properties (Letts 2018), performances (Moruzzi 2018; cf. Edidin 1997), or useful fictions (Kania 2008a; 2013a). Aaron Ridley (2003) argues that doing musical ontology is a waste of time; Andrew Kania (2008b) responds to Ridley's arguments.

In a highly influential exploration of the concept of the musical work, Lydia Goehr (1992) argues that the concept is more recent and contingent than most theorists have assumed. Stephen Davies (2001, 86–91) provides a useful critical discussion.

Nick Wiltsher (2016b) investigates the peculiar ontology of EDM (electronic dance music) – a form that seems to integrate live performance, recordings, and the audience in unusual ways.

7   Authenticity

Overview

In this chapter, we investigate further what is required to perform a work, focusing on the performance of historical works of classical music, where performers and theorists have questioned whether such works should be performed on the instruments and in the styles that would have been familiar to their composers, rather than modern instruments and styles. We then consider the issue of authenticity in popular song.

7.1 Works, Scores, and Performances

Toward the end of the previous chapter, we considered some ontological questions about musical works in general: Are they kinds of pure sonic event, or are aspects of their compositional context essential to them? Are they material objects or abstract entities? In this chapter, we return to the question of the musical constituents of such works: What notes, for instance, are essential to a given work, and thus must at least be *attempted* by musicians aiming to perform the work?[1] I mentioned previously that Sixpence None The Richer omit from the beginning of their recording of "Don't Dream It's Over" the bass riff that Crowded House include in their recording. But this surely wasn't an error – the covering band didn't fail to hear the bass riff on the original recording, nor was their bassist incapable of playing the riff. They simply didn't think it was an essential part of the song. And the fact that everyone treats the recording as of the same song as Crowded House's original track suggests that they were right. However, few in the world of classical music would consider it acceptable for the cellist in a performance of Clara Schumann's Piano Trio to omit the descending bass lines at the beginning of the first movement. All of the notes that Schumann wrote in the score of that work appear to be essential to it.

Stephen Davies has introduced an influential pair of concepts to help us think about such cases. He suggests that one musical work may be *thicker* or *thinner* than another, depending on how many properties are essential to it:

> If [a work] is thin, the work's determinative properties are comparatively few in number and most of the qualities of a performance are aspects of the performer's interpretation, not of the work as such. The thinner [a work is], the freer is the performer to control aspects of the performance.
>
> (S. Davies 2001, 20; cf. S. Davies 1991)

Thus, in Davies's terminology, the song "Don't Dream It's Over" is thinner than Schumann's Piano Trio. In order to perform the song, one must (try to) sing more or less the same words to more or less the same melody accompanied by more or less the same harmonies while, in order to perform the piano trio, one must (try to) play all the notes prescribed by Schumann in the finished score of the work. Indeed, popular songs are generally much thinner than classical works.

As the "more or less" suggests, there may be some ineliminable vagueness in what is prescribed in each of these cases.[2] There is typically no number or proportion of words, notes, or other musical elements of a given performance or recording that marks a clear boundary around what is essential to a given pop song. However, we can say, first, that not all lyrical or musical elements have equal weight as constitutive elements of a song and, second, that relational or "higher-level" features of a song are often more important to its identity than intrinsic or "lower-level" features (S. Davies 2001, 45–54). For instance, one way to change every musical element of a song, in one sense, is to transpose it to a different key. Crowded House's original recording of "Don't Dream It's Over" is in the key of E-flat major, while Sixpence None the Richer's cover is in F major – a step higher. But even people very familiar with both recordings may not notice this difference, precisely because Sixpence preserves the musical structure of the song – the relations between the notes, and thus between the chords and the melody. However, if one were to transpose only the first chord of one verse, keeping the rest of the song in the original key, or to transpose just the chords but sing the melody in the original key, everyone would notice something was wrong (even if they couldn't identify exactly what) because everyone would be able to tell that the functions of these harmonic elements in the song had been flouted (even though more of the notes would be the same as those in Crowded House's version).[3] The same point applies to the lyrics. It's one thing to sing "you'll never *reach* the end of the road" (as Sixpence does) instead of "you'll never *see* the end of the road" (as Crowded House does), but quite another to sing "you'll never *read* the end of the road" (as no one does). *Reaching* and *seeing* amount to more or less the same thing in this context, but the lyric about *reading* seems to refer to John Barth's novel, *The End of the Road*, which would significantly change the meaning of the performance (probably for the worse). So, as with musical elements, the contribution that linguistic elements make to the identity of a song is not simple, but a matter of how they fit into the song as a whole. Matters may be still more complicated given the complex relations between the different elements of the song, such as those between words and music considered in Chapter 1. For instance, changing a melody to which a line about "rising up" is sung may have a greater impact than changing a melody to some other line, just because (as we considered in Chapter 4, §4.1.2) music can itself rise up.

The point about the hierarchical structure of musical elements applies just as well to classical as to popular works. But, as noted above, classical works are generally much thicker than popular songs. Because the nature of such works is usually specified in a score, it's widely assumed that all the notes in the score are essential to the work. But even with a highly detailed score before us, it may not be possible to determine exactly which other features are essential to the work. Schumann's score contains detailed dynamics, phrasing, articulations, bowing, pedaling, and so on. There may simply be no fact of the matter about which of these are essential to the work. Nonetheless, this vagueness does nothing to cast doubt on the claim that Schumann's work is much thicker than the pop song.

This argument might seem puzzling, given that there's sheet music for "Don't Dream it's Over," just as there's a score for Schumann's Piano Trio. But though these musical notations both draw on similar conventions (using the same symbols for notes of different pitches and lengths, for example), they play very different roles in their respective musical practices.[4] In classical music, a score of the work is typically created by a composer in advance of any performances of it; in popular-music traditions, such as rock, sheet music is typically generated from a canonical recording by someone other than the original performers or composers. So in classical music, the score is used by a composer to communicate the essential features of the work to performers; one must follow the score if one wants to perform the work. In popular music, by contrast, the sheet music is secondary; while some may use it to figure out how to play a given song, it plays no essential role in the transmission of the work from composer to future performers.

7.2 Concepts of Authenticity

It's plausible that the classical tradition of composers using scores to communicate their works to performers arose and evolved in combination with composers' desires to create thicker and thicker works, that is, to control more of the features of performances of those works (S. Davies 2011e, 70). Arguably the most hotly debated issue in the performance of classical music in the twentieth century can be expressed as follows: Just how thick are works of classical music? In particular, do classical scores mandate not just that performers play certain notes in a certain order, but that they play them on particular kinds of instruments and in particular styles? This issue has become known as the debate over *authenticity* in the performance of classical music. The use of this term can be confusing from the start.[5] For one thing, the term "authentic" and its cognates have strongly positive connotations. This is no doubt part of the reason that proponents of a particular way of performing music – namely, on the kind of instruments and in the style that would originally have been used – chose it to describe their methods. But though the term is used primarily in positive evaluative contexts, it need not be (S. Davies 2001, 204–5). We can imagine two criminologists debating whether a particular person is an *authentic* serial killer or merely a run-of-the-mill murderer with many victims. One implication is that when we investigate authentic performance we need to ask at least two kinds of question: first, what makes a performance authentic and, second, what value such authenticity has, if any.

If we're trying to figure out whether someone is an authentic serial killer, we might start with whether or not they have killed anyone, but this obviously has nothing to do with whether a musical performance is authentic. This highlights another feature of the concept of authenticity: It is essentially relational. That is, it makes no sense to ask whether or not something is authentic, period; rather, we must ask whether it is an authentic thing of a certain kind (serial killer, work-performance, emotional expression, or whatever) (S. Davies 2001, 203–4). As with other relational properties, when we ask whether something is authentic without specifying the relevant kind, we assume – perhaps at our peril – that it is implicitly understood.

These points can help us distinguish different uses of "authenticity" in discussions of the arts. With respect to painting and sculpture, for instance, the term is typically used in connection with whether a work was truly created by a given artist or studio ("an authentic Georgia O'Keeffe"). This use occasionally comes up in music, for instance, when there is debate over whether a newly discovered manuscript or recording is an authentic Clara Schumann or Robert Johnson. In any art, even if a work's authorship is certain, the term can be used in connection with whether the work is a true expression of the artist's personality or a genuine reflection of the artist's culture. (We will turn to some of these questions in §7.5 and in Chapter 10.)

The most controversial application of the concept of authenticity to classical music, however, has been to *performances of works*. There has been debate over whether authentic performances of works should be understood in terms of (i) fulfilling the *intentions* of the composer, or reproducing the (kinds of) (ii) *sounds* that historical performers would have produced, (iii) *practices* that historical performers engaged in, or (iv) aural *experiences* that historical audiences would have had (Kivy 1995; Levinson 2019; Young 1988). But it has become a consensus view in philosophy of music that when classical musicians talk of an authentic performance, they should be understood as referring to an authentic *instance of the work* they are performing.[6] After all, the notion of instancing a work, as we have already seen, implicitly involves issues about composers' intentions, sounds, performance practice, and audience experiences.

7.3 Pure Sonicism, Timbral Sonicism, and Instrumentalism

The question of what is required for an authentic performance of a work thus largely reduces to the question of the essential features of a work. We have already looked at one general answer to this question: Sonicists claim that a musical work is a certain type of sequence of sounds.[7] To produce an instance of the type is simply to make the right sounds. But there are different varieties of sonicism. *Timbral sonicists* argue that the sounds that constitute musical works should be construed richly, to include their timbral features (Dodd 2007, 212–17). *Pure sonicists*, by contrast, argue not that instances of musical works must be made up of pure or timbreless tones, but rather that musical works are thinner than the timbral sonicist would have it: The timbral properties of a performance are irrelevant to its identity as an instance of a given work. Peter Kivy memorably summarizes pure sonicism in his claim that "[p]erforming a Bach fugue with a choir of kazoos … cannot, of itself, make the performance a performance of something else" (1988, 94).[8] Kivy goes further here than a pure sonicist needs to. In denying that a performance is of a particular work, one need not argue that it is thereby "a performance of something else." If Ferris Bueller takes out his clarinet in front of a crowd and (having never had a single lesson) blows through it while randomly hitting the keys, he is unlikely to produce an instance of the tune "Danke Schoen," even if that's what he's trying, in some sense, to play. But his failure to play that piece doesn't imply that he is playing some other piece.

Pure sonicists tend to be formalists, motivated by the idea that music's primary value is in aesthetic experience of its formal or structural features. If the essence of the Bach fugue is the relationships between the notes that constitute its complex contrapuntal structure, then any sounds that preserve that structure qualify as an instance of the work, no matter what instruments are used to produce them (Kivy 1988; cf. Kivy 2002, 67–109; Scruton 1997, 77–8). Kivy also notes that many composers in the Western classical tradition did not specify particular instruments in their scores, leaving such matters up to performers (1988, 76–82). This is particularly plausible with respect to composers in the Renaissance and Baroque periods, the music of which was the focus of the "early music movement" – the first modern defenders of authentic performance practice.

Stephen Davies responds to the latter argument by pointing out that though these composers gave a lot of leeway to the performers of their works, they did not take a completely laissez-faire attitude toward instrumentation (2001, 60–4). The title page of Bach's *Goldberg Variations* (c. 1740), for instance, describes the work as "for [a] harpsichord with 2 manuals [i.e., keyboards]" (Williams 2001, 3). It may be that this would be understood by Bach's contemporaries as a recommendation rather than a requirement – perhaps a performance of the score on a pipe organ would have been considered completely appropriate – but it does not follow that absolutely any instrument (or other means of producing the pitches and rhythms specified in the score) would be equally appropriate. The fact that the work was published under the title of "Clavierübung" (keyboard practice)[9] is strong evidence that the work is intended for performance on a keyboard instrument at the very least.[10] But while there may be some latitude in what Bach and his contemporaries meant by the term "Clavier," it is plausible that it did not include, say, an electronic synthesizer producing sounds like variously pitched dogs' barks. Moreover, Davies is happy to allow that works may vary with respect to the specificity of their instrumentation. For instance, from the Renaissance to the late Romantic period, works generally became thicker with respect to their instrumentation. There may be debate over whether it is appropriate to play the *Goldberg Variations* on a piano, but few would argue that one could produce an authentic performance of Beethoven's "Moonlight" sonata on a harpsichord.[11] It is very clear that Beethoven intended this piece to be played on a specific kind of keyboard instrument.[12] Such variation in instrumental specificity need not follow a strict historical pattern; even within a single composer's oeuvre there may be thinner and thicker works. It is plausible, for instance, that Bach's *Art of Fugue* (a collection of fugues and canons written in the 1740s) may be played on a range of solo instruments or by various kinds of ensembles, but other (earlier) works by Bach seem much more closely tied to their instrumentation. Perhaps the clearest examples are the solo works for violin and cello (c. 1720), but ensemble works such as the Brandenburg Concertos (c. 1713–1721) also seem designed to exploit the particular timbral possibilities of the instruments specified in their scores.

These last reflections suggest a response to the claim that musical works are pure sound structures: If a work's timbral properties play a role in determining essential properties of it, then those properties, too, must be essential to the work. For instance, near the beginning of the last movement of Brahms's First Symphony, a new theme is introduced on the French horn. Jerrold Levinson argues that the *nobility* of the theme in this passage depends in part upon the timbre of that particular instrument (1990b, 245–6). Kivy demurs that the nobility of the passage resides in its timbre-neutral musical features (pitches, rhythms, etc.). Indeed, Kivy observes that immediately after the passage in question, the flute plays the very same noble theme (1988, 86–8). Levinson responds that these two passages do not have exactly the same expressive effect. Kivy agrees, but simply insists that the emotional character of these passages is similar enough, and falls back upon pure sonicism: "where the emotive quality survives in sufficient degree, I would argue that [the] musical structure, of which it is a part, has survived. And it is musical structure, so conceived, that makes an instance of the work" (1988, 87). This seems to imply, as Levinson points out, that it would make no difference to whether a performance is a performance of this symphony to swap the contributions of the horn and the flute or, for that matter, to have the flute play both occurrences of the theme. The pure sonicist might reply that he can still say that performances following Brahms's orchestration are *better* than those in which the horn and flute parts are swapped; all parties agree that some equally authentic performances of a work are better than others.

Still, it is hard to square the sonicist's view with the value we attribute to the ways in which composers use instruments' timbres to create or inflect the expressive and other properties of their works. Perhaps we sometimes even value novel timbral effects for their own sake, as when new instruments are added to familiar ensembles. (We might think here of the introduction of the saxophone to the symphony orchestra in the late nineteenth century or – somewhat ironically in this context – that of the harpsichord to rock music in the 1960s.) Stephen Davies sums up the case for the importance of timbre with an analogy:

> In literature, the work cannot be replaced by a paraphrase in modern-speak because the story told is not separable from the manner of its narration. One can paraphrase Jonathan Swift, say, but one loses his work of art in doing so. What goes for literature applies yet more clearly to music. Because music does not have semantic content, its message resides entirely in its accent and inflection. As regards the "story" of an older instrumental work, there is simply nothing that could be paraphrased in a more up-to-date musical idiom. Musical works are not meaningless, as the sound of the wind is. Composers have something to "say," but, because what they say has no independently specifiable semantic content, it can be successfully communicated only in their own accents and idiolects, even if these are local to a particular time and place. It is the sounds of the instruments they knew and for which they wrote, as much as the syntax of their musical expression, that capture the tonal nuances of their utterances. To hear their voices at their clearest, we must listen to performances on period instruments.
>
> (2001, 71)

The last sentence of this quotation shows that Davies is no mere timbral sonicist. For if our goal is only to produce the kinds of sounds mandated by composers in their scores, even sounds in their full timbral richness, we can achieve it in ways other than by using instruments of the sort familiar to those composers. Most simply, we can imagine a "perfect timbral synthesizer" – an electronic instrument that can perfectly replicate the sounds of any given kind of instrument at the touch of a button.[13] Davies is thus defending not timbral sonicism, here, but *instrumentalism* – the view that an authentic performance of a work requires not just producing the sounds, in all their timbral detail, specified by a composer in the work's score, but producing those sounds *in the way* specified by the composer, which is typically a matter of playing particular kinds of instruments.[14] An authentic performance of Brahms's First Symphony requires not just certain horn-like sounds at a given point in the piece; it requires someone to produce those sounds *on a French horn* – a particular kind of physical artifact, mastery of which may require more effort, certainly effort of a different kind, than mastery of the perfect timbral synthesizer.

How can the instrumentalist justify the view that the sounds of a musical work must be produced in a certain way? Both Davies and Levinson appeal to composers' intentions: Composers specify in their scores what performances of their works require, and those scores often specify particular instrumentation. The timbral sonicist may object that this begs the question. Given that playing a French horn was the only way to achieve that timbre in Brahms's time, why suppose that the score reflects his intention *for that instrument to be played* rather than *for that timbre to be produced* (Dodd 2007, 218–24; Kivy 1988, 85–6)? Levinson also provides the same kind of argument for instrumentalism that we have seen him offer for contextualism: There are essential aesthetic and artistic properties of musical works that depend not just on the (timbral) sounds of the work, but also on those sounds' being produced in certain ways, namely, on the kinds of instruments for which the work was written (Levinson 1980, 14–19; 1990c, 399–400; cf. Walton 2012, 36–41). Take, for example, the excitement of a passage that depends on the passage's being *fast*. What counts as fast seems to depend in part on the instrument on which the passage is being played: Any organist can play faster with her fingers than her feet (on the keyboard and pedals, respectively); the best tuba player cannot play a chromatic scale as fast as the best trumpet player; and so on. Similarly, Levinson argues, the insouciance of a glissando played on the piano depends upon the insouciance of the gesture required to play it; the dialogic quality of some passages depends upon hearing them as being played in alternation by two instruments; and even hearing a note as high or low depends upon hearing it in the context of the range of the instrument on which it is played. (Middle C is a low note on the violin, but a high note on the double bass.)

Some instrumentalists resist this line of argument for their position, however. First, there are cases where the expressive or other properties of the music seem to be *at odds with* their manner of production (S. Davies 2001, 66). For instance, the opening of Stravinsky's *Rite of Spring* is scored for a bassoon playing very high in its register. This is extremely difficult, yet if played well the passage is ethereal, not tense or strained. Second, where we change the means of production, but without changing the resulting sound, we do not always get a change in aesthetic properties. Consider Levinson's example of a piano glissando. Here we have a rapidly rising series of notes on the piano, produced by moving one finger along the keyboard, to insouciant effect. But pianists can also produce rapidly rising passages by playing each note with a different finger, with a similarly insouciant effect. (Listen, for example, to the pianos in the last movement of Saint-Saëns's "Organ" Symphony.) This might lead us to be skeptical of the contribution of the instrumentation to this expressive effect (cf. S. Davies 2001, 220 n. 16). Third, is it really true that the gesture producing the glissando is itself insouciant? The difficulty of producing a controlled glissando on a piano suggests that, rather than the gesture contributing to the insouciance of what we hear, the insouciance of what we hear is what leads us to see the gesture as insouciant (when it is in fact highly controlled). Levinson might reply at this point that "the gesture" in this argument refers not to the actual action performed and experienced by the musician, but to the way this gesture appears to an audience member. However, this will merely push the discussion back one level. Is the relevant audience member one *familiar with* or *ignorant of* what it is like to produce a piano glissando? If the former, the objection remains, since the gesture will appear difficult rather than insouciant to such an audience member. If the latter, other arguments of Levinson's will be cast into doubt, such as the argument about the speed or excitement of a passage, depending as they do on a listener knowledgeable about how such sounds are produced.[15]

Davies raises a more general question for Levinson's grounding of aesthetic properties of music in the instruments used to produce it. Since instrumentalism is a general position, we might ask what it is ultimately based on. If the answer is the kind of aesthetic considerations just discussed, the problem is that there may not always be aesthetic differences when different instruments are used. It seems particularly unlikely that such differences will always occur between pairs of performances of the kind that originally motivated the debate over authentic performance practice – pairs of performances of the same work on historical and modern instruments – precisely because, for instance, baroque and modern violins are so similar (S. Davies 2001, 217–18). Davies's alternative answer appeals to the more general consideration of the intentions of the composer: In many cases, the composer mandates certain instruments because of the kind of properties we have been discussing, but her mandates are decisive independent of her reasons for them. However, Davies emphasizes that music is a social practice and thus governed by conventions. Though the conventions may change over time, their nature at any given time limits what a composer may mandate – even for good musical reasons (S. Davies 2001, 66–9). One example he gives is Benjamin Britten's composition of many works incorporating a solo tenor voice. Britten clearly had the distinctive vocal color of his partner Peter Pears in mind when writing these parts. Pears featured in the premières of many of these works and on their canonical recordings, often with Britten conducting. Davies's point is that none of this shows that other tenors must attempt to recreate Pears's distinctive tone when they perform these works (let alone that only Pears can authentically perform them).

Davies's answer raises the more general and fundamental question of why we should follow the composer's mandates at all. Everyone agrees that even perfect score-compliance allows room for performative interpretation, and that there are other performance values, so that two equally score-compliant performances of the same work may diverge considerably in their sound and value. But everyone also agrees that musicians can have good reasons for departing from the score. If there are no harpsichords around, better to play the Goldberg Variations on a piano than not at all. And it is doubtless interesting to hear what can be done with the musical structure of that work (melodies, rhythms, and harmonies) on a piano, with a string quartet, a brass band, and so on. Furthermore, whatever your view of work-authenticity, it comes in degrees. A performance with two wrong notes, other things being equal, will be less authentic an instance of the work than one with only one mistake. Similarly, if a harpsichord is essential to the Goldberg Variations, playing them on the piano is still more authentic – closer to the ideal – than a performance by Kivy's choir of kazoos. But suppose you think that performing that work on piano results in *better music* than performing it on harpsichord, because of the additional resources for dynamics and articulation that the piano provides. Why should you care about following the score *at all* in such cases? What is the value of such authenticity?

7.4 Score-compliance Authenticity and Interpretive Authenticity

Stephen Davies argues that it is simply a fact about classical music that participants in that practice are primarily interested in musical *works* – works for performance (2001, 247–52). As a result, one is simply not participating properly in the practice if one is not primarily concerned with producing instances of those works, that is, complying with the score (cf. Levinson 2019, 190–4). Lydia Goehr calls such fundamental goals of a musical practice *regulative ideals* (1992, 89–286); Julian Dodd calls them *constitutive norms* (Dodd & Irving, forthcoming).[16]

We might still reasonably ask, however, what reason we have to participate in a practice with such a goal. A group of Satanists might insist that yearly child-sacrifice is simply a regulative ideal or constitutive norm of Satanic practice. But, given the evil of killing innocent children, this will be a reason to *avoid* participating in that practice. Of course, we might argue that there's no analogous reason *not* to participate in classical work-performance practice, and one might cite extra-musical reasons for participating – perhaps it's a good way to make friends. But we might also hope for a positive *musical, artistic,* or *aesthetic* reason for participating in this particular practice. Guy Rohrbaugh (2020) suggests that the most significant such justification is that work-performance makes possible the *performative interpretation* of repeatable musical works – a source of musical value that would be inaccessible in the absence of a practice centrally concerned with the presentation of repeatable works in performance.

Dodd (2015; Dodd & Irving forthcoming) accepts that *score-compliance authenticity* (as he calls the concept we have thus far been discussing) is a constitutive norm of classical work performance; that is, if you don't aim at following the mandates of the composer as represented in the score, you're not properly participating in the practice of classical performance. There may be other things we properly value in classical performance, such as originality, spontaneity, and so on, but these are not constitutive norms, so they cannot trump score compliance; instead these values should be realized within the constraints of score compliance. However, Dodd points out that we can't assume that there is *only one* constitutive norm in classical performance practice. He suggests, on the contrary, that there is at least one further such norm, "interpretive authenticity," which is the injunction to perform a work *insightfully*, in such a way as to evince *understanding* of the work.[17] Since these norms embody different aims, it seems possible that they will come into conflict (cf. Kivy 1995, 108–42, 260–86). Since both are constitutive norms, it seems reasonable (at least sometimes) to favor interpretive authenticity over score compliance. The illustrative examples Dodd provides are varied (2015, 493–5). (1) Alfred Brendel, an accomplished pianist and writer, argues that we ought to ignore some tempi that Beethoven mandates in the scores of his piano sonatas, since any performances at those speeds will mask valuable detail (Brendel 2001, 33); (2) Andreas Staier, a distinguished practitioner of early music, departs from the very notes in the score of Mozart's Rondo alla Turca the better to convey its character, even as he plays it on the relatively uncommon, but score-compliant, fortepiano (an ancestor of the modern piano);[18] (3) Mark Evan Bonds, an esteemed musicologist, recommends using modern French horns instead of the scored bassoons at a particular spot in Beethoven's Fifth Symphony, since that brings out the structure of the movement more clearly.[19]

In order to identify the central issue raised by these examples, we should consider the extent to which they can be handled by score-compliance authenticity alone. First, there is some dispute over the tempo indications in Beethoven's scores, and in classical scores more generally. Beethoven was an early adopter of the metronome, and some have argued that the metronome he used was inaccurate. The current musicological consensus seems to be that this is incorrect, but it must be noted that although metronomic tempo *indications* are precise, musical conventions at Beethoven's time, no less than today, allow for significant leeway from this precision in performance (S. Davies 2013, 72; Fallows 2001b, §4.vi). Let us suppose then, that Beethoven knew what tempi he was mandating when he penned his metronome markings. Some argue further that since most composers add metronome markings late in the compositional process – "at the desk," rather than at the piano, on the podium, and so on – we should take such markings with a grain of salt.[20] If score compliance is a constitutive norm, however, this is neither here nor there. Surely composers, like other artists, make decisions about their works that are ill-advised; it does not follow that the results of those decisions are not parts of their works. So if Brendel is right that some of Beethoven's mandated tempi necessitate a loss of detail, there is a tension between following those tempi and making the details of his works clear.[21] Note, however, that the choice between notated tempo and notated detail seems more plausibly understood as a choice between compliance with two incompatible aspects of the score, rather than between score-compliance and interpretive authenticity.

Second, when Andreas Staier departs from the notes in the score of Mozart's Rondo alla Turca, does he fail to comply with that score? As with the case of Beethoven's metronome markings, this depends in part on the conventions of the time for reading scores. Some ornamentation of certain parts of a piece like this may be acceptable within the conventions of Mozart's time (S. Davies 2013, 73–4). But the point of this example is that Staier's particular ornamentation falls beyond this pale. Though most of the ornamentation is in a style that Mozart might have employed in an improvisation, its sheer extent clearly violates the norm of score compliance. But Dodd argues that the effect of such ornamentation on our modern ears recaptures the effect of Mozart's use of relatively exotic musical ideas in this piece (the "Turkish" elements that give the piece its nickname).[22] To make this point, however, Dodd must resist the idea that Staier is playing not Mozart's work, exactly, but a new *arrangement* of the work (cf. S. Davies 2013, 74). The version of this same piece that pianist Yuja Wang sometimes plays as an encore, for instance, is even more radically ornamented – a kind of Lisztian fantasy on Mozart's rondo. But Wang's performances are credited as an arrangement by Arcadi Volodos and Wang herself, an explicit acknowledgement that this is not Mozart's work.[23] Dodd's example is a nice one in that Staier does not present his performance in such a way, nor are its departures from Mozart's score as radical, so to claim that Staier's performance is of an arrangement might be thought to beg the question.

Third, what should a *score-compliance authenticist* – a defender of score-compliance authenticity as the sole non-negotiable ideal of classical work-performance – say about the use of modern instruments to perform historical works? Are musicians who play Bach on a modern piano, or use modern horns instead of bassoons at a particular spot in Beethoven's Fifth Symphony, failing to play the works they claim to be? If so, what are they doing? We should keep in mind the earlier points that there may be reasons (such as a shortage of harpsichords) to abandon authenticity, and that authenticity comes in degrees. However, there are two ways of understanding the latter point. One might, as Davies sometimes does, take it to mean that intentionally departing from the score *a little* results in a less than ideally authentic performance of the work, but a performance of the work nonetheless. (At such times, Davies draws the line between performance and non-performance of a given work at its *recognizability* by competent listeners familiar with the work.) For instance, Davies says that choosing to play Bach on a piano is a fault of taste: One needlessly loses some details of Bach's work (most obviously timbral properties, but perhaps also properties that depend on the "action" or mechanics of the harpsichord as opposed to the piano) but, in the grand scheme of things, the piano is a close enough cousin of the harpsichord that one still produces an instance of the work, and does not fall far short of authenticity (S. Davies 2001, 70). (Kivy's kazoo choir would presumably be a different story!)

However, a different kind of answer is available to the score-compliance authenticist. In accordance with a view considered in the previous chapter, one might hold that to perform a work is to (reasonably) intend to instantiate *all* the work-determinative properties mandated by the composer in the score. If one of those mandates is that the performance should be executed on a harpsichord, then to flout that mandate *intentionally* is to fail to perform the work (Wolterstorff 1975, 133). This conclusion may sound implausibly strong, but a proponent of this view could point out that such a performer may still succeed in instantiating many of, indeed almost all, the properties of the work. We might think of the performance as of a very minimal transcription or arrangement of the work. This is not how these terms are used in classical-music practice, but the point is that (on this view) deliberate departures from the score fall into a different category from mistakes (S. Davies 2001, 248). One may reasonably intend to comply completely with what the work demands and make a few mistakes, with the result being an imperfect (but very good) performance of the work; but if one does not intend to comply completely with what the work demands, what one produces, even if one executes one's intentions flawlessly, is not strictly speaking a performance of the work, since one is not even aiming at producing such a performance. Whether one should prefer this view or Davies's may turn on the best way of understanding what it means for score-compliance authenticity to be an *ideal*, or constitutive norm, of classical work-performance.

The case of Bonds's recommendation to use modern horns instead of bassoons at a certain point in Beethoven's Fifth Symphony is more complicated, since it depends upon facts about both sonata form and the evolution of the

French horn. The first movement of Beethoven's Fifth Symphony, like many other symphonies in the classical tradition, is in sonata form.[24] Bonds's recommendation concerns a fanfare that announces the opening of the second part of the recapitulation. The fanfare first occurs in the same place in the exposition, but – crucially – in a different key, where it is scored to be played majestically by the horns (Example 7.1a). In the recapitulation, by contrast, it is scored to be played (rather less majestically, it must be said) by the bassoons (Example 7.1b). Bonds argues that Beethoven *would* have given this passage to the horns, to mirror the exposition, but that he couldn't expect them to play it well because of the nature of the horns available. Essentially, in Beethoven's day a horn could only play a limited number of notes with the strength required for a fanfare. The two keys Beethoven chose for the exposition (the home key of C minor and its "relative major," E-flat major) can be handled comfortably by a single kind of horn (a horn "in E-flat"). However, the passage in question (in the recapitulation) is written in C *major* (C minor's "parallel major"), and thus not easily handled on the same kind of horn. As a result, given the constraints of the musical structure within which he was working, Beethoven had to reassign the fanfare, and chose the bassoons.

Horns are not what they used to be, however. In the nineteenth century, the "natural" horn with which Beethoven was familiar was gradually replaced by the "valved" horn. The crucial difference for our purposes is that the valved horn can play just about as easily in any key, thanks to the "valves," which function a little like a capo on a guitar (shifting the key of the instrument up or down) but are much more easily manipulated, via a set of "keys" (in the "button," rather than harmonic, sense). Modern orchestras can thus play the fanfare in question as Beethoven would have preferred it to be played, according to Bonds, namely on horns rather than bassoons.[25]

Example 7.1 Fanfare from Beethoven's Fifth Symphony, first movement, (a) at the opening of the second part of the exposition (mm. 59–63), and (b) at the same place in the recapitulation (mm. 303–7), both notated at sounding pitch.

Now, implicit in this argument is the premise that Beethoven gave the second fanfare to the *bassoons* as the instruments that would give closest to the same effect as the horns. But with trombones and trumpets in C already in the score, and not playing at this point, this premise is highly doubtful. The historical facts are also more complex than Dodd suggests. Natural-horn players could play a wide range of notes using "hand stopping" (altering the pitch by repositioning one's hand inside the horn's bell), though this technique radically affects the timbre of many pitches and was conventionally restricted to chamber music. In orchestral music, horns used different "crooks" to play in various keys (lengths of tubing that transform a horn in E-flat, say, into a horn in C). The same two horns in Beethoven's Fifth Symphony, in fact, are in E-flat in the first and third movements, and in C in the second and fourth. But changing crooks was a laborious process (the players get many measures of rest between crook changes) and thus was not practical at the point of the first movement under discussion. However, there are several other potential solutions to this compositional challenge, many of which have precedents in Beethoven's oeuvre. I have already mentioned the possibility of assigning the fanfare to the trumpets or trombones. But Beethoven might alternatively have (i) stuck with the horns and required hand-stopping,[26] (ii) not had the horns play together,[27] (iii) scored the work for more horns (e.g., two in E-flat and one in C),[28] or (iv) given the theme to the bassoons in both places. And, of course, there are more radical recompositional options, such as eliminating the fanfare or employing a different key structure.[29]

One might thus dispute Bonds's explanation of Beethoven's scoring of the fanfare in question (S. Davies 2013, 73). But granting the explanation for the sake of argument, the score-compliance authenticist's first reply to all this might be to admit that it is unfortunate that Beethoven did not have access to modern horns, but that since he did not, one cannot produce an authentic performance of his works by using such instruments. We may wonder what Michelangelo would have done had he had access to a digital video camera, but even with some evidence of his likely intentions in such a situation, no digital-video artwork is rightly attributable to him (S. Davies 2001, 222–4). Similarly, though much less radically, a putative performance of Beethoven's Fifth Symphony with the second fanfare reassigned to horns is a performance, strictly speaking, not of that work, but of a slight variation on it.[30]

Dodd disputes this point, however. He argues that the departures from the score practiced or recommended by Brendel, Staier, and Bonds, are grounded precisely in a deep understanding of their target works. Given the impossibility of performing Beethoven's piano sonatas *both* at the tempi he mandates *and* in such a way as to make their detail audible, one must choose between the two demands of the work. Either choice will leave out *something* that Beethoven mandated. Brendel thinks that the detail is more important than the speed – more important to *Beethoven's work*, properly understood. Thus to violate Beethoven's scored tempo indications in such cases is to be *more* faithful to his work than following the tempo indications at the expense of musical detail would be. Similarly, Mozart clearly intended the performer of the Rondo alla Turca to play the notes he wrote in the score of the work. But if a central point of writing those notes in particular was to give his audience an experience of novelty and exoticism, the modern performer faces a dilemma. Since those notes will no longer give audiences that experience, one must choose – in being faithful to the work – between the notes and the experience (Dipert 1980, 209–10). Staier judges that some departure from the notes is required to do justice to the work.

Note that the feature of the work supposedly in tension with score compliance is different in each of these cases. In the piano sonatas, the composer has arguably mandated something contradictory. In the Rondo alla Turca, two aspects of what Mozart intended (the notes and their effect) have become contradictory over time. If Bonds is right that Beethoven would have preferred the fanfare in question in his Fifth Symphony to be played on horns, the tension in this case is between Beethoven's compositional plans and the instrumental means available to him. As a result, Beethoven's intentions as embodied in the score are not contradictory; rather, the contradiction is between what Beethoven mandated in the score and what it seems likely he would have mandated in slightly different circumstances. To play the fanfare in question on modern horns is thus to be faithful to the work *as Beethoven first conceived it*, though it requires flouting aspects of the work *as Beethoven ultimately wrote it*.[31]

At this point, it seems that the dispute is largely over what constitutes the musical work. Davies argues that the work is constituted by the composer's mandates as expressed publicly in the score. Dodd implies that this view is in danger of missing the forest for the trees. The score describes the work at the level of surface detail, but the point of those details is to convey a deeper musical meaning or content. Davies would certainly agree that most musical works have a complex hierarchical structure, as we saw near the beginning of this chapter (2001, 45–58). But he denies that it makes sense to pursue composers' "higher-level" intentions, such as those regarding expressive effects, at the expense of "lower-level" intentions, such as those regarding which notes should be played. His primary argument is simply that classical works for performance are publicly accessible items, as befits their role in a social practice. They are specified in publicly accessible scores and thus it is their scores (properly understood) that determine the features of the work (S. Davies 2001, 221–2). In other words, composers aim to produce higher-level (e.g., expressive or formal) features *by means of* specific lower-level features (e.g., sequences of notes played on particular instruments). Davies also argues that embracing interpretive authenticity over score compliance could result in much more sweeping departures from the score than Dodd's examples suggest. For instance, the degree of tension in certain harmonies has changed over time. If we are to be true to the work's higher-level features at the expense of score compliance, then, it seems we should add, in performance, discordant notes to all music written before the twentieth century (S. Davies 2001, 232–3).

Since Dodd embraces both score-compliance and interpretive authenticity, he does not imply that performers must *always* add such notes (for instance), but to the extent that he allows this as one reasonable response to the tension between the two authenticities, he embraces what Davies sees as an absurd consequence of his view. However, if that view is to be a rival to Davies's, Dodd seems to owe us an account of *what a musical work is*, that is, of *what* the performer who chooses interpretive over score-compliance authenticity is being faithful *to*. As we have seen, his examples suggest a range of candidates, including what is represented in the score (which may contain tensions such as those that concern Brendel), the intended higher-level effects of a performance (as in Staier's Mozart performances), and the composer's ideal conception of the work before it is compromised by practical necessity (as in the case of Beethoven's bassoons). Dodd does not supply such an account. Instead, he grounds the value of interpretative authenticity in its ability to reveal "what is there to be understood in [the work, i.e., its] content" (2015, 487). But not everything that is revelatory of some aspect of a work is a performance of it. Most obviously, a written analysis of a work may reveal something about it to us, but it is not thereby a performance of the work. And performances of *arrangements of, fantasias or improvisations based upon*, or *works influenced by* a given work might reveal things to listeners about the target work without being performances of it (S. Davies 2013, 74; Kania 2008b, 70). So we cannot simply infer from the fact that a performance reveals something about a given work's content that it is a performance of that work – even if we recognize the work in the performance.

Now, Dodd himself has defended at length an ontology of musical works that seems much closer to Davies's "score-compliance" conception of them than any of the "interpretive" conceptions suggested by his discussions of authenticity (Dodd 2007). For instance, as we saw earlier in this chapter, as a timbral sonicist, Dodd thinks that a series of bassoon-timbre notes at the relevant point is essential to Beethoven's Fifth Symphony. This is difficult to square with the notion that faithfulness to the work could imply aiming to instance a series of horn-timbre sounds at that point. Two obvious solutions to the tension are to deny either (1) that interpretively authentic performances (must) aim at instancing the work, or (2) that the score correctly represents the work (at this point, at least). The first suggestion plainly contradicts the thrust of Dodd's argument, which defends interpretive authenticity as a kind of faithfulness to the work. The second is thus more promising for Dodd's purposes, and Dodd does gesture towards a development of this solution. When he talks of what is revealed in an insightful interpretation as (part of) a work's "content," he is careful to distinguish between "modest" and "rich" notions of work content. The *modest* content of a work "can be specified in advance of any performance, simply by consulting [the work's] score" in the case of a musical work (2015, 488, italics removed), or its text in the case of a literary work (Kania 2008b, 66–8, cited in Dodd 2015, 504, n. 9), while the *rich* content *cannot* be specified in advance of insightful interpretation; "its discovery is indefinitely extendable" (Dodd 2015, 503–4, n. 6). So perhaps Dodd's extant ontology of musical works is a theory of their *modest* content. He could thus claim that modest and rich content sometimes diverge and, when they do, that it is reasonable to pursue the latter at the expense of the former.

The score-compliance authenticist, by contrast, will insist that modest and rich content are not separable in the way that Dodd suggests. One need not deny that "interpretive authenticity" is fundamental to classical work-performance to defend this view; one need only argue that it is constrained by "score compliance." That is, a score-compliance authenticist could argue that the single, non-negotiable constitutive norm of classical work-performance practice is to evince an understanding of the work *through complying with the score*.

Independently of this central issue, we might consider an assumption in some of the arguments Dodd considers, namely that contemporary audiences are incapable of experiencing music that is culturally distant from them as its original or ideal audiences would have experienced them. For instance, Dodd implies that Staier thinks we can no longer hear the exoticism of Mozart's Rondo alla Turca if it is performed as written. This assumption has been persistent in the debate over classical authenticity, its most notable proponents being James O. Young (e.g., 1988) and Peter Kivy (1995, 47–79, 188–232), who both distinguish between sounds in an *acoustic* sense and in an *experiential* sense. Perhaps we can reproduce the (acoustic) sounds of historical performances, but the point of doing so is surely to give us a certain musical experience. If the latter is not possible, since we do not hear things the way historical audiences did, what is the point of achieving the former?

One reply Davies makes to these concerns is that we are not as bound by our historical context as they imply (2001, 234–7). He points out that we happily shift our attention between quite different kinds of contemporary music, whether from heavy metal to hard rock, rock to pop, or pop to classical. An experience of heavy metal, say, does not spoil our ears for hard rock – we can still hear it as "hard" within the context of rock more broadly, even though it is not as hard as heavy metal. The more distant a kind of music is from what we are used to, the more we will have to educate our ears in order to appreciate it. Hearing Beethoven's music as harmonically revolutionary may require learning why it was heard that way by contemporary audiences. Whether or not that requires explicit instruction in music theory (see Chapter 4, §4.6.2), it certainly requires listening to a lot of music from the relevant historical period. But this will still be easier (for a listener raised in an environment where Western music is ubiquitous) than learning to listen to Balinese gamelan with understanding, simply because Beethoven and the Beatles (but not the Balinese) share the same basic musical language.[32]

A second reply is that if we are interested in a particular historical work – or works as historically-contextualized artifacts more generally – then an inability to experience a work as its original, intended, or ideal audiences would have is no reason to change the work (Levinson 2019). Consider a literary analogy: David Foster Wallace's *Infinite Jest* (1996) is set in a (then) near-future North America that is heading toward full-blown dystopia. One central factor in the society's decline is its citizens' addiction to entertainment, particularly in the form of "cartridges" that are distributed over some kind of network. Reading the book at or shortly after the time in which it is set (around 2010) can be disorienting in a way that it would not have been to its original audience, since we are now aware of many actual developments in political history and technology since 1996 that the book's original readers could not have been. As a result, it is more difficult to maintain a coherent sense of the world of the novel reading it now than it would have been reading it in 1996.[33] One could solve this problem by slightly updating the novel – replacing all references to "teleputers" with references to "laptops," for instance; substituting the actual Donald Trump for the fictional demagogue Johnny Gentle; and so on.[34] But this would seem to be not *faithfulness to* Wallace's work, but rather *revision of* it. One could not claim, without qualification, to have read Wallace's famous novel if one had read only this updated version.[35]

7.5 Personal Authenticity in Popular Music

I said earlier that there's a growing consensus among philosophers that authenticity in classical performance is a matter of the production of a genuine instance of the work being performed. That this still leaves some difficult issues unsolved is obvious from Dodd's discussion of the apparent tension between score-compliance authenticity and interpretive authenticity. But when people talk of authenticity (genuineness, sincerity, keepin' it real) in connection with *popular* music, they are usually talking not of a relationship between the performance and *the work* of which it is a performance, but of a relationship between the performance (including the work being performed) and *the performer*. That is, when appreciating popular music, we often take it to be relevant whether or not the performance (including the song performed) is a genuine expression or manifestation of the performer's personality. This valorization of personal authenticity amounts to a musical ideal of *sincerity*.[36]

Peter Kivy discusses a variety of this "personal authenticity" that he takes to be an ideal within classical music, arguing that classical musicians and audiences value performance interpretations and styles that are original, authentic expressions of the unique individual performer (1995, 108–42, 260–86). Kivy seems to conflate sincerity and originality here. Though every individual is unique, it doesn't follow that every individual, even potentially, has a unique way of, say, interpreting the "Goldberg Variations." And though we may value unoriginal interpretations and styles for their sincerity, it's not obvious that we value them more highly than original – but insincere – interpretations and styles.

Philosophers who have discussed personal authenticity in popular music have generally avoided the issue of originality, focusing exclusively on sincerity (though see Gracyk 2009). Jeanette Bicknell (2005) puts the issue in terms of *convincingness*, arguing that while many songs may be convincingly performed by just about anyone, others require a kind of match between the song's content and the performer's persona.[37] This persona is not the thin persona posited by imagination theories of musical expressiveness (Chapter 2, §2.5), but rather the performer's public self, which we hear the song's content as issuing from and endorsed by:

> A singer's public persona is the face, body, and personal history … she presents to the audience. It includes such factors as gender, race, age, and ethnicity, as well as quirks of personality …. This information is conveyed by the singer's appearance, clothing choices, and the statements and activities reported by the media or circulated among fans. A public persona may transparently reflect a singer's true personality; more likely, it will be highly mediated and constructed.
>
> (Bicknell 2005, 262–3)

The "matching" Bicknell requires between persona and song content is no simple relationship. Bicknell doesn't mean that we identify the "I" or "narrator" of the song's lyrics with the performer or her persona. Nina Simone, for instance, gives powerful, convincing performances of her great song "Four Women," even though its text is narrated in the first person from the perspective of four different people. Bicknell's point is that we find Simone's performances of this song powerful in part because the artistic content it conveys is of a kind that Simone's public persona – that of a black, female, staunch civil-rights activist – is in a position to understand and endorse. Since other performers' public personae may also be in such a position, there can be compelling performances by other musicians. But some performances would fail to convince because the singer's public persona implies that he is likely not in such a position. Robin Thicke, for instance, whose public persona is masculine and at the very least tainted by accusations of misogyny and the theft of a black artist's music (Ortland 2016), may be incapable of singing the song convincingly.

It is a difficult question what convincingness requires in the relationship between a singer's public persona and the content of a song, most likely one that does not admit of a general answer. At any rate, it would certainly be too simplistic to conclude that songs narrated from a black or woman's point of view could not be performed by non-black or non-woman performers. Bicknell argues, for instance, that "a performer's gender is salient only in combination with other factors such as race and ethnicity, personality, and age" (2005, 264). Attempting to test the limits of this flexibility, she writes "I do not know of any male vocalists who have performed, say, 'Natural Woman,' nor can I imagine any who could and hope to convince an audience" (2005, 264). Yet surely a male drag artist who identifies as a man could give a convincing performance of that song – and not necessarily through performing it parodically.[38]

Why should the personal authenticity that underwrites convincingness be more important in popular song than in other kinds of musical performance? Bicknell hypothesizes that this is due to our deeply rooted sense that the voice is the primary vehicle of self-expression (2005, 267–8). Though we know that the singer is *performing*, and thus cannot automatically be assumed to be expressing herself in the details of the content of the song she performs, her central use of her *voice* in her performance makes it difficult to shake the impression that she is so expressing herself. Bicknell's resolution of this tension is to argue that though we do not typically take singing to be self-expression, we resist sharp contrasts between song content and singer's public persona (as in the hypothetical example of Robin Thicke performing "Four Women"). The plausibility of this hypothesis seems to be reduced by consideration of other artistic traditions, however. As Bicknell acknowledges, we do not apply the same standards of personal authenticity to *classical* singing. Given that classical singers use their voices no less than popular singers do, this suggests that other factors play a greater role here than the perceived self-expressive function of the human voice. Bicknell is also aware that this argument sits uncomfortably with the fact that "we accept for the most part that actors play at being someone else" (2005, 267). Of course, there are still limits to who we will accept acting certain roles. We may balk, for instance, at white actor Alec Guinness playing (Indian) Professor Godbole in *A Passage to India*.[39] But, given that actors' voices are also central to their performances and that their other main artistic tool is their bodies, it is somewhat puzzling that we should expect less rather than more sincerity from actors than from singers. Perhaps part of the explanation is that films, plays, and so on, usually create a more robust fictional world than song performances.

A more important clue may lie in the fact that Bicknell restricts the value of sincerity to only some popular songs. And if it's true that, for instance, there could be successful performances of "Natural Woman" by men, perhaps this restriction could be extended to only *some performances* of some popular songs.

Near the end of her first discussion of sincerity in song performance, Bicknell approvingly cites Mark Booth's claim that "song plays on my tendency to take it as a message *for me*" (qtd. in Bicknell 2005, 269); in a later discussion, she notes that jazz vocalists, like (sometimes) singers of popular songs, are explicit (outside their performances) about a personal emotional connection to the songs they sing, even though they typically sing songs composed by others (2015, 57–8). Perhaps it is not so much the nature of the song that leads us to look for sincerity in a song performance (when we do), then, but rather the context of the performance – a context that *includes* the singer's public persona. It would be silly to look for sincerity in Richard Cheese's performance of *anything* – his lounge-lizard versions of rock and pop classics such as Radiohead's "Creep" are clearly intended as arch, even camp, postmodern fripperies. Cheese does not claim to be sincere, nor do we expect him to be. Many pop entertainers, such as Walk the Moon, seem to be in the same boat. They produce singable, danceable, pop hits and no one cares whether they've ever actually been told to shut up and dance. By contrast, audiences took the young Bob Dylan (in part because of his public persona) to be *asserting* things through his performances – communicating what he took to be actual truths. If they had discovered that he didn't believe a word he sang, and was only in it for the money, it would have affected the convincingness of those performances (Gracyk 2017, §4).

What this suggestion amounts to is that the *functions* of a performance determine whether or not sincerity counts as a legitimate dimension of evaluation. (This should not be surprising given our discussion of value in Chapter 5.) If it functions, in part, as an assertion or self-expression, then sincerity will affect the performance's convincingness, as would be the case with, say, a political speech. Considering whether such assertion or self-expression is relevant to the *artistic* evaluation of a performance would return us to the issues discussed in Chapter 5. One upshot of this discussion seems to be that, as Theodore Gracyk puts it, "we need both the Bruce Springsteen model of utter sincerity and the David Bowie model of ironic play-acting" (2001, 216; cf. his 2009), that is, sincerity is a potentially valuable artistic property, but so is insincerity. And, as with many artistic properties, we may not be able to generalize about whether or not sincerity counts in favor of a given performance, even restricting our discussion to popular music.

7.6 Review and Looking Ahead

If personal authenticity is as inconstant a value in popular music as our discussion has suggested, then it is much less central to the tradition than work authenticity is to classical music. In Chapter 10, we will consider the issue of *cultural* authenticity in popular music. In the next chapter, however, we continue our investigation of musical performance by considering a musical practice in which the creation of music in the moment of performance seems to be valued over any work that might be performed: musical improvisation.

Questions

Explain the most general sense of "authentic," then explain what you think are the most important ways in which the concept applies to music. Is any of these the *primary* sense of authenticity in music?

Explain the differences between *pure sonicism, timbral sonicism,* and *instrumentalism* about works of classical music. Defend one view as superior to the others.

Explain the difference between *score-compliance* and *interpretive* authenticity. Are both "constitutive norms" of classical music? If so, can they come into conflict or do they cohere with one another? If they can come into conflict, may performers choose between them, or does one always trump the other?

What is personal authenticity? Does it generally confer artistic value on a popular-song performance? If so, why? If not, in what situations (if any) does it confer such value?

Notes

1 For simplicity, I often omit the alternative theory that performers must only attempt to instance *most* of what's essential to the work.
2 Nelson Goodman disagrees, arguing that allowing any divergence from the score in the performance of a work is fatal to a theory of a work's identity (1968, 186–7). For discussion, see S. Davies 2001, 153–9.
3 It doesn't necessarily follow that such a performance would fail to be of the song in question; the point here is the relative importance of various features of musical works.
4 I say that these two musical texts draw on *similar* rather than *the same* conventions since, for example, how to interpret the same rhythmic notation (e.g., whether or not "dotted notes" should be "swung") may differ between them, for reasons related to what follows, as well as the texts' different music-historical contexts.
5 In part to avoid some of this confusion, the issue is also referred to as one of "historical" or "historically informed" performance practice. For discussion, see S. Davies 2001, 208 and Young 2013, 452–3.
6 For critical discussion of this consensus, see Ravasio 2019b.
7 The term "sonicism" is a little misleading here. After all, as we will soon see, it is not mere (let alone "pure") *sounds* that constitute musical works according to the sonicist, but rather musical pitches, rhythms, etc.
8 Actual examples might include Wendy (formerly Walter) Carlos's early synthesizer album *Switched-on Bach* (1968) or the Swingle Singers' a capella performances of Bach's instrumental works.
9 Peter Williams argues that it is not obvious exactly how we should understand the "practice" ("-übung") part of the title, but the "keyboard" ("Clavier-") part is relatively unambiguous (2001, 1–34).

10 What's more, this indicates that the piece is intended to be played by only one person. You won't be getting the practice Bach had in mind if you and 50 of your closest friends play the piece on a single harpsichord, covering two keys each (cf. Godlovitch 1998, 36–7).

11 Consider, however, Olga Martynova's harpsichord performances of Romantic and modern works written for piano (e.g., the album *Everything You Wanted to Know about Harpsichord but were Afraid to Ask*).

12 How specific is this intention? For our purposes, it's enough that it is more specific than Bach's with respect to the *Well-Tempered Clavier* (assuming Bach would have sanctioned both harpsichord and organ performances of that work) and less specific than a particular individual instrument (e.g., the first piano Beethoven owned).

13 Recordings might seem a simpler example, but since most classical recordings are of people playing instruments, they are not as simple as they seem. We will consider recordings in detail in Chapter 9.

14 Better safe than sorry: The term "instrumentalism" here derives from the term (musical) "instrument"; it has nothing to do with the distinction between intrinsic and instrumental values discussed in Chapter 5.

15 Andrew Kania (2008c, 202) argues that the relationship between the music's aesthetic properties and how it is produced creates problems for Julian Dodd's timbral sonicism analogous to those discussed in Chapter 6, §6.3.3.

16 Though Dodd co-authored this essay with John Irving, I speak of "Dodd" throughout for simplicity.

17 Dodd considers this a type of *work authenticity* because it is a matter of being *faithful* to the work, a point to which we will return below.

18 Dodd cites Staier's liner notes to his 2005 recording as evidence of this reasoning. But when Staier discusses the Rondo alla Turca in particular, he implies that his departures from the score are not in the interest of authenticity or insight, but are rather a "personal comment" on how Mozart might have reacted (in performing the piece) to the fact that "we can no longer say whether we really like it or not[; w]e know it so much better than we would like to" due to its "triumphal progress around the world," "omnipresen[ce] from Acapulco to Tokyo," and "associat[ion] with dreary hotel lobbies or check-in queues" (Staier 2005, 12). Nonetheless, I follow Dodd's interpretation of Staier's intentions for the sake of argument.

19 Bonds gave this example in a personal communication to Dodd (according to a personal communication from Dodd to me!).

20 For useful overviews of the history of the metronome and tempo markings, see David Fallows 2001a and 2001b.

21 Davies denies that the mandated tempi necessitate the loss of detail, but I ignore that issue for the sake of the philosophical point (2013, 72).

22 As noted above, it seems to me that, on the contrary, Staier's performance is intended as a kind of crazed reaction to this piece's Muzakian ubiquity (as indicated in his liner notes).

23 See, for example, www.youtube.com/watch?v=Z7izUG6QStA.

24 See Chapter 4, §4.5, for a brief introduction to sonata form.

25 You can hear the passage in question played by bassoons around 4:33 on the Orchestre Révolutionnaire et Romantique's 1994 recording with John Eliot Gardiner conducting, and by modern horns around 5:06 on a recording by the Berlin Philharmonic with Herbert von Karajan conducting. The fanfare in the exposition can be heard on these recordings around 0:40 and 0:45 respectively. (Both recordings are on the Spotify playlist for this chapter: http://bit.ly/PWM-7.)

26 Compare Beethoven's Third Symphony, fourth movement, mm. 437–42.

27 That is, Beethoven could have had just one horn play for enough bars preceding and following the fanfare to allow the other horn to change crooks for the fanfare. Compare Beethoven's Third Symphony, first movement, mm. 370–510.

28 Compare Beethoven's Third Symphony.

29 Thanks to Drew Stephen and Nemesio García-Carril Puy for help with the corno-historical details here.
30 This reply depends on the version of score-compliance according to which a performance must be intended to follow *every* mandate in the score.
31 Note that the spirit of this argument might be better served – particularly for a timbral sonicist, such as Dodd – by playing the fanfare on *natural* horns *in C* (rather than modern horns throughout the symphony), though that would require employing one of the solutions to the compositional problem canvassed above.
32 This issue of the extent to which our ears are educable comes up in connection with a number of philosophical disputes about music. We have considered it already, for instance, in our discussion of hearing expressive, formal, and aesthetic properties (Chapter 2, §2.4.5; Chapter 4, §4.6; and Chapter 6, §6.3.3).
33 This problem is most similar to the one that motivates Staier to play different notes from those Mozart wrote. A literary parallel to Bonds's suggestion for the instrumentation of Beethoven's Fifth Symphony might be the production of a version of *Infinite Jest* edited to be more logically consistent.
34 Compare Davies's analogy between music and literature quoted in §7.3, above.
35 We do claim to have read literary works in translation, a change that might seem even more radical than my imagined updating of *Infinite Jest*. But most are happy to qualify such claims (e.g., "I've read Proust, but only in translation"). For further comparison of musical and literary cases, see S. Davies 2011f.
36 Compare Jenefer Robinson's "new Romantic" theory of expression, discussed in Chapter 3, §3.3.2.
37 Recall from Chapter 1 that this content amounts to more than just the meaning of the lyrics.
38 We will address the question of whether such a rendition – or, for that matter, Rod Stewart's 1974 version, "Natural Man" – would amount to the performance of a *different song* in Chapter 9, §9.4.
39 For discussion of race-mismatched casting, see Mag Uidhir 2013. Such "limits" can be exceeded for artistic effect, as in the mistaken-identity neo-noir *Suture*, in which the brothers mistaken for one another are played by actors who look nothing alike – one black and one white. But that doesn't show that the limits aren't there.

Further Reading

In a philosophical overview of authenticity in art, Denis Dutton (2003) helpfully addresses a range of concepts of authenticity in connection with a number of different arts.

Classic (and compendious) philosophical treatments of work authenticity in classical music include Kivy (1995) and S. Davies (2001, 60–71, 199–253). Though it appeared too late to be considered in this chapter, Julian Dodd's *Being True to Works of Music* (forthcoming) develops the view discussed in §7.4, arguing that (when the two conflict) interpretive authenticity always trumps score-compliance authenticity.

Wesley Cray (2019) develops the theory of the evaluative import of performance (and song) personas discussed by Bicknell and Gracyk.

8   Improvisation

Overview

In this chapter, we investigate the nature of musical improvisation before turning to the Western musical tradition most closely associated with improvisation – jazz – to consider the implications of the centrality of improvisation to jazz for its ontology and values.

We have considered the nature of musical works in some detail in the previous two chapters, since much musical performance is of such works. But in many musical traditions, we also find performances (and non-performance music-making) that aim not at instancing a pre-existing musical structure, but rather at bringing new music into being at the very moment it is played. The standard term for such music-making is *improvisation*. Many of the great composers of the Western classical tradition – Bach, Mozart, Beethoven – were famous for their improvisatory keyboard skills, and it was standard in a concerto – a work that showcases a solo instrument, accompanied by orchestra – to leave one or more "gaps" in the score, space for the soloist to improvise a *cadenza* based on the work's themes. (Sadly, improvisation is an almost lost art in the classical tradition. Aside from the performances of a few exceptional specialists, every time you hear a cadenza these days, far from being improvised, it is as highly rehearsed as the rest of the performance.) Many rock musicians improvise in both rehearsal and the studio as a way of generating musical material, but also during live shows; "jam bands" are known primarily for their extended improvisations in live performance. But the Western musical tradition most commonly associated with improvisation is surely jazz. In this chapter, we will first consider some philosophical issues raised by improvisation in general and then investigate the implications of the centrality of improvisation in jazz for its ontology and values.

8.1 What Is Improvisation?

The very notion of improvised musical performance can seem paradoxical. On the one hand, it seems essential to improvisation that it be spontaneous or unpremeditated. On the other hand, improvisation is an intentional action, that is, behavior that is under the control of the agent. After all, the notes that a skilled improviser plays are not random; they make some musical sense. We can usually distinguish between inspiration and error. Lee B. Brown identifies two views that might be considered polar-opposite solutions to this paradox, one of which he calls the "romantic perspective," the other of which we might call "eliminativism" (2011a, 60–1). The romanticist runs with the first part of the paradox: Improvisation is natural music-making, unconstrained by rules, preparation, or education. One problem with this view is that improvisation is obviously a skill that is improved by practice, coaching, and so on. And the fact that one can improvise (or fail to improvise) *on a particular tune*, or *in a particular style*, suggests that improvisation is at least often governed by rules in *some* sense. Brown points out that even in the freest jazz "a keyboardist is not normally allowed to interpolate Chopin's Ballade in G minor or to beat the piano with a baseball bat" (2011a, 60). But even if this problem could be solved, the romantic perspective leaves the original paradox untouched, since even natural, unconstrained actions are *actions*. If one is acting intentionally – making decisions, rather than being pushed around by forces completely beyond one's control – how can what one is doing be spontaneous? The eliminativist takes this last question to be rhetorical: Actions cannot be spontaneous, so there is no such thing as improvisation. (Thus they "eliminate" improvisation as an incoherent concept.) This view has the virtue of simplicity, but it is unsatisfying for the same reason – it seems to *over*simplify our musical experience. We do not think that all improvisers are frauds, presenting prepared performances disguised as spontaneous events.

The solution to the paradox seems to lie in getting clearer on what we mean by "spontaneous" or "unpremeditated" action. It can help to consider improvisation in the other arts and in non-artistic endeavors. Some philosophers of jazz have likened ensemble improvisation to ordinary conversation (Hagberg 1998, 480–1; Kraut 2007, 57–65). In conversation, you typically respond *spontaneously* to what your interlocutors say – of necessity, since you typically do not know what they are going to say in advance. You may have an idea of the kinds of things your interlocutor is likely to say, either in content or style. Perhaps she is an old friend whom you know to have conservative views and be something of a joker, while she knows you to be an earnest liberal. But it is unlikely that either of you would be able to predict exactly what the other would say at any given conversational moment – that is one of the joys of good conversation. At one limit, we can consider "conversation" with someone with whom we do not share a language. Some communication may be possible through gesture, facial expressions, and so on. But these will not be the most satisfying conversations. Even when we restrict our consideration to people fluent in the same language, some are better conversationalists than others. Perhaps this is in part due to natural talents, but it seems plausible that one can become a better conversationalist through observation and practice.

Where does spontaneity fit into all of this? It seems clear that when one responds to someone else in ordinary conversation, one's words typically (i) are under one's control (though one may of course occasionally misspeak), and (ii) draw on existing knowledge (e.g., of the language and conversational context), yet (iii) are decided upon just before one utters them. The spontaneity of one's utterance is a matter of the last factor. This spontaneity admits of degrees – one may hesitate before saying something, or pause to formulate the clearest way of expressing oneself – or it may be lacking, as when one utters a cliché or prepares a witticism in advance and then waits for an appropriate moment to unleash it. (Even in these last cases, however, the decision to deploy the witticism or cliché *now* is likely spontaneous.) The three general features of conversation identified above seem to fit musical improvisation in such a way as to solve the paradox with which we began. The improvising musician's actions are under her control and draw on her knowledge of how to play her instrument (or sing), of musical styles and conventions, and even of the piece of music being performed or her plans for this particular performance. But to the extent that she makes decisions about some aspect of her performance just before she creates it, her performance will be improvised.

We might ask just how much earlier than one's utterance – conversational or musical – one's decision to make it must occur in order to count as spontaneous. It seems unlikely that any precise answer to this question will be defensible. But it's plausible that any actions determined by decisions made before the performance begins fail to count as improvised in the relevant sense.[1] (There may be other senses, as when one forgets to bring one's drumsticks to a gig and improvises by using instead some cutlery that's ready to hand at the club.) We might also say that the shorter the gap between a decision and its execution, the more improvisatory the action. So a decision to add a quick grace note to the first note of the tune made just before playing it will count as more improvisatory than a decision made while playing the tune to add a different grace note when one next plays the tune. Even this way of putting things, though, makes the situation sound a lot cleaner than it is in reality. For instance, a musician may have a general but vague sense of how he wants a particular performance to go. If he is successful, we can say that that general but vague property of the performance was not improvised, even though we might say that every individual note was improvised. This may sound puzzling, but it is no more mysterious than someone setting out to write a song with verses in a minor key and a chorus in the relative major before they've decided anything about the melody, words, or other details of the song.

How can we tell whether or not a given performance is truly improvised, according to this conception? The short answer is that we won't always be able to. Andy Hamilton grapples with the putative case of jazz pianist Ray Bryant reproducing a famous recorded solo note-for-note in a jazz club setting where he was expected to improvise (Hamilton 2000, 176–9). Hamilton argues that "there is a genuine phenomenon of an *improvised feel*," arising from the ways in which competent improvisers respond to the challenge of continuing a coherent musical structure on the fly (2000, 178). However, as the Bryant case suggests, this feel can only be paradigmatic of, not *sufficient* for, improvisation. On the other hand, it's surely *possible* for an improviser to produce a musical structure so perfectly formed that one can hardly believe it was improvised rather than composed. This shows that an improvised feel cannot be *necessary* for improvisation, either. Whether such a performance would be a *good* improvisation is a question to which we will turn below.

Philosophers have questioned various aspects of the conception of improvisation outlined above. Perhaps most radically, Carol S. Gould and Kenneth Keaton deny that spontaneity is a necessary feature of improvisation. They argue instead that we should understand improvisation "not in terms of the degree of spontaneity of a performance, but rather in terms of how closely a given performance conforms to a score" (2000, 147). A minor problem with this view is the assumption that all performances (perhaps with the exception of completely improvised performances) derive from a score. Many jazz and rock musicians learn the tunes they play or improvise upon by ear, from other performances or recordings, yet we can clearly distinguish between a highly polished performance of a song learnt by ear and a quite free improvisation. Substituting "composition" for "score" in Gould and Keaton's formulation will solve part of this problem. But consider a classical violinist's improvised cadenza. Typically, apart from perhaps the first and last few notes, no detail of the cadenza is notated in the score (or mandated by the work) at all.[2] Yet it is conventional to improvise one's cadenza on the themes in the work. A useful theory of improvisation should surely let us distinguish between (i) the pre-existing themes of the work, and (ii) what the performer does with them in improvising her cadenza. Gould and Keaton's conception of improvisation seems unable to do this. Since no particular notes are required in order to perform this part of the work, every cadenza will conform to the score to the same degree. But a conception of improvisation that appeals to spontaneity can distinguish between a particular melodic motif, the shape of which is clearly not being made up on the spot (because we recognize it from earlier in the work) and the musician's real-time decision to employ it in this particular way (piled on top of itself, say, in a rapidly ascending sequence).

More generally, Gould and Keaton's view gives rise to the unintuitive consequence that a classical pianist, playing a meticulously rehearsed interpretation of a Beethoven piano sonata, is improvising to the extent that his interpretation involves details that go beyond what is required by the score. But since *every* performance of a scored work necessarily involves such details, every performance of such a work will count as improvised (to that extent). Gould and Keaton embrace this implication of their view, but, again, this seems to rob us of useful distinctions to make when trying to understand what musicians are doing. For we want to be able to cut an improviser more slack than someone who has meticulously prepared their performance, precisely because the former but not the latter is making decisions on the fly. What motivates Gould and Keaton to erase this distinction? They seem primarily concerned to close the gap they think some see between classical and jazz performances. According to the view they take as their target, in jazz performance a work is created as it is performed because the jazz performance is improvised, while classical performance is the mere instantiation of a musical structure encoded in a score. Gould and Keaton point out that, on the contrary, classical performers are themselves creative artists, necessarily interpreting scores in their performances, and there is a long history of improvisation in the classical tradition. They then point out that jazz musicians rarely, if ever, improvise *ex nihilo*, most commonly basing their performances on pre-existing musical material. These points are well taken, but they can be accounted for without rejecting the notion that improvisation is spontaneous. Indeed, at times Gould and Keaton themselves seem to waver on this point, for instance when they ask rhetorically: "is it not the case that a classical performer interpreting a work produces a unique sound event and does so *with an element of spontaneity?*" (2000, 145, italics added).

So much for the attempt to eliminate spontaneity from the heart of improvisation. James Young and Carl Matheson, by contrast, argue that our working conception of improvisation is too broad. They argue that an improvising performer is one "who spontaneously chooses *structural* properties" (italics added) of her performance:

> The structural properties of a performance include its melody, harmony, and length (in bars, not in temporal duration). A structural property is to be understood in contrast to an expressive or interpretive property. The expressive properties of a performance include tempo, the use of rubato, dynamics, and so on. We believe that the line between expressive and structural properties is a fuzzy one, but it must be drawn if we are to avoid the conclusion that virtually every musical performance involves improvisation.
>
> (Young & Matheson 2000, 127)

The concluding justification for restricting improvisation to structural properties is a puzzling one. Young and Matheson are surely right that many musical performances – particularly performances of classical works – will not involve any improvisation. Now, no two such performances – even of the same work by the same highly skilled performer under the same conditions on two successive nights – may be exactly the same, but this need not be due to spontaneous deployment of "expressive" properties. Mostly obviously, as Young and Matheson themselves point out, such performances may vary because of *mistakes*. But suppose this were not the case; perhaps *some* (expressive or interpretive) decisions in almost all, even meticulously rehearsed, classical performances are made spontaneously during the performance. Why not acknowledge that such performances thereby involve improvisation? One reason might be that this is surprising. Perhaps we typically think of jazz performances as improvisatory and classical performances as, by contrast, rehearsed. But insights can be as surprising as falsehoods. We don't typically think of ourselves as improvising when we engage in ordinary conversation, but if you are convinced by the reflections earlier in this chapter, you may now believe that that is in fact what we are doing. Moreover, our more sophisticated understanding of improvisation can help explain our pre-theoretical impression of the difference between jazz and classical performances. Jazz performances typically involve *more* improvisation – more spontaneous decisions about more aspects of the performance – than classical performances. Indeed, Young and Matheson's distinction between two kinds of musical property may help us to make more precise distinctions between the ways in which different performances are improvisatory.

We have been considering what improvisation is, but we might just as well have begun by asking what *an* improvisation is. That is, people use the term improvisation not just as a "mass noun," describing a kind of performative action, but also as a "count noun" that sorts performances into two mutually exclusive sets: the improvisations and the prepared performances. These two uses are often glossed over in the philosophical literature on jazz, and this may be behind some of the problems diagnosed with various theories and arguments above. For instance, even if you think that Young and Matheson are wrong to restrict the domain of improvisation (in the mass-noun sense) to "structural" musical features, it may well be that we typically call an entire performance *an* improvisation (count noun) only if a significant number of its structural features are largely improvised; it would be unusual, at the very least, to call a note-perfect performance of a Beethoven piano sonata *an improvisation*, even if every interpretive feature were improvised. Some who have considered the (count-noun) concept of *an* improvisation argue that at the heart of the concept is a musician's attitude toward the pre-existing musical material on which her performance is based (S. Davies 2001, 16–17; Brown 2011a, 66–7). If at base she intends to present a pre-existing musical composition to her audience (albeit by way of her own interpretation of it), then her performance is not an improvisation, whereas if she takes that material as a point of departure rather than a model, her performance is an improvisation. Again, this seems to allow for the possibility of sound-alike cases in which one performer gives a radical (and perhaps error-riddled) interpretation of a given composition while another produces a tame improvisation based on the same composition. Whether such a view is defensible will depend on whether we can say enough about the relevant intentions for a useful theoretical distinction. If we cannot, it may be that we have to settle for the idea that performances can be more or less improvisatory, leaving the concept of *an* improvisation as simply marking one end of a continuum.[3]

8.2 The Ontology of Jazz

We have seen that improvisation is a quite general concept (improvisation can be found in many different kinds of music and in non-musical activities) and also a matter of degree (a performance, or other action, can be more or less improvisatory). However, the centrality of improvisation to jazz has led some to ask whether the *ontology* of jazz, that is, the kinds of things there are in jazz and the relationships between them, is different from that considered in Chapters 6 and – particularly – 7. According to what David Davies calls the *classical paradigm*, a work is first composed and then may receive multiple performances that differ in artistically significant ways yet are all performances of the same work (2011, 23–70). The mere presence of improvisation in a performance does not show that it is not a performance of a work. Such improvisation may be called for by the stylistic conventions of the period in which the work was composed, as with the ornamentation of melodies in the baroque era, or mandated by the composer, as in the requirement to improvise a cadenza in many classical concertos. Jazz performance-practice is extremely varied, yet many theorists take a certain kind of performance to be paradigmatic: so-called *standard-form* jazz.[4] In such a performance, an ensemble first plays the *head* – the accompanied melody that will form the basis for the subsequent improvisations. There follow a number of *solos* by various members of the group – the harmonic and metrical pattern of the head is repeated continuously (in a series of *choruses*) while a single member of the group improvises melodically over this accompaniment. After all the solos, the group restates the head. There are considerable departures from this basic pattern within standard-form jazz. For instance, the opening or closing statements of the head may be omitted, or a pre-composed variation substituted for either or both; instead of a series of choruses improvised by one player, two players may "trade fours," improvising four measures each in a kind of musical call and response; and so on.

If standard-form jazz performances fit the classical paradigm as work performances, then the works that they are performances of must be extremely "thin." (Recall from Chapter 7 that a work's thickness is a matter of the proportion of properties mandated for its correct performance.) This is because the many performances of a given jazz *standard* – the name typically given to the putative works performed in standard-form jazz – vary considerably, much more than performances of classical works of the common-practice period. For one thing, there is the variation in the improvised choruses. In addition, not only is the instrumentation extremely flexible (indeed, it is not clear that any instrumentation is ruled out), the basic musical features of the standard are treated with considerable license. For instance, chord substitution – replacing a chord with a different one that may perform a similar harmonic function – is extremely common.[5]

One problem with viewing such performances as performances of even very thin works is that many of the works that the performances are putatively of were not written for this kind of treatment. Consider John Coltrane's classic recording of "My Favorite Things" (1961). The music of the well-known song from *The Sound of Music* is transformed in a number of striking ways: the rhythm is swung, minimal modal harmonies are substituted, giving an "oriental" feel to the music, the bridge ("when the dog bites ...") is postponed until the very end, and so on. Less subtly, of course, the *words* are missing from this rendition of the song! If Coltrane and his ensemble are performing some musical structure, then, it appears to be not Rodgers & Hammerstein's song, "My Favorite Things," but a stripped-down arrangement of that song.[6] Whether jazz performers are flouting many essential features of the works they claim to perform or accurately performing thin arrangements of those works, we seem to have a significant departure from the classical paradigm. For, as we saw in Chapter 7, one central aim of performances in the classical paradigm is to present the work that it is a performance *of.* (Recall that even the dispute between score-compliance and interpretive authenticists is over what *faithfulness to the work* entails.) In jazz performances of the kind we have been considering, by contrast, the standard on which the performance is based is treated more like a springboard for the performers' improvisational skills (S. Davies 2001, 16–17; Fisher 2018, 158–9), whether because the performers are free to ignore whatever features of it they like or because there is not much to it.

David Davies suggests that this argument cannot be made quite so quickly, since some standards, such as many classic numbers by Miles Davis and Thelonious Monk, were in fact composed specifically to be improvised upon by jazz musicians (D. Davies 2011, 155–7). Just as we properly appreciate a classical symphony through various performances of it, we properly appreciate these standards through various jazz improvisations upon them. This contrasts with "My Favorite Things," since that song can be properly appreciated as the work for performance that it is perhaps only in a non-improvisatory performance of it (including, at the very least, a singer); when we appreciate Coltrane's performance of the same name, we appreciate how Coltrane improvises on the basis of (parts of) that work, rather than appreciating the work through Coltrane's performance of it. Though Davies does not suggest it, we might develop a more unified account from such considerations by arguing that performances such as Coltrane's "My Favorite Things," rather than being inauthentic performances of thick works, are in fact authentic performances of new, thinner works – the stripped-down arrangements mentioned above. This view is more plausible to the extent that other jazz musicians take Coltrane's performance of "My Favorite Things" to be definitive in just this way, improvising on the same elements he originally took from the show tune, modified in some of the same ways (e.g., with the rhythm swung).

However, this way of thinking of improvisatory jazz performances – as performances of very thin works – sits uneasily with what Davies says elsewhere about the potential for performances to be works of art in their own right. He points out that though performances of typical classical works may exhibit artistically valuable properties, those properties – "coherence (in interpretation), originality, and individual style in particular – seem to be *performative* virtues rather than qualities that contribute towards *the articulation of a distinct artistic statement* by the performer," that is, towards the creation of a distinct work (D. Davies 2011, 146, italics added). The reason, according to Davies, is that the thickness of typical classical works leaves little room for the performer to make her own statement independently of the work she is performing. This means, of course, that *thinner* compositions leave *more* room for their performers to make their own artistic statements. Davies does not dwell on the implications of these considerations for the status of thin compositions as "works." But, presumably, the more room that a thin composition leaves open for its performer to make her own statement, the less content the composition itself has. Thus if Davies thinks we must withhold work-status from performances of very thick compositions, he seems committed to the corollary that we must withhold work-status from very thin compositions, perhaps including standards written specifically for jazz improvisation and the arrangements implicit in jazz performances such as Coltrane's "My Favorite Things."[7]

In the context in which Davies presents his views about when a performance may count as a work of art in its own right, he has already introduced and defended a particular theory of art. For our purposes, we may remain neutral on that question. We can take the term "work," more neutrally, to refer to *a primary focus of appreciation* in a given art practice.[8] Thus, when we debate whether standard-form jazz involves the performance of very thin works, or the creation of new works using existing (non-work) musical materials as ingredients, what is at stake is what is *central* to jazz practice, what people knowledgeable about jazz see as the focus of artistic activity in that practice. To shift domains for a moment, although many artistically valuable artifacts may be created within the artistic practice of painting (including sketches, studies, and perhaps even arrangements of people and objects as models), we think of instances of one particular kind of thing – *paintings* – as the *works of art* in this practice. From the ways artists and knowledgeable audiences treat these various things, we can see that it is the finished paintings that give the practice its point and which the other objects in the practice serve in various ways. There is plenty of vagueness here. We may not always be able to decide, for instance, whether or not a particular kind of object or activity is *the sole* primary focus of appreciation, or whether two things share that status. But the hope is that this way of approaching things allows us to think more clearly and carefully about the musical practices we care about. (We could understand Davies's defense of a particular theory of art, and its consequences for a theory of what counts as a musical work, as an attempt to eliminate some of this vagueness.[9])

There is no denying that most jazz standards are repeatable musical structures that get instanced in various highly improvisatory performances, whether those standards are (i) relatively detailed musical pieces, many aspects of which get ignored in jazz performances (e.g., the original song, "My Favorite Things"); (ii) stripped-down arrangements of such pieces (e.g., what's in common to different takes of "My Favorite Things" for the canonical Coltrane album); or (iii) pieces composed specifically for such performances (e.g., Miles Davis's "Blue in Green"). But if the above reflections on the concept of a work of art are defensible, then none of this shows that jazz standards are musical works. We might rather compare them to film screenplays. The screenplay often plays a crucial role in the creation of a film, and often includes many valuable artistic properties (structural, linguistic, etc.) that get transferred to the completed film. But, as with sketches or studies for oil paintings, screenplays perform a subsidiary role in the practice of film-making. They derive their importance from the contributions they make to finished films; it is *films* that are the works of art in that practice.[10] The seemingly obvious conclusion to draw is that in jazz it is the improvisatory performance that is the work of art, not the composition upon which that performance is based.[11]

Stefan Caris Love goes further and argues that it is not the complete performance, but rather the *individual solo* that is the primary focus of appreciation in jazz:

> [T]he straight-ahead solo remains at the center of much jazz pedagogy, performance, and criticism, and the beginning of a solo is a special moment in any jazz performance, charged with anticipation. ... Students do not transcribe and study entire performances but rather solos .... Jazz fans admire soloists and

their best solos. ... [N]o one expects an ensemble's complete performance to be a coherent artistic whole ... .

(2016, 62, 72; cf. Gioia 1988, 51)

If this is right, then we should think of standard-form jazz performances less as individual works and more as anthologies. Each solo is like a short story and the performance like a collection of stories sharing a theme, setting, or cast of characters.[12] As Love acknowledges, this view discounts the importance of interaction between the musicians in an ensemble during solo improvisations, but he sees this as a necessary corrective to an overemphasis in jazz studies on such interaction. He argues that the rest of the ensemble plays an almost exclusively supporting role during a typical solo and that there is little difference between improvising a solo alone and with a group. He contrasts jazz in these respects with improvisational comedy, in which each member of an ensemble continuously has the potential to play as important a role as any other member, and in which solo performance is uniquely challenging (Love 2016, 71–2).

Whether we think of the individual solo or the complete standard-form performance as the primary focus of appreciation in jazz, some have argued that we should still not think of improvisatory performances as jazz *works*: "A genuinely improvisational performance, even though based upon ... [a standard], is not itself a musical work, with everything that this concept implies. In particular ... such a performance is not re-identifiable in multiple instances" (Brown 2000a, 115).[13] The idea here seems to be that we should not lose sight of the fact that we would like our theories of jazz to cohere with our theories of music more generally. In particular, we would like to be able to use the term "musical work" to refer to the same kinds of things in different musical traditions. Of course, what counts as the *same kind of thing* depends on context. One might ask why the feature Brown picks out – repeatability – should be an essential property of musical works in addition to the property we have thus far been working with – being a primary focus of appreciation. However, it may be that the latter property is not fine-grained enough to do the work we are demanding of it. Consider classical music once more. It might be argued that there we have two equally primary objects of appreciation: the pieces being performed and the performances of them. If this is the case, then both kinds of things will count as musical works in the classical tradition (Kania 2011a, 397–9). There may be nothing objectionable about this in itself, but we will still want to distinguish between the "piece works" and "performance works" in classical music. We do so already, of course, with the terms "work" and "performance." Moreover, there is a tendency in theorizing about the arts more generally to think of artworks as enduring objects rather than ephemeral events (Thom 1993, 28). One motivation for some artists in the performance-art movement in the 1960s and 1970s was to reject the commodification of art in the form of objects that could be bought and sold – traditional art *works*. And, as we shall see below, the notion of an object that can be worked on over time is connected to the idea that artists should strive for perfection.

These considerations may not be decisive, however. While we will doubtless want to continue to distinguish between art objects and events, this distinction seems unlikely to be as central to our theorizing about art as the concept of a primary focus of appreciation in an artistic practice. Moreover, if commodification and perfectibility have been *rightly* criticized by artists and theorists such as those in the performance-art movement, it would be a mistake to entrench such values in our ontological theories of the arts. So, for instance, David Davies recommends introducing terms to distinguish between *works for performance* (such as traditional classical works and jazz standards composed for improvising upon), *work performances* (performances of these things), and *performance works* (performances that are works of art in their own right) (2011, 17–20). Julian Dodd goes further, maintaining that "a musical work is just a repeatable musical structure" specified by a composer as the condition on being a correctly formed performance (2014b, 277, 287–8). On Dodd's view, the questions we have been considering about what counts as a primary focus of appreciation in a given tradition are questions of *value*, not *ontology*. Jazz is ontologically just like classical music, according to Dodd (albeit with generally thinner works); the crucial difference between the two traditions is that in the classical tradition, the correct performance of thick works in all their detail is highly valued – indeed a constitutive norm of the practice[14] – while the jazz tradition values performance skills, such as improvisation, over such faithfulness.[15]

8.3 The Values of Jazz

Let us turn, then, from a focus on the ontology of jazz to what is valued in that practice. Many writers on this topic have pointed to two different values (or kinds of values) that seem to inform much jazz performance and appreciation, yet which seem to be in tension with one another. On the one hand, we have what might be called *product* values: features we take to make a performance good in virtue of the musical sounds that are produced, or features that would make an enduring musical work for repeated performance good. For instance, in a seminal paper, Philip Alperson writes that:

> in jazz, improvisations are criticized according to much the same criteria of internal purposiveness which may be applied to conventional [i.e., pre-composed] music: intelligible development, internal unity, coherence, originality, ingenuity, etc., the artful employment of prevailing idioms and the emergence of an individual style.
>
> (1984, 22)

On the other hand, we have what might be called *process* values – good-making features that cannot be made sense of apart from the notion that the thing being evaluated is a performance, an action being executed "in real time." Ted Gioia throws this feature of jazz appreciation into sharp relief by comparing jazz to other art forms. He asks us to:

> [i]magine T. S. Eliot giving nightly poetry readings at which, rather than reciting set pieces, he was expected to create impromptu poems – different ones each night, sometimes recited at a fast clip; imagine giving Hitchcock or Fellini a handheld motion picture camera and asking them to film something, anything – at that very moment, without the benefits of script, crew, editing or scoring; imagine Matisse or Dali giving nightly exhibitions of their skills – exhibitions at which paying audiences would watch them fill up canvas after canvas with paint, often with only two or three minutes devoted to each "masterpiece."
>
> (1988, 52)

Part of Gioia's point is that we could hardly expect the artistic *products* that even these great artists would produce under such conditions – the resulting poems, films, or paintings – to come anywhere near the level of their actual works, yet these conditions "are precisely those under which the jazz musician operates night after night, year after year" (1988, 52). As a result, we must appreciate jazz performances with these conditions in mind, just as we appreciate hewn marble sculptures and cast bronze sculptures in light of the very different potentials and qualities of their respective materials.

Some theorists have plumped for one kind of value to the exclusion of the other. What we might call a *product purist* argues that musical values apply to features of musical sounds. How those sounds are produced may be of interest, and an object of evaluation in its own right, but that process is not itself part of the music and thus not properly evaluated as such. Such a view is similar to the sonicism (including timbral sonicism) we encountered in Chapters 6 and 7, and might be criticized and defended using many of the same arguments. A *process purist*, by contrast, would be someone who argues that the product of an improvisation is more properly thought of as a *by*product, while the proper object of evaluation is the improvisatory actions of the musician. For instance, Gioia writes that:

> [a]n aesthetics of jazz would almost be a type of non-aesthetics. Aesthetics, in principle if not in practice, focuses our attention on those attributes of a work of art which reveal the craftsmanship and careful planning of an artist. ... [T]he virtues we search for in other art forms – premeditated design, balance between form and content, an overall symmetry – are largely absent in jazz.
>
> (Gioia 1988, 55)

Process purism seems even more problematic than product purism, since it is hard to see how one could consider a set of intentional actions – the process of musically improvising – in isolation from the goal and outcome of those actions, even if the reverse seems possible. Gioia himself seems inconsistent on this point, since he devotes a chapter of the book from which the above quotations are taken to "neoclassicism" in jazz, which he characterizes – very much in product terms – as "a music of balance, of care, of restraint. With an unabashed lyricism and a subtle sense of formal structure, the neoclassicist displays his affinity for jazz's rich traditions of vocal music" (Gioia 1988, 85).

Because of these problems, most jazz theorists have rejected both forms of purism, arguing for a synthesis of product and process values. Alperson does so by defending the thesis that we properly appreciate an improvisation as "the creation of a musical work as it is being performed" (1984, 27). He begins by pointing out that in attending to an improvisation we attend to a performance as both process and product. But since all performances have these two aspects, Alperson turns to a second distinction, between composition and performance. In the classical paradigm, these two things are kept well separated: Composition is what composers do, and results in works, while performance is what performers do, and results in performances. But Alperson thinks that, even considering just classical music, this separation is an oversimplification of actual musical practice. For composition almost always involves performance, if by that we mean the production of musical sounds, whether real or imagined. Almost all composers either play some music out loud to aid their composing, or run through in their heads how what they are writing will sound. Similarly, all performance involves composition, in the sense of determining how the resulting music sounds. This is clear in the case of improvisation, but Alperson points out the same is true of performance of classical works, since any work for performance is somewhat "thin," leaving performative options open for the performer (1984, 17–21).

Helpful though these observations are in spurring us to look at composition and performance in a new light, Alperson uses the two central terms too loosely to establish his thesis (Spade 1991). In arguing that composition involves performance, he clearly has our standard concept of composition in mind – the determining of the properties of a work for performance. Yet when he comes to argue for the necessity of composition in performance, he is using "composition" in a much looser sense, where it now means something like "determining the sonic properties of a performance." Similarly, while here he is using a standard sense of "performance" – the instancing of a work for performance – earlier, when arguing that composition requires performance, by "performance" he must mean simply "the production of some musical sounds," whether real or imagined, whether of the work being composed or not. And much of the "performance" that occurs during composition is in the service of *rejecting* the sounds "performed" from being constitutive of the work. We might also note that these equivocations make his argument a double-edged sword. For it seems to follow from Alperson's way of thinking that a standard performance of a classical work involves both composition and performance. If that's correct, then he may ironically have failed to defend a distinctive aesthetics of improvisation after all.

If these criticisms are sound, then improvisation and work-performance are alike not in that both involve composition, but rather in that *neither* involves composition. It is a necessary condition of a work-performance that there be some already-composed work that is being performed; no performer's decision, whether spontaneous or not, can affect the constitution of that work. Decisions about how a performance should sound, whether spontaneous or planned, are only compositional if the performance serves as a model for future performances in a relatively strict sense, which is not typically the case in jazz or classical practice (S. Davies 2001, 20–2).[16]

Drawing on the work of Lydia Goehr (1992), Andy Hamilton argues that theorists of jazz have conflated the creativity of the improviser with that of a composer because of the illegitimate dominance of the concept of the enduring work of art in modern philosophy of music, a problem that he also sees behind views such as Platonism and sonicism, which similarly attempt to separate the musical product from the messy human actions essential to its creation. Like Alperson, Hamilton posits a dichotomy to help us understand the differences between classical and jazz musical practices and then complicates it by suggesting that it is more of a spectrum. Hamilton's dichotomy distinguishes the "aesthetics of perfection" from the "aesthetics of imperfection" (Hamilton 2000, 169–73). The aesthetics of perfection comprises the values we see manifested in the classical tradition, including the notions of a musical work that can be perfected over time by the composer and of the perfectionist performer who strives above all never to make a mistake in her delivery of the work in performance. This simplistic view of classical music is then complicated by the acknowledgement that all works for performance of necessity leave room for the performer to make her own creative contributions in her interpretation of the work she performs, and that she may well improvise her creative contributions rather than work them out in advance. The aesthetics of imperfection, by contrast, is supposed to comprise the values we see manifested in improvisatory jazz practice.

But it is difficult to pin down exactly what Hamilton takes these values to be, in part because the notion of *imperfection* seems to imply an ideal of *perfection* from which one falls short. Hamilton attempts to address this issue by claiming that "imperfection" in this context means something closer to its etymological root of "unfinished" or "incomplete": "The aesthetics of imperfection finds virtues in improvisation which transcend ... errors in form and execution .... Indeed, it claims, these virtues arise precisely because of the 'unfinished state' of such performances" (2000, 171). It is not clear how far this gets us, though, since the concepts of being *unfinished* or *incomplete* seem just as value-laden as that of *imperfection*. Something unfinished or incomplete falls short of its inferred or intended *finished* or *complete* state. To claim that the aesthetics of imperfection comprises values that "transcend errors" seems only to postpone the question of what those values are.[17] Hamilton claims that the *improvised feel* of jazz, discussed above, is part of what we value in it, yet he also acknowledges that this feel can be illusory in being meticulously rehearsed, and is only truly valuable if it is actually generated by (spontaneous) improvisation. But then we seem to be back where we started: Surely an improvisation that did *not* include errors of form or execution – that sounded finished or complete, even though it was a genuine improvisation – would be more valuable than one with an improvised feel due to just such errors?

A way out of this tangled web of issues is provided by Lee B. Brown, who posits three "regulative ideals," more or less what I have been calling "values," in the jazz tradition. (Only the first two ideals will concern us here.) The first is simply the idea that the improviser should produce "formally" good music – a good musical "product": "An improviser [should] (a) present ... music intended to be worth hearing, by (b) determining a significant number of its features *as* he plays" (Brown 2000a, 119). Brown's second regulative ideal is that the improvising musician should *take risks*, that is, pursue musical avenues that are not obviously consistent with the first regulative ideal. Even if such a gambit fails, on this view, the risk-taking itself is valuable; on the other hand, if the performer succeeds in integrating their surprising move into the wider context of their improvisation, its total value will be greater than if the same result had been achieved without risk (whether because it was not improvised, or improvised by someone for whom this particular move was not risky, thanks to their greater improvisatory skills).[18] The valorization of risk can help us develop Hamilton's notion of the aesthetics of imperfection. Formal imperfection is a likely result of risk-taking; if it weren't, such actions wouldn't count as risks. So we should understand the imperfections of good jazz not in terms of the music's being somehow unfinished or incomplete, but rather as being produced under certain constraints – the regulative ideals that Brown has identified.

This can also help us with the puzzles Hamilton identifies in the notion of the "improvised feel" of jazz. Without the valorization of risk, it is unclear both why we should value the improvised feel of good jazz and also why we should be suspicious of, rather than impressed by, formal perfection in an improvisation. But keeping Brown's second regulative ideal in mind, we can see that the improvised feel is, in most cases, a sign that the improviser is pursuing the values of jazz. Likewise, we are suspicious of a formally perfect solo not usually because we do not believe it to be improvised, but rather because we suspect that its perfection is due less to the musician's ability to deal with any unforeseen challenges that might arise in the improvisatory situation, and more to his failure to push himself to take risks that provide such challenges.

For all that, it is still possible, as Brown acknowledges, for someone to take great risks and yet succeed in producing something musically perfect. But such performances will be "small miracles" (Brown 2000a, 117). It seems plausible that every actual musician has limits – there is no musically omnipotent improviser. It follows that everyone can always push themselves beyond their limits. Thus, confronted with a formally perfect improvisation, there seem to be two possibilities: Either this person did not take great enough risks, or they got lucky in producing perfection despite taking great risks. Given the regulative ideal of risk, we thus have cause to withhold praise of the perfection of such a musical product: Either this musician failed to follow this regulative ideal, or she is not responsible for the perfection that happened, by lucky chance, to result.[19]

8.4 Review and Looking Ahead

In this chapter, we have seen how the centrality of a particular kind of music-making to a tradition – improvisation and jazz, respectively – might be deeply intertwined with the ontology and values of that tradition. In the next chapter, we investigate a ubiquitous musical technology – sound recording – and consider its implications for Western musical traditions, particularly popular traditions, such as rock.

Questions

What is musical improvisation?

Is there a useful distinction between a performance that is *an* improvisation (in the count-noun sense) and one that is not?

Are most performances in the jazz tradition performances *of works*, in the sense in which most performances in the classical tradition are? If not, what is the ontological structure of jazz? If so, are there any philosophically interesting differences between jazz and classical works or performances?

What implications, if any, does the centrality of improvisation to jazz have for how we should understand and evaluate jazz music?

Notes

1 Even this condition requires finessing, however, since one can presumably improvise the first note of one's performance, as in one of the following examples.

2 In fact, there is often a highly detailed pre-composed cadenza in contemporary published scores of such works, but we should understand these as *recommendations* for musicians who cannot or will not improvise a cadenza, not requirements for anyone who would play the work.

3 Compare Gregory Currie's comments on mass- and count-noun senses of "narrative" (2010, 33–6).

4 John Andrew Fisher (2018, 157–8) criticizes this tendency.

5 For a refresher on functional harmony, see Chapter 4, §4.3.

6 It might be responded that Rodgers & Hammerstein intended many features of their original score – e.g., the words – to be mere recommendations, rather than work-determinative (though this seems more plausible with respect to (the composer) Rogers than (the lyricist) Hammerstein!), rendering the work thin enough that Coltrane's performance counts as fully authentic. But this strategy seems unlikely to succeed in all cases.

7 Davies does explicitly acknowledge the possibility of a middle ground where works may be thick enough to articulate an artistic statement, yet thin enough to allow for performers to articulate independent artistic statements while still performing them.

8 This use of the term "work" is common to many philosophers of music and the arts more generally. See, for example, Gracyk 1996 and D. Davies 2004. For criticism, see Fisher 2018, 153–7 and Dodd 2014b, 285–8.

9 For further discussion of these issues, see Brown 2011b, Kania 2012, and Brown 2012.

10 For a contrasting view of the artistic status of screenplays, see Nannicelli 2013, 61–188.

11 Such a view is arguably defended in Alperson 1984, Hagberg 2002, and S. Davies 2001, 16–19. For a defense of standards as a primary focus of appreciation in jazz, see Fisher 2018, 154.

12 Though he does not discuss them, Love presumably accepts that the opening and closing statements of the head also have significant artistic value.

13 Here Brown summarizes a view he argues for in Brown 1996.

14 On constitutive norms, see Chapter 7, §7.4.

15 John Andrew Fisher argues for a middle way between the views of Kania and Dodd: There are repeatable jazz musical works, yet "the jazz tradition [is] *sui generis* with respect to musical works and their performances" (2018, 158).

16 This is not to say that such "compositional improvisation" never happens. One case that receives some attention in the literature is J.S. Bach's improvisation of a three-voice fugue on a theme provided by Frederick the Great, later incorporated (perhaps with elaborations) into Bach's *Musical Offering*. Even in this case, however, as perhaps with Coltrane's "My Favorite Things," it seems unlikely that Bach conceived of the fugue *as he improvised it* as constituting a work for repeated performances, not least because it was not until Frederick went on to challenge him to improvise a *six*-voice fugue on the same theme that Bach demurred and began formulating his plan for *The Musical Offering*. For philosophical discussion of this case, see Kivy 1983, 124–8; S. Davies 2001, 13–16; and D. Davies 2011, 158–60. For an engaging historical account, see Gaines 2005.

17 Comparison with the Japanese "wabi" aesthetic might be helpful here. See Saito 1997 for a helpful introduction and Saito 2007, 164–204 for further discussion.

18 On musical risk-taking more generally, see Higgins 1991, 193–6.

19 For consideration of luck in appreciative, rather than creative, experiences, see Ribeiro 2018.

Further Reading

In *Jazz and the Philosophy of Art*, David Goldblatt and Theodore Gracyk have collected, updated, and integrated Lee Brown's essays on the philosophy of jazz, covering the definition and ontology of improvisation and jazz, as well as place of jazz in American culture and history (Brown, Goldblatt, & Gracyk 2018). Eric Lewis's *Intents and Purposes* (2019) is a recent attempt to develop a philosophical theory of jazz improvisation on its own terms, rather than in contrast to the classical paradigm.

9   Recordings

Overview

In this chapter, we investigate the nature of musical recordings and how differences in musical traditions (in particular, jazz, classical, and rock) have given rise to different approaches to the creation and appreciation of recordings. We end by considering the comparative value of live performances and recordings.

We have spent the last three chapters considering a range of issues raised by musical performance in general and musical performances of various kinds, particularly those of historical classical works and improvisatory jazz performances. I have sometimes used recordings as examples, since it is easy to think of musical recordings as simply sonic *records – traces* or *documents –* of musical performances. Now, traces or documents of things are different from the things they trace or document. (You wouldn't exchange someone you love for a photograph of them.) But, at the same time, they seem intimately connected with their subjects. What exactly is the nature of that connection, though? When we appreciate Crowded House's 1986 *recording* of "Don't Dream It's Over," are we basically appreciating a *performance*, which that recording records, as when I refer to my grandmother by pointing to the photograph of her on the mantelpiece? Or is the recording an object of musical interest in its own right, more like a photographic work of art, such as Diane Arbus's "Child with a Toy Hand Grenade"? Can we answer these questions generally, or do different recordings demand different answers? Given that most people across the globe now listen primarily to musical recordings, rather than live performances, these questions seem particularly urgent, especially if their answers have implications for the value of our musical experiences.

9.1 Transparency and Jazz Recordings

A live performance is a *singular* entity, in the sense that although two performances might be similar in all sorts of ways, they will remain two distinct
events. A musical work for performance, on the other hand, is a *multiple* entity,
in the sense that two distinct performances may be performances of *one and
the same* work. You may attend two different performances of Brahms's violin
concerto, but you can only ever hear one violin concerto by Brahms, because
he only wrote one. Recordings appear to be multiple entities, since, like musical
works, they are repeatable. When you play a CD of the Brahms violin concerto
twice, you get two instances of one and the same recording.[1]

Suppose we have an unedited sound recording of a live performance, such
as the tracks on *Complete Jazz at Massey Hall* (Parker 2003). When we listen
to the recording, we certainly have a different aural experience from that of
anyone in the audience at Massey Hall on May 15, 1953. But audience members in different parts of the hall that night had different aural experiences from
one another, too. They nonetheless all heard the same performance. When we
listen to the recording, do we similarly *hear the performance* given that night
by five jazz greats? One way to argue that we do is by appealing to Kendall
Walton's notion of a *transparent* medium. The basic idea would be that we
hear performances *through* recordings, just as we see things through windows.
Walton introduces the notion of transparency to defend the idea that we see
things through photographs, which he argues are like windows on to the past;
we literally, albeit indirectly, see the subject of a photograph through the photograph (Walton 1984). That this seeing is indirect does not disqualify it as
seeing, argues Walton, because we see things indirectly through other devices,
such as telescopes, microscopes, and periscopes. The more troubling issue is
whether the experience of "seeing" something in a photograph is literally an
experience of seeing, or whether this is just a compelling metaphor. After all,
we commonly talk of "seeing" something in a painting, or in our mind's eye,
but these claims are not literally true.

Walton argues that the difference between literal seeing and metaphorical
uses of the term is that the visual appearances presented to us in literal seeing
are "counterfactually dependent on the scenes they portray ... [and the] counterfactual dependence ... is independent of [for instance] the photographer's
beliefs" (1997b, 68).[2] That is, what appears in a photograph of something is
independent of what the photographer *believes* is in front of the camera, in
contrast with what appears in a painting of the same thing, which (for instance)
may include apparitions that exist only in the hallucinating painter's mind.
What the literal and metaphorical uses of "seeing" have *in common* is a resemblance in our visual experiences of subject and medium. As Walton points out,
we could program a computer to generate a linguistic description of a scene that

counterfactually depends on the scene (and not on anyone's beliefs about the scene). But no one would be tempted to say that they *see* the scene *through* the description (1984, 270–1). It is worth noting that transparency is not a matter of degree. To count as transparent, a medium must reach some threshold of resemblance between the appearance of the object and the appearance of the medium, but a stained old sepia photograph is just as transparent as a dirty funhouse mirror. You see things through it, whether accurately, dimly, or in a distorted fashion.

The extension of this notion of visual transparency to the realm of sound seems unproblematic. Sound recording technology, of the sort used in making recordings of performances, aims to mechanically reproduce the sounds in the environment where the recording was made, just as photographic technology aims to mechanically reproduce visual appearances. Thus, if we see through photographs, we hear through recordings.

However, Walton's original thesis that photographs are transparent is controversial. Most objections boil down to an alternative distinction between literal seeing and other kinds of visual experience. Contenders include the (alternative) criteria that literal seeing requires (1) the continuous transmission of light from the object seen to the eye (Gaut 2003, 637); or (2) the ability to spatially locate oneself with respect to the object seen on the basis of the visual experience alone (Carroll 1996, 61–2; Currie 1995, 65–9); or (3) *continuous* counterfactual dependence between the visual appearance under consideration and the object (S. Davies 2016, 180–3). All three of these criteria, and objections to them, can be translated into sonic and aural terms: (1) If the continuous transmission of sound waves is required for literal hearing, then you do not literally hear your mother when you talk to her on the phone, since the speaker in your phone does not emit the very same sound waves that issued from your mother's mouth, but rather new, qualitatively similar sound waves. (2) If the criterion of hearing is the ability to spatially locate yourself with respect to the object heard on the basis of your auditory experience alone, then you do not literally hear a person whispering in an echoey cathedral if you cannot point to where they are. (3) If continuous counterfactual dependence between sounds and aural experience is required, then whether or not you literally hear the other participants on a conference call depends on whether the technology employs a medium of recording or transmission (where the latter *preserves* but never *fixes* the signal).

Proposal (2) is unpromising. It is not clear that one ever locates oneself spatially with respect to an object solely on the basis of one's visual or auditory experience (cf. Lippman 1963). But even if one does, the line between such cases and others (where one cannot do so) does not seem to mark any natural boundary between literally seeing or hearing something and seeing or hearing a mere representation of that thing. Proposal (1) is more promising. As a principle, continuous transmission of light or sound seems like a good candidate for the criterion we seek, but when it comes to cases, it can seem arbitrary to place a sharp line between observing what's going on in the next room through a periscope and doing so through a closed-circuit video. Similarly, if I literally hear your mother through a "tin-can telephone" (because, unlike a regular phone, it *does* propagate the very sound waves that issue from your mother's mouth), it seems plausible that you also hear her over an ordinary telephone line or a web-based phone link.[3] Proposal (3) is in roughly the same boat: The presence or absence of continuous counterfactual dependence of a visual or auditory appearance on its object seems significant, yet it is difficult to argue that it distinguishes literal perceptual contact from mere representation without begging the question. It may be that there is simply no clear line between literal perceptual contact with an object and contact only with a representation of it. If so, however, it does not follow that these distinctions are without interest. For one thing, they may allow us to place various modes of contact on a continuum between uncontroversial literal perceptual contact and uncontroversial lack thereof. At least we can say that ordinary recordings bear the same sort of relation to the sounds they record as photographs do to their subjects. And even most of Walton's critics admit that this is a relation significant for its lack of intentional mediation (Warburton 2003).[4]

In what follows, I will assume for the sake of simplicity that sound recordings are transparent, that is, that we hear things through them.[5] I leave as an open question the extent to which, if recordings are *not* transparent, the following arguments can be preserved, substituting for the transparency claim a more nuanced account of the precise relation between a sound recording and the sonic events it records.

9.2 Studio Technology and Classical Recordings

Even if sound-recording technology is a transparent medium, it is rare that in listening to a musical recording we hear a single, continuous live performance. That is because most recordings, even if they begin with a live performance event, are altered in various ways using other technology. Charles Mingus, the bass player in the Massey Hall concert, was so dissatisfied with the loss of the lower frequencies on the original recording that he re-recorded his bass parts (in a studio, without an audience), "overdubbing" them onto the concert tapes (Parker 2003).[6] If recordings are transparent, then when one listens to the doctored version, one indirectly but literally hears the Massey Hall concert, but one also hears the parts Mingus recorded at a later date. The result, of course, is not a transparent record of a single, continuous live performance, even if that is how Mingus intended us to hear it and how we do, in fact, hear it.[7]

There are myriad ways in which musical recordings are edited. As with overdubbing, the musicians may record their parts separately to be combined by an engineer in the studio. Alternatively, the musicians may all play together, but record the same music several times, allowing for the combination of various "takes" into a final recording that, again, sounds like a single, continuous performance, but does not record one. The rise of digital technology has made electronic note-correction and other alterations of individual aspects of recorded music (e.g., "autotune") much easier than it used to be. All this raises the evaluative issue of whether recordings constitute *cheating* by enabling musicians to present a sequence of sounds as a single, continuous performance, when no such performance ever happened.

The centrality of improvisation to jazz only increases these concerns with respect to jazz recordings. Any departure from long takes of ensembles playing together (live or in the studio) is likely to be mentioned in liner notes or other media accompanying the release of the recording.[8] The musicians still choose *which* takes to release, but there is significant interest in "alternative" (i.e., initially unreleased) takes. And recordings, whether live or studio, featuring great first-take performances by ensembles with little or no experience playing together are considered jazz masterpieces (e.g., Les McCann & Eddie Harris's *Swiss Movement* and Miles Davis's *Kind of Blue*). Concerns about cheating are thus addressed in part by conventions about what can be expected from recordings released in the jazz tradition and what should be flagged as a departure from those expectations (cf. Bicknell 2015, 71–80).

Given the long history of classical music as a live-performance tradition before the invention of recording technology, one might expect classical musicians and audiences to take a similar attitude to recording as those knowledgeable about jazz. However, in the classical world, a complete performance of the work being recorded rarely occurs in the studio. Indeed, it is rare for a continuous take of even a single movement to make it to the final cut. Even "live" classical recordings have usually been "patched" with extra takes made under studio conditions at a later time (much like Mingus's overdubs). Putting live recordings to one side, Stephen Davies argues that because classical works are of the ontological kind *work-for-live-performance*, fully authentic instances of them must *be* live performances (2001, 20–36), just as they must employ the instruments mandated by the composer in the score (see Chapter 7, §7.3). Thus, no studio recording gives us access to a fully authentic instance of a classical work. This conflicts with how most classical audiences and musicians seem to treat classical studio-recordings, but Davies claims that "such talk relies on our willingness to treat the representations of performances found on recordings as acceptable substitutes for live performances" (2001, 319).

An alternative way to think of the relationships between classical works, performances, and recordings would be to take typical classical works to be simply *for performance*, and then argue that there are two kinds of work-performance – live and studio – either of which may instance a work in a fully authentic manner. The challenge facing this alternative is whether it makes sense to talk of a "studio performance" of a classical work. One feature of classical recordings that seems to count against their qualifying as work-performances is the looser spatio-temporal constraints on the music-making that goes on in the production of a recording, as opposed to a live performance. For instance, those who produce a live performance must all play together, in the same place and at the same time, without taking (nonmusical) breaks (Godlovitch 1998, 34–41; S. Davies 2001, 186–90). These constraints are not respected in the recording studio, so what happens in the recording studio, one might conclude, cannot be a performance. Aron Edidin suggests, on the basis of such considerations, that most classical studio-recordings are not recordings of work-performances, but simply *recordings of works* (1999, 30–6).

A defender of classical studio-recordings as work-performances might appeal to the distinction between performance as *process* and *product* (discussed in Chapter 8, §8.3; cf. Levinson 1987b, 76), arguing that the performance *product* we hear on a recording is connected to the performance *process* of the musicians in the studio in such a way that we are justified in claiming that we hear a performance when we listen to a classical recording.[9] On this view, the looseness of the spatio-temporal constraints on episodes of music-making in the studio is analogous to the similar looseness in rehearsals for live performances. In both cases, the point of the disjointed active music-making is the eventual production of the best possible performance-product. How the music-making contributes to that performance is different in each case but, on the view being considered, not in such a way as to disqualify the recording from counting as a performance. Perhaps, on this view, we ought to think of the development of classical studio-recording conventions as the discovery of a new type of performance, just as European explorers, familiar only with "old world" swans, learned in the antipodes that not all swans are white. While people always thought of live performances as the only kind of performance, with the introduction of recorded performances we see in hindsight that live performances are just one of (at least) two kinds.[10]

The concern may remain that if classical musicians can use any technological means available to create performance products that they have not created – perhaps *could* not create – in a live performance, they are betraying the centuries-old, skill-based tradition to which they purport to belong. As it turns out, however, just as the spatio-temporal constraints on live performance (appealed to by the critic of classical studio-recordings) developed implicitly within the performance tradition, new implicit conventions developed over the twentieth century, putting limits on what is acceptable in the production of a classical recording (e.g., the convention that only relatively long takes should be spliced together). The occasional classical-recording scandal is evidence of the existence of, and general adherence to, these conventions. (For example, there was an outcry when it was revealed that the high Cs in Isolde's part on a 1953 recording of *Tristan und Isolde* were sung not by the aging Kirsten Flagstad (who alone was credited for the part) but by the rising star Elisabeth Schwarzkopf.)[11] Perhaps the best explanation of these conventions is that they are attempts to establish a practice, given the resources of the recording studio, that honors both the tradition's long-standing valorization of live performance skills and the desire of performers and audiences (not of recent vintage itself!) to hear the best performances possible. The basic idea would be that one should not release a recording without explicit qualification if one would not be capable of producing such a performance-product live under ideal circumstances (S. Davies 2001, 192–4; Godlovitch 1998, 26–7).

If this defense of classical studio-recordings (as they are typically made) succeeds, such recordings are rightly thought of as giving access to performances of the works they purport to be of. Although the single, continuous phenomenal-performance they give listeners access to is not usually the result of a single, continuous performance-process (as in live performance), the conventions for producing such recordings that have developed in the classical-music world (rooted in the long-standing tradition of live performance) are such that it is appropriate to think of what we hear on a recording as a performance – a different kind of performance from a live performance, but a performance nonetheless.

9.3 Constructed Tracks and Rock Recordings

It might seem that our discussion of classical studio-recordings could easily be applied to studio recordings of "popular music," such as rock, pop, and hip hop.[12] For in the popular-music world, as in the classical, there are songs that receive multiple live performances, and recordings of those songs.[13] Theodore Gracyk has influentially argued, however, that these apparent similarities are deceiving (1996, 1–98; cf. Fisher 1998). Gracyk argues that the work of art in rock music (i.e., the primary focus of appreciation) is not a thin sound structure (a song) to be instanced in different performances, as in classical music, but the almost maximally thick sound structure of a recording, properly instanced through the playing of that recording.[14] (I will follow Gracyk in focusing on rock, but it seems plausible that this central claim will apply to other popular music traditions, such as pop, hip hop, electronica, etc.[15]) One crucial difference between such musical works *for playback* and traditional works *for performance* is that works for playback do not admit of interpretive variation in their instances. You can turn up the bass while playing your favorite track, but this will at best illustrate the sonic variation possible in authentic instances of the track; at worst it will produce a distorted instance of the track. Either way, you are not performatively interpreting the track.

Technology that enables works for playback did not originate, as rock did, in the mid-twentieth century. Mechanical music boxes have been around since at least the eighteenth century, for instance, and player pianos were developed in the mid-nineteenth century. But those technologies were typically applied to existing musical works for performance, allowing for the generation of what sounded more or less like performances of those works by someone with no musical skill. The development, in the mid-twentieth century, of sophisticated technology allowing for both complex editing of recorded sound and the purely electronic creation of sounds gave rise to the first sustained traditions of using a playback medium to create new works exploiting the distinctive possibilities of that medium. For instance, pioneers of the "electronic music" school – a branch of the classical avant-garde – began producing entirely synthetic recordings, using no actually recorded sounds as input (e.g., Edgard Varèse's *Poème électronique* (1958)). In the rival tradition of *musique concrète*, works for playback were created by manipulating pre-recorded sounds in various ways (e.g., Pierre Schaffer's *Étude aux chemin de fer* (1948)). It is uncontroversial that these works are for playback (rather than recorded performances in any sense), in part because they don't typically sound anything like a traditional musical performance – instruments historically used for live performance are rarely employed, and often traditional musical features (e.g., functional harmony) are absent. Rock recordings, by contrast, typically sound something like a recorded performance, employing, as they do, both widely accessible musical features, such as singable melodies, functional harmony, and steady meters, as well as instruments commonly heard live, such as electric guitars, drums, bass, and keyboards, not to mention the singing voice.

Gracyk makes the case that, nonetheless, rock recordings are properly appreciated as thick works for playback, rather than studio performances of thin songs, by appealing to the way rock musicians conceive of what they do (as reflected in their words and actions), along with the way that knowledgeable rock audiences (especially critics and historians) talk about the music. In particular, he points out that musicians and critics, even when they use terms such as "song" or "performance," almost always betray that they are really referring to *recordings*, by discussing details of the soundscape that could only be possessed by a particular recording. Gracyk argues that this musical tradition emerged from the live-performance tradition of "rock 'n' roll" with Elvis Presley's early recordings at Sun Studios, hitting its stride with Bob Dylan's first electric albums and the Beatles' shift of focus from live shows to the recording studio (1996, 1–36). If Gracyk is right, then Bob Dylan (with a little help from his friends) transformed not so much the concept of *literature* (as we saw Horace Engdahl claim in his speech awarding Bob Dylan's Nobel Prize in Literature (Chapter 1, §1.1)), but the concept of *music*, taking an artform with live performance at its heart and turning it into a tradition of making records. According to Gracyk, while recording technology may be put in the service of performance-centered musical traditions, such as jazz or classical music (just as photographic technology may be put in the service of painting, e.g., in reproducing paintings for posters and books), that technology is the *medium* of rock, just as photographic technology is the medium of photographic art (1996, 37–98). Thus, if Gracyk's conclusions are correct, rock is, in an important sense, an exception to the claim, with which I began Chapter 6, that music is a performing art.

Stephen Davies argues that rock is more like classical music than Gracyk allows, pointing to important rock practices that Gracyk ignores or sidelines, particularly the importance placed on live-performance skills (S. Davies 2001, 29–36):

> more groups play rock music than ever are recorded; almost every recorded group began as a garage band that relied on live gigs; almost every famous recording artist is also an accomplished stage performer; [and] although record producers are quite rightly acknowledged for the importance of their contribution, they are not usually identified as members of the band.
>
> (S. Davies 2001, 32)[16]

He also argues that cover versions and remixes are treated more like new interpretations of existing works – more like *performances* – than like new works in their own right (31–2).[17] Davies thus argues that rock works, like classical ones, are created for performance, but whereas classical works are for *live* performance, rock works are for *studio* performance, that is, they implicitly prescribe roles for producers and sound engineers to play, just as orchestral scores implicitly prescribe a role for a conductor (24–6).

Andrew Kania (2006) is sympathetic to Davies's reclamation of the importance of performance skills for rock, but argues that it has unacceptable consequences.[18] If rock songs are ontologically *for studio performance*, then live performances of such songs cannot be fully authentic instances of them. No matter how much technology is exported from the studio to the stage, there is a fundamental difference between making music in those two locations: In the studio, one can always in principle go back and change something until one is happy with the result, while live performance is essentially ephemeral; a mistake made on stage cannot be withheld from release. Davies might respond that this is not so dire a consequence of his view, since less than fully authentic instances of works can still be highly valued, as many performances of Bach's keyboard works on modern pianos demonstrate (see Chapter 7, §7.3). But Kania argues that we can find a place for the value of performance skills in rock without recourse to the notion of a work-for-studio-performance. He agrees with Gracyk that rock musicians primarily make *tracks* – ontologically thick works that are instanced in playings of recordings – and that these recordings are at the heart of the tradition. However, these tracks also instance *songs*. Rock songs – like jazz songs, but unlike classical songs – tend to be very thin ontologically, allowing alterations in instrumentation, lyrics, melody, and harmony. But while classical and jazz songs are works for performance *simpliciter*, rock songs are not works (in the sense of a primary focus of appreciation), nor are they *for* anything in particular. A rock track is not a special kind of performance of the thin song it instances, as Davies would have it. Rather, it is a studio construction: a thick work that *instances* a thin song, without being a *performance* of it. But none of this prevents a rock song from being instanced in a performance.

Thus, there are two places in Kania's account that leave room for valuing performance skills in rock. The first is in the construction of tracks. It might initially seem that if the performance skills that we value in the production of rock tracks – typically skill in singing and playing the guitar, drums, bass, and keyboards – are to be given their due, we must conceive of rock recordings as performances of some sort, and thus should be moved toward Davies's view of rock recordings as "studio performances." But we often value skills that go into the production of a non-performance artwork; just think of a painter's skill with the brush.[19] Moreover, Davies is well aware of this possibility in the realm of recorded music, for he acknowledges that works of *musique concrète* (for instance) are for playback, rather than for studio performance, yet that appreciating them requires understanding how they were produced (S. Davies 2001, 26).

The second place where there is room for esteeming performance skills in rock is, of course, in live performances. But though both Kania and Gracyk acknowledge the importance of rock concerts to the tradition, this presents a problem for their view: Why elevate recordings to pride of place, and grant live rock performances only a subsidiary role? Kania offers two arguments in addition to reiterating Gracyk's arguments that however important live rock is, recorded rock is much more central to the tradition, as evidenced by creative and appreciative practice. The first is based on a consideration of live rock performances themselves. It is clear that most rock performers, most of the time, perform their songs live with a "sound" similar to that of their recording of the song (much more similar to it than to a recorded cover of the song by different artists, for instance). What this amounts to is, first, the same song being performed as is instanced on the track and, second, the same kinds of sounds being used to fill out the skeleton of the song. But it is also clear that most artists do not attempt to create on stage a sonic doppelganger of a particular track. This can be done (as the performances of cover bands amply show), yet regular (non-cover) bands do not produce this kind of performance of songs they have recorded. Indeed, audiences expect live rock performances to differ from tracks in certain ways. Some of the more common changes are an extended introduction, often concealing which song is being performed, added verses, instrumental solos, invited audience participation, a new ending to replace the track's fade-out, and so on. Thus, we can see that although live rock-performances do not attempt to mimic a studio recording of a song, they do take the track as primary in some sense. This is unsurprising, given that the track represents the artists' considered opinion about what sounds good enough to constitute an enduring addition to their oeuvre.

Kania's second argument for the view that recorded rock is primary and live rock secondary is a thought experiment inviting you to imagine four different scenarios. Two concern the classical-music world, and two the rock-music world. For each tradition suppose, first, that all recording technology has been destroyed without hope of recovery. Then, suppose an alternate scenario in which recording technology survives, but all live performances are eliminated from the world. In the case of classical music, Kania claims, the elimination of recordings would not greatly affect the music-making practices of the tradition; this would merely be a return to the old days. The elimination of live performances, on the other hand, might conceivably have an effect, over time, on the kinds of works and recordings produced. (Kania puts this point somewhat hesitantly since, as we have just seen, the long history of the live performance tradition in classical music has arguably made its recording practices quite robust.) In the rock scenarios, the situation is roughly reversed, according to Kania. With the end of live performances, musicians could continue to make albums as they have for the past several decades. Were the recording studios to be shut down, however, live rock performances could no longer draw on recordings as they do now. A different, more performance-centered art would need to emerge were rock to survive. In short, classical recording-practice depends upon classical live-performance practice, while rock live-performance practice depends upon rock recording-practice.[20]

Gracyk, Davies, and Kania have different things to say about how performance skills enter into the recording-centered practice of rock. Franklin Bruno (2013) and Christopher Bartel (2017), however, argue that Gracyk, Davies, and Kania are mistaken in their basic agreement that recordings are the primary focus of appreciation in the rock tradition. Bruno argues that songs – thin structures of melody, harmony, and lyrics – are an equally primary focus of appreciation in rock. Bartel adds live performance to the list, arguing that recordings, songs, and live performances are equally important in the rock world.

Bruno provides two kinds of argument for placing songs at the same level of appreciative importance as recordings in rock. The first is criticism of an argument he sees underlying the recording-centered ontologies of Gracyk, Davies, and Kania:

The thinness of songs renders them incapable of supporting distinctively artistic forms of appreciation and evaluation. [So] an account of the appreciation and evaluation of rock music must appeal to properties of thick recordings, rather than those of the thin songs that may underlie them.

(Bruno 2013, 67)

Bruno provides several objections to this argument (70–2). First, classical compositions' thinness doesn't prevent their being the works in that tradition, so it's unclear why rock songs' thinness should. Second, if ontological thinness is really standing in for musical simplicity, then it's implausible that all rock songs are so simple as to be disqualified from the realm of artworks. Third, even if rock songs are simple, this could as easily be a sign of their appealing minimalism rather than their banality. Finally, even if it were true that all rock songs are boringly simple, that would not show that they cannot be artworks, that is, primary foci of appreciation in their tradition; at best it would show that rock is a tradition with a lot of boring works.

Bruno's criticisms of his target argument are plausible. However, it's not clear that any of the philosophers with whom he disagrees employ that argument.[21] While Gracyk, Davies, and Kania agree (as does Bruno) that songs are thinner than their recordings (and than many classical works) and argue that, in general, thinner pieces offer less to be appreciated than thicker pieces (e.g., S. Davies 2001, 22), none of them base their claims about the centrality of recordings on this point, and some are quite explicit about this (e.g., Kania 2006, 408). Rather, the evidence they provide for their claims is what musicians and audience members do and say with regard to the music. Fortunately, Bruno, too, gives positive evidence of this kind for his view, discussing six features of rock practice that suggest that songs are foci of appreciation, the first three from appreciative discourse and the last three from creative practice (2013, 67–8):

1   Some rock musicians are evaluated on the basis of their songwriting (as opposed to track-making) abilities.
2   Some songs are evaluated highly, even when the best known recordings of them are evaluated poorly.
3   Recordings are often evaluated with respect to how they realize a given song (e.g., the appropriateness of instrumentation and vocal style).
4   There is a robust rock practice of *covering* songs, which can only be understood in terms of making a new recording (or performance) of a song that has at least one existing recording.
5   There are critically acclaimed rock songwriters who do not perform or make recordings.

6   There is often a clear distinction in the production of a rock record between an earlier stage of song composition and a later stage of arrangement and recording.

Bartel endorses most of what Bruno has to say about songs and adds that similar considerations show that live performances are as central to rock practice as recordings and songs. He suggests, for instance, that Gracyk, Davies, and Kania are attracted to a recording-centered ontology because they consider an unrepresentative sample of rock bands (Bartel 2017, 147–9). While a recording-centered ontology may fit the practices of "gods of rock" and "electro" bands – those, such as Led Zeppelin, who can afford the studio time required to create songs and recordings of them from scratch in the studio, and those, such as Björk, who create songs (or arrangements) that no one would expect to be performed live without significant technical assistance – it does not fit the practices of "garage" and "touring" bands – those, such as many punk bands, whose recordings only document live performances or styles, and those, such as the Dave Matthews Band, who hone a song on tour before creating a recording that instances it. The ways in which garage and touring bands' music is created and appreciated shows, according to Bartel, that in those areas of the rock world, recordings are subsidiary to live performances (in the case of garage bands) or on an equal footing with them (in the case of touring bands). Similarly, Bartel argues, Kania's argument that live performance practice in rock depends upon rock recording practice, and not vice versa, is compelling only if we consider the live shows of gods-of-rock and electro bands. With garage bands, the dependence runs in precisely the opposite direction – recordings serving as mere documents of live performances or live-performance styles – while, with touring bands, studio production techniques may result in thick tracks that are objects of appreciation in their own right, but those tracks do not serve as the standard against which live performances are judged (Bartel 2017, 149–52). Bartel concludes that rock is "a three-value tradition," that is, that recordings, songs, and live performances all lie at the core of rock practice.

We might question some of the observations Bruno and Bartel make about rock practice. For instance, Bartel argues that hardcore punk groups of the early 1980s, such as Black Flag, though not commercially successful, were highly influential in the rock world and thus should not be sidelined when considering rock practice in general. And "it would be a mistake to try to understand [hardcore punk records such as the EP *Minor Threat*] from the point of view of a recording-centered ontology" (Bartel 2017, 151). These are "garage" bands in Bartel's taxonomy, their records transparent documents of a live-performance style (if not of actual live performances). If a recording-centered ontology is right, "then *Minor Threat* should be viewed as a complete failure due to its poor production quality. ... [T]he guitars are not doubled, all of the instruments are panned in the center ..., it is difficult to distinguish the drummer's crash cymbal from the hi-hat," and so on (Bartel 2017, 151).

But Bartel seems here to be conflating a recording-centered *ontology* with a particular recording *aesthetic*. Gracyk, Davies, and Kania may emphasize the wide range of *possibilities* that the recording studio offers to rock musicians, but none argue that the best recordings are those that *make use of* the widest range of possibilities in a single recording. That would be like saying that the best orchestral works are those that feature the maximum number of instrumental combinations and the widest dynamic range. Some late Romantic works may aim for such a "maximalist" aesthetic, but late-twentieth-century minimalist works (for instance) employ a more limited sound palette. In either case, however, assessment of the composer's use of instrumentation relies on understanding the range of possibilities available. Indeed, one of Gracyk's central examples is Bob Dylan, who seems to qualify as a "touring" artist in Bartel's taxonomy. Dylan writes great songs, developing many of them on the road and performing them live in a wide variety of arrangements and styles, but though his classic recordings achieve a kind of "live sound" (rather than being polished studio artifacts like those of Björk), Gracyk nonetheless argues that when we look at both Dylan's own statements about what he is trying to achieve and critics' assessments of Dylan's achievements, we see that it is Dylan's *records* (which, of course, instance his songs), not his live performances (nor a live performance captured on the record), that is their focus.

The evidence from punk practice that Bartel provides could also be interpreted as supporting a recording-centered ontology. Bartel quotes Tony Cadena of The Adolescents recalling their first recording session, where he had to put a sound engineer in his place: "there'd be somebody who wanted to 'fix' us. ... We got to a point where we said, 'We're going to do it this way. Just turn the machine on'" (qtd. in Bartel 2017, 150). Cadena clearly wants a raw sound, but he equally clearly wants it *on the record he's making*. Similarly, it is obvious that Bartel's description of the details of the sound of the *Minor Threat* EP is a loving one; Bartel, like the members of Minor Threat, *admires* the sound of this recording in all its detail, and would not willingly exchange it for a glossier, more commercial sound. Bartel might respond that it is not the sound of the *recording* he admires, but the sound of the performance (or style) that he hears in or through the recording. But, like the critics Gracyk quotes, much of his description is recording-specific. A live-performance style cannot feature undoubled guitars, or a panning of instruments in the center – those are features these punk *recordings* possess in deliberate defiance of the contemporaneous mainstream rock aesthetic.

Be that as it may, Bartel is clearly right that such punk bands' recording aesthetic followed their live-performance aesthetic, and not vice versa. More generally, Bruno and Bartel are clearly correct that songs and live performances are significant foci of appreciation in the rock world. Of course, as Bartel acknowledges, "Gracyk, Davies, and Kania would all likely agree that songwriting and performing are important and valued activities within rock" (2017, 143). This suggests that the title of his article – "Rock as a Three-Value Tradition" – is somewhat misleading. No one denies that these three things are valued in the rock tradition. Indeed, at the end of his article, Bartel suggests that there may be *further* practices central to rock. But what makes a practice "central"? Creative and critical attention is paid to album covers, stage lighting, and musicians' hairstyles, but presumably Bartel would not infer from this that rock is a *six*-value tradition. One might continue this discussion by investigating the *relative centrality* of these different kinds of things as foci of appreciation in rock, and perhaps whether there is some threshold outside which something no longer counts as central *at all*. Alternatively, one might argue that this debate has proceeded at too general a level. There is no primary focus of appreciation in *rock*; rather, recordings are the primary focus of appreciation in gods-of-rock and "electro" rock, songs are the primary focus in touring-band rock, live performance is the primary focus of appreciation in garage rock, and so on. The limiting case of this kind of view is ontological *particularism*, according to which there are no useful generalizations about the kind of thing that is an artwork in a given tradition; we must appreciate each artistic object or event on its own terms.[22] Deciding which of these avenues is most promising, not to mention pursuing it, likely requires both careful, detailed sociological analysis of rock practice and reflection on the methodology of musical ontology.[23]

9.4 Covers

The practice of rock artists "covering" other artists' material has come up several times in the preceding section, since it is the recording practice in rock that looks most like the classical practice of performers giving different interpretations of a single work. Stephen Davies, for instance, claims that rock artists' and audiences' attitudes toward covers are one of "[t]wo factors [that] lend strong support" to his account of rock as a studio-performance tradition (2001, 31), while Franklin Bruno suggests that any plausible account of covers must acknowledge the importance of the song that provides the link between the original and cover version (2013, 68–9).

Anyone who thinks that the relations between songs, performances, and recordings are different in rock practice than in classical practice thus owes us an account of covers. Andrew Kania claims that, rather than being different studio performances of the same song, covers are distinct tracks (i.e., studio constructions) that intentionally instance the same song. He defends this view by means of an extended analogy with film remakes (Kania 2006, 407–9; cf. S. Davies 2001, 33).[24] A remake is a new film that shares many important properties with a pre-existing film. The narrative and the title are the most commonly transferred properties, but much can be altered, including setting, dialogue, and even important aspects of the narrative. For instance, in the 1999 remake of *The Thomas Crown Affair* (1968), what was a happy ending only for Steve McQueen's womanizing Thomas Crown becomes, with the addition of a new final scene, a happy-couple ending for Pierce Brosnan's more sensitive Crown and Rene Russo's Catherine Banning.[25] Audiences, of course, compare the original and the remake.[26] However, according to Kania, there is an important difference between comparisons of an original film with its remake and comparisons of two performances of a symphony, for instance. When one performance is preferred over another for, say, its sensitive handling of tempo changes in a certain section, the two are being compared as instances *of the same work*. One listener might agree with another that, in itself, the first performance of the section is more exciting but that, ultimately, the second is truer to the work as a whole. However, similar judgments are not made in the comparison of an original film and a remake. Two critics might disagree about whether the chase scene in the remake is more exciting, or better edited, than the parallel sequence in the original, or which chase scene is better suited to the pacing of the film of which it is a part, but there is no talk of which movie is truer to "the work" – for there is no obvious referent for this term in cinema, other than a given movie. The thin narrative that original and remake share is not a primary focus of appreciation in film, the way a symphony is in classical music. The narrative is more like a "subject" in painting, such as the crucifixion, that is treated in different ways by different painters, yet is not in itself a work of art.

In sum, Kania claims that people knowledgeable about cinema treat an original and its remake as works in their own right, comparing them directly, rather than comparing them by reference to a third, different kind of entity – the narrative – to which both are related in some fashion. The two films are the kind of thing that is the primary focus of appreciation in cinema; the narrative is not. The implication for rock music is that we compare cover versions with their originals without thinking of them as performances of the songs they instance. The parallels between the way films and rock tracks are created are relevant here. A film may begin as a screenplay and the artistic vision of a director, but we do not think of the screenplay as a primary focus of appreciation in cinema (*pace* Nannicelli 2013, 61–188). Similarly, a track may have its genesis in someone writing a song with pen and paper at the piano, but this does not show that the resulting recording is a performance of a thin song. So the rock practice of covering tracks, according to Kania, bolsters the view that rock tracks, like films, are works in their own right, rather than performances of other, independent works.

Kania's account of covers is relatively simple: A cover is a track that intentionally instances the same song as a previous track. Theodore Gracyk, by contrast, thinks that although this is how the term was originally used, the notion of a cover has become more complex. Preferring the term "remake" for Kania's simple concept, Gracyk argues that sometime in the 1960s, covers became an artistically interesting *species* of remake.[27] What distinguishes a *cover* in the artistically interesting sense from a *mere* remake is that the cover is intended by its creators to be understood in relation to the "original," i.e., the track featuring the same song that has become the *standard* version in the rock tradition.[28] According to Gracyk, "covers are extended allusions to previous works" (2012–13, 40). Allusions are subtle references to other things. If I ask you if you've read *Lolita*, I simply *refer* to that novel. But when the protagonist of The Police's "Don't Stand So Close to Me" mentions "the book by Nabokov," in the context of his troubling experiences with a student, he *alludes* to the novel. In the arts, allusions are often achieved by using uncredited quotations or adaptations of parts of other works, as when Dave Dobbyn alludes to the Elvis classic, "Love Me Tender" (1956) in his own "Loyal" (1998), with the line "I love you tender, but we must walk away." According to Gracyk, whereas

> [n]ormally, an allusion is a brief or relatively small aspect of a text[, c]overs are
> … saturated allusions. Every aspect of the performance is to be treated as referencing all aspects of the earlier recording at parallel points in the performance.
> (2012–13, 41)

Thus, Tiffany's 1987 recording of Tommy James and the Shondells' "I Think We're Alone Now" (1967) is a mere remake, according to Gracyk, because Tiffany could not have expected her audience to be aware of the original track, and thus could not have reasonably intended them to hear her version in comparison with it. But The Rubinoos' 1977 recording of the same song *is* a cover, because they *did* reasonably expect their audience to hear it as harking back to the innocence of the original, in sharp contrast to the dominant punk aesthetic of the time (2012–13, 41–3). Understanding covers as saturated allusions, Gracyk argues, clarifies one resource that popular music – often thought to be simpler than classical or jazz music – has for producing complex musical meanings, thanks to its recording-centered ontology (2012–13, 43).[29]

According to Cristyn Magnus, P. D. Magnus, and Christy Mag Uidhir (henceforth "the Mags," to save some space!), covers are even more complicated than Gracyk suggests. The Mags argue for a four-category taxonomy of covers (Magnus, Magnus, & Mag Uidhir 2013). The simplest category is *mimic* covers, which aim at reproducing the sound of the *original*, rather than a new interpretation of the song. Gracyk would classify recorded mimic covers of the song as (mere) remakes. But the Mags point out that mimic covers are typically performed live by *cover bands*, rather than recorded, and claim that such performances are clearly surrogates for hearing the original band perform live (2013, 362–3). The last point seems a little quick. The "original" that the live performance mimics is a *track*, not a live performance, and, as noted above, few groups attempt to mimic their recordings in live performance. So the cover band's live performance seems to be a surrogate not for hearing the original band live, but for hearing the original track. But then it is puzzling why audiences need a surrogate, since the *track* is widely available. Perhaps, instead, the audience wants to make vivid the illusion that the original track is a transparent document of a single, continuous performance. Whatever the reason for the popularity of cover bands, it does seem reasonable to consider mimic covers a significant category of performance, to be judged in terms of faithfulness to the original track.

The Mags' second category is *rendition* covers (2013, 363–5). These are tracks (or performances) that instance the same thin song as the original, but depart from (rather than mimic) the original's realization of that song.[30] Such covers can be properly evaluated in two different ways, according to the Mags: (i) in comparison with the original track, or (ii) as a rendition of the thin song on the original track (but not in comparison with the original rendition). Gracyk's saturated-allusion covers seem to fit the Mags' characterization of renditions, but it's not clear that the Mag's theory of the *evaluation* of renditions applies to them, since it is impossible to properly appreciate an allusion without considering what it is an allusion *to*. We might, then, subdivide the category of rendition covers into *mere* renditions and saturated-allusion renditions. But we might also wonder whether the appreciation of *any* rendition cover would be necessarily incomplete without comparison to the original.

The Mags might resist this line of thought by appealing to the fact that allusions are widely considered to be essentially intentional. For example, if I compare the world to a theatrical stage, I only make a Shakespearean *allusion* if I intend a reference to Jaques's famous speech in *As You Like It*. If I've never even heard that metaphor before, the resemblance is coincidental and not an allusion – even if my audience *supposes* that it is an allusion. Now, all theorists might agree that if a track *coincidentally* sounds like a rendition cover of a track that the creators of the new track had never heard of, it would not technically be a cover. But what about two more likely scenarios? In the first, the artist intends her track to be heard in comparison with the original track. In the second, the artist intends her track to be heard as instancing the same thin song instanced on the original track, but not in comparison with the original track in particular. The new track in the first case is a saturated allusion, but it is not so clear that the new track in the second case is. Certainly there is a crucial intentional connection between the new track and the original: The artist intends to instance the song on the original track. But it is not obvious that such an intention is enough for allusion. A novelist may use a plot twist that he enjoyed in another novelist's work without *alluding to* the novel he is imitating. The difference seems to be that to make an allusion, one must intend not just to *create* a certain resemblance between one's new work and one's extant target, but also that one's audience will *recognize* the intended resemblance. In the second case, the artist intends her audience to be able to distinguish the thin song she instances from the thick properties of her particular instance (her track), but she does *not* intend that the audience think of the original track's rendition of that song as particularly relevant to her track's appreciation. Such an artist intends her version of the song to be compared to others (actual and possible), much as a classical performer intends his performances of a given work to be compared to other performances of the same work. The relevant comparison class is all possible performances (or recordings), but no single performance (or recording) counts for these purposes as *the original*. Thus not all renditions are saturated allusions – that depends on the intentions of a given track's creator.

Gracyk might respond that, given the recording-centered nature of rock and the widespread practice of identifying certain tracks as the "the original" versions of given songs (features of rock practice that the Mags acknowledge), no one could *reasonably* intend her cover of a song with such an original version to be appreciated *only* as a recording of the song, and not primarily in comparison with the original. This would conflict, however, with Gracyk's characterization of Tiffany's "I Think We're Alone Now" as a mere remake. Moreover, recall that not all songs – even those previously recorded – have versions that rise to the level of an "original" or standard version against which all others will be measured. So Gracyk must make room for rendition covers that are not saturated allusions, whether or not the only tracks in this category are covers of songs that have no widely acknowledged standard recording, while the Mags must allow that the full appreciation of saturated-allusion renditions requires comparison with the original.

You might have thought that mimic and rendition covers exhaust the field, since a cover either does or doesn't aim to mimic the original recording of a given song. But the Mags argue that there are two further categories of cover: Both *transformative* and *referential* covers are recordings *not* of the song on some previous track, but of a *different* song "sufficiently derivative" of the song on the original track (2013, 365).[31] The Mags' central example of a *transformative* cover is Aretha Franklin's "Respect" (1967). Franklin's classic recording is widely considered an original in its own right, but it is also a cover of Otis Redding's 1965 recording of his song "Respect." The Mags, however, argue that Franklin made such significant changes to the meaning or content of

Redding's song that her recording is an instance of a different (albeit derivative) song.[32] Their case is entirely based on additions and changes Franklin made to Redding's lyrics. The additions include her spelling out "respect," the line "take care, TCB [i.e., take care of business]" and the "sock it to me" hook; the changes include the transformation of "give me my proper respect" to "give me my propers." These differences seem too minor to justify the claim that Franklin is recording a different song; they're of kinds that occur in many rendition covers. The crucial changes are those that transform the perspective of the song. Where Redding claims that "what you want, honey you've got it; and what you need, baby, you've got it," Franklin asserts that "what you want, baby, *I* got; what you need, do you know *I* got it."[33] Redding's plea is that "all I'm asking is for a little respect when I come home," while Franklin's demand is that "all I'm asking is for a little respect when *you* come home (just a little bit!)." Where Redding gives his woman permission to cheat on him when he's gone, as long as he gets respect at home, Franklin says she has no interest in cheating on her man; where Redding asks for respect in return for his money, in Franklin's version it is she who has the money. Moreover, Franklin values her man's kisses no higher than her money, allowing her to end the song with the warning that if he doesn't respect her, he might come home one day to find her gone – a warning that is absent from Redding's version. These changes amount to more than just a switch from a man addressing his woman to a woman addressing her man (otherwise, Tiffany's "I Saw Him Standing There" would count as a transformative cover of the Beatles' "I Saw Her Standing There"); they amount to the transformation of the song from an assertion of patriarchal authority into a feminist anthem.

Is it really the *song* that is thus transformed, though, or do both recordings instance the *same* song, differing only in how that song is realized? Compare the two recordings of "Respect" with Gloria Gaynor's 1978 disco hit "I Will Survive" and Cake's 1996 alt-rock cover. In this case, the cover alters very few lyrics, but the musical setting of those lyrics could hardly be more different.[34] Gaynor's recording is almost operatic, with its recitative-like opening section followed by the strutting aria of the main body of the song. No wonder it became, first, another feminist anthem and, later, an anthem for gay men in the AIDS era. But where one has no doubt that the protagonist of Gaynor's recording will survive – indeed is bursting with such strength that she cannot help but joyously express it – one gets the feeling that the protagonist of the Cake version is barely fooling himself. With its lackluster rock beat and sloppy, behind-the-beat singing, it seems questionable whether the protagonist will even make it to the end of the song.[35] In short, the Cake cover of "I Will Survive" seems as different in content from Gaynor's original as Franklin's "Respect" does from Redding's. But does it thereby follow that Cake's recording is of a *different song* than Gaynor's? It seems at least as plausible that the brilliance of Cake's recording resides in large part in the fact that they found a way to record *the very same song* while communicating an entirely different meaning.

But if the song remains the same, how can two recordings of it differ so drastically in their content? The obvious answer is that the song is very thin, which allows for the various realizations of it in performance or recording to differ radically. After all, classical audiences are willing to hear a relatively small number of works over and over again in performance (live or recorded), precisely for the different interpretive possibilities that such works enable, even though most of those works are much thicker than popular songs. Indeed, Gracyk has argued at length that the content of most popular songs in recording-centered traditions is intentionally open-ended and future-directed, since, as mass art, it is intended to reach a wide and diverse audience (2001, 1–80; 2013a). And it seems plausible to think of Cake's cover as, broadly, an *ironic* recording of the same song that Gaynor recorded sincerely. Franklin's recording of "Respect" is not *ironic*, but we might think that she similarly takes the content of a thin song – Redding's – and *uses it* to communicate a radically different message. Finally, it seems possible that the Mags are misled into thinking that Franklin's "Respect" is a recording of a different song than Redding's because her version has become the standard that later covers take as their target (from which most people learn the song, etc.). That Cake's cover of "I Will Survive" has not replaced Gaynor's recording as the standard recording might explain why we would be less willing to countenance that it is a recording of a different song.

While all of the above considerations seem reasonable, none of them seem decisive. Ultimately, the question raised by the Mags' positing of the category of transformative covers is how popular songs should be individuated, that is, under what circumstances we have two recordings of one song as opposed to recordings of two different (albeit related) songs. Consider parodies. The Mags claim that though Weird Al Yankovich's "Yoda" (1985) is clearly derivative of the Kinks' "Lola" (1970) – indeed, you would entirely miss the point of the former if you did not realize it was a parody of the latter – the changes that Yankovich made to the song are so great that it is no longer *sufficiently* derivative to count as a cover. (Most obviously, *all* of the lyrics are changed.) The Mags claim that though the notion of a song's being "sufficiently derivative is admittedly vague, … common usage suffices to draw a rough boundary" (2013, 366). However, while that is plausible for parodies, it doesn't apply to cases such as "Respect" or "I Will Survive," where common usage treats the supposedly *transformative* cover versions as renditions of *the same song*. So it seems that the defense of the category of "transformative cover" will require more work on the song-individuation question. As with the question of whether recordings are the sole primary focus of appreciation in rock, answering this question will depend mostly on how knowledgeable rock artists and audiences treat songs and recordings of them.

The Mags' final category is *referential* covers (2013, 367–8). Like transformative covers, a referential cover supposedly instances a different song sufficiently derivative of the song on the original track. The crucial change to the song in question that puts referential covers in a class of their own is that it becomes *about* the original track. Sid Vicious's 1978 cover of Frank Sinatra's famous 1969 recording of "My Way," for instance, is not just a new recording of a famous song in a radically different genre (according to the Mags), it is also a critique of the values expressed by the original recording. Referential covers raise the same questions as transformative covers: Do the differences between Vicious's and Sinatra's recordings really imply that Vicious's recording is of a different (albeit derivative) song, or is it just one more way in which the same thin song can be realized? Are the references to Sinatra's track part of the *song* instanced on Vicious's recording, or part of *the way in which the song is instanced* on that recording? Presumably the answers to these questions will be the same as those we give about transformative covers.

Note that if "transformative" and "referential" covers are of the same songs as their originals, then we end up with a simpler theory of covers, closer to Gracyk's theory, but incorporating the Mags' insights: There are mimic (or remake) covers and rendition covers. Mimic covers are properly appreciated with respect to how well they mimic the original. A rendition cover may be a saturated allusion to its original or not. If not, it can be fully appreciated independently of the original track; but if it *is* a saturated allusion, it cannot be fully appreciated without comparison to the original. We might retain the labels "transformative" and "referential," but these will name not covers that instance different songs from their originals, but rather *different interpretive strategies* a given rendition cover takes toward the song it instances.

9.5 The Comparative Value of Live and Recorded Music

Thus far, we have investigated some general aspects of recording technology, and the ways in which recordings are made and appreciated in a range of musical traditions. Another question that has exercised philosophers of music is whether live performances or recordings provide better musical experiences (Brown 2000b; S. Davies 2001, 295–340; Glasgow 2007; Gracyk 1997; Hamilton 2003). Discussions of this question sometimes seem to assume that music consists entirely of work-performances. This assumption need not beg the question in favor of *live* performances since, as we have seen, it might be argued that some recordings are themselves work-performances, or give us access to work-performances. Nonetheless, the assumption does ignore arguments that there is music (such as much jazz) consisting of performances that are not of works, and music (such as much rock and pop) consisting of works for playback, rather than for performance. Obviously, if there are musical works whose medium is recorded sound, and which thus cannot be performed live, it makes no sense to ask whether they are better experienced through live performance or recordings.[36] I focus in this section, then, on the comparison of live performances and recordings of music that can be performed live. Philosophers have discussed three dimensions along which recordings and live performances differ: their sonic properties, their potential for interpersonal interaction, and their (un)repeatability. I consider here only the *artistic* value of recordings and live performances, ignoring, for instance, the social costs and benefits of individual (e.g., earbud) versus communal (e.g., concert) musical experiences.

There are appreciable differences between the auditory (and tactile or somatic) experience of actual recordings and live performances, not to mention the absence of the visual element from most recordings. For this reason, musical recordings are sometimes compared to photographic reproductions of paintings. But perhaps they are more closely analogous to DVD editions of films, which we tend to treat as genuine instances of the works they purport to be of, and are rarely dismissed as "mere" reproductions. Nothing on the artistic order of brushwork, for instance, is lacking from films seen on a small screen; likewise for typical musical recordings (cf. Gracyk 1996, 24). And though some fine details of timbre, for instance, may be lost, recordings enable us to hear some other features (through judicious microphone placement, say) that we might miss at a live performance. Finally, the use of studio technology enables musicians to hone a performance that can be heard an indefinite number of times.

If appreciation of a performance requires understanding how the sounds are produced, whether for the performance's expressive features (as we considered in Chapter 7) or recognizing that it is an improvisation (Chapter 8), then the absence of the visual element from most music recordings is cause for concern. But if we are already acquainted with how a piano is played, we need not *see* every piano performance; we can *hear* what the performer is doing (Gracyk 1997, 146–7).[37] And it is not obvious that even in the live performance situation we *see* that the performers are improvising. Moreover, note that if this concern is compelling it will have far-reaching implications. It is the received view in contemporary philosophy of the arts that one must understand something of how a work was created in order to properly appreciate it. But the creation of many kinds of art (paintings, novels, etc.) is not directly accessible to audiences. Thus, either the received view is incorrect, or indirect knowledge of the creation of works can be sufficient for their proper appreciation.

Recordings may eliminate two kinds of interactivity available to audiences of live performances: The musicians on a recording are unable to respond to their audience, and audiences of recordings are (typically) unable to interact with one another as the music unfolds. The latter kind of interaction may be valuable in all sorts of ways, but its loss seems unlikely to affect one's appreciation of the music (though see Cochrane 2009). Anyway, Theodore Gracyk points out that there are alternative venues in which audiences of recordings can interact, such as online discussion groups (1997, 147–8). It is more difficult to determine the extent and value of musician–audience interaction at live performances. There are obvious examples, such as the call and response often initiated by rock artists on stage, but these seem of little artistic value. Artistically significant interaction, as when the "mood of the room" affects the performance, seems likely to be more prevalent in more intimate venues and in improvisatory performances. It might be argued that such interaction affects the performance being experienced, rather than being an object of appreciation itself. Nonetheless, if the effects of such interaction are typically *good*, and absent from recordings, this is one reason to favor live performances of such music over recordings.

A range of concerns arise from recordings' repeatability. One is that repeated listening to a recording will jade us to its aesthetic qualities (Sessions 1950, 70–1). But this is a contentious claim (S. Davies 2001, 305–7; Glasgow 2007, 168–9). We seem capable of appreciating other artistic objects, including musical works for performance, on repeated exposure to them, so why not the music captured on recordings? Even if repeated exposure to the same recordings *does* jade us, the advantages accruing to the repeatability of recordings likely outweigh this disadvantage. The repeatability of recordings, and the portability that follows upon it, allow us to listen to the performances of people whom we could never hear live, for any number of reasons; it allows us to compare two performances side by side that we could not hear that way live; it allows us to hear a much larger number of works and performances than we could hear live; and so on.

It might be argued that the repeatability of recordings has larger-scale effects than the ones just considered. Lee Brown argues that the ubiquity of recordings has led many jazz scholars to erroneously treat the improvisatory performances captured on jazz recordings as performances of repeatable works (2000b, 119–22).[38] If this is so, then it seems that we should ask such scholars to reflect more deeply on the ontology of the tradition with which they are engaged; such errors cannot be laid at the feet of recording technology or artists.

In the classical world, it is surely the repeatability of recordings that drives performers to "perfect" their recordings, that is, to fix the small errors that would pass in a moment in a live performance, yet become anticipated landmarks in a repeatable recording. As a result, it is argued, live audiences' tolerance for small errors has decreased, leading to a decline in creative risk-taking by musicians in live performance. It is undeniable that classical performance styles and interpretations have become more uniform since recording technology arrived. Ironically (for the technology's detractors), some of the best evidence for this is recordings (Philip 1992). The factors plausibly involved in this shift are complex, but it is hard to deny that recordings have played a significant role. One remedy would be to acknowledge the close relationship between live performances and recordings of classical music, while at the same time maintaining an awareness of their differences (S. Davies 2001, 307–14). On the part of musicians, this might involve adopting a different attitude in live performance than in the recording studio: taking more chances and experimenting with new approaches on stage, while acknowledging that only certain kinds of approaches and interpretations will bear the multiple listenings that recordings allow. This is no small recommendation for most classical musicians, since there is a close connection between what such musicians do live and in the studio. And such changes would of course require audiences to understand and embrace this increased experimentation and diversity in live performances. But note that such practices are standard in the rock world.

9.6 Review and Looking Ahead

In Chapters 6 through 8, we considered various issues raised by different kinds of musical performance. In this chapter we have looked at how those issues are complicated by the introduction of recording technology – technology that now mediates the majority of musical experiences around the world. Though we have, as usual, raised more questions than we have answered, it is clear that recordings play different roles in various musical traditions and practices. Indeed, the role of recordings in other musical traditions and practices, most notably various popular traditions such as punk, hip hop, and EDM (electronic dance music) remains a largely untapped but potentially rich field for philosophical study.

In the remaining chapters we turn to two areas of enquiry on which we must bring to bear many of the issues we have considered to this point in the book. In Chapter 10, we consider the relationship between music and morality. In Chapter 11, we return to a question first raised in Chapter 1: What is music?

Questions

What does it mean to say that sound recordings are *transparent*? What conditions must a medium meet in order to count as transparent? Are (some) sound recordings in fact transparent?

Consider a recording of a classical work that is spliced together from several takes. When one listens to the recording, does one hear a *performance* of the work in question?

What does it mean to identify some kind of thing as the (or a) *work* in a given musical tradition? What is (or are) the work(s) in the rock tradition: songs, live performances, recordings, or something else ?

Is the relationship between a rock or pop song and an edited studio-recording of that song the same as, or different from, the relationship between a classical work (e.g., a symphony) and an edited studio-recording of that work?

What is a *cover version* of a given rock or pop recording? Can a cover of a given recording (the "original") be an instance of a different song than appears on the original?

Consider a popular-music tradition or genre with which you are familiar (other than rock or pop), such as hip hop, punk, EDM, etc. How, if at all, would your answers to the previous three questions change if they were about your chosen tradition or genre?

Are live performances or recordings a better way to experience music?

Notes

1 For arguments against even these basic points, see Mag Uidhir 2007. One complication is that you can have two *copies* of the same recording (e.g., two CDs off the same production line). A playing of either copy will instance the same recording. But these copies are not instances of the recording in the relevant sense, since they are not sound events. (Thanks to Matteo Ravasio for this point.) For further discussion, in connection with audiovisual recordings, see Carroll 1996, 66–70.
2 Walton does not claim that intentions play no role in photography, just that there is one particular role they do not play, which distinguishes photographs from "handmade" images.
3 For a consideration of many issues about the identity, individuation, and transmission of sounds glossed over here, see O'Callaghan 2007.
4 One exception is Stephen Davies (2016 p, 180–3), but he argues that the lack of intentional mediation in photography is not significant in the context of arguing that intentional representations, like paintings, can be just as transparent as photographs.
5 More precisely, I assume that sound recordings *can be* transparent. If there is no original sound event captured on a "recording" (e.g., in the case of a track produced purely electronically), then there is nothing for the recording to be transparent *to*.
6 Doubtless there were sound engineers and perhaps other people listening to Mingus as he recorded these parts, but it is not clear that they qualify as an audience, as discussed in Chapter 6. (The recording cited in the text features the original, undoctored recordings.)
7 It is an interesting question whether this experience of edited recordings as single, continuous performances is a perceptual illusion (like the visual experience of movement in a film) or an imaginative experience (as when we imagine of an actor that she is the doctor she plays).
8 Jazz fusion is an exception, since it is defined in part by its embrace of studio technology.
9 For discussion of whether recordings meet the intended-audience condition on performances, see Chapter 6, §6.1.
10 For an analogous argument about artistic predicates, see Danto 1964.
11 For consideration of a range of cases aimed at establishing the existence of classical recording conventions, see Kania 1998, 37–51.
12 For disputes about the term "popular music," see Fisher 2011.
13 I talk of "songs" throughout, although there is some purely instrumental popular music; what I say is intended to apply to both kinds.
14 Recall from Chapter 7, §7.1, that the more properties of an instance of an ontologically-multiple entity are determined by that entity, the thicker it is.

15 Note that Gracyk uses the term "rock" to refer not to a style or genre (*rock* as opposed to *heavy metal*), but to a wider artistic tradition (*rock* as opposed to *classical* or *jazz*).

16 As we turn from Gracyk's basic argument to criticisms and developments of his view, the extent to which our discussion will apply to popular traditions other than rock (pop, hip hop, electronica, etc.) becomes less clear.

17 We will consider cover versions at greater length below.

18 I know, I know: *I'm* Andrew Kania. But in the interest of neutrality, I will discuss my own published views in the third person.

19 Some philosophers (notably Gregory Currie (1989) and David Davies (2004)) see such skills as so important that they argue we should conceive of all artworks as performances in some sense.

20 There are also, of course, recordings of live rock performances. There is no space here to consider these, but one thing worth noting is that, unlike recordings of live jazz or classical performances, the primary source for live-rock recordings is typically not microphones in the hall, but the *soundboard* that takes the signals from onstage sources (electric instruments and microphones) and processes them for amplification through the venue speakers. There is thus an additional factor distancing the experience of the live audience from that of the recording audience.

21 Note, however, that David Davies (2011, 100–1) also attributes something like this argument to Kania.

22 Kania (2008a, 435) considers Lee B. Brown a particularist about jazz.

23 For two relevant debates over the methodology of art- and musical ontology, see D. Davies 2004, 16–24, Dodd 2013, and D. Davies 2017; and Brown 2011b, Kania 2012, and Brown 2012.

24 Compare the analogy between jazz standards and screenplays in Chapter 8, §8.2.

25 There can also be extremely faithful remakes and covers. For instance, Gus Van Sant's 1998 remake of Alfred Hitchcock's *Psycho* (1960) recreated the original (almost) shot for shot, and we have already considered Sixpence None the Richer's 2003 cover of Crowded House's "Don't Dream It's Over" (1986).

26 The word "original" is not intended evaluatively here; a remake can be better – even more *original* – than the "original" film or track. The term merely refers to a film that gets remade or a track that gets covered.

27 This musical application of the term "remake" should not be confused with the cinematic concept discussed above.

28 The "original" need not be the *first* track to feature the song in question. For instance, Gracyk takes Jimi Hendrix's recording of "All Along the Watchtower" (1968) to be the standard version, even though Bob Dylan's 1967 recording of this (his own) song is well known.

29 Gracyk intriguingly argues that we can understand some works in other non-performance arts as saturated allusions. He gives the example of Tom Stoppard's play, *Rosencrantz and Guildenstern Are Dead* (1966), which we can understand as a saturated allusion to Shakespeare's *Hamlet*.

30 Henceforth, I will talk only about cover *tracks* for simplicity, though the Mags allow for live-performance covers in all their categories.

31 As with renditions, the Mags claim that one can properly evaluate a transformative cover *either* in comparison with its target original *or* simply as a recording of a song. The criticisms of this claim with respect to rendition covers presumably transfer directly to transformative covers. I consider the appreciation of referential covers below.

32 "Derivative," like "original," is not an evaluative term here.

33 As elsewhere, I talk of "Redding" and "Franklin" for simplicity, but they are presumably performing in some sense as fictional protagonists or narrators of their respective songs' story and message.

34 One could be forgiven for thinking that the Mags think song content is generated exclusively by lyrics. They bolster their case for Franklin's cover being transformative, for instance, by pointing out that the changes she made to the song "go well beyond the change to a few

chord progressions" or "merely a difference in musical style or idiom" as opposed to "a significant difference in content" (365). But I take it that the Cake cover I am about to discuss demonstrates that musical changes can be just as "transformative" as lyrical ones.

35 The negative adjectives I use to describe this recording are intended to convey the feeling of the track. I have no doubt that these sounds were carefully crafted by the musicians. Indeed, I think it is a brilliant reimagining of "I Will Survive."

36 One might still compare, in general, the value of works for playback and works for performance, but there is no space to do so here.

37 Opera and ballet are in a different category with respect to this question, since they are not purely musical arts: A proper instance of an opera or ballet is staged. Thus, an adequate recording of such a work must be an audio-visual one (S. Davies 2001, 320).

38 Even if Julian Dodd (2014b) is right that most jazz performances are of works, he still allows that these are highly improvisatory performances, and it is the improvisatory elements that Brown accuses jazz scholars of treating as work-like.

Further Reading

An important essay on jazz recordings is Lee B. Brown's "Phonography, Repetition and Spontaneity" (2000b), revised and expanded as Chapter 9 of Brown, Goldblatt, and Gracyk 2018 (208–33). In *Musical Works and Performances* (2001, 25–36, 295–340), Stephen Davies discusses many issues concerning musical recordings, with a focus on classical music.

Topics about musical recordings that have yet to receive their due in the philosophical literature include sampling and the integration of recordings into live performance in DJing. Zed Adams (2018) and Nick Wiltsher (2016b), respectively, make a good start on these topics.

10 Music and Morality

Overview

In this chapter we consider the morality of musical works themselves, their production, and their reception. Specifically, we ask (1) whether a moral flaw in a piece of music need be an artistic flaw; (2) whether singing along to morally flawed songs is itself morally bad; (3) whether instrumental classical music contributes to the oppression of women; and (4) whether it is morally acceptable for white musicians to play music that is part of black culture.

During the "war on terror," one of the standard ways in which CIA and US-military personnel psychologically manipulated detainees at various sites around the world – ways that many believe amounts to torture – was to play music at high volumes in their cells and interrogation rooms, constantly or randomly (Cusick 2008). A wide range of music was used, including music from children's TV shows (e.g., *Barney and Friends*), pop songs (e.g., Britney Spears), heavy metal (e.g., Metallica), and "Arabic music" (qtd. in Cusick 2008, 12). Some functions of this treatment, such as sleep deprivation, presumably depend little on the content of the music, or even on the sounds' being music at all. Others, such as the attempt to break down the target's sense of self, may depend on the nature of the music. Some strands of Islamic thought, for instance, construe music for entertainment, especially music performed by women, as sinful (Cusick 2008, 12–14). Whether or not you think torture is justified in some circumstances, some uses of music are uncontroversially immoral, for instance, taking your neighbor prisoner and subjecting him to your latest compositions against his will merely for your own amusement. Perhaps you can think of many other uncontroversially immoral ways in which music could be used. My aim in this chapter is to consider some more controversial claims about morality and music, focusing particularly on music put to more standard artistic uses. That is, I ask whether the typical actions of musicians and audiences, and even whether musical works, performances, and recordings themselves, can be morally bad.

One way in which any of these things could be morally bad is by *harming* people. For instance, if listening to death metal causes people to become murderers, then that music is morally bad, as is the creation and distribution of it, and perhaps even the choice to listen to it. Now, it is fairly obvious that death metal does not, by itself, turn people into murderers. But figuring out whether it plays *any* role in increasing violence is a difficult empirical question, better addressed by social scientists than philosophers. I thus put such causal questions aside where possible.

If you think that only the *consequences* of an action, such as harming others, are relevant to its moral value, then you are a *consequentialist*. Consequentialism is controversial. According to *deontology*, a major rival of consequentialism, it is the *intentions* with which you act (crucially the intention to follow a moral rule), rather than the consequences of your action, that are morally relevant. Of course, your intentions will typically be intimately connected to the consequences of your action – you intend to *do something*, after all – but the contrast between the two theories can be illustrated by a simple example. Suppose you see an unattended baby drowning in a swimming pool. You immediately dive in to save the baby, not realizing that the pool is very shallow. Cracking your head on the bottom, you knock yourself out and quickly drown, as does the baby. Did you perform a morally good action? The consequentialist seems obliged to answer "no": As a consequence of your actions, two people are dead; had you walked on, only one death would have occurred. The deontologist seems obliged to answer "yes": Though two people are dead, your intention – to save a drowning innocent – was impeccable. Neither answer strikes most people as wholly adequate (and, indeed, both the consequentialist and deontologist would rightly complain that I have applied their theories simplistically), but the point for our purposes is that it is not obvious that *only* the consequences of actions are morally relevant.[1]

Some philosophers argue further that *feelings* are morally evaluable, even if they affect neither consequences nor intentions. A *virtue ethicist*, for instance, will argue that someone who *grudgingly* saves a drowning baby is morally worse than someone who does so wholeheartedly, even if this difference is imperceptible to others and has no effect on the rescue. The relevance of feelings arises frequently in philosophical discussions relating art and morality, since many argue that affective responses to art are often crucial to its appreciation (see Chapter 3, §3.3.1, and Chapter 5, §5.2.2), and such responses may be morally evaluable independently of the kind of causal connection between the experience of art and later actions, discussed above.

10.1 Are Moral Flaws Artistic Flaws?

Can a piece of music be morally bad not because of how it was created, or for the effects it has, but *in itself*?[2] A positive answer may seem easier to defend with respect to song, since songs have *words* that can represent morally objectionable situations. But the mere representation of a morally bad situation does not make the representation morally bad. A discussion of the morality of torture in an ethics class, for instance, might require talking about morally reprehensible treatment of people, but this does not make the ethics class morally reprehensible, since the treatment *represented* in the discussion is not necessarily (hopefully not in fact!) *endorsed* in the discussion. One can – sometimes one must – represent something morally reprehensible in order to *repudiate* it. The same distinction is often invoked in discussions of fictions that represent morally reprehensible actions. Some pornography, for instance, is condemned on the grounds that it endorses sexual violence against women by presenting it as erotic, while the rape scene in *The Accused* (1988) is widely acclaimed for conveying the horror of sexual violence. Similarly, while the Beatles' "Run for Your Life" could be criticized for implying that violence is an acceptable masculine response to unrequited love, Suzanne Vega's "Luka" is praised for its empathetic representation of domestic violence. The difference between a representation that endorses and one that repudiates its subject typically involves artistic features such as the point of view from which the situation is represented, the emotions it is intended to elicit (and in fact elicits) in a competent audience, and the way in which the representation of the situation relates to other parts of the work.

If *endorsing* the good or bad is itself good or bad, then, given the considerations just mentioned, artistic matters are relevant to figuring out whether an artwork is morally good or bad. Is the converse true? That is, does the moral value of an artwork affect its artistic value? Philosophers have defended three kinds of answer to this question.[3] *Autonomists* say *no*: the moral value of an artwork is irrelevant to its value as art. Artistic value is *autonomous*, i.e., unconnected to other types of value, such as the moral. *Ethicists*, by contrast, argue that the moral value of a work *is* relevant to its artistic value, at least when its moral attitude is artistically integrated with the work in some way (Gaut 2007, 82–9). Ethicists claim that a moral flaw of this kind is an artistic flaw in the work and that a moral merit is an artistic merit. *Contextualists* agree with ethicists that the moral value of a work may affect its artistic value, but they argue that the relation between the two is not so straightforward: Depending on the *context* (i.e., the other features of the work), a moral flaw can make a work artistically *better* and a moral merit can make it artistically *worse* – claims that the ethicist denies.[4]

Autonomists are usually monists about the value of art – they think there is a single value of art, and it's not moral value. Autonomists have typically been formalists, arguing that the single value of art is a narrowly construed aesthetic value. But even if one rejects monism, it's not obvious that moral value is relevant to artistic value. Everyone agrees that artworks have *economic* value, for instance, yet few people think that a work's price affects its artistic value. So ethicists and contextualists owe us an argument for the artistic relevance of a work's moral value.

One such argument appeals to *cognitivism* about artistic value, the position (encountered in Chapter 5) that art can be valuable in virtue of teaching us things. It's plausible that if art teaches us anything it (sometimes) teaches us about morality; thus if cognitivism is true, a work's moral-cognitive merits (or flaws) are artistic merits (or flaws), provided the lessons it teaches are artistically integrated into the work (Gaut 2007, 165–202). Such an argument would likely favor ethicism over contextualism, since a moral-cognitive flaw in a work would amount to its teaching us something *false*, and it is difficult to see how that could be an artistic merit (cf. Gaut 2007, 184–6).

A second argument for ethicism – the *merited-response argument* – appeals to the point that the value of artworks depends, in part, on their eliciting certain responses in their audiences. For instance, a film or song often attempts to elicit sympathy for its hero or narrator.[5] If the work fails in that attempt because the response in question is "unmerited," the work is flawed. The ethicist argues that the moral qualities of the work will often be a factor in whether such elicitation is successful. For instance, we may sympathize with the poetically plainspoken narrators of Nina Simone's "Four Women," but be repelled by the creepy misogyny of the narrator of the Beatles' "Run for Your Life." In the latter case, the moral flaw (creepy misogyny) is an artistic flaw because it precludes a central response that the artwork attempts to elicit (sympathy with the narrator). It is important to note that the responses in question, as with other theories we have considered, are not necessarily those of actual audiences. Otherwise, the creepy misogyny of "Run for Your Life" might count as an artistic merit – for creepy misogynists, at least. Rather, the appeal is, again, to a *competent* audience, though in this case they are competent with respect to not just music, but also morality. (If you deny that there is such a thing as moral value, the debates considered in this chapter are all moot.)

The contextualist agrees with the ethicist that the responses elicited in a competent audience are relevant to the work's artistic success, and that moral considerations often play a role in these responses, but she disagrees that the two types of value always mirror one another, as the ethicist claims.[6] To establish contextualism, then, all we need is a single case in which a work's moral merit is an artistic flaw, or a moral flaw is an artistic merit. Candidates of the first kind include the "preachy ([e.g.,] Jenny Holzer), pat (Charles Dickens), sentimental (Norman Rockwell), or flat-out boring" (Eaton 2009, 22). Much Christian rock comes in for such criticism. The songs may be morally impeccable, and their moral qualities artistically integral to them, yet they seem *less* good artistically for that. Candidates of the second kind include *transgressive* works – works that violate moral norms, often to foreground or criticize them. Punk band the Meatmen's double whammy of "Morrissey Must Die" and "How Soon Is Now" (a Smiths cover that, among other changes, replaces the line "I am human and I need to be loved" with "I am inhuman and I need to be killed") appears to promote murder in order to provocatively question the value of Morrissey's persona as a sensitive, sexually ambiguous man.

Ethicists reject these examples in three ways. First, the ethicist may clarify that the merits and flaws in question are *pro tanto* contributors to a work's value (Gaut 2007, 57–66). That is, a preachy work is artistically good *insofar as* it is morally good, but it is bad insofar as it is preachy. In an assessment of the work's overall artistic value, both merit and flaw must be taken into account. Second, the ethicist may appeal to a hierarchy of prescribed responses (Gaut 2007, 230). If "Morrissey Must Die" initially enjoins your amusement at the notion of killing the sensitive singer only to later elicit your shame at your casual misanthropy, then the initial immoral response is ultimately repudiated and thus part of an all-things-considered moral *merit* in the song. Third, the ethicist may simply reject the contextualist's proposed examples. If the Meatmen only mean to be provocative – to spur us to imagine taking murderous revenge on Morrissey for his whiny self-involvement, but not actually to endorse such behavior – then it's not obvious that the song is morally flawed. (See the following section for further discussion.) Alternatively, if the Meatmen *do* endorse the murder of Morrissey in this song, then the ethicist will surely stick to his guns and deny that this could be an artistic merit, given the unmerited nature of the prescribed sympathetic response.

To the extent that instrumental music can express morally evaluable attitudes, ethicist and contextualist arguments may be applied to it. For instance, since the sixth number of Mussorgsky's *Pictures at an Exhibition* (orchestrated by Ravel) is program music, representing (in some sense) a pair of Jewish figures, we can understand concerns that it is anti-Semitic. Similarly, if some apparently "pure" music (e.g., Shostakovich's Tenth Symphony) in fact has narrative content, as we saw Jenefer Robinson argue in Chapter 2, §2.6.2, we might morally evaluate the emotional responses to its protagonist that it prescribes. But if we think there are examples of music alone, without any such representational resources, we might wonder if this debate is relevant to it, since it seems unable to represent a morally evaluable situation and thus a morally evaluable attitude towards that situation.

María José Alcaraz León (2012), however, argues that pure music's ability to express emotional and other mental states is sufficient for the application of ethicist and contextualist arguments to it. Alcaraz León points out that we morally assess people's expressive behavior – criticizing someone's character, for instance, if they mourn their dead hamster with a grief more appropriate to the loss of a child. But even if music can express the same level of grief, it cannot represent the *object* of that grief. We thus cannot morally criticize the music's expression since, for all we know, it is appropriate to its object. Alcaraz León responds that we also criticize expressive behavior independently of the objects of the states expressed. She gives the examples of someone manifesting a "frenetic or calm character" or "distrustful or unnatural" attitude (182). But someone has a frenetic or calm *character* only insofar as he behaves frenetically or calmly *in a range of situations*. So, again, without the ability to represent those situations, it is unclear whether music can manifest such traits. Another suggestion Alcaraz León makes is that just as we sometimes morally criticize the *way in which* people express their emotions, independently of the objects of those emotions, we might morally criticize the way in which a passage expresses an emotion. She puts the point in terms of whether "the way in which the work is expressing some mental state [is] adequate or inadequate" (185). Now, if the adequacy in question is to the object of the emotion, we are again returned to the initial problem. If it is rather to the emotion itself, then we require an independent grasp on the emotion expressed and the way in which it is expressed.

Perhaps what Alcaraz León has in mind is that the expressiveness of a passage occurs in a musical and expressive context (the rest of the work), and thus may be more or less appropriate to that context. This could in turn affect whether the responses called for by the passage are merited or unmerited. For instance, a section in Elgar's concert overture *In the South*, consisting of a few portentous themes each repeated several times in different keys, is arguably *overblown* or *bombastic*, in that the high expressivity does not seem appropriate to the slight musical development thus far, yet it also seems to call for an awed response.[7] Whether this artistic flaw is a *moral* flaw depends upon whether our refusal to be awed by the music is accurately characterized as moral.

10.2 Can Singing along Be Immoral?

Though the debate over the artistic status of moral merits and flaws draws on audiences' responses to artworks, it is about the moral and artistic value of artworks themselves. Aaron Smuts (2013), by contrast, considers the ethics of a mode of engagement with art that seems peculiar to music: singing along to a recording. As we have seen throughout this book, the appreciation of art is not as passive as one might initially have thought. Still, singing along to a song is peculiar in the audience's instancing parts of the song being performed *along with* a perfectly good instance of it by the performers. This is unlike the recitation of poetry, say, which is not typically done over the top of someone else's recitation. It is also unlike our engagement with "interactive" artforms such as videogames, where our actions influence the instance of the work. Perhaps the closest artistic practice to singing along is the cult-movie "quote-along" – a screening of a film at which fans recite famous (or all) lines from it. But singing along to recordings is surely much more common (Smuts 2013, 122).[8]

Smuts argues that in singing along to, say, "Run for Your Life," one adopts in imagination the role of the narrator of the song (in this case, a creepy misogynist threatening to kill his girlfriend if she leaves him).[9] Now, it is obviously wrong to threaten to kill someone for ending a romantic relationship, but in singing along to this song, one might argue, one does no such thing – one at most *imagines* threatening to kill someone for that reason.[10] We've already seen that such imaginings are not necessarily wrong. One may imagine something morally bad for positive moral ends, such as sympathizing with a survivor of violence. And the ethicist argues that a work that asks us to imagine something morally bad is thereby itself morally bad only if it endorses the morally bad. But in singing along to "Run for Your Life," we do not simply imagine a morally bad situation; we imagine *performing* immoral actions (threatening someone with death), in a way that seems to be endorsed by the song itself, and we *take pleasure* in imagining performing those actions (Smuts 2013, 121–3).[11]

Still, one might maintain, to enjoy doing something wrong is entirely different from enjoying *imagining* doing something wrong. Consequentialists may argue that no one is affected by our *imagined* actions, but it seems possible, at the very least, that someone who routinely enjoys imagining torturing babies, say, might develop a hardened character, becoming less sensitive to actual babies' cries. If so, then that person's actions, guided by their changed character, could easily affect other people, too. Smuts acknowledges this possibility, but does not rely on it to make his case, setting aside, as I have done, controversial empirical claims (2013, 123–4).

Deontologists may argue that, since they are not part of one's action-guiding intentions, one's imaginings are morally irrelevant. Smuts argues, however, that enjoying imagining morally bad situations (including performing immoral actions) is *intrinsically* morally bad. As we saw in Chapter 5, arguing for something being an intrinsic value is especially difficult, since one cannot appeal to the commonly agreed value of *other* things to ground one's claim (lest one make the value instrumental after all). But Smuts claims that "[w]e merely need to consider a few cases to see that" evil imaginings are themselves evil (2013, 124). He first asks us to imagine (!) a gruesome accident. No one is to blame, but an onlooker quietly takes pleasure in the victim's suffering. Smuts claims that the onlooker should at the very least feel guilty for taking pleasure in this situation. She is not to blame for anything, but her character deserves *disesteem* – a term of moral condemnation that is the equivalent of blameworthiness, but applicable to people's characters rather than their actions (Smuts 2016, 382). Of course, in this case the onlooker enjoys not just *imagined*, but *actual* suffering. But Smuts next introduces cases that he considers equally compelling but that involve only imagined suffering. Compare two possible worlds, each of which contains just a single person. In one world, the person spends her free time imagining "cats playing with rubber bands on sunny windowsills"; in the other, the person spends her free time imagining "torturing children with a pair of pliers and a blowtorch" (2013, 124–5). Smuts thinks that the second world is clearly morally worse than the first, even though we need fear no evil consequences of its inhabitant's actions, since there is no one else in her world to harm.

If everyone shares Smuts's intuitions in these cases, then he has secured his central moral-theoretic claim – that enjoying imagining performing immoral actions is itself immoral. But note that he hasn't really argued for it; he has simply appealed to our intuitions. Thus, if there is significant disagreement among thoughtful, reasonable people about the second thought-experiment, Smuts has provided no reason that they should follow his argument any further. And some thoughtful, reasonable people *do* resist Smuts's second thought-experiment, claiming precisely that the fact that the accident victim's suffering is *real*, while the tortured children's suffering is only *imagined*, makes all the moral difference. For that matter, some thoughtful, reasonable people – notably consequentialists and deontologists – resist the conclusion Smuts draws from his *first* thought-experiment. Since the onlooker's pleasure involves no morally bad consequences or intentions, it is morally neutral. Smuts's arguments thus seem to turn on quite general questions in ethical theory.

Smuts (2013, 125–7) argues further that:

1   When we sing along to a song, imagining being the song's narrator, we are engaged in *surrogate fantasy*, that is, we would like what we are imagining to actually happen.
2   Desiring to perform immoral actions is itself immoral.
3   Thus, singing along to songs in which the narrator performs immoral actions is itself immoral.

Is premise (1) true? That is, do first-person imaginings tend to be surrogate fantasies? Smuts reports "I cannot recall ever assuming the persona of a film character, much less the villain in a slasher movie," in contrast to his experience of singing along to songs (2013, 127). But *imagining being* a character in a film or novel is surely a very common experience, especially when "first-person" techniques are used, such as first-person narration in a novel or point-of-view shots in a film. So Smuts must mean something more by "assuming the persona" of a character. One possibility is suggested by the notion of "self-involving" fictions, which generate fictional truths *about the reader*, prescribing that she imagine being a character in the fiction as it unfolds. The most well-known examples are videogames, along with choose-your-own-adventure stories and role-playing games (Robson & Meskin 2016). It is notable that these examples are all *interactive*, that is, the audience appreciates the work *by instancing it*, as opposed to traditional, non-interactive artforms, in which the audience appreciates something instanced or created by others (Gaut 2010, 140–51). But there are also non-interactive self-involving fictions.[12] Italo Calvino's novel *If on a Winter's Night a Traveler* (1979), for instance, is narrated in the rare "second person." This implies that the main character of the book – a reader struggling to get through an Italo Calvino novel – is *you*: "You are at your desk, you have set the book among your business papers ..." (Calvino 1979, 7).[13]

Are songs self-involving fictions? There are arguably *some* such songs (e.g., Carly Simon's "You're So Vain"), but most, like most novels and stories, are not. Smuts argues, however, that singing along is unlike ordinary appreciation of novels and films. In singing along, we imagine being the narrator of the song as he tells its story. This mode of appreciation is more like acting out part of a movie than imagining what it would be like to be a character (another similarity between singing along and movie quote-alongs). One turns what is not in itself self-involving into a self-involving fiction by imaginatively using it in a certain way.

But even if this is the case, it is implausible that self-involving fictions typically elicit surrogate fantasy. First, if you don't know what will happen in a given videogame or second-person novel, we cannot infer that you would like to do in real life what you do in the fiction. Now, often one has *some* sense of what will happen in such fictions. If I download the videogame *Zombie Massacre 3*, I can be sure that in playing the game I will imagine slaughtering zombies. And when I play it for the 25th time, I have an even better sense of what is in store. When one sings along to a song, one typically knows in some detail what the song involves (otherwise, one would not be able to sing along to it). And one typically sings along to songs that one enjoys – in part because one often chooses the songs that one listens to. But far from bolstering Smuts's argument, these points should give us serious pause. It's certainly *possible* that people who enjoy repeatedly playing first-person shooters desire to shoot things in real life, but that seems at least as controversial an empirical claim as those Smuts puts to one side about the causal connection between imagining doing things and actually doing them.

What about premise (2)? Perhaps *actually desiring* to do something immoral is worse than *enjoying imagining* doing it. But the most plausible reason for this is that we think that desires are more likely to lead to actions than imaginings are. If this is what makes surrogate fantasies of performing immoral actions themselves immoral, then the argument relies, once more, on the contentious empirical claims that we are putting to one side. Alternatively, one might claim that desiring to perform immoral actions is *intrinsically* worse than enjoying imagining them, but this is unlikely to convince anyone who believes that imagining performing immoral actions is intrinsically morally neutral, since the latter view seems grounded in the idea that only what happens in the external world, as opposed to in our minds, is morally relevant. Once more, Smuts's argument seems to turn on quite general questions in ethical theory.

The issues we have considered so far depend on the idea that music has intrinsic moral value. In the remainder of the chapter, we turn to the morality of the creation and consequences of music. These topics include a huge range of issues, both general moral issues and those pertaining to specific aspects of humanity, such as race, gender, sexuality, age, and disability. Much of the extensive scholarly literature on these topics is sociological, examining the details of how race, gender, and so on affect the production and reception of music. There is space here only to consider how philosophy can contribute to our understanding of two specific questions: (1) whether instrumental classical music contributes to sexist oppression, and (2) whether white people can sing music from black traditions.

10.3 Does Instrumental Classical Music Oppress Women?

The musicologist Susan McClary (1991) has influentially argued that many canonical works of instrumental classical music are not only intrinsically morally flawed but actually contribute to the oppression of women.[14] To understand McClary's argument, we must understand some basic concepts in feminist theory. Perhaps the most important is that of *oppression*, which can be usefully contrasted with *discrimination*. Let "discrimination" name the intentional treatment of an individual as inferior on the basis of some aspect of their identity (sex, race, etc.). Oppression, by contrast, is the disadvantage and injustice suffered by a *social group* (e.g., women or black people), due to the norms and institutions of a society – even one that comprises mostly well-intentioned (e.g., non-sexist) individuals (Young 1988, 271–6). Membership in a social group is (i) largely determined by how one is perceived by others, and (ii) contributes to one's social identity. For instance, someone's Asian-Americanness is generally perceived to be part of who they are, in a way that being an employee of Walmart is not.[15] Putting all this together: A man who denies a woman a promotion because he thinks women can't handle great responsibility *discriminates* against her; a man who holds the door open for a woman because that's the polite thing to do, by contrast, contributes to the *oppression* of women if (despite his good intentions) this social norm reinforces the notion that women are less capable than men, thus contributing to unjust differential treatment of women and men. Note that women can contribute to sexist oppression. Many

260 Music and Morality

feminists would argue, for instance, that much of women's participation in the cosmetics industry (i.e., purchasing and regularly applying makeup) contributes to sexist oppression by reinforcing the pressure on women to spend more time and money than men on their appearance.

As the generality of the concept suggests, oppression can occur in a wide variety of ways. Of particular relevance to us, given our concern with the cultural realm, is *psychological oppression*, which occurs when members of the oppressed group internalize the conception of themselves as inferior. One example is the ubiquity of *stereotypes* (Bartky 1990, 106–7). When women are, for instance, constantly portrayed in films as victims requiring rescue by a man, it likely reinforces the idea – among women as well as men – that women are incapable of controlling their own destinies. (Such representations may be plausible in the first place only because of the existence of the stereotype being reinforced.) Another example is *cultural domination* and the resulting *alienation* (Bartky 1990, 107–8). When all the heroes of mainstream films are men, audiences – women and men alike – are constantly encouraged to sympathize with male heroes, even if female heroes remain a theoretical possibility. Women, however, are likely to experience more alienation or cognitive dissonance in sympathizing with a male hero, since they are well aware that – in virtue of being women – they are significantly unlike such heroes.

The first step in McClary's case that classical instrumental music contributes to the oppression of women is an argument that elements of such music are frequently *gendered*. The term "gender" is sometimes used as a synonym for "sex," that is, a system of biological categories connected to reproductive roles. But in feminist scholarship, "gender" refers to various conceptual systems connected to, but distinct from, sex. Most relevant for our purposes is the notion of gender as a system of cultural norms that classify things as "masculine" or "feminine." (I will use these terms exclusively for gender-norm concepts, reserving "male" and "female" for biological-sex concepts.) For instance, in the contemporary United States, high heels, knitting, and the color pink are all feminine, while work boots, wood-splitting, and the color blue are all masculine. What this means, in a nutshell, is that it is generally understood (in this culture) that it is more natural, normal, or appropriate for women to wear high heels, knit, and like pink things than for men to, and vice versa for the masculine items.

In practice, gender norms are much more complicated than this brief characterization suggests. For instance, the color pink is probably more strongly gendered feminine than the color blue is masculine (e.g., it is more acceptable for women to wear blue than for men to wear pink). And one can endorse such gender norms and still think that it is possible, in some cases even appropriate, for a man to knit a scarf while wearing pink high heels. (Perhaps the man is an anti-feminist illustrating the absurdity of rejecting gender norms.) However, one can *acknowledge* that gender norms *exist* without *endorsing* them. Indeed, the point of drawing attention to gender norms is often to undermine them. Most feminists argue that gender norms are not natural, but culturally constructed (as evidenced by cultural variation), and thus that it is up to us to decide whether or not we should endorse them. In many cases, of course, feminists argue that we should *reject* them because they contribute to the oppression of women. Wearing high heels, for instance, arguably emphasizes eroticized parts of the female body and certainly makes it more difficult to engage in many activities – not least walking! So the norm that women ought to wear high heels reinforces the ideas that they should emphasize their appeal as objects of heterosexual male desire and that they are less physically capable than men. The norm that women are natural knitters, together with other norms, reinforces the notion that a woman's place is in the domestic sphere as a caretaker and caregiver. The norm that women should like pink things at the very least emphasizes the importance of sexual difference (the greater the scope of gender norms, the more important sexual difference appears), and if there are further connections (natural or cultural) between, say, colors and psychological traits (e.g., that pink is a soft, gentle color), it may also reinforce further gender norms (e.g., that women are soft and gentle).

McClary's point is that musical elements are no less gendered than footwear, activities, or colors. Recall, for example, the first movement of Mozart's *Eine kleine Nachtmusik* (discussed in Chapter 4, §4.5, as an example of sonata form). Consider the first themes of the primary and secondary theme groups (Example 10.1). Taking each theme in turn, ask yourself whether it is masculine or feminine. (Remember that this is a question about what cultural norms exist; you need not *endorse* these norms to acknowledge them.) McClary bets that most people familiar with Western music will – correctly – identify the primary theme as masculine and the secondary theme as feminine, perhaps in part because the first theme is bold and assertive (masculine traits), while the second is gentle and delicate (feminine traits).[16] Indeed, she claims that such identifications can be made by "any five-year-old [with] sufficient experience from watching Saturday morning cartoons" (1991, 68). McClary also draws attention to the gendering of musical features in Western music theory from the seventeenth to late-twentieth centuries (1991, 7–12). For instance, the major–minor duality of the tonal system has been explicitly connected with the masculine–feminine duality since at least the eighteenth century, and "normal" cadences (ending on a strong beat) were labelled "masculine" in contrast to "feminine" cadences (ending on a weak beat) until at least the 1970s (McClary 1991, 9–12; cf. Rieger 1985, 139–40).

The mere gendering of musical elements, like that of colors, could be argued to contribute to sexist oppression by reinforcing the importance of sexual difference, but the problem McClary focuses on is how the relationships between

Example 10.1 Mozart, *Eine kleine Nachtmusik*, K. 525, first movement: (a) the first theme of the primary theme group, and (b) the first theme of the secondary theme group. These themes occur at the beginning of, and 50 seconds into, the recording on the Spotify playlist for this chapter, respectively.

these elements over the course of a piece of music reinforce the notion of the feminine as a dangerously destabilizing force that must be brought under masculine control. Consider the form of the first movement of *Eine kleine Nachtmusik*. In Chapter 4, I noted that sonata form is often described in terms of tension and resolution. The initial tension is generated (in the exposition) by the introduction of the secondary theme group in a key other than the tonic; the tension is finally resolved (in the recapitulation) by the secondary thematic material reappearing in the tonic key. Merely add to this picture the idea that primary themes tend to be masculine and secondary themes feminine, and it is easy to understand McClary's claim that sonata form contributes to the oppression of women: Sonata form typically tells the story of an assertive masculine entity destabilized by a (misleadingly) gentle feminine entity but who, after a period of uncertain interaction with the feminine (the development section), triumphantly reclaims stability by bringing the feminine under his control (1991, 68–9; cf. Rieger 1985, 139, and Citron 1994, 16–24). Given that sonata form is the most common and highly esteemed form in classical music and its scholarship, McClary argues that its gendered narrative, like those of Hollywood movies, reinforces the ideas that men are active heroes and women passive yet dangerous obstacles that must be brought under masculine control, thus contributing to the psychological oppression of women.

McClary is obviously providing new critical interpretations of much classical instrumental music. Feminism is not just a theoretical perspective, however, but a political movement. If we are convinced by McClary's argument, then, how should her conclusions affect our actions? Perhaps surprisingly, given the seriousness of her moral criticism of much of the Western classical canon, McClary does not suggest that we should abandon these works, as either performers or listeners. She is ultimately concerned primarily to demonstrate that these works are not simply abstract formal structures, cut off from the social worlds of their creators or audiences, as traditional music theory often seems to suggest.[17] But this does not imply that she considers traditional, formal interpretations of such works to be *false* – indeed, her feminist interpretations *depend* on traditional formal interpretive techniques. Rather, she is arguing that such techniques can give us, at best, a *partial* understanding of the works they purport to describe and explain. If we embrace McClary's interpretations, then, we may respond differently to the music, since we may judge, for instance, that insofar as the positive responses called for by the transposition of the secondary themes to the tonic in the recapitulation are unmerited (in the ethicist's sense), this feature of the work is an artistic flaw.[18] Finally, though McClary writes mainly from the position of a sophisticated *listener*, feminist theorists have also argued that such interpretations should lead us to *perform* classical works differently, in ways that *resist* their patriarchal or misogynistic content, by, for instance, fore-grounding or parodying it (Cusick 1994; cf. Neufeld 2011 and Bicknell 2015, 114–15).

The first reaction to McClary's argument of many people familiar with classical music is to reject the first step of attributing gendered content to musi-cal themes. One might acknowledge that a certain theme in an *opera*, say, is masculine because it is associated with a male character. But the fact that, if pressed, one can categorize the themes of *Eine kleine Nachtmusik* as mascu-line or feminine doesn't show that they *are* masculine or feminine. Perhaps, if pressed, one could categorize those themes as, say, canine or feline; that wouldn't show that they have "domesticated animal" content.[19]

One reply McClary might give is analogous to a reply that someone might give to the argument that the emotional content of a song derives solely from its words: The fact that we can judge whether or not some music is more or less appropriate for a given opera-character's gender shows that it must have gendered content independent of its use in the opera. The critic might respond, however, that the cases are not sufficiently analogous. The mere facts (i) that music has affective content (such as assertiveness or boldness), and (ii) that there are music-independent gender norms (such as assertiveness and boldness being masculine), might be enough to explain our judgments of the appropriateness of a given theme for a masculine char-acter. Even granting this response, however, McClary may have enough room to defend her main conclusion. For if (i) in sonata form, bold asser-tiveness normally succeeds by taking control of gentle yet disruptive deli-cacy, and (ii) there are music-independent gender norms (such as that bold assertiveness is masculine and gentle delicacy feminine), then it might still be argued that sonata form, given its ubiquity and the high esteem in which it is held, reinforces the notion that the feminine is a dangerous threat to order that must be brought under masculine control, and thus contributes to the oppression of women.

A second reply that McClary might give to skepticism about music's gendered content is to remind us that music theorists have long described music in gendered terms. Fred Maus, however, points out that this evidence is ambiguous (2011, 577–8). It might show that music theorists have long detected the gendered content of music, but it might equally show that music *theory*, rather than music itself, is gendered – and possibly oppressive.[20] This move opens up a range of possibilities for reinterpreting the works McClary criticizes. One option would be to resist the interpretation of, say, assertive themes as masculine and gentle themes as feminine. Another would be to retain these interpretations, but reinterpret the structure of sonata form as one of, say, voluntary union between the masculine and feminine rather than coercion of the latter by the former.

A second way to resist McClary's argument would be to appeal to empirical evidence that few people hear the key relationships identified in the kind of formal analysis that underpins McClary's argument (see Chapter 4, §4.6.1). McClary could respond that it is the experiences of *competent* listeners that are relevant to assessing the content of a work, but this may simply throw into sharper relief the question of the value of formal features of music (see Chapter 5, §5.3.1). Note that construing the recapitulation as feminine submission to the masculine relies on valuing harmonic over melodic (or thematic) structure, a feature of Western music theory that has recently been questioned. Indeed, Maus suggests that McClary's arguments contribute to a mounting case for giving more weight to alternatives to traditional formal analysis in the understanding of music (Maus 2011, 577–8).

10.4 Can White People Sing the Blues?

In Chapter 7, §7.5, we considered whether a performer's persona, including her race or ethnicity, should affect the appreciation of her popular-song performance. These attributes feature even more centrally in another question that is asked about various kinds of music (among other cultural products), namely, whether the appropriation of music across cultural boundaries is morally acceptable.[21] There is a long history of such appropriation in Western music. Consider, for example, Mozart's Rondo alla Turca (discussed in Chapter 7, §7.4), so named for its appropriation of "Turkish" stylistic features – considered hip and exotic at the time. Joel Rudinow raises the acceptability of a more recent instance of such appropriation in the subtitle of a 1994 article: "Can White People Sing the Blues?" Though Rudinow's concern is with blues performance, his question also resonates with those who see rock music as a tradition founded on morally unacceptable appropriation of the blues and other musical practices from black culture by white musicians. Similar issues have more recently been discussed with respect to white appropriation of hip-hop culture (e.g., Robertson 2014; Taylor 2005). I will follow Rudinow in focusing primarily on the blues, but much of the discussion should apply to other instances of cultural appropriation.[22]

Rudinow's question – Can white people sing the blues? – admits of two broad readings.[23] The *descriptive* reading asks whether white blues is *possible*. As Rudinow immediately points out, the mere existence of famous white blues artists, such as Stevie Ray Vaughan, Bonnie Raitt, and Eric Clapton, suggests that the answer is obviously *yes* (1994, 127). But a subtler version of the descriptive reading asks whether the music these people play is *really* the blues, given that they are white and that the blues is a historically black musical tradition.[24] A negative answer to this subtler descriptive question would thus amount to the claim that though what these white musicians are doing is derived from the blues, it cannot be authentic (genuine, true) blues, precisely because its creators are white. The second, *normative* reading of the question is whether it is *morally acceptable* for white musicians to play the blues, given its historical blackness. This might seem to assume a positive answer to the first question: If white people *can't* play the blues, then there's no need to ask whether they *may*. But, again, a subtler interpretation is possible. One might argue, first, that white musicians are incapable of playing authentic blues and, second, that they ought not even *attempt* to play the blues (or that they ought not play music closely derived from the blues).

There is broad consensus that one way of answering the descriptive question negatively is racist. If you think that white people can't play the blues because the biology of black people gives them a certain musical capacity that white people lack (thanks to their different biology), then you are committed to the ideas that (i) races are biological categories, and (ii) biological differences between those categories ground significant differences in intellectual and cultural capacities. Though it is currently a minority view, some philosophers still defend a version of the first of these two ideas (e.g., Spencer 2018), but the second idea is now universally rejected in serious scholarship (James 2017, ¶4).

If there is no essential connection between racial biology and culture, then (whether or not you think there are biological races) any argument that white people can't sing the blues must begin from a social or cultural, rather than biological, conception of blackness. Rudinow thus addresses the question of whether people who do not belong to black culture can (either at all, or morally acceptably) participate in a black cultural practice. This in turn requires some clarity on what cultures are, how people belong to them, and what it is to participate in a cultural practice. Theodore Gracyk defines a culture as:

> the ideas, values, and associated behavioral patterns expected of members of an ongoing, self-identified group. These expectations [or norms] are transmitted

to new members of the [group] through the use of symbols, by modes of organizing behavior [i.e., practices], and through their embodiments in artifacts.

(2001, 110)

Rudinow puts the point in terms of ethnicity: "a matter of acknowledged common culture, based on shared items of cultural significance such as experience, language, religion, history, habitat, and the like. Ethnicity is essentially a socially conferred status – a matter of communal acceptance, recognition, and respect" (1994, 128). It is widely accepted that one's culture or ethnicity often contributes to one's sense of self. We can thus think of cultures as social groups, in the sense explained in the previous section.[25]

10.4.1 The Proprietary Argument

One way to argue that white people *shouldn't* sing the blues, then, is to argue that the blues, as a cultural practice, *belongs* to black culture, and thus that white appropriation of the blues is *theft* (Rudinow 1994, 129–32).[26] This view is summarized in the title of an essay by Amiri Baraka: "The Great Music Robbery" (1987). Baraka argues that:

> attempts by the bourgeoisie to claim and coopt, in a growingly more obvious way, black music as the creation of whites [331] ... is illegitimate to the degree that national oppression still exists in the U.S. and to the extent that any black anything can be appropriated without exact reciprocal compensation! [329] ... It is the lack of democracy that makes all this criminal. Labor is still being stolen, resources vandalized, and the colored still ain't got nothin' but bad reputations. From black art alone the African-American people should be as wealthy (literally) as anyone in the United States.
>
> (332)

We can separate the two charges of theft and deception that Baraka makes here. To claim that the blues was created by white people, when one knows that it was a black cultural creation, is to *lie*, which is morally wrong. Baraka's point about the financial compensation of black people for the appropriation of their music is presumably independent of the charge of deception: Admitting that you stole something does not rectify the wrong of your theft; you should at the very least return what was stolen.

One problem with applying this simple moral precept to the cultural appropriation of music is that it's not clear what would count as *returning* stolen music. Stealing the blues from black culture is quite different from stealing a particular black person's iPod. The appropriation is not of a physical piece of property, but rather of a way of making music – a musical style – including compositional, instrumental, and vocal techniques. The solution is surely to augment the original precept: If returning a stolen item is impossible, you should, as Baraka implies, compensate the victim of your theft for its loss. Conveniently enough, there is a long tradition of intellectual-property rights and law on which such a solution could draw, including musical applications of such theory and law (Gracyk 2001, 105–8; Rudinow 1994, 130–2). Inconveniently, however, this tradition is rooted in *liberal individualism*, that is, the idea that "the individual [is] an independent entity in competition with other individuals, and … social and political life [is] a sphere in which this competitive pursuit of self-interest is coordinated" (Festenstein 2018, §1). This moral and legal tradition can thus handle the "theft" or illegitimate use by individuals or corporations of material copyrighted by other individuals or corporations (e.g., unlicensed performances of copyrighted songs) but it has little to say about the ownership of musical styles by cultures. Moreover, the application of such legal theory to black musical practices is not obviously an unmitigated good. It can be used to address wrongs against black artists, but black artists have also suffered at its hands – perhaps disproportionately (Headlam 2002, 184).[27] A larger-scale theoretical problem is that many theorists of racial and other kinds of oppression consider the acceptance of liberal individualism to be a major contributor to such oppression, since it ignores the existence and power of social groups. It would thus be difficult for such theorists to appeal to these considerations as part of a case against immoral cultural appropriation.[28]

10.4.2 The Experiential-Access Argument

An alternative approach is to argue that the blues is black in virtue of being essentially *about* black experience, thus one can or should not produce authentic blues unless one belongs to black culture:

> The experiential access argument says in effect that one cannot understand the blues or authentically express oneself in the blues unless one knows what it's like to live as a black person in America, and one cannot know this without being one.
>
> (Rudinow 1994, 132)[29]

One might question whether *all* blues is, or was, about black experience. Some blues, for instance, seems to be more about gender and sexuality. One might also question whether there is no way to understand the experience of people in cultures to which one does not belong. Some argue, on the contrary, that empathetic understanding of others' experiences is essential to combatting oppression. Rudinow criticizes the argument for a third reason, namely for being what contemporary race-theorists would call "essentialist." As the name suggests, essentialism is the idea that there is some single (if complex) feature or kind of experience that is *essential* to being a black person. When biological concepts of race were rejected by race theorists, they faced a challenge: How could one talk about (let alone fight) the oppression of black people if one denied that race was real? (If there are no races, there are no black people, so they can't actually be oppressed any more than unicorns can.) A popular solution was to locate the essence of blackness not in biology but in social or cultural features. Nonetheless, essentialism about race is commonly criticized on the grounds that there is no (even complex) feature or experience that all and only black people have in common. Rudinow suggests that the features of black experience most plausibly posited as essential to understanding or performing the blues would be features of the experiences of those who originated the blues, such as "the experience of slavery or sharecropping or life on the Mississippi delta during the twenties and thirties" (1994, 133). The problem, of course, is that although making such experiences essential to the understanding or performance of authentic blues would exclude most contemporary white people from the blues, it would also exclude most contemporary *black* people from the blues. Rudinow concludes that the blues, as a continually developing cultural practice with porous borders, cannot be the exclusive preserve of black musicians.

10.4.3 The Moral-Deference Argument

Paul C. Taylor (1995) objects to the way that Rudinow frames the issues. Part of his case perhaps amounts to an argument similar to Jeanette Bicknell's that we considered in Chapter 7, §7.5, namely that some black audiences will find *any* white blues performance *unconvincing* because of the racial aspect of any white performance persona. But another part makes a moral argument that white people should not participate in the blues. Taylor proposes that "the blues is a *racial project* [i.e., 'a cultural space within which the meaning of race is articulated'], and [thus] *moral deference* is owed to black contributions to the project," that is, non-black musicians ought to assume that black musicians are competent to pursue this project – in particular to articulate the moral pain of oppressed black people – on their own, and defer to them when it comes to pursuing the project (Taylor 1995, 314, italics added).[30]

The notion that to be black is to belong to a group that has a particular history of oppression provides Taylor with a way of linking the blues essentially to black people while avoiding an implausible essentialism about blackness (e.g., that all black people have experience of sharecropping).[31] If the blues is about this particular history of oppression – about being black – then black musicians have priority within the tradition. As Rudinow puts it, "Taylor's argument concludes that white blues is in effect the usurpation of the 'voice' of black people. It is talking out of turn" (2010, 139).[32]

Even assuming that all blues is a racial project, Taylor's argument leaves at least two avenues open for a defense of morally acceptable white blues. First, the notion of *deference* that Taylor appeals to is much more subtle than the thesis that no white person can ever play authentic blues. As Rudinow observes:

> although the Butterfield [blues] band is everybody's first and favorite example of a "white blues band," it was always racially mixed. The classification "white" flows from the fact that the bandleader, who sang lead vocal and played one of the lead solo instruments (harmonica), was a white man. But ... Paul Butterfield got to be a bandleader in large part because he commanded respect as a player. You don't get Howlin' Wolf's rhythm section if you can't play.[33] And Butterfield earned respect as a player in a way typical of oral musical traditions generally. He apprenticed, and got better and better, until his playing began to do credit to Junior Wells and Little Walter [two of Butterfield's black idols and mentors].
>
> (2010, 144)

It seems possible that the acceptance of some white blues musicians by the black blues community implies that those musicians have deferred appropriately to black participants in the practice in the course of becoming accomplished blues musicians themselves.[34] Indeed, Rudinow suggests that this sort of cross-cultural exchange might be positively beneficial for combatting racial oppression (1995, 317). We should not, however, lose sight of the fact that it is easy to *claim*, perhaps even *believe*, that one is being appropriately deferential when in fact one is not.

Second, Taylor's argument leaves untouched the possibility of a (morally acceptable) tradition that is derived, but distinct, from authentic blues (Rudinow 1995, 317). If white musicians accept that Taylor's argument shows that no white person can play authentic blues, they might yet continue to make music as they have been, while taking care to clarify that what they are doing is not true blues, but white music based heavily on certain aspects of the blues.

10.4.4 The Cultural-Intimacy Argument

In a recent paper, C. Thi Nguyen and Matt Strohl consider how to justify a certain kind of objection to cultural appropriation that resembles Taylor's point about the deference owed to participants in a racial project. Nguyen and Strohl distinguish objections to instances of cultural appropriation that are independently grounded from those that are expressive (Nguyen & Strohl 2019, 983–8). *Independently grounded* objections rely on something outside the objection itself that could be disputed, for instance, that a particular kind of appropriation *harms* the target culture or its members. If it turns out that the appropriation does not result in the alleged harm, then such objections must be abandoned. But some objections to cultural appropriation seem to be *expressive*, meaning that they are intended or taken to be self-justifying. For instance, the very fact that a member of a culture *expresses the opinion* that an instance or kind of cultural appropriation is unacceptable is sometimes taken to be reason for thinking that it *is* unacceptable. Nguyen and Strohl's central claim is that the force of expressive objections to appropriation of some cultural practices is grounded in the *intimacy* among members of the culture generated by those practices (2019, 988–93).

The appeal to the intimacy of cultural groups draws on Julie Inness's work on interpersonal intimacy (1992, 74–94). Inness argues that the most plausible basis for the variety of things that get covered by claims of a "right to privacy" (whom we choose to kiss or have sex with, to whom we show our diaries or love letters, how we choose to raise our children, etc.) is the *intimacy* of the actions involved, that is, the fact that they involve "a choice on the agent's part about how to embody her love, care, or liking … because [what the choice is about] draws its meaning and value from the agent's care, love, or liking" (1992, 91). Nguyen and Strohl argue that:

> in the case of larger groups, what makes a practice intimate is that it functions to embody or promote a sense of common identity and group connection among participants in the practice, and thereby renders it meaningful and valuable to these participants.
>
> (2019, 989)

In either case, the relevant actions or practices (e.g., writing love letters or playing the blues) partly constitute the identity of the individual or group because of the actions' or practices' meaningfulness to the individual or group. The basic idea, then, is that such meaningfulness and self-determination are so valuable that we ought to take claims by insiders about how outsiders should interact (if at all) with the intimate actions or practices in question (e.g., read the love letters or play the blues) to have moral force.

This conclusion is too strong as it stands – unqualified and in full generality – since it seems to allow anyone in a given culture to forbid anyone outside the culture from interacting in any way with a given cultural practice. There are both plausible counterexamples and logical problems with this strong version of the claim. Counterexamples include cases when access to a sacred space is essential for investigating a murder, or when members of a previously isolated culture offer outsiders certain artifacts in ignorance of their financial value in the outside world. In these cases, the general principle implies that a culture can prevent police from investigating a serious crime, and that the outsiders can take the offered artifacts without informing members of the originating culture of their financial value. Logical problems include the possibility of one member of a group inviting outsiders to appropriate some musical style while another member forbids it. The general principle implies that such appropriation is both morally acceptable and morally unacceptable.

The counterexamples can be replied to by appealing to relatively uncontroversial features of moral reasoning. For instance, the idea of a person's consenting to some state of affairs is typically taken to include the proviso that the person has not been deceived about the state of affairs. Thus, if the outsiders' withholding of information about the financial value of the culture's offered artifacts counts as deception, the insiders' consent is undermined. Nguyen and Strohl also suggest that the principle is most plausibly interpreted as *defeasible* and *pro tanto* (2019, 990). To say that it is defeasible is to say that it can be *defeated* or overruled by other moral considerations. For instance, the state's moral obligation to solve the murder might overrule the culture's prohibition on outsiders entering their sacred space (though they may still be under obligation, say, not to divulge information about it in ways irrelevant to their investigation). To say that the principle is *pro tanto* is to say that it has moral force even when ultimately defeated (see §10.1). For instance, the police's entering the sacred space might still be a morally bad thing, even if it is ultimately justified by other moral considerations.

The logical problems are more difficult to deal with, since they raise questions such as (i) who belongs to a given cultural group and who does not (the *boundary problem*), and (ii) when a cultural group has acted, e.g., forbidding a certain appropriation (the *agency problem*). Nguyen and Strohl acknowledge the difficulty of the boundary problem but offer little by way of a solution (2019, 997). Its importance for issues of cultural appropriation is clear, however. Any plausible account of cultural groups seems likely to accept that they are vague, overlapping, and in constant flux. For instance, there are different ways to understand what happened if or when some members of black culture originally invited white outsiders to play the blues. Perhaps blues culture was extended outside black culture, or perhaps those white musicians joined black culture, or perhaps a new, "blues-like" cultural group was created. Deciding which of these descriptions is correct means deciding whether there can be authentic white blues.

Regarding the agency problem, Nguyen and Strohl cite a growing body of work defending the notion of *group agency*, that is, the notion that groups meeting certain criteria can be treated as rational agents with belief- and desire-like states, giving them the ability to perform actions (2019, 995–9). But they acknowledge that most cultural groups do not meet the relevant criteria, since they lack the institutional structure of groups such as the United States government, Microsoft, or the NAACP. Gracyk concludes from similar considerations that cultural groups cannot act:

> The only plausible sense in which cultures "act" … is that *representatives of the culture*, such as key agents controlling education and the arts, do so. Key individuals may make choices on behalf of the culture. … But the culture, in the holistic sense …, does not "make a choice."
>
> (2001, 115)

Nguyen and Strohl disagree, suggesting that a "sub-agential" group, such as the blues community, "approximates a univocal decision when a considerable number of group members voice such a decision and there is an insignificant amount of dissent from within the group" (2019, 998). This criterion is obviously vague, but that doesn't show that it is useless or even incorrect. For one thing, there may be cases where the criterion clearly applies, despite its vagueness (e.g., when only a single member of a culture dissents from the overwhelming majority). For another, this vagueness may reflect the actual vagueness of groups and their agency.

In sum, if Nguyen and Strohl's theory is correct, then (as with the moral-deference argument) determining who may participate in the blues will turn on difficult questions about the membership and actions of black culture.

10.4.5 Swamping and Dilution Arguments

The arguments considered thus far criticize white appropriation of the blues for morally unacceptable aspects of *exporting* the musical style *from* black culture. The *dilution* and *swamping* arguments criticize white appropriation of the blues for morally unacceptable aspects of the *encroachment* of white blues *on* black culture (Gracyk 2001, 109–28).[35] One version of the dilution argument claims that white appropriation of black musical styles typically results in bad music and thus harms black culture by giving it a bad name. It is difficult to judge such general claims about the artistic effects of cross-cultural appropriation. As we've seen, there seem to be at least some white blues musicians who are highly respected within black culture. It also seems plausible that plenty of bad music is produced in every musical culture, whether or not it appropriates styles from other cultures. Even if the general claims in the argument are true, it might seem that the best response to this state of affairs is to criticize the quality of white blues, while reminding people that it is white rather than black blues.

Gracyk interprets Baraka (1990) as giving a different version of the dilution argument: Black culture is essentially, or at its best, an art of resistance to oppression, particularly white oppression (cf. Taylor's moral-deference argument). If white musicians appropriate aspects of black culture, those aspects no longer qualify as resistant to white oppression. Thus the appropriation of black musical styles dilutes the cultural power of those styles (Gracyk 2001, 113). Putting aside, once more, the plausibility of attributing a single meaning to all blues, Gracyk responds that this charge will have force only if the appropriation of the music by white musicians has not been sanctioned by the black community (Gracyk 2001, 125). Note that this response does not *deny* that white appropriation dilutes the cultural power of black musical styles. It merely points out that there is nothing morally objectionable in this if black culture sanctions such appropriation, thus returning us to issues of cultural deference and intimacy.

Swamping occurs when a dominant culture is so pervasive that it becomes difficult for members of a non-dominant culture to participate in their own cultural practices. Paradigm examples involve cultures that have become minorities in their own lands after colonization. Gracyk gives the example of an Ojibwe boy growing up in northern Minnesota. In some sense he has a choice about whether to get involved in traditional Ojibwe music, but the context in which he makes that choice – one in which he rarely hears Ojibwe music, but is inundated in the mass media by non-Ojibwe music – makes it highly unlikely that he will choose to get involved in traditional Ojibwe music. The boy's situation thus contrasts starkly with that of a white girl in the same context, who is more or less automatically enculturated into her own culture's music (Gracyk 2001, 120–2).

Claims that white appropriations of black music, such as rock and roll, swamp the black music from which it is derived, such as the blues, are more difficult to defend, partly because of the difficulty of issues, considered above, about what counts as authentic blues, and partly because it is not easy to judge the extent to which people's choices are constrained by their cultural environment. Gracyk argues that if swamping is the result of (unconstrained) choices by the swamped culture, then members of that culture have no grounds for complaint. To assume that they are incapable of making good choices about their cultural practices (e.g., selling blues records or inviting white people to participate in the blues) is unacceptably paternalistic. Gracyk also cites black blues paragons such as Muddy Waters and B. B. King lamenting the lack of interest in the blues among black people in the 1960s, and expressing gratitude for white interest in the blues at that time (2001, 126). But claims about whether and how the relevant choices are constrained by the socio-economic and cultural position in which the relevant people find themselves are bound to be controversial, and their confirmation would require, at the very least, detailed sociological analysis.

10.4.6 Conclusions: Black, White, and Blues

In this section, we have considered many complicated arguments in a very short space. Some of the arguments seem weak, such as the propriety argument against white appropriation of the blues and the version of the dilution argument that claims that inferior white imitations of the blues give black culture a bad name. Other arguments, such as those that white appropriations of the blues have swamped black musical culture, are defensible in principle, but making them convincingly seems to require detailed sociological evidence. The remaining cultural-deference and -intimacy arguments are also promising, but require more philosophical work on the nature of cultural groups, as well as sociological evidence about particular groups and practices. My personal tentative answer to Rudinow's original question is that white people can, morally acceptably, play music derived from black musical traditions such as the blues, but that this requires deference to black culture of the sort that Taylor (1995) and Nguyen and Strohl (2019) articulate. (We should not forget that merely *claiming* to exercise such deference – even sincerely – is not to demonstrate it.) Whether or not such music is ultimately classified as authentic blues seems less important than acknowledgment by white musicians and audiences of how the music is rooted in a long history of the oppression of black people by white people.

10.5 Conclusions: Music and Morality

More than in any other chapter, we have just skimmed the surface of the issues raised here. Yet there is surprisingly little philosophical literature on the intersection of morality and music in particular. Perhaps one reason is that many of these questions seem ultimately to turn on more general philosophical issues, such as the nature of the morally good, or on empirical claims, such as the effects of a particular cultural development.[36] At the very least, however, we have seen that general ethical views and arguments can fruitfully be applied to music. Perhaps such applications can in turn contribute to debates over the more general philosophical issues.

In the next, final chapter, we return to an issue left hanging at the end of the first: the nature of music. Though this is a highly theoretical topic, we will see that, even there, issues of ethics and other values may be unavoidable.

Questions

Explain the issue about which autonomists, ethicists, and contextualists disagree; then explain those three different positions on the issue. Defend one position as superior to the others.

Can ethicism or contextualism be applied to purely instrumental music, or are words (or some other representational medium) essential for those views to gain purchase on an artwork?

Is singing along to a song recording ever intrinsically morally unacceptable?

Explain and critically discuss Susan McClary's argument that instrumental classical music contributes to the oppression of women.

What is the cultural appropriation of music? Which of the arguments considered here against the acceptability of (some) such appropriation is the strongest? Does it ultimately succeed?

Notes

1 Both the consequentialist and deontologist might point out that we succeed in our baby-saving endeavors much more often than not. The consequentialist can thus insist that we should of course still attempt to save drowning babies, even if there may be the occasional case where the outcome is morally bad, while the deontologist can point out that the would-be savior's death in this case is an unfortunate (if not immoral) byproduct of a morally good action. Detailed introductions to ethics are legion; one good example is Shafer-Landau 2018.

2 Though they sometimes have distinct meanings in ethics, I use the pairs of terms "ethical" and "moral," "right" and "good," and "wrong" and "bad" as synonyms throughout.

3 Helpful introductions to this debate, to which my exposition is indebted, are Gaut 2013 and 2007.

4 This position is unrelated to the *ontological* contextualism discussed elsewhere in this book.

5 The narrator of a song cannot be simply identified with its composer or performer, as we saw in Chapters 1 (§1.3.3), 7 (§7.5), and 9 (§9.4).

6 A sophisticated defense of contextualism is Jacobson 1997.

7 The approximately two-minute passage (mm. 284–379) begins between the 6- and 7-minute mark on most recordings.

8 I follow Smuts in often talking of *songs*, though "track" or "recording" would be more precise.

9 Smuts's argument will thus not apply in cases where listeners do *not* imagine being the song's narrator. But it seems plausible that there are cases where listeners *do* imagine this.

10 If you think the narrator of the song might be joking, consider verse three: "Let this be a sermon / I mean everything I've said / Baby, I'm determined / And I'd rather see you dead."

11 It's not *necessary* to take pleasure in singing along to a song, but I presume that most people sing along voluntarily and, at least in part, because they enjoy it. Anyway, Smuts is only concerned with such cases.

12 Moreover, there are non–self-involving interactive fictions, such as a choose-"your"-own-adventure story in which you make decisions about a third-person character.

13 Being an Italo Calvino book, things do not remain this simple. There is some discussion of whether "you" really refers to *you*, the reader. At certain points, "you" is another character named Ludmilla.

14 McClary does not explicitly draw the distinction between intrinsic and consequential moral flaws, but she makes both kinds of moral criticism.

15 One may, of course, reject one's Asian-Americanness as defining oneself, even in part, but this will not eliminate others' identification and treatment of one as Asian-American. Similarly, even if one embraces one's employment by Walmart as part of their identity, that aspect is unlikely to be acknowledged by others.

16 McClary does not discuss this specific example, but I believe my treatment of it is in the spirit of her view.

17 McClary's project is thus akin to Jenefer Robinson's revival of a Romantic theory of expression (discussed at the end of Chapter 3).

18 For analogous interpretations of several works of Beethoven from the perspective of disability (rather than gender) studies, see Straus 2011, 45–62.

19 Thanks to Faith Broddrick for this way of putting the point.
20 McClary herself criticizes music theory as oppressive to women, on these and other grounds (1991, 9–17), though it is sometimes unclear whether she is attributing gender to aspects of music or music theory.
21 Though it is popularly used as a pejorative term, I follow most philosophers in using "appropriation" in a morally neutral sense. That is, there is no prima facie contradiction in speaking of morally acceptable appropriation.
22 We will investigate the concept of a *culture* below, but note that by "black" culture I mean African-American culture, as opposed to African cultures or other cultures in the African diaspora, such as Black British or African-Caribbean cultures. Some argue that, where it names a culture, "black" should be capitalized; I follow Paul Taylor (2016) in spelling it with a lower-case "b."
23 I ignore one subtlety of the question: whether the answer should change with the substitution of other races or ethnicities for "white." It might initially seem that the only relevant distinction here is between black and non-black people. But if, for instance, the concept of oppression is central to one's answer, then perhaps whether the performer belongs to an oppressed group is more important than her particular race or ethnicity.
24 I ignore the distinction between performing original works and those of others. The question is about the possibility or acceptability of white musicians' playing *in the blues style*.
25 We will return to questions about cultural membership and boundaries in §10.4.4.
26 Since the blues did not arise *ex nihilo*, but emerged in black culture around the turn of the twentieth century as a fusion of historically African and European elements (Evans 2002, 22–4; Van der Merwe 1992), we might ask whether those styles were appropriated for the blues in a morally acceptable way. This question likely raises the same questions all over again, however, so I proceed on the assumption that the blues is unproblematically a historically black cultural practice.
27 The application of copyright law to the central hip-hop practice of *sampling* has also been controversial. Helpful introductions include Crum 2008 and E. Lewis 2019, 35–56.
28 The correct response to this state of affairs might be to change the law. Such changes will require justification, however; you could see the discussion that follows as a consideration of potential such justifications.
29 Ewan Allinson (1994) gives an experiential-access argument with respect to hip hop.
30 It is unclear whether Taylor would still endorse this argument. In a more recent essay on hip hop, Taylor seems to take it for granted that Eminem, a white rapper, is *not* "somehow out of place in the hip-hop world" (2005, 81), even while defending hip hop as part of black culture. His position in this essay is surprisingly similar to Rudinow's, even while Rudinow, in a later consideration of the issues (2010, 136–41), grants the force of Taylor's 1995 arguments!
31 Taylor has, in fact, developed his own theory of race in great detail (Taylor 2013). For an introduction to such "constructivist" theories of race, see James 2017, §2.
32 Gracyk points out that audiences (in this case, white audiences) also have an obligation to understand the music they profess to be interested in, which inevitably includes learning about its cultural significance, context, and history (2001, 155–60).
33 The bassist and drummer of the Butterfield Blues Band had toured with the great blues artist Howlin' Wolf.
34 Perhaps this explains Taylor's (2005) attitude towards Eminem, noted above.
35 Such arguments are related to the concept of cultural domination, discussed in §10.3, above.
36 Philip Alperson (2014) offers a different diagnosis of this problem and proposes a solution.

Further Reading

Kathleen Higgins (1991) covers many of the issues discussed in this book from the perspective that music is a "better central model for ethics than the moral dilemma …

[and the] atemporal, abstract 'solutions' to" such dilemmas that characterize much philosophical ethics (7).

Peter Kivy (2008) argues that pure music is incapable of any effect on our moral knowledge, behavior, or character. Jerrold Levinson (2013, 51–5), Philip Alperson (2014), and James Harold (2016) defend pure music's moral power.

Gender and sexuality in connection with music (and the other arts) are woefully under-discussed by philosophers. Important work by philosophically inclined music-scholars includes a survey of feminist perspectives on music by Wayne Bowman (1998, 356–94) and two seminal collections of essays: Brett, Wood and Thomas (2006; first edition 1994) and Barkin and Hamessley (1999).

Paul C. Taylor's *Black Is Beautiful* (2016) is an indispensable introduction to black aesthetic theory, though only the last chapter is devoted to music (and has little to say about cultural appropriation). Nick Wiltsher (2016a) discusses cultural authenticity and appropriation in EDM (electronic dance music). Stephen Davies devotes a chapter of his *Musical Works and Performances* (2001, 254–94) to cultural authenticity, including a detailed case-study of Balinese gamelan music.

11 The Definition of Music

Overview

In this chapter, we investigate philosophers' attempts to define music, that is, to give an informative account of what distinguishes music from non-music. We consider what role may be played in a definition of music by concepts such as sound, silence, hearing, listening, basic musical features (such as pitch and meter), and art; different forms a definition might take; and criticisms of the ways in which philosophers have pursued the definition of music.

On July 16, 2007, the popular and critically acclaimed band the White Stripes took the stage on George Street in St John's, the capital of the Canadian province of Newfoundland and Labrador. The ecstatic crowd cheered them on as guitarist Jack White and drummer Meg White drew back their arms in preparation to begin the show, played a single loud note, and put down their instruments.[1] The show was over. Before they took their bow, to riotous applause and cheering (including calls for "one more note!"), Jack White announced that the duo had now "officially played in every province and territory in Canada." Few would deny that the White Stripes performed in St John's that day. But did they perform *music*?

In Chapter 1, I made the case that any philosophy of music requires a notion of the medium of "pure" music, not least for understanding hybrid media, such as song. That notion has played a role in many discussions throughout this book, but thus far the content of the notion has remained unarticulated. In this chapter we turn squarely to face the question: What is music?

11.1 Definitions

In response to questions of classification, such as whether the White Stripes' "one-note show" is an instance of music, the traditional Western philosophical response is to offer a *definition* of the phenomenon in question, in terms of necessary and sufficient conditions. A necessary condition is one that must be met for a candidate to count as an instance of the kind in question. For instance, to be an *aunt*, one must be female. But being female is not *sufficient* (i.e., *enough*) to count as an instance of the kind – there are lots of women who are not aunts. And not just any sufficient condition will be useful for a definition. After all, being *my* aunt is sufficient for being *an* aunt, but presumably my aunt does not feature in any satisfactory definition of being an aunt. Traditionally, philosophers have sought definitions comprising conditions that are individually necessary and jointly sufficient. We might propose, then, that (i) being female, and (ii) having a niece or a nephew, are individually necessary and jointly sufficient conditions for being an aunt, and thus constitute a satisfactory definition of the concept.

Even this simple example raises a number of issues about definitions in terms of necessary and sufficient conditions. First, our proposed definition might be accused of circularity. A definition is circular if the concept being defined appears in the definition. Circularity does not imply falsity. After all, the definition *X is an aunt if and only if (iff) X is an aunt* is obviously true.[2] The problem is that a definition is supposed to be *helpful* in some way. For instance, a definition might (1) "illuminate the shared *nature*" of the things that it captures, e.g., the "essence" of aunthood; (2) help us "*in practice* to identify whether ... something is of the kind," e.g., give us a test for aunthood; (3) "isolate the criteria *implicit in decisions* about which marginal or novel things are of the kind," e.g., explain how we in fact decide whether or not someone is an aunt; or (4) aid us in *teaching* the concept to those unfamiliar with it, e.g., teaching people from a culture without the concept of an aunt how to use the term (McKeown-Green 2014, 397–8, italics altered). It should be clear that the definition *X is an aunt iff X is an aunt* will not help us in any of these ways, because of its circularity. The earlier proposal, in terms of nieces and nephews, is not *explicitly* circular, but it may be *implicitly* so. After all, someone who does not understand the concept "aunt" is unlikely to understand the concepts "niece" and "nephew." We might, of course, offer further definitions of those concepts, but if we define a niece as someone who (i) is female, and (ii) has an aunt or an uncle, and a nephew as someone who (i) is male, and (ii) has an aunt or an uncle, then the concept of an aunt is implicit in the earlier proposal, and thus the accusation of circularity stands.

We can eliminate the concepts of "niece" and "nephew" from our definition-in-progress, however: X is an aunt iff (i) X is female, and (ii) X has a sibling or sibling-in-law with a child. This revision still contains terms that must themselves be understood, but one need not already understand the concept "aunt" in order to understand those terms. The assumption is that these are more basic concepts that we may take for granted in the context of this particular enquiry. (This is not to say that these concepts are more easily defined, as debates over the nature of sex and gender demonstrate.) The revision raises a second issue relevant to many definitions. Should a definition of "aunt" include relations by marriage, or is it a strictly biological concept? One might conduct a survey to see how competent English speakers use the term, but one will find that they use it not only in both these ways, but in many others (for instance, for a "woman who is regarded with respect or affection similar to that often accorded to an aunt [in the kinship sense] despite not being linked by this specific kinship" (*Oxford English Dictionary*). This last meaning of "aunt" is clearly derivative from the kinship sense, but that does not show that it is any less legitimate or useful a concept. Most philosophers draw two morals from this sort of example: First, there are often many closely related concepts represented by a single term and, second, there may be no answer to the question of which of these concepts is *the* concept in question. Rather, which concept we are interested in may depend on our project. A geneticist may need the biological concept of aunthood, while the sociologist may need the concept that includes not just biological aunts and aunts by marriage, but also "non-kinship" aunts. The practical upshot for the project of defining music is that, as we consider various proposals and cases, we should keep in mind both what we want such a definition for, and that there may be other, equally legitimate projects that demand different definitions (cf. Currie & Killin 2017).

A third general issue that must be addressed is the cultural scope of the concept of music being defined. Though I have focused on Western music throughout this book, what philosophers have been interested in is not a definition of the concept of *Western music*, but a definition of the *Western concept* of music. Simplifying greatly, Western cultures seem to share a concept captured by the English word "music." But many other cultures do not seem to have a similar concept. For example, the Blackfoot peoples of North America have a word that "means something like singing, dancing, and ceremony all rolled into one" (Nettl 2000, 466), but no word for music alone. Even if a culture does not have a *concept* of music, however, it may nonetheless have *music*, that is, the kind of thing picked out by the Western concept, just as members of the culture have adrenalin in their bodies, even if they have no *concept* of adrenalin; or as they have dreams even if they have no concept of dreams (perhaps because they see no noteworthy difference between waking and sleeping experiences). The plausibility of such a universal concept of music will turn in part on the details of the concept. If, for instance, it is a necessary condition on music that it be produced with the explicit intention *that it be music*, then no culture without the concept could produce music. If, by contrast, music turns out to be something (like adrenalin) that one can produce without having a concept of it, its cultural universality cannot be immediately ruled out.

A common starting point for those interested in investigating the nature of music is the idea that music is *the art of sound*.[3] As it turns out, the only unproblematic word in this phrase is "of"! First of all, it seems clear that music involves not only *sounds* but also silences. Second, there are other sonic arts, making talk of music as *the* art of sound seriously misleading. Most obviously, spoken poetry is an art of sound, but there is also some question about whether all non-linguistic sonic art is music. Third, as we saw in Chapter 5, §5.1.2, it is plausible that there are many instances of music that are not instances of art. These three points are helpful places to start thinking about more sophisticated definitions of music.

11.2 The Art of *Sound*? Music, Silence, and Deafness

11.2.1 Music and Silence

Jerrold Levinson (1990d) begins constructing his definition of music from a different old saw about the nature of music – that music is *organized sound*. Though he points out that this is clearly insufficient – the sounds of machinery, speech, and animals are all organized, but none are thereby music – Levinson retains the condition as *necessary* for music. But he immediately qualifies the claim in a footnote:

> I certainly understand ["organized sound"] to comprise the organization of sound *and silence*, or sounds and silences taken together; there are very few imaginable musics, and no actual musics, for which silence – the space between sounds – would not be a structural principle.
>
> (1990d, 270 n. 3)

One might question Levinson's claim that no actual musics lack silence as "a structural principle." It is rare for a rock or pop track to include even a moment's literal silence. But perhaps Levinson means only that no entire musical tradition lacks at least one example of musical silence, or that no matter how rare silences are in a given tradition, such silences are – or would be – musically meaningful. It is also possible that by "silence," Levinson means not the lack of musical sound, but rather a gap in the active production of musical sound. The Beatles' "A Hard Day's Night," for instance, opens with a majestic chord followed, a couple of seconds later, by the beginning of the first chorus. Those pregnant seconds are certainly a "space between sounds" in one sense – a lack of events that would be notated in a transcription of the song – but, in another, those seconds are filled with sound, as the chord rings on. Be that as it may, silence in the strong sense – a lack of musical sound altogether – does play a role in much Western music. A powerful example occurs at the climax of Barber's "Adagio for Strings" (Example 11.1): A tense, drawn-out cadence is played very loudly (*sff*), high on all the instruments, there is a rest (notated with a pause), then the same cadence is repeated very softly (*pp*) two octaves lower.[4] The time taken between the end of the playing of the last high chord and the beginning of the first low chord makes a huge difference to the effect of this passage. Depending on the venue and interpretation, that time may be filled with the ringing of the high chord, or it may include some silence between the complete dying away of the high chord and the beginning of the low chord. In the latter case, the specific qualities of the silence undeniably play an expressive role in the music. More generally, one cannot omit the silences from a piece of music without affecting important musical features such as rhythm, form, and emotional expression.

Jennifer Judkins (1997) points out that there are different kinds of silences in music, which tend to have different kinds of effects. *Measured* silences include ordinary rests; *unmeasured* silences may be *internal*, as with the silence in Barber's Adagio just described, or *framing* silences, such as the time taken between the end of the last note of a song and the audience's applause. Which category a given silence belongs to may be a matter of performative interpretation. For instance, the silence between the two statements of the opening motif of Beethoven's Fifth Symphony (like the pause on the final note of each statement) may be performed as measured or unmeasured (Example 11.2). We might consider a further category of "quasi-measured" silences (Kania 2010, 343). When a note is marked staccato, for instance, one must play it shorter than its notated length – one starts the note "on time," but finishes it early. The note and silence together add up to the notated length (hence "measured"), yet the silence may not be conceived of by the performer as a particular length, such as an eighth-note (hence "quasi-"). Many articulations will result in such quasi-measured silences.

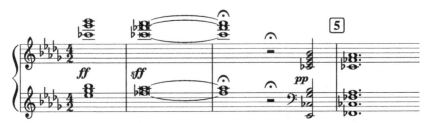

Example 11.1 The climax of Barber's "Adagio for Strings." (Adapted from "Adagio for Strings," © 1939, G. Schirmer.) The passage occurs around 6:17–42 on the recording on the Spotify playlist for this chapter.

Example 11.2 The opening theme of Beethoven's Fifth Symphony, first movement.

Given that there are musical silences of different kinds, and that they are *musical* silences precisely because they must be attended to in the appreciation of the music in which they occur, one may wonder if, just as it is possible to have music without silence, it is possible to have music without sound, that is, purely silent music. It is impossible to broach this subject without discussing John Cage's notorious *4'33"* (1952). Despite often being referred to – even by Cage himself – as his "silent piece," most music scholars agree that *4'33"* is not silent, but filled with sounds.[5] Though early versions of the piece differ somewhat, the published version is unambiguous (Kania 2010, 344–5; cf. Gann 2010, 167–87). It consists of three movements, during which the performer is to remain silent; however, the point of the work is to appreciate the ambient sounds of the performance environment. Most theorists thus take these ambient sounds to be the content of the work, rather than the silence of the performer. I will thus (briefly) return to whether *4'33"* is music when we consider, below, what makes a sound *musical*.[6]

Andrew Kania observes that there are other arguably silent pieces of music – some predating *4'33"* by decades (2010, 349–50).[7] He argues that the best candidate for the title of first silent piece of music is Erwin Schulhoff's "In futurum," the middle movement of *Fünf Pittoresken* (*Five Picturesques*, 1919), a suite for piano (Example 11.3). The four other pieces take popular dances as their basis (foxtrot, ragtime, and so on). "In futurum," however, consists entirely of rests. Many elements of the piece point to a facetious intent: Though consisting entirely of rests, each measure on each staff is subdivided in different and quite complex ways; the clefs of the piano staves are switched; the time signatures are nonsensical and incommensurable (though the rests in every measure add up to a whole note); the score contains not only rests, fermatas, breath marks, and a grand pause, but also upside-down fermatas, exclamation points and question marks, and "notes" whose heads are smiley- and frowny-faces; and, finally, the tempo and stylistic indications are: "Timeless tempo; the whole piece freely with expression and feeling throughout, to the very end!" But even if "In futurum" is a joke, that doesn't show that it's not music.[8]

Given that "In futurum" is silent, however, how could one think that it is music? That is, aren't sounds a necessary condition on music? Levinson hedges a little. As we have seen, he argues that silence must be allowed as a component of musical works, but it does not follow that there could be works consisting

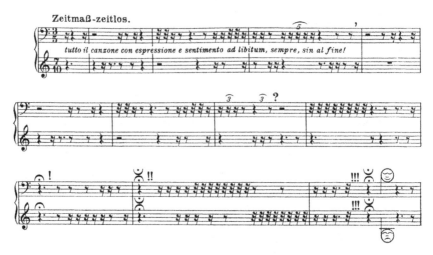

Example 11.3 Erwin Schulhoff, "In futurum," excerpt (© 1991, Ries & Erler).

entirely of silence. (You might argue that holes are a necessary component of authentic Swiss cheese without thereby committing yourself to the notion that a cheese could consist of *nothing but* holes!) Levinson allows that "we can include [*4'33"*] in music if we like, as a limiting case of the organization of sound-and-silence," but confusingly goes on to acknowledge that Cage's piece is not silent after all (1990d, 270 n. 3). It is thus unclear whether Levinson would acknowledge the possibility of a truly silent piece. Kania emphasizes the point, mentioned above, that we must admit silences into the realm of music because, like musical sounds, musical silences must be attended to, in order for the music they (typically) partially constitute to be understood (2010, 343). As a result, Kania rejects the necessity of sounds for music, arguing instead that music must be intended to be *heard* and (in some cases) *listened to* in a certain way.[9] This raises two further questions – one about the nature of silence, the other to do with music and hearing more generally.

The first question is whether silence can be heard or listened to at all. The challenge is that if the objects of hearing are *sounds*, and silence is the absence of sounds, then silence cannot be heard. "Hearing silence," on this view, is loose talk for *not hearing anything*; though we may listen *for* sounds and fail, we cannot listen *to* silence. If the challenge succeeds, even Kania's definition does not allow for silent music. Answering the challenge adequately would require developing a theory of auditory perception, which I am in no position to do here (or elsewhere!).[10] But note that anyone who accepts that musical silences must be attended to in the appreciation of music that contains them must answer this challenge in some way. And even if musical silences are typically bounded by musical sounds, we have so far seen no reason that they cannot be bounded in other ways. For instance, David Tudor, the first performer of *4'33"*, framed its movements (and, hence, his silences) by lowering the lid of the piano at the beginning of each movement and raising it at the end, gestures that have become standard for pianistic performances of the work.

11.2.2 Music and Deafness

The second question is whether appeals to hearing and listening in a definition of music contribute to the marginalization of d/Deaf people. Such concerns are at the heart of disability studies, a relatively recent area of scholarly enquiry that considers the oppressive social construction of disability, just as feminist or race theory considers the oppressive social construction of gender or race. Scholars in disability studies do not deny that there are objective differences between disabled people and, say, a statistical norm; their concern is rather with the ways in which those differences manifest themselves in social and cultural attitudes, norms, and practices – especially unjust ones – including conceptions of disability. (Compare race studies: No one denies that people have different skin colors, for instance; the disputes are over what race really is (if anything) and how it manifests itself, especially in unjust ways, in society and culture.) Where an able-bodied person might see a disabled person's use of a wheelchair as a *handicap* necessitated by their *disability*, for instance, a disability-studies theorist (not to mention the wheelchair user) might argue that it is the ubiquity of stairs and curbs that are the handicap, unjustly restricting the movements of wheelchair users just as "white only" signs unjustly restrict the movements of people of color.[11] Evelyn Glennie, a highly respected percussionist, highlights the social construction of disability by pointing out that while virtually no one discusses her work without relating it to her deafness, no one would consider the size of her arms and hands a "disability," though – while "normal" – they also present performance challenges that she must overcome (Straus 2011, 147).[12]

A wide range of topics has been covered in the burgeoning musicological literature at the intersection of music and disability, including (1) how the identity of composers and performers, and the reception of their works and performances, are shaped by their disabilities; (2) the representation of disability in musical works and performances; (3) the musical experiences of people with disabilities; and (4) the notion that disability itself is performative, "something you do rather than something you are" (Howe, Jensen-Moulton, Lerner, & Straus 2016, 4–5). There is only room here to scratch the surface of one issue related to the definition of music, namely the musical experiences of d/Deaf and hard-of-hearing people.[13] As these terms suggest, there is great diversity among both (i) people's hearing abilities and (ii) the cultures and practices – musical and otherwise – that surround those abilities. Hearing abilities differ from person to person (and from ear to ear) and range across many dimensions, including frequency, loudness, and timbre. Someone is *profoundly deaf* in the audiological sense if they cannot hear sounds below 91 decibels (a measure of loudness roughly equivalent to that of a passing subway car or motorcycle). The term "Deaf" (with a capital "D") refers to members and aspects of Deaf culture, a "global community united by its use of sign language," while "deaf" (with a lowercase "d") refers to those who do not identify as members of Deaf culture, and who typically use both phonetic (rather than sign) language and hearing aids (Holmes 2017, 173). (The term "d/Deaf" is an abbreviation for "deaf and Deaf" or "deaf or Deaf," depending on the context.) Some people whose hearing abilities fall outside the statistically normal, but short of profound deafness, identify as "hard of hearing," rather than "deaf." But self-identification in the categories *Deaf*, *deaf*, and *hard of hearing* does not match up neatly with hearing ability. In particular, Deaf culture has traditionally resisted the characterization of "hearing loss" or "impairment" as a deficit, arguing instead that "to be 'Deaf' is to belong to a linguistic-cultural minority," while the non-culturally deaf and hard of hearing may accept the characterization of their hearing as deficient, sometimes attempting to "pass" as hearing with the help of hearing aids, including technology such as cochlear implants and practices such as speech therapy (Holmes 2017, 176–9).

Jessica Holmes identifies three persistent, interrelated stereotypes about deafness, grounded in ignorance or overgeneralization, that affect popular notions of d/Deaf musical experiences and abilities: "[1] deaf people experience the world as total aural silence *and* pure visual-tactile sensation; [2] deaf people automatically aspire to hearing norms; and, [3] through their inborn sensory acuities, deaf people compensate for hearing loss in extraordinary ways" (2017, 209). The second stereotype is invalidated by the very existence of Deaf culture, though it must be acknowledged that many deaf and hard-of-hearing people *do* aspire to mainstream cultural hearing norms. The range of hearing abilities in the d/Deaf population puts paid to the first stereotype, and even the most profoundly deaf people possess some auditory abilities. Moreover, though d/Deaf people commonly use other sensory modalities, particularly the visual and tactile, to enhance their musical experiences, this is also true of the hearing population. The appeal of thumping beats, for instance, which combine a visceral tactile experience with an auditory one, is clearly not restricted to d/Deaf audiences. Similarly, as we saw in Chapter 7, §7.3, some philosophers argue that a visual or kinesthetic knowledge of how musical sounds are produced plays an essential role in their expressive character and other aesthetic properties (Bergeron & Lopes 2009; Levinson 1980, 14–19; 1990a, 399–400). More generally, philosophers of perception increasingly acknowledge the existence and ubiquity of "multisensory" experiences, that is, unitary perceptual experiences in which more than one sensory modality is essentially involved (Briscoe 2017).[14]

Unsurprisingly, given the diversity of the d/Deaf population, there is a wide range of d/Deaf musical practices and attitudes toward music. It is worth emphasizing at the outset that "hearing is integral to many deaf people's experiences of music: for some, hearing remains the most efficient and familiar way to engage with music" (Holmes 2017, 210). In particular, those outside Deaf culture may use hearing-aid technology to enhance their aural experience of music. d/Deaf people's hearing abilities understandably sometimes lead to a preference for music with certain features, such as loud, low bass lines, though some reject taking these features to the extremes, since the bodily effects of such amplified vibrations can be disorienting and even harmful (Holmes 2017, 195). But many d/Deaf listeners, especially those who were once hearing, also *imagine* auditory experiences, aided by memory or scores (Straus 2011, 169–70). Hearing people also have imagined auditory musical experiences, of course, though they likely engage in such experiences less often during episodes of musical listening.

As already noted, many d/Deaf people, particularly among the culturally Deaf, integrate visual and tactile experience into their musical experiences more prominently than do hearing listeners. One important example is *song signers*, who use sign language to communicate song content to d/Deaf listeners, in ways that typically incorporate musical features such as tempo and rhythm – though not necessarily the same tempo or rhythm as those of the signed song (Holmes 2017, 191; Maler 2016). Non-culturally deaf and hard-of-hearing listeners may also attend to the mouthing of lyrics by the singer or someone else (Holmes 2017, 201). Other common visual elements include on-stage dancers and rhythmic lighting (again, practices hardly exclusive to d/Deaf musical communities). Joseph Straus points out that almost all listeners commonly understand music kinesthetically, through moving our bodies with or to the music, or through watching others move theirs (2011, 169).[15] Common tactile methods of appreciation among the d/Deaf include the already mentioned experience of loud, low-frequency sounds and the use of hand-held balloons to amplify musical vibrations. Again, the importance of these aspects of musical experience to many d/Deaf listeners may lead to certain musical preferences (e.g., for dance music), though it is worth emphasizing that "d/Deaf people rarely privilege vibration over other sensory modalities, while, for some, vibration on its own does not qualify as music" (Holmes 2017, 209).

Despite the variety of d/Deaf musical experiences, some members of Deaf culture reject music as part of "audist" culture – "the hearing way of dominating, restructuring, and exercising authority over the deaf community" – a particular form of ableism (the disability-rights equivalent of sexism, racism, etc.) (Holmes 2017, 198 n. 112). For such people, "music is fundamentally at odds with the primacy of vision in Deaf culture" (2017, 200). At one point, Holmes seems to reject this viewpoint as an unenlightened response to "the deep-seated cultural linkage of music with aurality," countering that "hearing is not itself hegemonic; it is rather the cultural values ascribed to hearing – in this case the assumed interdependence of music and hearing – that overlook and devalue [d/Deaf] listeners" (2017, 210). But the rejection of this perspective seems a rare departure from Holmes's disability-studies methodology of letting the d/Deaf speak for themselves, and at odds with other information she presents. For instance, Holmes notes that some accomplished d/Deaf dancers rely not on directly experiencing the music they dance to (whether through hearing or touch), but rather on visual and kinesthetic cues such as signed beat counts or the movement of their partner's body. She cites members of Gallaudet University's all-deaf Dance Company explaining that it's simply not possible "even with a state-of-the-art heavy bass sound system" to hear or feel the music sufficiently to dance competently to it (2017, 194–5).

What implications does the diversity of d/Deaf experiences of, and attitudes toward, music have for the *definition* of music? First, the worry that putting concepts of sound, hearing, or listening at the heart of music will marginalize d/Deaf people seems based, in part, on the misconception that no d/Deaf people can hear, and thus live in a world of silence. Similarly, if sound is not necessarily or exclusively experienced aurally, then putting sound at the heart of musical experience seems less problematic for the musical experiences of d/Deaf people. Perhaps even more helpful, however, would be to reconceive hearing and listening along multisensory lines. Not only does this seem an independently promising line of enquiry in the philosophy of perception, but it would demonstrate that d/Deaf and "hearing" musical experiences are not as different as we – d/Deaf and hearing alike – might at first have thought.

Despite these positive conclusions, there remains the troubling possibility that though d/Deaf people will not be *excluded* from the realm of music by these theoretical suggestions, they might yet be *marginalized*: To the extent that sound and aural experience are central to music, d/Deaf people's experiences of it may seem deficient. It is worth noting in this connection that most – perhaps all – listeners fall short of the ideals of musical experience posited by, for instance, music-theoretic analyses of complex works. Just as no actual reader could be expected to experience everything in one reading of James Joyce's novel *Ulysses* that has been plausibly found there by literary scholars, no listener could be expected to experience everything at one performance of Beethoven's Ninth Symphony that has been plausibly found in the work by music scholars. Some music theorists, including some disability-studies theorists, have criticized methods of music scholarship that posit such rich content in musical works for idealizing a kind of "prodigious" or superhuman hearing (Straus 2011, 150–2), but rather than abandoning such theories as marginalizing d/Deaf (and most other!) listeners, we might understand them as illustrating that when confronted with the richness of great musical works, we are *all* incapable of appreciating everything they have to offer, at least in a single experience.

And yet the objection may still be raised that such theories put d/Deaf listeners at more of a disadvantage than hearing listeners, if the features that such scholarship attributes to great musical works include those less accessible to d/Deaf listeners. Though I cannot hope to resolve this issue here, I will make two final remarks. First, the mere fact that much music (or many aspects of it) is inaccessible to d/Deaf people does not *in itself* marginalize them. Rather, it is, as Holmes puts it, "the cultural values ascribed to hearing" experiences and practices that lead to marginalization (2017, 210). For instance, if (contrary to what we have just seen) d/Deaf people *were* completely incapable of appreciating music, then Nietzsche's remark that "without music, life would be a mistake" (1889, 160) would imply that d/Deaf people cannot lead meaningful lives. But that would surely be reason to question Nietzsche's claim, rather than accept the implication.

Second, the possibility that music scholars (among others) have overlooked valuable musical practices and experiences should serve as a spur to investigate a wider range of musical works, performances, and experiences – most obviously, in this case, those with d/Deaf composers, performers, audiences, and content. Thus, Joseph Straus summarizes the goals of developing theories of "disablist hearing" as (i) empowering the disabled, acknowledging their ability and right to represent themselves; (ii) emphasizing "what disability can provide to the listener, not what the listener can do despite the disability"; and (iii) recognizing that musical experience is more diverse than most music scholarship suggests (2011, 179–81).

Where might the exploration of this diversity lead us? Deaf artist Christine Sun Kim argues that "sound is not a prerequisite for music. Music can be an exclusively visual-spatial experience" (Holmes 2017, 196). However, as we have already seen, some members of Deaf culture reject even the less radical claim that vibrations alone can constitute music. The definition of music, then, cannot be *settled* by appealing to the experiences of any particular group of people; we must rather take as many different perspectives into account as we can while pursuing a definition of music.

11.3 *The* Art of Sound? Music, Language, and Sound Art

Suppose that we can resolve the issue of whether and how to integrate sound, silence, hearing, and listening into a definition of music. We still face the question of what distinguishes *musical* sounds.[16] One obvious place to start is with the basic, perhaps essentially musical, features of musical sounds that we considered in Chapter 4, such as pitch, harmony, rhythm, and meter. There are two initial objections to making such features necessary for any sound that qualifies as music: that they will make the resulting definition of music too narrow, or that they will make it too broad. They will make the definition too narrow if we require too many such features in order for something to count as music. As Jerrold Levinson puts it, "it should be apparent that there are no longer any intrinsic properties of sound that are required for something possibly to be music, and none that absolutely excludes a sonic phenomenon from that category" (1990d, 271):

> Gregorian chant and shakuhachi solos are music but lack harmony. Takemitsu's *Water Music* (derived from taped raindrop sounds), African drumming, and Webern's pointillistic *Five Pieces*, op. 5, lack melody but are nonetheless music. Certain kinds of atmospheric modern jazz and synthesizer compositions have virtually no rhythms, yet they are music also. Melody, rhythm, and harmony are important features of a lot of music, but they nonetheless remain only typical features for music in general, not necessary ones.
>
> (1990d, 270–1)

One obvious move to make in light of this objection is to require of musical sounds not any *particular* musical feature but *at least one* such feature. Note that all the examples Levinson gives lack some feature typical of Western music (harmony, melody, and rhythm, respectively), but they all also *possess* some such feature (melody, rhythm, and pitch).

However, even if we require only that sounds possess at least one basic musical feature, such as pitch or rhythm, in order to qualify as music, the second objection remains: Many sounds that no one would call music seem to have such features, making the definition too broad. My first printer, for instance, seemed to serenade me with the devilish melody in Example 11.4 whenever I committed my thoughts to paper. But surely my printer didn't make music. Worse (from the point of view of a tidy definition of music), these non-musical sounds seem capable of *being transformed into music*. Had I been a composer, I might have built a musical structure around *and including* my printer's sounds, just as Leroy Anderson did with a typewriter (in *The Typewriter*).

But perhaps the objection that the necessity of musical features will make a definition of music too broad ignores the complexity of those features, which

Example 11.4 The sound of my first printer, notated as music.

we investigated in Chapter 4. Recall that (musical) pitch is not the same thing as (sonic) frequency; it relies on the psychological phenomena of *octave equivalence* (by which we hear the A above middle-C and the A below it as the same *kind* of pitch) and *categorical perception* (by which we hear continuous frequencies as falling into discrete categories within the octave).

There are different ways to integrate these psychological phenomena into a theory of pitch or music, as we have seen with respect to various aspects of music, such as emotional expressiveness. Is pitch a *subjective* phenomenon, so that if I hear my printer as playing a tune, but you hear it as making noise, those sounds are music *for me* but not *for you*? Or is pitch an *intentional* phenomenon, so that the printer's sounds are music only if intended to be heard as pitched by their creator or appropriator? Most philosophers have preferred an intentional characterization of music. For instance, even though bongo drums have specific frequencies, one should not hear them as pitched, because that is not how they are intended to be heard by composers and performers who employ them. By contrast, though no dog intends its bark to be music, the barks cunningly arranged to sound like "We Wish You a Merry Christmas" on *Christmas Unleashed* are music because they were intended to be heard as pitched by the Jingle Dogs (assuming this name refers to the people responsible for producing the record, and not the canine contributors!).

If we think of music as rooted in certain cognitive capacities, should we be more tempted by a subjective approach? Not necessarily. If, by analogy, language is rooted in certain cognitive capacities, we could still argue that instances of language are anything that is *produced*, rather than *understood*, using those capacities. One point in favor of this approach is that we should acknowledge the possibility that sounds people make could be instances of language or music that we do not understand, rather than saying that because we do not understand them, they are not (at least to us) language or music.

The idea of requiring just one of several basic musical features as necessary for music is so simple that it is surprising Levinson does not consider it. But perhaps he ignores this approach because he thinks that there are clear examples of music with *no* basic musical features. It's notable that he doesn't give an example, however. Indeed, it is difficult to find uncontroversial examples, but consider the "noise music" of Merzbow as a candidate. "Merzbow" is the stage name of Masami Akita, a prolific artist who performs live and produces (hundreds of!) studio recordings. Whether or not his work is *music* is, of course, an open question at this point in our discussion. But it is called *noise* music because it consists largely of sounds – processed electronically, though sometimes with acoustic sources – that consist of a wide range of randomly distributed frequencies – they are "white noises." Though even white noise can be heard as pitched in some contexts, it is much more naturally heard as unpitched – more like a snare drum than a bongo. While some of Merzbow's work, e.g., "Munchen" from the album *1930*, arguably has basic musical features – most notably rhythm – some of it, e.g., the "Introduction" to the same album, clearly does not.

If this last track is properly called music, we must reject the necessity of *any* basic musical features for music. Ultimately, this seems to be Levinson's reason for omitting basic musical features from his definition. Instead, Levinson emphasizes the *function* of musical sounds. According to Levinson, music is:

> [i] sounds [ii] temporally organized [iii] by a person [iv] for the purpose of enriching or intensifying experience through active engagement (e.g., listening, dancing, performing) [v] with the sounds regarded primarily, or in significant measure, as sounds.
>
> (1990d, 273)[17]

If, on the other hand, the track in question is *not* music, we might explore an alternative such as Kania's definition, focusing this time on condition 3(a):

> Music is (1) any event intentionally produced or organized (2) to be heard, and (3) *either* (a) to have some basic musical feature, such as pitch or rhythm, *or* (b) to be listened to for such features.
>
> (2011b, 12)[18]

11.3.1 Pitch, Tonality, and Language

We will consider Levinson's central, functional condition (iv) in the following section; but what about the final condition that musical sounds must be "regarded primarily, or in significant measure, as sounds"? Taken out of the context of Levinson's argument for it, this condition can seem rather mysterious. How else would an artist intend her artistic sounds to be regarded? But Levinson introduces this condition to deal with "the poetry problem" (1990d, 272), that is, the fact that recitations of poetry may meet all the other conditions of his definition, yet they should not count as music.

Levinson is surely right that we must exclude spoken poetry from the realm of music, but it's not clear that he has chosen the best method for doing so. Note, first, that when we listen to most music with understanding, we do not listen to it as "pure sound." We hear the sounds as possessing all sorts of features, along a spectrum from basic features (e.g., pitch and rhythm), through more complex features (e.g., melodies and harmonies), all the way up to high-level features such as emotional content and musical form. To be fair, Levinson does not use a phrase such as "pure sound." But it is difficult to see what else he might mean by regarding sounds "as sounds." If the point is merely to exclude linguistic sounds from the definition, we could do so explicitly, for instance by appealing to our best linguistic theories and requiring that music must *not* be intended to be regarded as *that* kind of sound.

One might worry that excluding linguistic sounds from the realm of music implies that we must deny that *song* is music. But this worry can be allayed if we accept the notion that music is a medium that can be combined with other media. This does imply that song is not *purely* musical, but not in any pejorative sense. The sung words of a song have both musical and linguistic content, while the instrumental accompaniment has only musical content. The overall content of the song, however, is more than simply the sum of these contents, as we saw in Chapter 1.

There are many works of art that play with the distinction between linguistic and musical content. For instance, the technique of *Sprechstimme*, invented by Schoenberg for *Pierrot lunaire* (1912) blurs the boundary between speech and song by exaggerating the expressive contours of speech. Kurt Schwitters's *Ursonate* (1922–32) achieves a similar effect by organizing nonsense syllables (quasi-linguistic sounds) in a highly rhythmic fashion. Steve Reich's "Come Out" (1966) is a track that repeats a sample of speech over and over again, but slightly out of phase in the left and right stereo channels (before proceeding to other techniques of fragmentation and repetition). Even before the phasing is perceptible, the repetition of the linguistic fragment confuses the listener's perception of it as language – one hears it as rhythmic – but as the channels get further out of phase, or later as the sample is further fragmented and repeated in various ways, the sounds are less and less recognizably linguistic and seem more and more musical. (One fascinating effect of this is that, because one can't forget that the sounds are linguistic, they retain a kind of "aura" of the spoken word even though one might not be able to identify them as speech if presented out of context.) A final example is the opening of Glenn Gould's radio documentary *The Idea of North* (1967). Here Gould weaves various recordings of people talking about living in the far north of Canada into a kind of sonic tapestry. While the effect might be described as contrapuntal, the result does not seem naturally described as literal music, unlike (arguably) some of the previous examples.

A final issue that must be addressed when distinguishing music from language is the nature of "tonal" languages. In spoken English, as in many languages, variation in frequency can be used in different ways (e.g., for emphasis or to indicate a question), but such variation is not heard in terms of musical pitch (i.e., categorical perception in a division of the octave). In tonal languages, such as Mandarin, frequency plays a more central role: uttering a given syllable with one of four "tones" determines which word is being spoken. But these "tones" do not meet the criteria for musical pitches either. In particular, what is essential to such language tones is certain frequency *contours*, rather than categorical perception in a division of the octave (Stainsby & Cross 2009, 55–6).

Comparing the two approaches to defining music, note that Levinson's definition divides artistic sounds into two classes: oral literature and music. Music turns out to be artistic sounds that aren't linguistic. Kania's definition, in appealing to specifically *musical* features, by contrast, allows for a third category – sound art – comprising artistic sounds that are intended to be understood neither as language nor as pitched, rhythmic, and so on (cf. Hamilton 2007, 40–6, 59–62). Merzbow's "noise music," then, would strictly speaking be *sound art*, according to this theory, not *music* at all, as would the ambient sounds that constitute the content of a performance of *4'33"* (Kania 2010, 344–9). The distinction between music and sound art is highly contested, particularly by artists working near the border of these domains. But many philosophers have taken *tonality* (a feature of passages of music that is closely related to pitch) to be central to the nature of music (e.g. Graham 2007; Hamilton 2007, 40–65; Scruton 1983; 1997, 1–79), just as language is central to the nature of literature, with the result that a space is carved out for sound art as the artistic use of sounds not connected in the right way to either tonality or language. According to these philosophers, it is the sounds of sound art, not music, that are appropriately regarded *as* (pure) *sounds*.[19]

11.3.2 Rhythm, Meter, and "Temporal Organization"

Given his denial that any "intrinsic properties of sounds" are essential to music, it is perhaps surprising to see Levinson require music's *temporal organization*, since this might sound like the requirement of another basic musical feature we explored in Chapter 4, namely, rhythm or meter. But Levinson means something quite different by this phrase. In the course of constructing his definition, Levinson claims that "[m]usic as we conceive it seems as essentially an art of time as it is an art of sound." He thus aims to exclude from the realm of music "colorful instantaneous combinations of sounds – i.e., chords of vanishingly brief duration" (1990d, 273). Given Levinson's own gloss here, together with the reasonable assumption that the notion of a literally instantaneous sound is incoherent, perhaps we should interpret the condition as excluding sounds that are extremely short, though not of any particular duration. Such sounds are surely far from being paradigms of music for anyone. Yet there are actual candidates for the status of music that arguably violate this condition, such as the White Stripes' one-note show. Moreover, this interpretation of the temporal-organization condition puts the defender of the condition in an awkward position. If a chord held for five minutes counts as music, but a "vanishingly brief" chord does not, what is the minimum duration of a piece of music? Any answer specifying a particular length will be unacceptably arbitrary. Nor does it seem plausible that a chord becomes less musical as it gets shorter.

An alternative interpretation of the condition is that "temporal organization" or "development" requires, at the very least, two temporally distinct musical events, such as two notes or chords, constituting temporal parts of a larger musical whole. Again, sonic artworks violating this condition are non-paradigmatic at best, yet, again, there are several candidates, such as La Monte Young's *Composition 1960 #7*, which requires just two notes to be played simultaneously on the piano and "to be held for a long time." It might be argued that there is temporal development in this piece, since one point of interest is how the inevitably "impure" sound changes over time, as a result of the decay of, and interference between, the sound waves produced by the various strings of the piano responsible for producing the two notes. But there are other pieces where such development is minimized, whether through the use of electronic sound sources or ensemble effects. For instance, Yves Klein's *Monotone-Silence Symphony* (c. 1957) consists of a D-major chord played by a chamber instrumental and vocal ensemble for five to seven minutes (followed by 44 seconds of silence).

A further question that this condition raises is why Levinson privileges one kind of musical organization over others. For instance, even if La Monte Young's *Composition 1960 #7* is not *temporally* organized, it is *tonally* organized. That is, it comprises two distinct *pitch* events – a B and an F-sharp. It is not clear why these sounds have less of a claim to music status than, say, the performance of a piece that requires the same note to be played twice in close succession. To be fair, Levinson's explicit argument appeals not to single instances of temporally unorganized sounds, but an art consisting *entirely* of instantaneous works:

> an art in which the point was to produce colorful instantaneous combinations of sounds – i.e. chords of vanishingly brief duration – ... to be savored independently. My intuition is that we would not regard this art as a type of music .... It would be the auditory equivalent of jam tasting or rose smelling – the receiving of a sensory impression, sometimes complex, but one for which temporal development was not an issue.
>
> (1990d, 273)

But even if Levinson is right that (1) such an art (and hence its works) would fail to be music, it does not follow that (2) *individual* instantaneous works (e.g., *Composition 1960 #7*), appearing in a rich musical culture in which almost all works are temporally organized, could not be music.

Is Levinson right about even the first claim? It would certainly be difficult to think of such a tradition as a musical one if its practitioners would simply not know what to make of two chords played one after the other, or if there were something about the minds of these practitioners that made it the case that *it would simply never occur to them* to do so.[20] But we can imagine a culture in which religious strictures forbid any temporal organization of sounds. People from this culture can perfectly well understand the musical potential of temporal organization and its continuity with their sonic art. It may well be, then, that such a tradition would be a musical one.

In sum, it seems that Levinson's requirement that musical sounds be temporally organized should either be removed, thus admitting "instantaneous" and other non-temporally-organized sounds into the realm of music, or developed into a requirement for more robustly characterized basic musical features, thus excluding (some) sound art from the realm of music.

Developing Kania's disjunctive basic-musical-features approach to the definition of music would require developing theories of those features, as well as establishing which are sufficient for sounds' being music. We began the former task in Chapter 4; we will consider the latter task in §11.5, below. Next, however, let us examine the assumption, common to many theories of music, that music is essentially *an art*.

11.4 The *Art* of Sound? Music and Art

Levinson's central requirement for sounds' being music is the *functional* condition that the sounds must be organized "for the purpose of enriching or intensifying experience through active engagement (e.g., listening, dancing, performing)" (1990d, 273). Because of the kind of experience it describes, this condition is widely considered *aesthetic*;[21] it is central to Levinson's definition because it is the heart of his response to the problem of music with no basic musical features.[22]

Levinson rejects the characterization of this condition as *aesthetic*, because he takes aesthetic experience to be a more restrictive notion, involving "contemplative and distanced apprehension of pure patterns of sound, or ... specific attention to [the sounds'] beauty or other aesthetic qualities" (1990d, 272). Making the more restrictive notion essential to music's function, Levinson thinks, would exclude music with other primary functions, such as Bach's cantatas, Maori haka, or disco. Andy Hamilton, sympathetic to Levinson's approach in this respect, suggests that a better way of dealing with this tension is to deflate the notion of aesthetic experience. Hamilton claims that:

> the aesthetic is ordinary and ubiquitous .... [T]he consequences of direct social function [such as inculcating religious experience, fortifying warriors, or enabling dancing] – and of the imperfect separation of the ethical, aesthetic and cognitive value spheres before the eighteenth century – are overrated by Levinson and other writers.

(2007, 56)

But even given Hamilton's broad conception of aesthetic experience, there seem to be examples of music that neither are intended to elicit, nor in fact elicit, any such experience. For instance, Levinson asks us to imagine "a sequence of sounds devised by a team of psychological researchers ... such that when subjects are in a semiconscious condition and are exposed to these sounds, the subjects enter psychedelic states of marked pleasurability" (1990d, 273). The point is supposed to be that if the researchers do not intend their subjects to attend actively to the sounds they're producing (and perhaps take steps, such as administering drugs, to ensure that their subjects *cannot* attend actively to them), then the sounds they produce cannot be considered music. But a lot seems to turn on how these sounds are characterized. Given Levinson's description of this example, one might imagine the researchers producing a wash of ambient, synthesized sound. But suppose we imagine the head researcher, having drugged up the subjects, sitting down at her Steinway grand and playing the slow movement of a Beethoven piano sonata. Here it seems clear that the researcher is producing music, even though she doesn't intend anyone to actively engage with it.[23] A more prosaic case of the same kind is that of a parent singing his child to sleep. The parent clearly does not want the child to engage actively with the sounds of the lullaby – on the contrary, he wants the child to stop actively engaging with the world in general! Yet lullabies are surely instances of music. To take a third example: Levinson counts his definition's exclusion of Muzak from the realm of music as a point in its favor (1990d, 273), but it seems more plausible that Muzak is *bad* music.[24]

There is a host of cases similar to these non-aesthetic uses of music. Consider "musical" doorbells, ringtones, public-address punctuators, and computer notification sounds. In many cases, it is doubtful that the hearers of these sounds are intended to actively engage with them. But it seems likely that intuitions about whether such things count as music will vary according to "how musical" they are. For instance, a ringtone that is a digital sample of a pop recording seems likely to strike more people as music proper than a ringtone that is an electronically synthesized pentatonic scale. For those who are skeptical about the minimal end of the spectrum (e.g., S. Davies 2012a, 538–9), it's worth quoting Brian Eno on his composition of the start-up sound for the Windows 95 operating system:

> The thing from the agency said, "We want a piece of music that is inspiring, universal, blah-blah, da-da-da, optimistic, futuristic, sentimental, emotional," this whole list of adjectives, and then at the bottom it said "and it must be 3¼ seconds long." I thought this was so funny and an amazing thought to actually try to make a little piece of music. It's like making a tiny little jewel. In fact, I made 84 pieces. I got completely into this world of tiny, tiny little pieces of music. I was so sensitive to microseconds at the end of this that it really broke a

logjam in my own work. Then when I'd finished that and I went back to working with pieces that were like three minutes long, it seemed like oceans of time.
(Selvin 1996, paragraph breaks removed)

A final kind of example worth considering is musical exercises, such as the
practicing of scales and arpeggios. Intuitions may be less clear here than in
the cases just considered, because we may not think of such exercises as even
pieces of music, let alone musical works or performances. But they certainly
contain pitches and rhythms, and these are constitutive of them in the same way
pitches and rhythms are constitutive of musical works – part of the point of
practicing scales is to make sure you can play the right notes.

One might try to save the aesthetic condition in the face of these putative
counterexamples by arguing in each case that they are in fact intended to enrich
or intensify someone's experience. We might count the heightened desire to
purchase goods as an *intensification* of the shopper's experience on exposure to
Muzak (though we would have to drop the active-engagement condition), and
argue that the lullaby's soothing of the baby qualifies as *enriching* her experience in a certain sense. But this would be a Pyrrhic victory; the result would be
a vacuous conception of aesthetic experience as something like *any psychological change*. This is not what the defenders of such a condition have in mind, no
matter how broad their conception of aesthetic experience.

If these counterexamples are convincing, then we should reject the notion
that music is essentially aesthetic. This would not necessarily imply that music
is not essentially *artistic*, since most philosophers now reject the idea that art
is essentially aesthetic. However, it is notable that the very philosophers who
defend aesthetic conditions on music begin with the notion that music is essentially an art. For instance, Levinson begins his defense of the aesthetic condition
with the claim that "music in the primary sense is an art (or artistic activity)"
(1990d, 271); Scruton states that "[m]usic is an art of sound" (1997, 16); and
Hamilton claims that "music is essentially an art while speech is not" (2007,
57). Hamilton emphasizes that the conception of art employed here, like his
conception of the aesthetic, is a broad one, "with [a] lower-case 'a'," including
any "practice involving skill or craft whose ends are essentially aesthetic, and
that especially rewards aesthetic attention" (2007, 52), presumably in contrast
to Art with an upper-case "A" – something like a narrow conception restricted
to a closed list of fine arts designated as such at some point in the history of
Western art-theory. But even Hamilton's "small a" artistic conception of music
will either exclude many of the examples just considered or risk vacuity.

It may be no coincidence that essentially artistic conceptions of music are
pursued by *aestheticians* or philosophers *of the arts*. Music psychologists, for
instance, are much less likely to assume that music is necessarily artistic. A
comparison with other arts is helpful here. In reference works on aesthetics and

the philosophy of art, such as the *Oxford Handbook of Aesthetics* (Levinson 2003) or the *Routledge Companion to Aesthetics* (Gaut & Lopes 2013), there are chapters on such topics as metaphor, fiction, narrative, and pictorial representation. Neither the editors of these volumes, nor the authors of the chapters on these topics, believe that metaphor, fiction, and so on, are essentially artistic. Examples of non-artistic metaphors, narratives, and pictorial representations are legion, and it doesn't take much imagination to see the same holds true of fiction. An instructional video might exemplify all four concepts, yet fail to be a work of art, or even artistic in any weaker sense. The point is even more obvious if we turn to a topic such as *language*. There is plenty of language that is non-artistic, and the same sentence can be art in one context but not in another. This idea is commonplace in discussions of the definition of art. Most definitions of art are logically independent of any particular artworks or artforms.[25] Art is characterized in a general way that can apply to artifacts in any medium, precisely because there are clear examples of non-artistic pictures, stories, and so on. It is *possible*, of course, that music is an exception to this rule, but no one has argued this explicitly; Levinson, Scruton, and Hamilton simply *assume* that music is essentially artistic.[26]

This assumption is particularly puzzling in Levinson's case, since he elsewhere defends a definition of art that is inconsistent with his definition of music. His definition of art allows a broader range of goals to artworks than the aesthetic goal embedded in his definition of music, yet he claims that music is the art of sound. According to Levinson, "something is art iff it is or was intended … for overall regard as some prior art is or was correctly regarded" (2002, 13), and he defends this view, in part, precisely because he does not think that aesthetic (or other functional) definitions of art allow room for the variety of modes of attention intended for and appropriate to the variety of artworks.[27] But surely this general point applies to sonic artworks as well as it does to pictorial or linguistic ones. Again, this suggests that music should be characterized independently of the concept of art, just as language and pictures are, and then a distinct account should be given of when or what music qualifies as art – quite plausibly a general account that applies equally to language, pictures, and other media.[28]

Though Kania does not explicitly embrace the idea that music is essentially artistic, and elsewhere defends the idea that music should be considered, like language and pictures, a medium that can be put to artistic and non-artistic uses (2013b, 639–40), his definition may face objections similar to those just raised against aesthetic theories of music. Recall that, according to Kania, music is "(1) any event intentionally produced or organized (2) to be heard, and (3) *either* (a) to have some basic musical feature, such as pitch or rhythm, *or* (b) to be listened to for such features" (2011b, 12). He defends the disjunctive third condition as a way of accommodating the examples that push Levinson toward an aesthetic definition of music, i.e., examples of music that lack any basic musical features. Instead of arguing for an aesthetic condition, Kania suggests that sounds (or silences) that are intended by their creators to be listened to *for* such features, even though they lack them, are music. He gives the example of Yoko Ono's track "Toilet Piece/Unknown" from the album *Fly* (1971). Though it consists of nothing but an unedited recording of a toilet flushing, Kania argues that Ono's presentation of those sounds on an album that otherwise features mostly uncontroversial examples of music suggests that she intends listeners to approach them as they would musical sounds (i.e., listening for melodies, rhythms, harmonies, and so on), even though she is well aware that such listening will be frustrated.

There is nothing paradoxical about intending your audience to look or listen for something that isn't there; indeed, it's a staple of much modernist art – just think of Godot, for whom the audience, along with the characters, waits in Beckett's play. But it is difficult to think of examples that are not examples of *art*. Indeed, the structure of Kania's proposal is strikingly similar to that of Levinson's definition of art. Levinson allows for both (i) "transparent" art-creative intentions that audiences regard the work in some specific way (e.g., for its emotional expression), which just happens to be a way in which some previous art is correctly regarded, and (ii) "opaque" intentions, for instance that audiences regard the work in ways some previous art is correctly regarded, *whatever those ways are*; Kania allows for (i) music that is intended to have basic musical features, even if they're not intended to be listened to (e.g., Muzak), and (ii) music that is intended not to have basic musical features, but to be listened to *for* them (e.g., Ono's "Toilet Piece"). So although Kania's definition is not specifically *aesthetic*, it does seem torn between defining music as a *medium* and as *artistic uses of* that medium. Indeed, immediately following his introduction of the disjunctive third condition, Kania observes that "[c]ondition 3a should capture most music across history and the globe," including, presumably, music that is not art, "while 3b should capture the remaining modernist and postmodern musical experiments," such as Ono's "Toilet Piece" (Kania 2011b, 11).

A final implication of divorcing the concept of music from that of art is that it makes more plausible one claim that most philosophers have rejected, namely, that non-human animals can make music. Most philosophers have rejected the possibility of such music on the basis that non-human animals lack the complex intentional capacities required for music-making (S. Davies 2012b, 32–3; Gracyk 2013b, 1–34; Hamilton 2007, 49–51; Kania 2011b, 7; Levinson 1990d, 269–70; Scruton 1983, 89–90).[29] We have musical names for certain animal sounds (e.g., "bird song" or "whale song"), but not others (e.g., the dog's bark and cat's meow), according to this view, because the former but not the latter share superficial features with the kinds of music with which we are familiar (though all these animal sounds may simply be, say, warning signals), just as we describe sounds as "musical" without implying that they are literally music (e.g., the babbling of a brook).[30] But if music is basically a matter of cognitive capacities with an evolutionary history, independently of their cultural uses, then it seems an open – and at least partly empirical – question whether other animals share those capacities (Currie & Killin 2016, 19–20).

11.5 Beyond Necessary and Sufficient Conditions

So far, we have considered some recurring themes in attempts to define music, focusing on extant definitions in terms of necessary and sufficient conditions. Now we turn to some theories that attempt to characterize music in other ways. First, we will look at a couple of philosophical theories of music that are not put in terms of necessary and sufficient conditions. Then we will consider some objections to the philosophical methods common to all these attempts and some suggestions for how to proceed in future.

11.5.1 Prototype and Portmanteau Theories of Music

Andy Hamilton (2007) argues that, since it is a cultural phenomenon, we cannot expect a definition of music in terms of necessary and sufficient conditions. He thus restricts himself to arguing for three "salient features" of music: (1) being intentionally produced (52–3), (2) for aesthetic ends (52–6), and (3) consisting of a preponderance of tonally organized sounds (56–9), where that means something like pitches, as characterized in Chapter 4. Puzzlingly, Hamilton makes no mention of rhythm in his chapter on the concept of music, yet he devotes a separate chapter of the same book to rhythm, where he argues that "rhythm is essential" to music, as well as to poetry and dance (2007, 119), "the one indispensable element of all music" (122), and that "music could be defined as [!] the rhythmicization of sound" (121). The most charitable way to understand this, it seems to me, is to consider rhythm, broadly construed, not a necessary feature of all music, as Hamilton literally claims here, but rather as one further salient feature of music, on a par with tonal organization in his account.

Hamilton's approach is reminiscent of the prototype theory of performance that we considered in Chapter 6, §6.1. Something that possesses *all* of Hamilton's salient features will be paradigmatic or prototypical music, while something with only one such feature will be a borderline case, at best (Currie & Killin 2017, 164–7). However, the features Hamilton identifies vary greatly in their degree of salience. Something's merely being intentionally produced, or even intentionally produced for aesthetic ends, gives us little reason to think that it is music. Most sculpture, for instance, will have those features. Thus Hamilton must admit that tonal organization and (I have suggested) rhythm, are much more salient in determining whether something is music. So Hamilton's and Kania's approaches are similar in putting a lot of weight on basic musical features.

In a helpful article, Stephen Davies (2012a) surveys a range of approaches to defining music. He considers the functional approach (e.g., aesthetic definitions), the approach appealing to basic musical features (the "structural" approach), and the socio-historical approach (similar to Levinson's definition of art), among others.[31] Davies rejects each such approach as too simple to match the complexity of music, but he does not conclude that we should abandon the search for a definition. Rather, he suggests, in what we might call a "portmanteau" theory, that we need to combine the best ideas from a variety of approaches:

> The best bet, I think, for defining music would appeal to the intentional use of structural/generative principles viewed historically against the background of musical traditions that are construed sufficiently broadly that they take in not only the immediate practices connected with music making but also the cultural forces that facilitate and structure this.
>
> (S. Davies 2012a, 552)

This suggestion bears a broad resemblance to Kania's definition in appealing both to basic musical features (the "structural/generative principles") and cultural rejigging of those features. The main difference is that Davies implies there will need to be a lot more detail in both parts of the theory than Kania provides. Kania does admit that his references to basic musical features are a kind of promissory note to be filled in by theories of pitch, rhythm, etc., provided by scholars in music theory, psychology, and ethnomusicology. But his final disjunctive condition, allowing for music without basic musical features but intended to be listened to *for* them, is much narrower than what Davies has in mind by "background ... musical traditions" and "cultural forces."

11.5.2 The Methodology of Defining Music

Like Davies, Jonathan McKeown-Green (2014) begins his discussion of the definition of music with counterexamples to the necessity and sufficiency of Kania's proposal.[32] Suppose, for instance, that Kania settles on *meter* as one of the basic musical features to appear in his definition. Both Davies and McKeown-Green argue that this would imply that (i) messages in Morse code will count as music when they clearly should not, and (ii) pitchless, metrically irregular musical works will not count as music when they clearly should (S. Davies 2012a, 538; McKeown-Green 2014, 394). Kania's only hope here is to develop or appeal to a theory of meter complex enough to rule all the right cases in and out.

McKeown-Green raises an even more difficult problem for definitions such as Kania's and Levinson's, however. He notes that implicit in their arguments for their definitions – namely, their reliance on intuitions and musical practices as evidence – is the assumption that "the nature of music is settled by our conception of music" (McKeown-Green 2014, 395, italics removed). Yet Levinson happily excludes Muzak from the realm of music and Kania's definition rules silent music in, even though these are both controversial conclusions from the point of view of ordinary intuitions and practices. If the nature of music *is* settled by our conception of it, an adequate definition should not imply such revisionary conclusions, according to McKeown-Green, but rather leave the borderline cases at the borders (2014, 399–400).

The only way that McKeown-Green sees to fix such a definition, given the assumption, is to make it so detailed that it would essentially become a socio-cultural history of music and thus cease to be a useful definition (McKeown-Green 2014, 397–400). The reason is that what we think of as music (and non-music) is heavily culturally conditioned. For instance, in the early twentieth century, Arnold Schoenberg invented *twelve-tone serialism*, a new form of composition that rejected tonality (including functional harmony) as an organizing principle.[33] Many people found – and still find – serial music inaccessible. Though serialism has apparently secured a permanent place in the history of music, it seems possible that it might have ended up classified as non-music, much as Hamilton and Kania argue that we should distinguish sound art from music. Thus, in order to capture what makes serialism music, a definition must make reference not just to its complex, more-or-less intrinsic features (such as pitch and rhythm), but also to the socio-cultural, historical forces that ultimately saw serialism accepted into the musical fold. For instance, following World War II, serialism was embraced by a new generation of classical composers while rock and roll emerged as the new popular music, contributing to the specialization and marginalization of classical music. Thus it seems that our definition of music must now include reference to World War II.

McKeown-Green illustrates the significance of this point by imagining someone in the mid-nineteenth century coming up with a definition such as Kania's. That definition rules serialism *in* as music (since serial music is intended to have basic musical features), but if serialism's counting as music depends on such contingent historical matters as the effects of World War II on musical practices, then a theorist in the mid-nineteenth century could hit upon the correct definition of music only by luck, since he couldn't know how twentieth-century history would go. Thus, McKeown-Green concludes, no definition of this sort could be "future proof." Will the possibility of silent music be embraced by future listeners and music scholars? This may depend on future contingencies no less predictable than those that resulted in serialism's being accepted as music, so even if a proposed definition gets the answer right, it too can only do so by luck, since things could easily have turned out differently. And if the definition's being right is a matter of luck, we can have no *reason*, here and now, for accepting it as correct.

Moreover, suppose that, in response to McKeown-Green's criticisms, we develop a socio-cultural, historical account of music and clarify that it is intended only as a definition of music *as currently conceived*, not as future-proof. Such a definition would be useless, since it would not serve any of the four functions of a philosophical definition mentioned earlier: It would not (1) illuminate music's nature, (2) give us a practical test for something's being music, (3) explain how we in fact decide whether or not something is music, or (4) help us teach the concept of music to those unfamiliar with it (McKeown-Green 2014, 397–8).

McKeown-Green largely ignores the prototype and portmanteau theories of music defended by Hamilton and Davies. But they, too, seem vulnerable to these objections. McKeown-Green says that "Hamilton's view is not one of my targets: he is not proposing a definition of music in terms of necessary and sufficient conditions; also, his argument is not especially beholden to intuitions or existing institutional rulings" (2014, 402 n. 8). However, first (as McKeown-Green notes in the same place), Hamilton's definition appeals to basic musical features as central to music, in ways that seem to leave it vulnerable to the accusation of not being future-proof.[34] And, second, it is not clear what Hamilton appeals to in defense of his view beyond intuitions and practices. Turning to Davies's proposal, it is not difficult to see his sketch of a definition – with its acknowledgement of the importance to the concept of music of arbitrary cultural forces – as headed in the direction of a socio-cultural history of the sort criticized by McKeown-Green as neither future-proof nor useful.

McKeown-Green's arguments are not wholly negative, however. In addition to the possibility of patching up the kinds of definitions we have already examined, he suggests two further ways of pursuing a definition of music (2014, 400–2). Both require rejecting the assumption that McKeown-Green identifies in Levinson's and Kania's arguments, namely, that the nature of music is settled by our conception of it. Of the two ways, the more distant from traditional philosophical methodology turns the project of defining music into a scientific endeavor. McKeown-Green's analogy is Noam Chomsky's theory of "I-languages." Chomsky argues that linguistics has developed to the point where "all scientific approaches have simply abandoned ... what is called 'language' in common usage" (qtd. in Scholz, Pelletier, & Pullum 2016, §2.2.2). That is, Chomsky offers a theory of language, but does not intend it to be beholden to any ordinary intuitions about language (e.g., that French and Spanish are languages). Indeed, he rejects the idea that there is *anything* theoretically worthwhile to say about our ordinary concept of language. Protests against the unintuitiveness of the theory should carry no more weight, on this view, than protests against the unintuitiveness of physical theories such as quantum mechanics. Physicists do not deny the bizarre appearance of quantum theory; they simply insist that the evidence makes it our best current hypothesis of (certain aspects of) the physical world. If music is like language (on Chomsky's view), then philosophers may have something to contribute to the development of a theory of music (just as philosophers of physics contribute to the development of quantum mechanics), but the bulk of the work will surely fall to those in empirical fields such as psychology and neuroscience.

McKeown-Green's other suggestion is a kind of middle way between the traditional philosophical approach and the scientific approach. According to the "Canberra Plan," championed by philosophers David Lewis and Frank Jackson, the development of adequate theories of things requires not just traditional philosophical conceptual analysis, nor just scientific enquiry, but a combination of the two.[35] We must first figure out our conception of some target of enquiry in order to figure out what sorts of evidence will count as relevant to developing a theory of that target. But our conception does not automatically constitute the correct theory; with the conception in hand, we must examine the evidence. That may involve further philosophical enquiry (e.g., doing some fundamental metaphysics), but will likely also involve empirical enquiry. From this perspective, Chomsky's theory of I-languages may be true and valuable, but it cannot properly be called a, let alone *the*, theory of *language*, if it is not a theory of the sorts of things we are referring to when we ordinarily talk about language. With respect to music, the Canberra Plan suggests that we should pursue the kinds of conceptual analysis that we have seen Levinson, Hamilton, Kania, and Davies engage in until we get a rough consensus – perhaps a point we have already reached – and then turn to empirical disciplines to find out what's really going on, in detail, in the ballpark outlined by that consensus.[36]

11.6 Conclusion

Most of the topics discussed by philosophers of Western music, and hence most of the topics covered in this book, arise from considering Western artistic musical practices. But if music is a medium, like language and pictures, that can be put to artistic and non-artistic uses, then an exclusive focus on artistic musical practices runs the risk of grossly distorting our view of the nature of music itself. Moreover, if music is a medium rather than an art, then it is not clear that philosophy is the discipline best suited to pursuing its definition. While philosophers, here as elsewhere, may have useful contributions to make in guiding and checking empirical research into the medium of music, such research is surely in the domain of more-empirical disciplines such as music theory and music psychology. Even if this is true, however, this leaves philosophers – as I hope is demonstrated throughout this book – with plenty of work to do on a host of fascinating and important questions and puzzles raised by music.

Questions

What, in your view, is the most plausible definition of music in terms of necessary and sufficient conditions? What are the strongest objections to that definition? Can the definition withstand the objections?

What are the best arguments against the possibility of a definition of music in terms of necessary and sufficient conditions? What is the best response to such arguments? What is the most defensible position on this issue?

Are the silences in music *part of* the music? If so, how should they be incorporated into a definition of music? If not, why can't they be omitted from the music?

What implications do the musical experiences of d/Deaf people have for the definition of music?

Is music essentially an art, or is it a medium (like language or pictures) that can be put to artistic and non-artistic ends? What implications does your answer have for the definition of music?

Notes

1   That is, there was only a single, short "beat." But both Jack and Meg White played on the beat – Jack a single note (F?) and Meg a quickly damped cymbal crash and kick-drum hit. Several amateur videos of the show are available on YouTube. A professional film of it is included on the band's 2009 DVD, *Under Great White Northern Lights*.

2   "Iff" is a standard philosophical abbreviation for "if and only if." It functions as a "conceptual equals sign," that is, what appears to its left is equivalent to what appears to its right (just as "2+2" is equivalent to "4" in "2+2=4"). The connection to necessary and sufficient conditions is that "if" introduces a sufficient condition (e.g., X is a rectangle if X is a square), while "only if" introduces a necessary condition (e.g., X is a square only if X has four sides). Thus "if and only if" introduces a (possibly complex) condition that is both necessary and sufficient.

3   See, for example, Levinson 1990d, 269; Hamilton 2007, 40; and Scruton 1997, 16 (though none of these philosophers endorse the idea in this simplistic form).

4   Interestingly, there is no pause on the rest in the string quartet movement of which the more famous string-orchestra version is Barber's own arrangement.

5   A notable exception is Julian Dodd (2018).

6   Many people think that the work is for piano (or, at least, pianist!) and, for obvious reasons, that its length is unambiguous. But Cage notes, in the paragraph that constitutes most of the score, that: "The title of this work is the total length in minutes and seconds of its performance. ... However, the work may be performed by any instrumentalist or combination of instrumentalists and last any length of time" (Cage 1960). An excellent 2004 performance by the BBC Symphony Orchestra is unfortunately no longer available on YouTube. Recordings of the piece on Spotify are unreliable.

7 Again, in the interest of neutrality, I discuss my own views in the third person.

8 There is a long history of musical jokes, one of the most famous being Mozart's *Musikalisches Spaß* ("Musical Joke," K522).

9 We will consider Kania's complete definition below.

10 Useful starting points are O'Callaghan 2016 and Sorensen 2009.

11 Two clarifications: (1) I do not mean to imply that curbs and "white only" signs are equally oppressive, only that they are both argued to be oppressive in the same way, i.e., by unjustly restricting people's movement. (2) The term "disability" is unfortunately ambiguous. Disability-studies theorists and many disabled people reject the negative connotations of the term (partly arising from its etymology), yet, as the term "disability studies" suggests, many have also reclaimed the term for their own purposes, much as the sexually diverse have reclaimed the term "queer."

12 Whether "normal," in such contexts, is a neutral objective classification or a value-laden culturally-constructed classification is a matter of dispute. See, for example, Straus 2011, 6–8, 152–7.

13 Throughout the following discussion, I am heavily indebted to Holmes 2017.

14 Investigating the third stereotype would take us too far afield. See Holmes 2017, 182–90, and Straus 2011, especially 1–62 and 125–81.

15 Compare Tiger Roholt's theory of understanding grooves (2014), discussed in Chapter 4, §4.2.

16 "Musical" sometimes means *not music, but like music*; here I intend the strict sense – a sound that *is music*.

17 The numbering of the conditions is mine, though Levinson argues for each condition individually in the preceding pages.

18 I assume throughout that Merzbow's work does not meet Kania's condition 3(b).

19 Whether *any* artistic sounds could be "pure" is disputed by Stephen Davies (1997b, 448–53).

20 This would make them a bit like the dove in one of Roger Scruton's examples: "Does the dove hear the subtle rhythm that we perceive in his call? ... If he heard that rhythm, would he not be persuaded of the merits of another?" (1983, 90).

21 We first considered the notion of aesthetic experience in Chapter 5, §5.1.1.

22 It is worth noting that one could argue for a definition that appealed to *both* an aesthetic condition *and* basic musical features. Roger Scruton (1997, 1–96) and Andy Hamilton (2007, 40–65) defend such theories, though they resist giving *definitions* of music in terms of necessary and sufficient conditions, for reasons we will consider in the next section.

23 Note that if Levinson is correct, it will be extremely difficult, if not logically impossible, to test the effects of music on an unengaged listener. For if you intend them to be unengaged, what you produce will be disqualified as music!

24 Scruton implies that Muzak is (bad) music (1997, 374–5); Kania agrees (2011b, 10). Hamilton is "not sure whether to argue that muzak is not music" (2007, 55).

25 A notable exception is Lopes 2014.

26 Hamilton wavers a little. At one point he says that "[m]y concern here is with the question 'what is music?', understood as on the level of 'what is language?' and 'what is depiction?' – though it is, I believe, inextricably linked with the question 'how do we conceive of music?', in a way not paralleled by the questions about language and depiction" (2007, 46).

27 This definition can at best characterize *most* art, since there must be some first art or "*ur*-art" to get the process going. Levinson addresses this issue elsewhere (e.g., 1979, 242–4). For references to the extensive discussion of Levinson's definition, see Levinson 2002.

28 One practical problem for this view is that we do not have distinct words in English for *music in general* and *music that is art*, as we do in the cases of language and literature, or pictures and paintings (or prints or drawings). However, as these examples show, we don't have particularly systematic language for these distinctions, either, and we do not get too confused. While "literature" means something like "artistic language," terms such as "painting" and "prints" name certain art forms (the equivalents of "poetry," "novels," and so on). Perhaps we should

talk of "the musical arts" as we do of "the visual arts." (German has two words, *Musik* and *Tonkunst* that etymologically suggest the distinction between music and "tone art." But the latter term is now somewhat archaic; it is certainly not used to mark the distinction being discussed here.)

29 For cautious dissent, see Higgins 2012, 17–35. Davies argues that the "songs" of male humpback whales are the best actual candidates for non-human art, because their variation and hierarchical structure is "suggestive of the musical generativity that ... is absent from birdsong" (2012b, 34).

30 The assumption that music is art may thus lurk behind the tendency of philosophers of art to defend Intentional rather than subjective definitions of music.

31 Davies devotes a separate section to the approach of appealing to "musical universals," but it seems to me that this is an instance of the structural approach.

32 Davies discusses Levinson's definition at the same time; McKeown-Green turns to Levinson's definition later in his essay.

33 Some later serialists reintegrated functional harmony with serialism.

34 Hamilton's definition is also vulnerable to counterexamples, of course (Currie & Killin 2017, 164–7).

35 For short introductions to the Canberra Plan, see Papineau 2016, §2.3, and Kingsbury and McKeown-Green 2009; the classic book-length introduction and defense is Jackson 1998.

36 McKeown-Green thinks that Davies's proposal is of this Canberra-Plan type. I have my doubts since, as discussed above, it seems vulnerable to the kinds of criticism McKeown-Green levels against Levinson's and Kania's definitions.

Further Reading

Michael Nyman's *Experimental Music* (second edition, 1999) is an excellent introduction to avant-garde music (depending on your definition of music!) of the latter half of the twentieth century. Douglas Kahn's *Noise, Water, Meat* (1999) is a history of noise- and sound art from the late-nineteenth to mid-twentieth century; Brandon LaBelle picks up where Kahn leaves off and continues through the early twenty-first century in *Background Noise* (2006).

Two philosophical articles devoted to musical silence and silent music are Jennifer Judkins's "The Aesthetics of Silence" (1997) and Andrew Kania's "Silent Music" (2010). An excellent introduction to John Cage's *4'33"* is Kyle Gann's *No Such Things as Silence* (2010); philosophical discussions of the piece include articles by Noël Carroll (1994), Stephen Davies (1997b), Andrew Kania (2010), and Julian Dodd (2018).

There has been very little discussion by philosophers of disability (including deafness) in connection with music. Good starting points by musicologists include Jessica Holmes's article "Expert Listening beyond the Limits of Hearing" (2017), Joseph Straus's monograph *Extraordinary Measures* (2011), the collection of essays *Sounding Off* (Lerner & Strauss 2006), and *The Oxford Handbook of Music and Disability Studies* (Howe, Jensen-Moulton, Lerner, & Straus 2016).

Bibliography

So that the chronology of the dialogue between philosophers is clearer in the text, I have slightly adapted Chicago format in my references. The date following the author's name is the date of first publication. Where the text I have cited is a later reprint, the date of the reprinting publication is listed after the publisher. For example, Hume's essay "Of the Standard of Taste" was originally published in 1757, but I have cited its reprinting in a 2008 anthology, as follows:

Hume, David. 1757a. "Of the Standard of Taste." *Aesthetics: A Comprehensive Anthology.* Ed. Steven M. Cahn & Aaron Meskin. Malden, MA: Blackwell, 2008. 103–12.

Where a journal article has been republished in a collection, I prefer to cite the original article, since so many journals are now available online, at least to people affiliated with academic institutions.

Abell, Catharine. 2013. "Depiction." *The Routledge Companion to Aesthetics.* Ed. Berys Gaut & Dominic McIver Lopes. 3rd edition. New York: Routledge. 362–72.

Adajian, Thomas. 2005. "On the Prototype Theory of Concepts and the Definition of Art." *Journal of Aesthetics and Art Criticism* 63: 231–6.

Adams, Zed. 2018. "Surface Noise." *British Journal of Aesthetics* 58: 255–70.

Alcaraz León, María José. 2012. "Music's Moral Character." *Teorema* 31: 179–91.

Allinson, Ewan. 1994. "It's a Black Thing: Hearing How Whites Can't." *Cultural Studies* 8: 438–56.

Alperson, Philip. 1984. "On Musical Improvisation." *Journal of Aesthetics and Art Criticism* 43: 17–29.

Alperson, Philip. 2014. "Music and Morality." *Ethics and the Arts.* Ed. Paul Macneill. New York: Springer. 21–31.

Aristotle. 2018. *Poetics.* Trans. James Hutton. Ed. & rev. Michelle Zerba & David Gorman. New York: Norton.

Baraka, Amiri. 1987. "The Great Music Robbery." *The Music: Reflections on Jazz and Blues.* New York: Morrow. 328–32.

Baraka, Amiri. 1990. "Jazz Criticism." *New Perspectives on Jazz.* Ed. David N. Baker. Washington, DC: Smithsonian Institution Press. 55–70.

Barkin, Elaine & Lydia Hamessley, eds. 1999. *Audible Traces: Gender, Identity, and Music.* Zürich: Carciofoli Verlaghaus.

Bartel, Christopher. 2017. "Rock as a Three-Value Tradition." *Journal of Aesthetics and Art Criticism* 75: 143–54.

Bartky, Sandra. 1990. "On Psychological Oppression." *Feminist Theory: A Philosophical Anthology*. Ed. Ann E. Cudd & Robin O. Andreasen. Malden, MA: Blackwell. 105–13.

Baugh, Bruce. 1993. "Prolegomena to Any Aesthetics of Rock Music." *Journal of Aesthetics and Art Criticism* 51: 23–9.

Baugh, Bruce. 1995. "Music for the Young at Heart." *Journal of Aesthetics and Art Criticism* 53: 81–83.

Bent, Ian D. & Anthony Pople. 2018. "Analysis." *Grove Music Online*. www.oxfordmusiconline.com/grovemusic/view/10.1093/gmo/9781561592630.001.0001/omo-9781561592630-e-0000041862. Oxford University Press. Accessed May 16, 2018.

Bergeron, Vincent & Dominic McIver Lopes. 2009. "Hearing and Seeing Musical Expression." *Philosophy and Phenomenological Research* 78: 1–16.

Bicknell, Jeanette. 2005. "Just a Song? Exploring the Aesthetics of Popular Song Performance." *Journal of Aesthetics and Art Criticism* 63: 261–70.

Bicknell, Jeanette. 2015. *Philosophy of Song and Singing: An Introduction*. New York: Routledge.

Bigand, Emmanuel & Bénédicte Poulin-Charronnat. 2009. "Tonal Cognition." *The Oxford Handbook of Music Psychology*. Ed. Susan Hallam, Ian Cross, & Michael Thaut. Oxford: Oxford University Press. 59–71.

Boghossian, Paul. 2010. "The Perception of Music: Comments on Peacocke." *British Journal of Aesthetics* 50: 71–6.

Bonds, Mark Evan. 2014. *Absolute Music: The History of an Idea*. Oxford: Oxford University Press.

Bowman, Wayne D. 1998. *Philosophical Perspectives on Music*. Oxford: Oxford University Press.

Brendel, Alfred. 2001. *Alfred Brendel on Music*. Chicago: A Cappella.

Brett, Philip, Elizabeth Wood, & Gary C. Thomas, eds. 2006. *Queering the Pitch: The New Gay and Lesbian Musicology*. 2nd edition. New York: Routledge.

Briscoe, Robert Eamon. 2017. "Multisensory Processing and Perceptual Consciousness: Part II." *Philosophy Compass* 12.12: e1–e13.

Brown, Lee B. 1996. "Musical Works, Improvisation, and the Principle of Continuity." *Journal of Aesthetics and Art Criticism* 54: 353–69.

Brown, Lee B. 2000a. "'Feeling My Way': Jazz Improvisation and Its Vicissitudes – A Plea for Imperfection." *Journal of Aesthetics and Art Criticism* 58: 113–23.

Brown, Lee B. 2000b. "Phonography, Repetition and Spontaneity." *Philosophy and Literature* 24: 111–25.

Brown, Lee B. 2011a. "Improvisation." *The Routledge Companion to Philosophy and Music*. Ed. Theodore Gracyk & Andrew Kania. New York: Routledge. 59–69.

Brown, Lee B. 2011b. "Do Higher-Order Music Ontologies Rest on a Mistake?" *British Journal of Aesthetics*. 51: 169–84.

Brown, Lee B. 2012. "Further Doubts about Higher-Order Musical Ontology." *British Journal of Aesthetics* 52: 103–6.

Brown, Lee B., David Goldblatt, & Theodore Gracyk. 2018. *Jazz and the Philosophy of Art*. New York: Routledge.

Bruno, Franklin. 2013. "A Case for Song: Against an (Exclusively) Recording-Centered Ontology of Rock." *Journal of Aesthetics and Art Criticism* 71: 65–74.

Budd, Malcolm. 1985. "Understanding Music." *Proceedings of the Aristotelian Society*. Supplementary volume 59: 233–48.

Budd, Malcolm. 1995. *Values of Art: Pictures, Poetry, and Music*. London: Penguin.

Budd, Malcolm. 2003. "Musical Movement and Aesthetic Metaphors." *British Journal of Aesthetics* 43: 209–23.

Cage, John. 1960. *4'33"*. Glendale: Edition Peters.

Calvino, Italo. 1979. *If on a Winter's Night a Traveler*. Trans. William Weaver. New York: Harcourt, Brace, Jovanovich, 1981.

Caplan, Ben & Carl Matheson. 2006. "Defending Musical Perdurantism." *British Journal of Aesthetics* 46: 59–69.

Caplan, Ben & Carl Matheson. 2011. "Ontology." *The Routledge Companion to Philosophy and Music*. Ed. Theodore Gracyk & Andrew Kania. New York: Routledge. 38–47.

Carroll, Noël. 1988. *Mystifying Movies: Fads and Fallacies in Contemporary Film Theory*. New York: Columbia University Press.

Carroll, Noël. 1990. *The Philosophy of Horror or Paradoxes of the Heart*. New York: Routledge.

Carroll, Noël. 1994. "Cage and Philosophy." *Journal of Aesthetics and Art Criticism* 52: 93–8.

Carroll, Noël. 1996. "Defining the Moving Image." *Theorizing the Moving Image*. Cambridge: Cambridge University Press. 49–74.

Carroll, Noël. 2003. "Art and Mood: Preliminary Notes and Conjectures." *Monist* 86: 521–55.

Cheyne, Peter, Andy Hamilton, & Max Paddison, eds. 2019. *The Philosophy of Rhythm: Aesthetics, Music, Poetics*. Oxford: Oxford University Press.

Citron, Marcia J. 1994. "Feminist Approaches to Musicology." *Cecilia Reclaimed: Feminist Perspectives on Gender and Music*. Ed. Susan C. Cook & Judy S. Tsou. Urbana, IL: University of Illinois Press. 15–34.

Cochrane, Tom. 2009. "Joint Attention to Music." *British Journal of Aesthetics* 49: 59–73.

Coleridge, Samuel Taylor. 1817. *Biographia Literaria: Or, Biographical Sketches of My Literary Life and Opinions*. Ed. Nigel Leask. Rutland, VT: Charles E. Tuttle, 1997.

Collingwood, R.G. 1938. *The Principles of Art*. Oxford: Oxford University Press.

Cone, Edward T. 1960. "Analysis Today." *Music, A View from Delft: Selected Essays*. Chicago: University of Chicago Press, 1989. 39–54.

Cooke, Deryck. 1959. *The Language of Music*. Oxford: Oxford University Press.

Covach, John & Andrew Flory. 2015. *What's that Sound? An Introduction to Rock and Its History*. 4th edition. New York: Norton.

Cray, Wesley D. 2019. "Transparent and Opaque Performance Personas." *Journal of Aesthetics and Art Criticism* 77: 181–91.

Cray, Wesley D. & Carl Matheson. 2017. "A Return to Musical Idealism." *Australasian Journal of Philosophy* 95: 702–15.

Crum, Joshua. 2008. "The Day the (Digital) Music Died: *Bridgeport*, Sampling Infringement, and a Proposed Middle Ground." *Brigham Young University Law Review* 2008: 943–69.

Currie, Adrian & Anton Killin. 2016. "Musical Pluralism and the Science of Music." *European Journal of the Philosophy of Science* 6: 9–30.

Currie, Adrian & Anton Killin. 2017. "Not Music, But Musics: A Case for Conceptual Pluralism in Aesthetics." *Estetika* 54: 151–74.

Currie, Gregory. 1989. *An Ontology of Art*. New York: St. Martin's Press.

Currie, Gregory. 1993. "The Long Goodbye: The Imaginary Language of Film." *British Journal of Aesthetics* 33: 207–20.

Currie, Gregory. 1995. *Image and Mind: Film, Philosophy, and Cognitive Science*. Cambridge: Cambridge University Press.

Currie, Gregory. 2003. "Interpretation in Art." *The Oxford Handbook of Aesthetics*. Ed. Jerrold Levinson. Oxford: Oxford University Press. 291–306.

Currie, Gregory. 2010. *Narratives & Narrators: A Philosophy of Stories*. Oxford: Oxford University Press.

Cusick, Suzanne G. 1994. "Gender and the Cultural Work of a Classical Music Performance." *Repercussions* 3: 77–110.

Cusick, Suzanne G. 2008. "'You are in a place that is out of the world … ': Music in the Detention Camps of the 'Global War on Terror'." *Journal of the Society for American Music* 2: 1–26.

Dammann, Guy. 2016. "The Nobel Prize for Literature, at Long Last, Has Been Awarded to a Complete Idiot." *The Spectator*. https://blogs.spectator.co.uk/2016/10/nobel-prize-literature-long-last-awarded-complete-idiot/. Accessed August 28, 2017.

Danto, Arthur. 1964. "The Artworld." *Journal of Philosophy* 61: 571–84.

Davies, David. 2004. *Art as Performance*. Malden, MA: Blackwell.

Davies, David. 2007. *Aesthetics and Literature*. London: Continuum.

Davies, David. 2011. *Philosophy of the Performing Arts*. Malden, MA: Wiley-Blackwell.

Davies, David. 2013a. "Categories of Art." *The Routledge Companion to Aesthetics*. Ed. Berys Gaut & Dominic McIver Lopes. 3rd edition. New York: Routledge. 224–34.

Davies, David. 2013b. "The Dialogue between Words and Music in the Composition and Comprehension of Song." *Journal of Aesthetics and Art Criticism* 71: 13–22.

Davies, David. 2017. "Descriptivism and Its Discontents." *Journal of Aesthetics and Art Criticism* 75: 117–29.

Davies, David. Forthcoming. "Analytic Philosophy of Music." *Oxford Handbook of Western Music and Philosophy*. Ed. Tomas McAuley, Nanette Nielsen, & Jerrold Levinson, with Ariana Phillips-Hutton. Vol. 1. Oxford: Oxford University Press.

Davies, Stephen. 1980. "The Expression of Emotion in Music." *Mind* 89 (new series): 67–86.

Davies, Stephen. 1987. "The Evaluation of Music." *Themes in the Philosophy of Music*. Oxford: Oxford University Press, 2003. 195–212.

Davies, Stephen. 1991. "The Ontology of Musical Works and the Authenticity of Their Performances." *Noûs* 25: 21–41.

Davies, Stephen. 1994. *Musical Meaning and Expression*. Ithaca: Cornell University Press.

Davies, Stephen. 1997a. "Contra the Hypothetical Persona in Music." *Emotion and the Arts*. Ed. Mette Hjort & Sue Laver. Oxford: Oxford University Press. 95–109.

Davies, Stephen. 1997b. "John Cage's *4'33"*: Is It Music?" *Australasian Journal of Philosophy* 75: 448–62.

Davies, Stephen. 1999. "Rock versus Classical Music." *Journal of Aesthetics and Art Criticism* 57: 193–204.

Davies, Stephen. 2001. *Musical Works and Performances: A Philosophical Exploration*. Oxford: Oxford University Press.

Davies, Stephen. 2002a. "The Multiple Interpretability of Musical Works." *Is There a Single Right Interpretation?* Ed. Michael Krausz. University Park: Pennsylvania State University Press. 231–50.

Davies, Stephen. 2002b. "Profundity in Instrumental Music." *British Journal of Aesthetics* 42: 343–56.

Davies, Stephen. 2003. "Ontologies of Musical Works." *Themes in the Philosophy of Music*. Oxford: Oxford University Press. 30–46.

Davies, Stephen. 2006. "Artistic Expression and the Hard Case of Pure Music." *Contemporary Debates in Aesthetics and the Philosophy of Art*. Ed. Matthew Kieran. Malden, MA: Blackwell. 179–91.

Davies, Stephen. 2010. "Emotions Expressed and Aroused by Music: Philosophical Perspectives." *Handbook of Music and Emotion: Theory, Research, Applications*. Ed. Patrik N. Juslin & John Sloboda. Oxford: Oxford University Press. 15–43.

Davies, Stephen. 2011a. "Cross-cultural Musical Expressiveness: Theory and the Empirical Program." *Musical Understandings & Other Essays on the Philosophy of Music*. Oxford: Oxford University Press. 34–46.

Davies, Stephen. 2011b. "Emotional Contagion from Music to Listener." *Musical Understandings & Other Essays on the Philosophy of Music*. Oxford: Oxford University Press. 47–65.

Davies, Stephen. 2011c. "Music and Metaphor." *Musical Understandings & Other Essays on the Philosophy of Music*. Oxford: Oxford University Press. 21–33.

Davies, Stephen. 2011d. "Musical Understandings." *Musical Understandings & Other Essays on the Philosophy of Music*. Oxford: Oxford University Press. 88–128.

Davies, Stephen. 2011e. "Notations." *The Routledge Companion to Philosophy and Music*. Ed. Theodore Gracyk & Andrew Kania. New York: Routledge. 70–9.

Davies, Stephen. 2011f. "Versions of Musical Works and Literary Translations." *Musical Understandings & Other Essays on the Philosophy of Music*. Oxford: Oxford University Press. 177–87.

Davies, Stephen. 2012a. "On Defining Music." *The Monist* 95: 535–55.

Davies, Stephen. 2012b. *The Artful Species: Aesthetics, Art, and Evolution*. Oxford: Oxford University Press.

Davies, Stephen. 2013. "Performing Musical Works Authentically." *British Journal of Aesthetics* 53: 71–5.

Davies, Stephen. 2015. "Defining Art and Artworlds." *Journal of Aesthetics and Art Criticism* 73: 375–84.

Davies, Stephen. 2016. *The Philosophy of Art*. 2nd edition. Malden, MA: Wiley.

De Clercq, Rafael. 2007. "Melody and Metaphorical Movement." *British Journal of Aesthetics* 47: 156–68.

Dean, Jeffrey. 2003. "The Nature of Concepts and the Definition of Art." *Journal of Aesthetics and Art Criticism* 61: 29–35.

DeBellis, Mark. 1991. "Conceptions of Musical Structure." *Midwest Studies in Philosophy* 16 (Philosophy and the Arts): 378–93.

DeBellis, Mark. 1995. *Music and Conceptualization*. Cambridge: Cambridge University Press.

Deutsch, Diana. 2013. "The Processing of Pitch Combinations." *The Psychology of Music*. Ed. Diana Deutsch. 3rd edition. New York: Academic Press. 249–325.

Dewey, John. 1934. *Art as Experience*. New York: Minton, Balch.

Dipert, Randall R. 1980. "The Composer's Intentions: An Examination of Their Relevance for Performance." *Musical Quarterly* 66: 205–18.

Dodd, Julian. 2007. *Works of Music: An Essay in Ontology*. Oxford: Oxford University Press.

Dodd, Julian. 2013. "Adventures in the Metaontology of Art: Local Descriptivism, Artefacts and Dreamcatchers." *Philosophical Studies* 165: 1047–68.

Dodd, Julian. 2014a. "The Possibility of Profound Music." *British Journal of Aesthetics* 54: 288–322.

Dodd, Julian. 2014b. "Upholding Standards." *Journal of Aesthetics and Art Criticism* 72: 277–90.

Dodd, Julian. 2015. "Performing Works of Music Authentically." *European Journal of Philosophy* 23: 485–508.

Dodd, Julian. 2018. "What *4'33"* Is." *Australasian Journal of Philosophy* 96: 629–41.

Dodd, Julian. Forthcoming. *Being True to Works of Music*. Oxford: Oxford University Press.

Dodd, Julian & John Irving. Forthcoming. "Authenticity." *The Oxford Handbook of Western Music and Philosophy*. Ed. Tomas McAuley, Nanette Nielsen, & Jerrold Levinson, with Ariana Phillips-Hutton. Vol. 2. Oxford: Oxford University Press.

Dubiel, Joseph. 2011. "Analysis." *The Routledge Companion to Philosophy and Music*. Ed. Theodore Gracyk & Andrew Kania. New York: Routledge. 525–34.

Dutton, Denis. 2003. "Authenticity in Art." *The Oxford Handbook of Aesthetics*. Ed. Jerrold Levinson. Oxford: Oxford University Press. 258–74.

Dyck, John. 2014. "Perfect Compliance in Musical History and Musical Ontology." *British Journal of Aesthetics* 54: 31–47.

Dylan, Bob. 1971. *Tarantula*. New York: Macmillan.

Dylan, Bob. 2014. *The Lyrics: Since 1962*. Ed. Christopher Ricks, Lisa Nemrow, & Julie Nemrow. London: Simon and Schuster.

Eaton, A.W. 2009. "Almodóvar's Immoralism." *Talk to Her*. Ed. A.W. Eaton. New York: Routledge. 11–26.

Edidin, Aron. 1997. "Performing Compositions." *British Journal of Aesthetics* 37: 323–35.

Edidin, Aron. 1999. "Three Kinds of Recording and the Metaphysics of Music." *British Journal of Aesthetics* 39: 24–39.

Ekman, Paul. 1993. "Facial Expression and Emotion." *American Psychologist* 48: 384–92.

Engdahl, Horace. 2016. Award Ceremony Speech. *Nobelprize.org*. www.nobelprize.org/nobel_prizes/literature/laureates/2016/presentation-speech.html. Nobel Media. Accessed August 28, 2017.

Ereshefsky, Marc. 2017. "Species." *The Stanford Encyclopedia of Philosophy*. Ed. Edward N. Zalta. Fall 2017 edition. https://plato.stanford.edu/entries/species/. Accessed July 2, 2018.

Evans, David. 2002. "The Development of the Blues." *The Cambridge Companion to Blues and Gospel Music*. Ed. Allan Moore. Cambridge: Cambridge University Press. 20–43.

Fabb, Nigel & Morris Halle. 2008. *Meter in Poetry: A New Theory*. Cambridge: Cambridge University Press.

Fallows, David. 2001a. "Metronome (I)." *Grove Music Online*. www.oxfordmusiconline.com.libproxy.trinity.edu/grovemusic/view/10.1093/gmo/9781561592630.001.0001/omo-9781561592630-e-0000018521. Accessed December 1, 2016.

Fallows, David. 2001b. "Tempo and Expression Marks." *Grove Music Online*. www.oxfordmusiconline.com/subscriber/article/grove/music/27650. Accessed December 1, 2016.

Feagin, Susan L. 1983. "The Pleasures of Tragedy." *American Philosophical Quarterly* 20: 95–104.

Festenstein, Matthew. 2018. "Dewey's Political Philosophy." *The Stanford Encyclopedia of Philosophy*. Ed. Edward N. Zalta. Fall 2018 edition. https://plato.stanford.edu/entries/dewey-political/. Accessed June 20, 2019.

Fisher, John Andrew. 1998. "Rock 'n' Recording: The Ontological Complexity of Rock Music." *Musical Worlds: New Directions in the Philosophy of Music*. Ed. Philip Alperson. University Park: Pennsylvania State University Press. 109–23.

Fisher, John Andrew. 2011. "Popular Music." *The Routledge Companion to Philosophy and Music*. Ed. Theodore Gracyk & Andrew Kania. New York: Routledge. 405–15.

Fisher, John Andrew. 2018. "Jazz and Musical Works." *Journal of Aesthetics and Art Criticism* 76: 151–62.

Gaines, James R. 2005. *Evening in the Palace of Reason: Bach Meets Frederick the Great in the Age of Enlightenment*. New York: HarperCollins.

Gambaccini, David. 1974. "Paul McCartney: The Rolling Stone Interview." *Rolling Stone*. January 31, 1974. Available at www.rollingstone.com/music/features/the-rolling-stone-interview-paul-mccartney-19740131. Accessed February 21, 2018.

Gann, Kyle. 2010. *No Such Thing as Silence: John Cage's 4'33"*. New Haven, CT: Yale University Press.

Garner, Bryan A. 2016. *Garner's Modern English Usage*. 4th edition. (Previous editions titled *Garner's Modern American Usage*.) Oxford: Oxford University Press.

Gaut, Berys. 1993. "The Paradox of Horror." *British Journal of Aesthetics* 33: 333–45.

Gaut, Berys. 2003. "Film." *The Oxford Handbook of Aesthetics*. Ed. Jerrold Levinson. Oxford: Oxford University Press. 627–43.

Gaut, Berys. 2007. *Art, Emotion and Ethics*. Oxford: Oxford University Press.

Gaut, Berys. 2010. *A Philosophy of Cinematic Art*. Cambridge: Cambridge University Press.

Gaut, Berys. 2013. "Art and Ethics." *The Routledge Companion to Aesthetics*. Ed. Berys Gaut & Dominic McIver Lopes. 3rd edition. New York: Routledge. 394–403.

Gaut, Berys & Dominic McIver Lopes, eds. 2013. *The Routledge Companion to Aesthetics*. 3rd edition. New York: Routledge.

Gioia, Ted. 1988. *The Imperfect Art: Reflections on Jazz and Modern Culture*. Oxford: Oxford University Press.

Gioia, Ted. 2006. *Work Songs*. Durham, NC: Duke University Press.

Glasgow, Joshua. 2007. "Hi-Fi Aesthetics." *Journal of Aesthetics and Art Criticism* 65: 163–74.

Godlovitch, Stan. 1998. *Musical Performance: A Philosophical Study*. New York: Routledge.

Goehr, Lydia. 1992. *The Imaginary Museum of Musical Works: An Essay in the Philosophy of Music*. Revised edition. Oxford: Oxford University Press, 2007.

Goldman, Alan. 1992. "The Value of Music." *Journal of Aesthetics and Art Criticism* 50: 35–44.

Goldman, Alan. 2002. "The Sun Also Rises: Incompatible Interpretations." *Is There a Single Right Interpretation?* Ed. Michael Krausz. University Park: Pennsylvania State University Press. 9–25.

Goodman, Nelson. 1968. *Languages of Art: An Approach to a Theory of Symbols*. 2nd edition. Indianapolis: Hackett, 1976.

Gould, Carol S. & Kenneth Keaton. 2000. "The Essential Role of Improvisation in Musical Performance." *Journal of Aesthetics and Art Criticism* 58: 143–8.

Gracyk, Theodore. 1996. *Rhythm and Noise: An Aesthetics of Rock*. Durham, NC: Duke University Press.

Gracyk, Theodore. 1997. "Listening to Music: Performances and Recordings." *Journal of Aesthetics and Art Criticism* 55: 139–50.

Gracyk, Theodore. 2001. *I Wanna Be Me: Rock Music and the Politics of Identity*. Philadelphia: Temple University Press.

Gracyk, Theodore. 2007. *Listening to Popular Music: Or, How I Learned to Stop Worrying and Love Led Zeppelin*. Ann Arbor, MI: University of Michigan Press.

Gracyk, Theodore. 2009. "The Song Remains the Same, but Not Always." *Led Zeppelin and Philosophy: All Will Be Revealed*. Ed. Scott Calef. Chicago: Open Court. 31–45.

Gracyk, Theodore. 2012–13. "Covers and Communicative Intentions." *Journal of Music and Meaning* 11: 22–46.

Gracyk, Theodore. 2013a. "Meanings of Songs and Meanings of Song Performances." *Journal of Aesthetics and Art Criticism* 71: 23–33.

Gracyk, Theodore. 2013b. *On Music*. New York: Routledge.

Gracyk, Theodore. 2017. "Performer, Persona, and the Evaluation of Musical Performance." *Contemporary Aesthetics* 15. www.contempaesthetics.org/newvolume/pages/article.php?articleID=801. Accessed May 25, 2018.

Gracyk, Theodore & Andrew Kania, eds. 2011. *The Routledge Companion to Philosophy and Music*. New York: Routledge.

Graham, Gordon. 2007. "Music and Electro-sonic Art." *Philosophers on Music: Experience, Meaning, and Work*. Ed. Kathleen Stock. Oxford: Oxford University Press. 209–25.

Hagberg, Garry L. 1998. "Improvisation: Jazz Improvisation." *Encyclopedia of Aesthetics*. Ed. Michael Kelly. New York: Oxford University Press. Volume 1, 479–82.

Hagberg, Garry L. 2002. "On Representing Jazz: An Art Form in Need of Understanding." *Philosophy and Literature* 26: 188–98.

Hagberg, Garry L. 2013. "Metaphor." *The Routledge Companion to Aesthetics*. Ed. Berys Gaut & Dominic McIver Lopes. 3rd edition. New York: Routledge. 351–61.

Hamilton, Andy. 2000. "The Art of Improvisation and the Aesthetics of Imperfection." *British Journal of Aesthetics* 40: 168–85.

Hamilton, Andy. 2003. "The Art of Recording and the Aesthetics of Perfection." *British Journal of Aesthetics* 43: 345–62.

Hamilton, Andy. 2007. *Aesthetics and Music*. London: Continuum.

Hamilton, Andy. 2011. "Adorno." *The Routledge Companion to Philosophy and Music*. Ed. Theodore Gracyk & Andrew Kania. New York: Routledge. 391–402.

Hanslick, Eduard. 1854. *On the Musically Beautiful: A Contribution Towards the Revision of the Aesthetics of Music*. Trans. & ed. Geoffrey Payzant, from the 8th edition (1891). Indianapolis: Hackett, 1986.

Harold, James. 2016. "On the Ancient Idea that Music Shapes Character." *Dao* 15: 341–54.

Harrison, Daniel. 1997. "After Sundown: The Beach Boys' Experimental Music." *Understanding Rock: Essays in Musical Analysis*. Ed. John Covach & Graeme M. Boone. Oxford: Oxford University Press. 33–57.

Headlam, Dave. 2002. "Appropriations of Blues and Gospel in Popular Music." *The Cambridge Companion to Blues and Gospel Music*. Ed. Allan Moore. Cambridge: Cambridge University Press. 158–87.

Hick, Darren Hudson. 2017. *Artistic License: The Philosophical Problems of Copyright and Appropriation*. Chicago: University of Chicago Press.

Higgins, Kathleen Marie. 1991. *The Music of Our Lives*. Philadelphia: Temple University Press.

Higgins, Kathleen Marie. 2012. *The Music between Us: Is Music a Universal Language?* Chicago: Chicago University Press.

Higgins, Kathleen Marie. 2017. "Global Aesthetics – What Can We Do?" *Journal of Aesthetics and Art Criticism* 75: 339–49.

Hills, David. 2017. "Metaphor." *The Stanford Encyclopedia of Philosophy*. Ed. Edward N. Zalta. Fall 2017 edition. https://plato.stanford.edu/archives/fall2017/entries/metaphor/. Accessed February 26, 2018.

Holmes, Jessica A. 2017. "Expert Listening beyond the Limits of Hearing: Music and Deafness." *Journal of the American Musicological Society* 70: 171–220.

Howe, Blake, Stephanie Jensen-Moulton, Neil Lerner, & Joseph Straus, eds. 2016. *The Oxford Handbook of Music and Disability Studies*. Oxford: Oxford University Press.

Hume, David. 1757a. "Of the Standard of Taste." *Aesthetics: A Comprehensive Anthology*. Ed. Steven M. Cahn & Aaron Meskin. Malden, MA: Blackwell, 2008. 103–12.

Hume, David. 1757b. "Of Tragedy." *Selected Essays*. Ed. Stephen Copley & Andrew Edgar. Oxford: Oxford University Press, 1998. 126–33.

Huovinen, Erkki. 2008. "Levels and Kinds of Listeners' Musical Understanding." *British Journal of Aesthetics* 48: 315–37.

Huovinen, Erkki. 2013. "Concatenationism and Anti-architectonicism in Musical Understanding." *Journal of Aesthetics and Art Criticism* 71: 247–60.

Inness, Julie C. 1992. *Privacy, Intimacy, and Isolation*. Oxford: Oxford University Press.

Jackendoff, Ray. 2011. "Music and Language." *The Routledge Companion to Philosophy and Music*. Ed. Theodore Gracyk & Andrew Kania. New York: Routledge. 101–12.

Jackson, Frank. 1998. *From Metaphysics to Ethics: A Defence of Conceptual Analysis*. Oxford: Oxford University Press.

Jacobson, Daniel. 1997. "In Praise of Immoral Art." *Philosophical Topics* 25: 155–99.

James, Michael. 2017. "Race." *The Stanford Encyclopedia of Philosophy*. Ed. Edward N. Zalta. Spring 2017 edition. https://plato.stanford.edu/entries/race/. Accessed June 20, 2019.

Judkins, Jennifer. 1997. "The Aesthetics of Silence in Live Musical Performance." *Journal of Aesthetic Education* 31.3: 39–53.

Kahn, Douglas. 1999. *Noise, Water, Meat: A History of Sound in the Arts*. Cambridge, MA: MIT Press.

Kania, Andrew. 1998. "Not Just for the Record: A Philosophical Analysis of Classical Music Recordings." M.A. thesis. University of Auckland.

Kania, Andrew. 2006. "Making Tracks: The Ontology of Rock Music." *Journal of Aesthetics and Art Criticism* 64: 401–14.

Kania, Andrew. 2008a. "The Methodology of Musical Ontology: Descriptivism and Its Implications." *British Journal of Aesthetics* 48: 426–44.

Kania, Andrew. 2008b. "Piece for the End of Time: In Defence of Musical Ontology." *British Journal of Aesthetics* 48: 65–79.

Kania, Andrew. 2008c. Review of *Works of Music* by Julian Dodd. *Journal of Aesthetics and Art Criticism* 66: 201–3.

Kania, Andrew. 2010. "Silent Music." *Journal of Aesthetics and Art Criticism* 68: 343–53.

Kania, Andrew. 2011a. "All Play and No Work: An Ontology of Jazz." *Journal of Aesthetics and Art Criticism* 69: 391–403.

Kania, Andrew. 2011b. "Definition." *The Routledge Companion to Philosophy and Music*. Ed. Theodore Gracyk & Andrew Kania. New York: Routledge. 1–13.

Kania, Andrew. 2012. "In Defence of Higher-Order Musical Ontology: A Reply to Lee B. Brown." *British Journal of Aesthetics* 51: 97–102.

Kania, Andrew. 2013a. "Platonism vs. Nominalism in Contemporary Musical Ontology." *Art and Abstract Objects*. Ed. Christy Mag Uidhir. Oxford: Oxford University Press. 197–219.

Kania, Andrew. 2013b. "Music." *The Routledge Companion to Aesthetics*. Ed. Berys Gaut & Dominic McIver Lopes. 3rd edition. New York: Routledge. 639–48.

Kania, Andrew. 2015. "An Imaginative Theory of Musical Space and Movement." *British Journal of Aesthetics* 55: 157–72.

Kant, Immanuel. 1790. *Critique of the Power of Judgment*. Trans. Paul Guyer & Eric Matthews. Ed. Paul Guyer. New York: Cambridge University Press, 2000.

Karl, Gregory & Jenefer Robinson. 1995a. "Levinson on Hope in *The Hebrides*." *Journal of Aesthetics and Art Criticism* 53: 195–9.

Karl, Gregory & Jenefer Robinson. 1995b. "Shostakovich's Tenth Symphony and the Musical Expression of Cognitively Complex Emotions." *Journal of Aesthetics and Art Criticism* 53: 401–15.

Karl, Gregory & Jenefer Robinson. 2015. "Yet Again, 'Between Absolute and Programme Music'." *British Journal of Aesthetics* 55: 19–37.

Kingsbury, Justine. 2002. "Matravers on Musical Expressiveness." *British Journal of Aesthetics* 42: 13–19.

Kingsbury, Justine & Jonathan McKeown-Green. 2009. "Jackson's Armchair: The Only Chair in Town?" *Conceptual Analysis and Philosophical Naturalism*. Ed. Robert Nola & David Braddon-Mitchell. Cambridge, MA: MIT Press. 159–82.

Kivy, Peter. 1980. *The Corded Shell: Reflections on Musical Expression*. Princeton: Princeton University Press. (Reprinted, with four additional essays, as *Sound Sentiment: An Essay on the Musical Emotions*. Philadelphia: Temple University Press. 1989).

Kivy, Peter. 1983. "Platonism in Music: A Kind of Defense." *Grazer Philosophische Studien* 19: 109–29.

Kivy, Peter. 1988. "Orchestrating Platonism." *The Fine Art of Repetition*. Cambridge: Cambridge University Press, 1993. 75–94.

Kivy, Peter. 1990. *Music Alone: Philosophical Reflections on the Purely Musical Experience*. Ithaca: Cornell University Press.

Kivy, Peter. 1993. "The Fine Art of Repetition." *The Fine Art of Repetition*. Cambridge: Cambridge University Press. 327–59.

Kivy, Peter. 1995. *Authenticities: Philosophical Reflections on Musical Performance*. Ithaca: Cornell University Press.

Kivy, Peter. 1997. *Philosophies of Arts: An Essay in Differences*. Cambridge: Cambridge University Press.

Kivy, Peter. 1999. "Feeling the Musical Emotions." *British Journal of Aesthetics* 39: 1–13.

Kivy, Peter. 2001. "Music in Memory and *Music in the Moment*." *New Essays on Musical Understanding*. Oxford: Oxford University Press.

Kivy, Peter. 2002. *Introduction to a Philosophy of Music*. Oxford: Oxford University Press.

Kivy, Peter. 2003. "Another Go at Musical Profundity: Stephen Davies and the Game of Chess." *British Journal of Aesthetics* 43: 401–11.

Kivy, Peter. 2008. "Musical Morality." *Revue Internationale de Philosophie* 62: 397–412.

Kivy, Peter. 2009. *Antithetical Arts: On the Ancient Quarrel between Literature and Music*. Oxford: Oxford University Press.

Kivy, Peter. 2015. *De Gustibus: Arguing about Taste and Why We Do It*. Oxford: Oxford University Press.

Knobe, Joshua & Shaun Nichols. 2017. "Experimental Philosophy." *The Stanford Encyclopedia of Philosophy*. Ed. Edward N. Zalta. Winter 2017 edition. https://plato.stanford.edu/archives/win2017/entries/experimental-philosophy/. Accessed November 30, 2018.

Korsgaard, Christine M. 1983. "Two Distinctions in Goodness." *Philosophical Review* 92: 169–95.

Korsmeyer, Carolyn. 2011. *Savoring Disgust: The Foul and the Fair in Aesthetics*. Oxford: Oxford University Press.

Kostka, Stefan, Dorothy Payne, & Byron Almén. 2018. *Tonal Harmony: With an Introduction to Twentieth-Century Music*. 8th edition. New York: McGraw-Hill.

Kraut, Robert. 2007. *Artworld Metaphysics*. Oxford: Oxford University Press.

Kroon, Fred & Alberto Voltolini. 2016. "Fiction." *The Stanford Encyclopedia of Philosophy*. Ed. Edward N. Zalta. Winter 2016 edition. https://plato.stanford.edu/archives/win2016/entries/fiction/. Accessed February 26, 2018.

LaBelle, Brandon. 2006. *Background Noise: Perspectives on Sound Art*. New York: Continuum.

Lamarque, Peter. 2009. *Philosophy of Literature*. Malden, MA: Blackwell.

Langer, Susanne K. 1942. *Philosophy in A New Key: A Study in the Symbolism of Reason, Rite, and Art*. 3rd edition. Cambridge, MA: Harvard University Press, 1957.

Langer, Susanne K. 1953. *Feeling and Form: A Theory of Art Developed from* Philosophy in A New Key. New York: Scribner's.

Lerdahl, Fred & Ray Jackendoff. 1983. *The Generative Theory of Tonal Music*. Cambridge, MA: MIT Press.

Lerner, Neil & Joseph N. Straus, eds. 2006. *Sounding Off: Theorizing Disability in Music*. New York: Routledge.

Letts, Philip. 2018. "The Property Theory of Musical Works." *Journal of Aesthetics and Art Criticism* 76: 57–69.

Levinson, Jerrold. 1979. "Defining Art Historically." *British Journal of Aesthetics* 19: 232–50.

Levinson, Jerrold. 1980. "What a Musical Work Is." *Journal of Philosophy* 77: 5–28.

Levinson, Jerrold. 1982. "Music and Negative Emotion." *Philosophical Quarterly* 63: 327–46.

Levinson, Jerrold. 1987a. "Song and Music Drama." *The Pleasures of Aesthetics*. Ithaca: Cornell University Press, 1996. 42–59.

Levinson, Jerrold. 1987b. "Evaluating Musical Performance." *Journal of Aesthetic Education* 21: 75–88.

Levinson, Jerrold. 1990a. "Hope in the Hebrides." *Music, Art, and Metaphysics*. Ithaca: Cornell University Press. 336–75.

Levinson, Jerrold. 1990b. "What a Musical Work is, Again." *Music, Art, and Metaphysics*. Ithaca: Cornell University Press. 215–63.

Levinson, Jerrold. 1990c. "Authentic Performance and Performance Means." *Music, Art, and Metaphysics*. Ithaca: Cornell University Press. 393–408.

Levinson, Jerrold. 1990d. "The Concept of Music." *Music, Art, and Metaphysics*. Ithaca: Cornell University Press. 267–78.

Levinson, Jerrold. 1992. "Musical Profundity Misplaced." *Journal of Aesthetics and Art Criticism* 50: 58–60.

Levinson, Jerrold. 1993. "Performative versus Critical Interpretation in Music." *The Interpretation of Music*. Ed. Michael Krausz. Oxford: Oxford University Press. 33–60.

Levinson, Jerrold. 1996. "Musical Expressiveness." *The Pleasures of Aesthetics*. Ithaca: Cornell University Press. 90–125.

Levinson, Jerrold. 1997. *Music in the Moment*. Ithaca: Cornell University Press.

Levinson, Jerrold. 2002. "The Irreducible Historicality of the Concept of Art." *British Journal of Aesthetics* 42: 367–79.

Levinson, Jerrold, ed. 2003. *The Oxford Handbook of Aesthetics*. Oxford: Oxford University Press.

Levinson, Jerrold. 2006a. "Musical Expressiveness as Hearability-as-expression." *Contemporary Debates in Aesthetics and the Philosophy of Art*. Ed. Matthew Kieran. Malden, MA: Blackwell. 192–206.

Levinson, Jerrold. 2006b. "Concatenationism, Architectonicism, and the Appreciation of Music." *Revue Internationale de Philosophie* 238: 505–14.

Levinson, Jerrold. 2010. "Artistic Worth and Personal Taste." *Journal of Aesthetics and Art Criticism* 68: 225–33.

Levinson, Jerrold. 2013. "Popular Song as Moral Microcosm: Life Lessons from Jazz Standards." *Royal Institute of Philosophy Supplement* 71: 51–66.

Levinson, Jerrold. 2019. "In Defense of Authentic Performance: Adjust Your ears, Not the Music." *Of Essence and Context: Between Music and Philosophy*. Ed. Rūta Stanevičiūtė, Nick Zangwill, & Rima Povilionienė. Cham, Switzerland: Springer. 185–95.

Lewis, Clarence Irving. 1946. *An Analysis of Knowledge and Valuation*. La Salle, IL: Open Court.

Lewis, Eric. 2019. *Intents and Purposes: Philosophy and the Aesthetics of Improvisation*. Ann Arbor: University of Michigan Press.

Lippman, Edward A. 1963. "Spatial Perception and Physical Location as Factors in Music." *Acta Musicologica* 35: 24–34.

Livingston, Paisley. 2005. *Art and Intention: A Philosophical Study*. Oxford: Oxford University Press.

London, Justin. 2012. *Hearing in Time: Psychological Aspects of Musical Meter*. 2nd edition. Oxford: Oxford University Press.

London, Justin. 2016. Review of *Groove* by Tiger Roholt. *Journal of Aesthetics and Art Criticism* 74: 101–4.

Lopes, Dominic McIver. 2014. *Beyond Art*. Oxford: Oxford University Press.

Love, Stefan Caris. 2016. "The Jazz Solo as Virtuous Act." *Journal of Aesthetics and Art Criticism* 74: 61–74.

Lowe, E.J. 2002. *A Survey of Metaphysics*. Oxford: Oxford University Press.

Maconie, Robin. 1990. *The Concept of Music*. Oxford: Clarendon Press.

Mag Uidhir, Christy. 2007. "Recordings as Performances." *British Journal of Aesthetics* 47: 298–314.

Mag Uidhir, Christy. 2012. "Introduction: Art, Metaphysics, and the Paradox of Standards." *Art and Abstract Objects*. Ed. Christy Mag Uidhir. Oxford: Oxford University Press. 1–26.

Mag Uidhir, Christy. 2013. "What's so Bad about Blackface?" *Race, Philosophy, and Film*. Ed. Dan Flory & Mary Bloodsworth-Lugo. New York: Routledge. 51–68.

Magnus, Cristyn P.D. Magnus, & Christy Mag Uidhir. 2013. "Judging Covers." *Journal of Aesthetics and Art Criticism* 71: 361–70.

Maler, Anabel. 2016. "Musical Expression among Deaf and Hearing Song Signers." *The Oxford Handbook of Music and Disability Studies*. Ed. Blake Howe, Stephanie Jensen-Moulton, Neil Lerner, & Joseph Straus. Oxford: Oxford University Press. 73–91.

Mathisen, Thomas J. 2011. "Antiquity and the Middle Ages." *The Routledge Companion to Philosophy and Music*. Ed. Theodore Gracyk & Andrew Kania. New York: Routledge. 257–72.

Matravers, Derek. 1991. "Art and the Feelings and Emotions." *British Journal of Aesthetics* 31: 322–31.

Matravers, Derek. 1998. *Art and Emotion*. Oxford: Clarendon Press.

Matravers, Derek. 2011. "Arousal Theories." *The Routledge Companion to Philosophy and Music*. Ed. Theodore Gracyk & Andrew Kania. New York: Routledge. 212–21.

Maus, Fred Everett. 1988. "Music as Drama." *Music and Meaning*. Ed. Jenefer Robinson. Ithaca: Cornell University Press, 1997. 105–30.

Maus, Fred Everett. 2011. "Music and Gender." *The Routledge Companion to Philosophy and Music*. Ed. Theodore Gracyk & Andrew Kania. New York: Routledge. 569–80.

McClary, Susan. 1991. *Feminine Endings: Music, Gender, and Sexuality*. Minneapolis: University of Minnesota Press.

McGonigal, Andrew. 2013. "Truth, Relativism, and Serial Fiction." *British Journal of Aesthetics* 53: 165–79.

McKenna, Michael & Derk Pereboom. 2016. *Free Will: A Contemporary Introduction*. New York: Routledge.

McKeown-Green, Jonathan. 2014. "What Is Music? Is There a Definitive Answer?" *Journal of Aesthetics and Art Criticism* 72: 393–403.

Mew, Peter. 1985. "The Expression of Emotion in Music." *British Journal of Aesthetics* 25: 33–42.

Meyer, Leonard B. 1956. *Emotion and Meaning in Music*. Chicago: University of Chicago Press.

Mill, John Stuart. 1863. *Utilitarianism, On Liberty,* and *Considerations on Representative Government*. Ed. H.B. Acton. Rutland, VT: Everyman's Library.

Moruzzi, Caterina. 2018. "Every Performance Is a Stage: Musical Stage Theory as a Novel Account for the Ontology of Musical Works." *Journal of Aesthetics and Art Criticism* 76: 341–51.

Nannicelli, Ted. 2013. *A Philosophy of the Screenplay*. New York: Routledge.

Neill, Alex. 2013. "Tragedy." *The Routledge Companion to Aesthetics*. Ed. Berys Gaut & Dominic McIver Lopes. 3rd edition. New York: Routledge. 415–24.

Neill, Alex & Aaron Ridley, eds. 2008. *Arguing About Art: Contemporary Philosophical Debates*. 3rd edition. New York: Routledge.

Nettl, Bruno. 2000. "An Ethnomusicologist Contemplates Universals in Musical Sound and Musical Culture." *The Origins of Music*. Ed. Nils L. Wallin, Björn Merker, & Steven Brown. Cambridge, MA: MIT Press. 463–72.

Neufeld, Jonathan A. 2011. "Living the Work: Meditations on a Lark." *Journal of Aesthetic Education* 45: 89–106.

Newcomb, Anthony. 1984. "Sound and Feeling." *Critical Inquiry* 10: 614–43.

Nguyen, C. Thi & Matt Strohl. 2019. "Cultural Appropriation and the Intimacy of Groups." *Philosophical Studies* 176: 981–1002.

Nietzsche, Friedrich. 1889. *Twilight of the Idols*. In *The Anti-Christ, Ecce Homo, Twilight of the Idols, and Other Writings*. Trans. Judith Norman. Ed. Aaron Ridley & Judith Norman. Cambridge: Cambridge University Press, 2005. 153–229.

Nussbaum, Charles. 2007. *The Musical Representation: Meaning, Ontology, and Emotion*. Cambridge, MA: MIT Press.

Nussbaum, Charles. 2015. "Musical Perception." *The Oxford Handbook of Philosophy of Perception*. Ed. Mohan Matthen. Oxford: Oxford University Press. 495–514.

Nyman, Michael. 1999. *Experimental Music: Cage and Beyond*. 2nd edition. Cambridge: Cambridge University Press.

O'Callaghan, Casey. 2007. *Sounds: A Philosophical Theory*. Oxford: Oxford University Press.

O'Callaghan, Casey. 2016. "Auditory Perception." *The Stanford Encyclopedia of Philosophy.* Ed. Edward N. Zalta. Winter 2016 edition. https://plato.stanford.edu/entries/perception-auditory/. Accessed March 26, 2019.

Orr, Robert. 2017. "After Dylan's Nobel, What Makes a Poet a Poet?" *The New York Times.* March 24, 2017. www.nytimes.com/2017/03/24/books/review/after-dylans-nobel-what-makes-a-poet-a-poet.html?mcubz=0&_r=0. Accessed August 28, 2017.

Ortland, Eberhard. 2016. "Blurred Lines: A Case Study on the Ethics and Aesthetics of Copying." *The Aesthetics and Ethics of Copying.* Ed. Darren Hudson Hick & Reinold Schmücker. New York: Bloomsbury. 225–47.

Papineau, David. 2016. "Naturalism." *The Stanford Encyclopedia of Philosophy.* Ed. Edward N. Zalta. Winter 2016 edition. https://plato.stanford.edu/entries/naturalism/. Accessed March 26, 2019.

Parker, Charlie. 2003. *Complete Jazz at Massey Hall.* Recorded May 15, 1953. The Jazz Factory. Compact disc. JFCD22856.

Passmore, John. 1967. "Philosophy." *The Encyclopedia of Philosophy.* Ed. Paul Edwards. New York: Routledge. Vol. 5. 216–26.

Patel, Aniruddh D. 2007. *Music, Language, and the Brain.* Oxford: Oxford University Press.

Peacocke, Christopher. 2009. "The Perception of Music." *British Journal of Aesthetics* 49: 257–75.

Pegg, Carole. 2001. "Overtone-singing." *Grove Music Online.* www.oxfordmusiconline.com/grovemusic/view/10.1093/gmo/9781561592630.001.0001/omo-9781561592630-e-0000049849. Oxford University Press. Accessed April 2, 2018.

Philip, Robert. 1992. *Early Recordings and Musical Style: Changing Tastes in Instrumental Performance, 1900–1950.* Cambridge: Cambridge University Press.

Pratt, Carroll C. 1931. *The Meaning of Music: A Study in Psychological Aesthetics.* New York: McGraw-Hill.

Pratt, Carroll C. 1952. *Music as the Language of Emotion.* Washington, DC: The Library of Congress.

Predelli, Stefano. 1995. "Against Musical Platonism." *British Journal of Aesthetics* 35: 338–50.

Radford, Colin. 1975. "How Can We Be Moved by the Fate of Anna Karenina?" *Proceedings of the Aristotelian Society* supplementary volume 49: 67–80.

Ravasio, Matteo. 2018. "On Evolutionary Explanations of Musical Expressiveness." *Evental Aesthetics* 7. http://eventalaesthetics.net/wp-content/uploads/2018/03/Matteo-Final_6-29.pdf. Accessed May 15, 2018.

Ravasio, Matteo. 2019a. "Appearance Emotionalism in Music: Analysis and Criticism." *Journal of Aesthetic Education* 53: 93–105.

Ravasio, Matteo. 2019b. "Historically Uninformed Views of Historically Informed Performance." *Journal of Aesthetics and Art Criticism* 77: 193–205.

Ribeiro, Anna Christina. 2018. "Aesthetic Luck." *Monist* 101: 99–113.

Ricks, Christopher. 2003. *Dylan's Visions of Sin.* New York: HarperCollins.

Ridley, Aaron. 1995a. *Music, Value, and the Passions.* Ithaca: Cornell University Press.

Ridley, Aaron. 1995b. "Profundity in Music." *Arguing about Art: Contemporary Philosophical Debates.* Ed. Alex Neill & Aaron Ridley. 1st edition. New York: McGraw-Hill. 260–71.

Ridley, Aaron. 2003. "Against Musical Ontology." *Journal of Philosophy* 101: 203–20.

Ridley, Aaron. 2004. *The Philosophy of Music: Theme and Variations.* Edinburgh: Edinburgh University Press.

Rieger, Eva. 1985. "*Dolce Semplice*? On the Changing Role of Women in Music." *Feminist Aesthetics*. Ed. Gisela Ecker. Trans. Harriet Anderson. London: The Women's Press. 135–49.

Robertson, Diarra Osei. 2014. "Cash Rules Everything around Me: Appropriation, Commodification, and the Politics of Contemporary Protest Music and Hip Hop." *Soul Thieves: The Appropriation and Misrepresentation of African American Popular Culture*. Ed. Tamara Lizette Brown & Baruti N. Kopano. New York: Palgrave Macmillan. 31–49.

Robinson, Jenefer. 1995. "Startle." *Journal of Philosophy* 92: 53–74.

Robinson, Jenefer. 2005. *Deeper than Reason: Emotion and Its Role in Literature, Music, and Art*. Oxford: Oxford University Press.

Robson, Jon & Aaron Meskin. 2016. "Video Games as Self-Involving Interactive Fictions." *Journal of Aesthetics and Art Criticism* 74: 165–77.

Roholt, Tiger. 2011. "Continental Philosophy and Music." *The Routledge Companion to Philosophy and Music*. Ed. Theodore Gracyk & Andrew Kania. New York: Routledge. 284–93.

Roholt, Tiger. 2014. *Groove: A Phenomenology of Rhythmic Nuance*. New York: Bloomsbury.

Roholt, Tiger. 2017. "On the Divide: Analytic and Continental Philosophy of Music." *Journal of Aesthetics and Art Criticism* 75: 49–58.

Rohrbaugh, Guy. 2003. "Artworks as Historical Individuals." *European Journal of Philosophy* 11: 177–205.

Rohrbaugh, Guy. 2020. "Why Play the Notes? Indirect Aesthetic Normativity in Performance." *Australasian Journal of Philosophy* 98: 78–91.

Rudinow, Joel. 1994. "Race, Ethnicity, Expressive Authenticity: Can White People Sing the Blues?" *Journal of Aesthetics and Art Criticism* 52: 127–37.

Rudinow, Joel. 1995. "Reply to Taylor." *Journal of Aesthetics and Art Criticism* 53: 316–18.

Rudinow, Joel. 2010. *Soul Music: Tracking the Spiritual Roots of Pop from Plato to Motown*. Ann Arbor: University of Michigan Press.

Russell, Bruce. 2017. "*A Priori* Justification and Knowledge." *The Stanford Encyclopedia of Philosophy*. Ed. Edward N. Zalta. Summer 2017 edition. https://plato.stanford.edu/archives/sum2017/entries/apriori/. Accessed April 28, 2018.

Saito, Yuriko. 1997. "The Japanese Aesthetics of Imperfection and Insufficiency." *Journal of Aesthetics and Art Criticism* 55: 377–85.

Saito, Yuriko. 2007. *Everyday Aesthetics*. Oxford: Oxford University Press.

Schlosser, Markus. 2015. "Agency." *The Stanford Encyclopedia of Philosophy*. Ed. Edward N. Zalta. Fall 2015 edition. https://plato.stanford.edu/entries/agency/. Accessed December 1, 2016.

Scholz, Barbara C., Francis Jeffry Pelletier, & Geoffrey K. Pullum. 2016. "Philosophy of Linguistics." *The Stanford Encyclopedia of Philosophy*. Ed. Edward N. Zalta. Winter 2016 edition. https://plato.stanford.edu/entries/linguistics/. Accessed March 26, 2019.

Schopenhauer, Arthur. 1819. *The World as Will and Representation*. Volume 1. Trans. & ed. Judith Norman, Alistair Welchman, & Christopher Janaway. New York: Cambridge University Press, 2010.

Schopenhauer, Arthur. 1844. *The World as Will and Representation*. Volume 2. Trans. & ed. Judith Norman, Alistair Welchman, & Christopher Janaway. New York: Cambridge University Press, 2018.

Scruton, Roger. 1983. "Understanding Music." *The Aesthetic Understanding*. Manchester: Carcanet Press. 77–100.

Scruton, Roger. 1997. *The Aesthetics of Music*. Oxford: Oxford University Press.

Scruton, Roger. 2004. "Musical Movement." *British Journal of Aesthetics* 44: 184–7.

Selvin, Joel. 1996. "Q and A with Brian Eno." *San Francisco Chronicle*. June 2 1996. www. sfgate.com/music/popquiz/article/Q-and-A-With-Brian-Eno-2979740.php. Accessed March 28, 2012.

Sessions, Roger. 1950. *The Musical Experience of Composer, Performer, Listener*. Princeton: Princeton University Press.

Shafer-Landau, Russ. 2018. *The Fundamentals of Ethics*. 4th edition. Oxford: Oxford University Press.

Sharpe, R.A. 1982. Review of *The Corded Shell* by Peter Kivy. *British Journal of Aesthetics* 22: 81–2.

Shelley, James. 2010. "Against Value Empiricism in Aesthetics." *Australasian Journal of Philosophy* 88: 707–20.

Shepard, Roger N. & Jacqueline Metzler. 1971. "Mental Rotation of Three-Dimensional Objects." *Science* 171 (new series): 701–3.

Smuts, Aaron. 2013. "The Ethics of Singing Along: The Case of 'Mind of a Lunatic'." *Journal of Aesthetics and Art Criticism* 71: 121–9.

Smuts, Aaron. 2016. "The Ethics of Imagination and Fantasy." *The Routledge Handbook of Philosophy of Imagination*. Ed. Amy Kind. New York: Routledge. 380–91.

Sober, Elliott. 2005. *Core Questions in Philosophy: A Text with Readings*. 4th edition. Upper Saddle River, NJ: Pearson Prentice Hall.

Sorensen, Roy. 2009. "Hearing Silence: The Perception and Introspection of Absences." *Sounds and Perception: New Philosophical Essays*. Ed. Matthew Nudds & Casey O'Callaghan. Oxford: Oxford University Press. 126–45.

Spade, Paul Vincent. 1991. "Do Composers Have to Be Performers Too?" *Journal of Aesthetics and Art Criticism* 49: 365–9.

Spencer, Quayshawn. 2018. "Are Folk Races like Dingoes, Dimes, or Dodos?" *Norton Introduction to Philosophy*. Ed. Gideon Rosen, Alex Byrne, Joshua Cohen, Elizabeth Harman, & Seana Shiffrin. 2nd edition. New York: Norton. 571–8.

Spignesi, Stephen J. & Michael Lewis. 2004. *100 Best Beatles Song: A Passionate Fan's Guide*. New York: Black Dog & Leventhal.

Staier, Andreas. 2005. "Ornamentation and Alteration in Mozart – Can We, Should We, Must We?" Liner notes to his recording of Mozart piano sonatas K. 330, K. 331 "alla turca" & K. 332. Harmonia Mundi HMC 901856. 11–12.

Stainsby, Thomas & Ian Cross. 2009. "The Perception of Pitch." *The Oxford Handbook of Music Psychology*. Ed. Susan Hallam, Ian Cross, & Michael Thaut. Oxford: Oxford University Press. 47–58.

Stecker, Robert. 1996. "What Is Literature?" *Revue Internationale de Philosophie* 50: 681–94.

Stecker, Robert. 1997. *Artworks: Definition, Meaning, Value*. University Park, PA: Penn State Press.

Stecker, Robert. 2003a. *Interpretation and Construction: Art, Speech, and the Law*. Malden, MA: Blackwell.

Stecker, Robert. 2003b. "Value in Art." *The Oxford Handbook of Aesthetics*. Ed. Jerrold Levinson. Oxford: Oxford University Press. 307–24.

Stecker, Robert. 2010. *Aesthetics and the Philosophy of Art: An Introduction*. 2nd edition. Lanham, MD: Rowman and Littlefield.

Stecker, Robert. 2013. "Interpretation." *The Routledge Companion to Aesthetics*. Ed. Berys Gaut & Dominic McIver Lopes. 3rd edition. New York: Routledge. 309–19.

Stevens, Catharine & Tim Byron. 2009. "Universals in Music Processing." *The Oxford Handbook of Music Psychology*. Ed. Susan Hallam, Ian Cross, & Michael Thaut. Oxford: Oxford University Press. 14–23.

Straus, Joseph N. 2011. *Extraordinary Measures: Disability in Music*. Oxford: Oxford University Press.

Stravinsky, Igor. 1936. *An Autobiography*. New York: Norton, 1962.

Szabó, Zoltan Gendler. 2003. "Nominalism." *The Oxford Handbook of Metaphysics*. Ed. Michael J. Loux & Dean W. Zimmerman. Oxford: Oxford University Press. 11–45.

Taylor, Charles & Murray Campbell. 2001. "Sound." *Grove Music Online*. www.oxfordmusiconline.com/grovemusic/view/10.1093/gmo/9781561592630.001.0001/omo-9781561592630-e-0000026289. Accessed November 4, 2016.

Taylor, Paul C. 1995. "… So Black and Blue: Response to Rudinow." *Journal of Aesthetics and Art Criticism* 53: 313–16.

Taylor, Paul C. 2000. *Race: A Philosophical Introduction*. 2nd edition. Malden, MA: Polity.

Taylor, Paul C. 2005. "Does Hip Hop Belong to Me? The Philosophy of Race and Culture." *Hip Hop and Philosophy: Rhyme 2 Reason*. Ed. Derrick Darby & Tommie Shelby. Chicago: Open Court. 79–91.

Taylor, Paul C. 2016. *Black Is Beautiful: A Philosophy of Black Aesthetics*. Malden, MA: Wiley Blackwell.

Thom, Paul. 1993. *For an Audience: A Philosophy of the Performing Arts*. Philadelphia: Temple University Press.

Thom, Paul. 2007. *The Musician as Interpreter*. University Park, PA: Pennsylvania State University Press.

Thomasson, Amie L. 2004. "The Ontology of Art." *The Blackwell Guide to Aesthetics*. Ed. Peter Kivy. Oxford: Blackwell. 78–92.

Thompson, William Forde. 2013. "Intervals and Scales." *The Psychology of Music*. Ed. Diana Deutsch. 3rd edition. New York: Academic Press. 107–40.

Tillman, Chris. 2011. "Musical Materialism." *British Journal of Aesthetics* 51: 13–29.

Tolstoy, Leo. 1898. *What Is Art?* Trans. Richard Pevear & Larissa Volokhonsky. London: Penguin, 1995.

Tormey, Alan. 1971. *The Concept of Expression: A Study in Philosophical Psychology and Aesthetics*. Princeton: Princeton University Press.

Trivedi, Saam. 2011a. "Resemblance Theories." *The Routledge Companion to Philosophy and Music*. Ed. Theodore Gracyk & Andrew Kania. New York: Routledge. 223–32.

Trivedi, Saam. 2011b. "Music and Imagination." *The Routledge Companion to Philosophy and Music*. Ed. Theodore Gracyk & Andrew Kania. New York: Routledge. 113–22.

Trivedi, Saam. 2017. *Imagination, Music, and the Emotions: A Philosophical Study*. Albany: State University of New York Press.

Urmson, J.O. 1973. "Representation in Music." *Philosophy and the Arts*. Ed. Julian Mitchell. London: Macmillan. 132–46.

Van der Merwe, Peter. 1992. *Origins of the Popular Style*. Paperback edition. Oxford: Oxford University Press.

Vermazen, Bruce. 1986. "Expression as Expression." *Pacific Philosophical Quarterly* 67: 196–224.

Vernezze, Peter & Carl J. Porter, eds. 2006. *Bob Dylan and Philosophy: It's Alright, Ma (I'm Only Thinking)*. Chicago: Open Court.

Walton, Kendall L. 1970. "Categories of Art." *Philosophical Review* 79: 334–67.

Walton, Kendall L. 1978. "Fearing Fictions." *Journal of Philosophy* 75: 5–27.

Walton, Kendall L. 1984. "Transparent Pictures: On the Nature of Photographic Realism." *Critical Inquiry* 11: 246–76.

Walton, Kendall L. 1988a. "What Is Abstract about the Art of Music?" *Journal of Aesthetics and Art Criticism* 46: 351–64.

Walton, Kendall L. 1988b. "The Presentation and Portrayal of Sound Patterns." *Human Agency: Language, Duty and Value*. Ed. Jonathan Dancy, J.M.E. Moravcsik & C.C.W. Taylor. Stanford: Stanford University Press. 237–57.

Walton, Kendall L. 1990. *Mimesis as Make-Believe: On the Foundations of the Representational Arts*. Cambridge, MA: Harvard University Press.

Walton, Kendall L. 1993. "Understanding Humor and Understanding Music." *The Journal of Musicology* 1: 32–44.

Walton, Kendall L. 1994. "Listening with Imagination: Is Music Representational?" *Journal of Aesthetics and Art Criticism* 52: 47–61.

Walton, Kendall L. 1997a. "Spelunking, Simulation, and Slime: On Being Moved by Fiction." *In Other Shoes: Music, Metaphor, Empathy, Existence*. Oxford: Oxford University Press, 2015. 273–87.

Walton, Kendall L. 1997b. "On Pictures and Photographs: Objections Answered." *Film Theory and Philosophy*. Ed. Richard Allen & Murray Smith. Oxford: Oxford University Press. 60–75.

Walton, Kendall L. 1999. "Projectivism, Empathy, and Musical Tension." *In Other Shoes: Music, Metaphor, Empathy, Existence*. Oxford: Oxford University Press, 2015. 118–50.

Walton, Kendall L. 2012. "Two Kinds of Physicality in Electronic and Traditional Music." *In Other Shoes: Music, Metaphor, Empathy, Existence*. Oxford: Oxford University Press, 2015. 36–51.

Warburton, Nigel. 2003. "Photography." *The Oxford Handbook of Aesthetics*. Ed. Jerrold Levinson. Oxford: Oxford University Press. 614–26.

Webster, James. 2001. "Sonata Form." *Grove Music Online*. www.oxfordmusiconline. com/grovemusic/view/10.1093/gmo/9781561592630.001.0001/omo-9781561592630-e-0000026197. Oxford University Press. Accessed March 28, 2018.

Weitz, Morris. 1956. "The Role of Theory in Aesthetics." *Journal of Aesthetics and Art Criticism* 15: 27–35.

White, David A. 1992. "Toward a Theory of Profundity in Music." *Journal of Aesthetics and Art Criticism* 50: 23–34.

Wildman, Nathan & Richard Woodward. 2018. "Interactivity, Fictionality, and Incompleteness." *The Aesthetics of Videogames*. Ed. Jon Robson & Grant Tavinor. New York: Routledge. 112–27.

Williams, Peter. 2001. *Bach: The Goldberg Variations*. Cambridge: Cambridge University Press.

Wilson, George & Samuel Shpall. 2016. "Action." *The Stanford Encyclopedia of Philosophy*. Ed. Edward N. Zalta. Winter 2016 edition. https://plato.stanford.edu/archives/win2016/entries/action/. Accessed December 1, 2016.

Wiltsher, Nick. 2016a. "The Aesthetics of Electronic Dance Music I: History, Genre, Scenes, Identity, Blackness." *Philosophy Compass* 11: 415–25.

Wiltsher, Nick. 2016b. "The Aesthetics of Electronic Dance Music II: Dancers, DJs, Ontology, and Aesthetics." *Philosophy Compass* 11: 426–36.

Wolterstorff, Nicholas. 1975. "Toward an Ontology of Art Works." *Noûs* 9: 115–42.

Wolterstorff, Nicholas. 1987. "The Work of Making a Work of Music." *What Is Music?* Ed. Philip Alperson. New York: Haven. 101–29.

Wolterstorff, Nicholas. 2015. *Art Rethought: The Social Practices of Art*. Oxford: Oxford University Press.

Wordsworth, William. 1802. "Preface." *Lyrical Ballads*. Ed. Michael Mason. New York: Longman, 1992. 55–87.

Young, Iris Marion. 1988. "Five Faces of Oppression." *Philosophical Forum* 19: 270–90.

Young, James O. 1988. "The Concept of Authentic Performance." *British Journal of Aesthetics* 28: 228–38.

Young, James O. 1995. "Between Rock and a Harp Place." *Journal of Aesthetics and Art Criticism* 53: 78–81.

Young, James O. 2013. "Authenticity in Performance." *The Routledge Companion to Aesthetics*. Ed. Berys Gaut & Dominic McIver Lopes. 3rd edition. New York: Routledge. 452–61.

Young, James O. 2014. *Critique of Pure Music*. Oxford: Oxford University Press.

Young, James O. & Carl Matheson. 2000. "The Metaphysics of Jazz." *Journal of Aesthetics and Art Criticism* 58: 125–33.

Zangwill, Nick. 2001. *Metaphysics of Beauty*. Ithaca: Cornell University Press.

Zangwill, Nick. 2004. "Against Emotion: Hanslick Was Right about Music." *British Journal of Aesthetics* 44: 29–43.

Zangwill, Nick. 2007. "Music, Metaphor, and Emotion." *Journal of Aesthetics and Art Criticism* 65: 391–400.

Index

4'33" (John Cage) 283–5, 306n6, 308

absolute music *see* music, pure
abstract objects 169–71
abstractness *see* representation; value of music, and abstractness
"Adagio for Strings" (Barber): expressiveness of 32, 40, 46, 54, 70, 73; silence in 282, 306n4
Adams, Zed 249
Adorno, Theodor 155n18
aesthetic experience: and aesthetic properties 171–2; different conceptions of 296–8; and value of music 132–3
aesthetic properties 40, 63n15; and instrumentation 187; and sonicism vs. contextualism 171–5
aesthetic value 132–5, 140, 253
aesthetics of perfection and imperfection 218–19
affective appraisals 43–4, 86, 88–9
African-American culture *see* black culture
African drumming 290
Alcaraz León, María José 254–5
Alhambra, the 149
"All Along the Watchtower" 248n28
alliteration 17, 20
allusions 173, 238–40, 243, 248
Alperson, Philip 215, 217–18, 276n36, 277
ambient sounds 283, 294
Anderson, Leroy 290
animals, music of 300–1, 308n29
anti-Semitism 254
appropriation (meaning of term) 276n21; *see also* cultural appropriation
a priori see knowledge, non-empirical
Arbus, Diane 222
arguments (in philosophy) 8–9
arousalism 33–7, 40, 64n25
art, categories of *see* categories of art
art, definition of 134, 298–300
Art of Fugue (Bach) 184

artistic value and moral value (relationship between) *see* moral value and artistic value
artworks, ontology of 169, 212–15, 236, 248n19; *see also* musical works
assonance 17
As You Like It (Shakespeare) 38, 239
Auden, W.H. 2, 25n4
audiences: performer interaction with 244–5; and performance 158–63
audism 287
authenticity: in classical music 181–3, 196; cultural 200, 277; personal 197–200; *see also* expressionism; sincerity; score-compliance and interpretive 188–97, 203, 211
autonomania 14, 19, 24, 26n27
autonomism 252–3

Bach, J.S.: cantatas 296; improvisation by 221n16; instrumentation of 184, 191, 201n8, 230; Partita no. 2 for solo violin 174; *see also* Brandenburg Concertos; Goldberg Variations; "Jesu, Joy of Man's Desiring"
"Ballad of a Thin Man" (Bob Dylan) 136
ballet, recordings of 249n37
Baraka, Amiri 266–7, 272
Barber, Samuel 32, 63n5; *see also* "Adagio for Strings"
Bartel, Christopher 232, 234–6
Baugh, Bruce 156
Beach Boys, the 18–19, 116
Beatles, the: and harmony 113; lyrics of 21; and metrical irregularity 69; and musical form 116; focus on recordings 229
Beethoven, Ludwig van: Fifth Symphony 167, 189, 191–5, 202n25, 203n33, 282–3; incidental music by 61; "Moonlight" Sonata 68, 184; Ninth Symphony 288; Piano Sonata no. 30 (op. 109) 118–19, 122, 150; revolutionary harmony of 196–7; tempo indications 189–90, 193–4

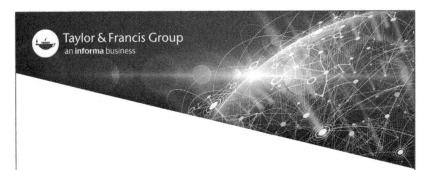

Made in United States
North Haven, CT
26 April 2022

18589688R00202